AF148708

Gender and Politics

Series Editors

Johanna Kantola
Senior Lecturer in Gender
University of Helsinki, Finland

Sarah Childs
Professor of Politics and Gender
University of Bristol, UK

Editorial Advisory Board

The *Gender and Politics* series celebrates its 5th anniversary at the 4th European Conference on Politics and Gender (ECPG) in June 2015 in Uppsala, Sweden. The original idea for the book series was envisioned by the series editors Johanna Kantola and Judith Squires at the first ECPG in Belfast in 2009, and the series was officially launched at the Conference in Budapest in 2011. In 2014, Sarah Childs became the co-editor of the series, together with Johanna Kantola. Gender and Politics showcases the very best international writing. It publishes world class monographs and edited collections from scholars - junior and well established - working in politics, international relations and public policy, with specific reference to questions of gender. The 15 titles that have come out over the past five years make key contributions to debates on intersectionality and diversity, gender equality, social movements, Europeanization and institutionalism, governance and norms, policies, and political institutions. Set in European, US and Latin American contexts, these books provide rich new empirical findings and push forward boundaries of feminist and politics conceptual and theoretical research. The editors welcome the highest quality international research on these topics and beyond, and look for proposals on feminist political theory; on recent political transformations such as the economic crisis or the rise of the populist right; as well as proposals on continuing feminist dilemmas around participation and representation, specific gendered policy fields, and policy making mechanisms. The series can also include books published as a Palgrave pivot.

More information about this series at
http://www.springer.com/series/14998

Michaela Köttig • Renate Bitzan • Andrea Pető
Editors

Gender and Far Right Politics in Europe

palgrave
macmillan

Editors
Michaela Köttig
Frankfurt University of Applied
Sciences, Frankfurt, Germany

Andrea Pető
Central European University
Budapest, Hungary

Renate Bitzan
Technische Hochschule Nuremberg
Nuremberg, Germany

Gender and Politics
ISBN 978-3-319-82849-7   ISBN 978-3-319-43533-6   (eBook)
DOI 10.1007/978-3-319-43533-6

Cover illustration: © Tetiana Vitsenko / Alamy Stock Photo

Printed on acid-free paper

This Palgrave Macmillan imprint is published by Springer Nature
The registered company is Springer International Publishing AG
The registered company address is: Gewerbestrasse 11, 6330 Cham, Switzerland

'In times of re-arising nationalisms and the simultaneousness of advanced standards of women's emancipation and anti-feminist backlash, the book tremendously helps to be aware of common and differing gender politics within Europe's far right.'

– Prof. Ursula Birsl, Philips-University, Germany

'For far too long, the relationship between gender and today's extreme right has been neglected. Replete with examples drawn from across Europe, this is an impressive work. Important, timely and deeply thought-provoking, this book is long overdue.'

– Professor Nigel Copsey, Teesside University, UK

'This timely volume sheds light on a largely overlooked, yet critical, aspect of the extreme right in Europe today: gender. The well-researched chapters make it abundantly clear the extreme right skillfully employs gendered discourses and appeals as part of their political arsenal.'

– Professor Margaret Power, Illinois Tech, USA

PREFACE AND ACKNOWLEDGMENTS

Finished at last! The way has been long and arduous, but finally we have succeeded in gathering together papers from a total of 12 European countries on right-wing extremism and gender, a subject which receives far too little attention in academic discussions.

The inspiration for this book came from the international workshop 'Gender and Far Right Politics in Europe' which was held in September 2012 in Nuremberg, Germany. We would therefore like to express our gratitude once again to those organizations which supported the workshop financially or otherwise: the Competence Center for Gender & Diversity at the Georg Simon Ohm Technische Hochschule Nuremberg; the research network 'Women and Right-Wing Extremism'; the foundation 'Nuremberg—City of Peace and Human Rights'; the mayor of Nuremberg; the Georg Simon Ohm Technische Hochschule Nuremberg; the Bayern Forum of the Friedrich-Ebert Foundation; the Hans Böckler Foundation and the Amadeu Antonio Foundation. We also thank the Frankfurt University of Applied Sciences for supporting this book project.

Our warm thanks go to all the authors for their perseverance and their contributions to this project. We are grateful to Ruth Schubert for her language editing services, and last but not least we say thank you to Alice Blum, who believed in this project and worked for it tirelessly, during all its ups and downs.

Without all this help, the project would not have been possible and would never have come to fruition. Thank you everybody.

Michaela Köttig
Frankfurt am Main, Germany

Renate Bitzan
Nuremberg, Germany

Andrea Petö
Budapest, Hungary

April 2016

CONTENTS

CONTRIBUTORS

EDITORS/AUTHORS

Renate Bitzan, PhD, is professor of social sciences with a focus on gender and diversity at the Technische Hochschule Nuremberg Georg Simon Ohm, Nuremberg, Germany. One of her main research interests is women/gender in the political far right since the early 1990s. She took part in the European research project 'Migration and Interculturality in UK, Spain and Germany. Case Studies in the World of Labour' (1999–2003); its results were published in German, Spanish and English. She has presented papers at numerous German and international conferences. She has been a founding member of the German research network 'Women and Right-Wing Extremism' since 2000. She is (co-)organizer of national and international conferences on gender and the far right.

Michaela Köttig, PhD, is professor of communication, communication techniques and conflict management at the Frankfurt University of Applied Sciences, Germany. Her principal field of research is female right-wing extremism in Germany. She also focuses on political socialization, family sociology and family history, as well as on the influence of these factors on peer interactions. In her research she employs biographical, intergenerational and ethnographical methods. She was a visiting professor at the Pontifícia Universidade Católica do Rio Grande do Sul (PUCRS) in Porto Allegre (Brazil) (2013). She is one of the early members of the German research network 'Women and Right-Wing Extremism'. Between 2010 and 2014 she was the vice-president of the Research Committee on Biography and Society (RC 38) of the International Sociological Association (ISA).

Andrea Petö is professor at the Department of Gender Studies at Central European University in Budapest, Hungary, a Doctor of Science of Hungarian Academy of Sciences. Her works have appeared in 15 different languages. Her recent book is co-edited with Ayse Gül Altinay: *Gendered Wars, Gendered Memories. Feminist Conversations on War, Genocide and Political Violence*, Routledge, 2016. In 2005, she was awarded the Officer's Cross Order of Merit of the Republic of Hungary by the President of the Hungarian Republic and the Bolyai Prize by the Hungarian Academy of Sciences in 2006.

AUTHORS

Maria Alvanou, PhD, is a judicially recognized court evaluator for terrorism cases and female criminality in Greece. She is an EENet and ITSTIME member and has been lecturing at the National Security School and in Greece on issues relating to terrorism and national security threats. Her research and scholarly interests include female criminality, terrorism, social unrest, violence due to the economic crisis, anarchist movements, extremist violence, right-wing violent movements and prison facilities for security prisoners.

Silke Baer, Dipl. social pedagogy/social work, MA journalism/ communication sciences/North American studies; certified trainer in mediation, is co-founder and CEO/pedagogical lead of Cultures Interactive e.V., NGO. Since 2001 she has worked in the field of youth cultural and community-based approaches in prevention and de-radicalization, piloting "Model Projects" around issues of right-wing-extremism, racism, religious fundamentalism and militant Jihadism. With colleagues she developed a specific approach combining post-traditional civic education, youth cultural empowerment workshops (RAP, DJ, Graffiti, Skateboarding) and psychological informed group work settings to work with vulnerable young people. Since 2015 Cultures Interactive e.V. is one of 15 organizations announced by the ministry for family affairs for federal tasks of prevention and de-radicalization work.

Kathleen M. Blee, PhD, is distinguished professor of sociology and associate dean for Graduate Studies and Research, University of Pittsburgh. Her areas of interest are gender issues, social movements including racist, anti-Semitic and right-wing movements, racial violence and microsociology.

Alice Blum Frankfurt University of Applied Sciences (FRA-UAS). MA student, works and teaches at FRA-UAS. Main topics are national settlement, the new right, intersectionality and critical theory in social work.

Frauke Buettner graduated from the Free University of Berlin with a degree in political sciences. She has worked as a consultant to develop communal strategies against racist and right-wing extremist ideologies in Germany and has done research on contemporary forms of right-wing extremism and effective counter-strategies in Spain. She is working as a freelancer specializing in the prevention of right-wing extremism and racism with a special focus on women.

Robert Claus, MA in European Anthropology and Gender Studies, studied in Berlin, Istanbul and Buenos Aires. He is working in the "Competence Group for Fan Cultures and Social Work" at Leibniz gGmbH, Hannover. His research and publications focus on gender, masculinity, migration, racism, right-wing extremism, football fan cultures and social movements.

Andrea S. Dauber, PhD lectures and researches at the University of California, San Diego, and is Program Director of a Prevention and Early Intervention Mental Health Program for incarcerated individuals in San Diego County. Her research concentrates on gender and crime, including terrorism, left- and right-wing extremism and homicide, the media, family and social inequality. In one of her recent publications she examines Pierre Bourdieu's concept of symbolic violence by applying it to the study of Nazi and Neo-Nazi women in Germany.

Valérie Dubslaff is working for a PhD at the Université Paris-Sorbonne and the Ludwig-Maximilians-Universität München. She taught at various universities in Germany and France (Regensburg, Saarland, Paris-Sorbonne, Caen) and is chairwoman of the 'Interdisciplinary Research Community Germany-France' (GIRAF-IFFD) for young researchers and academics in the Humanities and Social Sciences in France and Germany.

Boka En holds an MSc in Gender and Sexuality Studies from Birkbeck, University of London, and is currently working towards an MA in Science and Technology Studies at the University of Vienna. Boka's research interests revolve around categorisation, boundary-drawing and identity construction, as well as the intersections/interactions between art, academia and activism.

Michael En holds an MA in Critical Sociolinguistics from Goldsmiths, University of London, and is a PhD candidate in Transcultural Communication at the Centre for Translation Studies, University of Vienna, working on how hegemonic ideas of 'nativeness' influence the (self-)perception of language users. Michael's main research interests include the linguistic construction of (sexual/political/...) identities and discourses on social minorities.

Anikó Félix is a political analyst and sociologist. She studied minority politics (MA) and is presently writing her PhD thesis in sociology. She is dealing with far-right movements from a gender approach. She has participated in projects dealing with Roma population, youth activism, holocaust education and social media. Furthermore she is a member of the MTA-ELTE Peripato Research Group.

Michaela Glaser, MA in social sciences/politics, researcher, project manager of the Centre for the Prevention of Right-Wing Extremism and Xenophobia, Deutsches Jugendinstitut (German Youth Institute), Halle/Saale. Her main research areas are educational and social work approaches in countering right-wing extremism and violent Islamism; young people's pathways into violent extremism.

Judith Goetz is a specialist in comparative literature and political science. She is a member of the editorial team for Context XXI, LICRA (League against Racism and Anti-Semitism) and FIPU (research group ideologies and policies of inequality, www.fipu.at), a Mauthausen satellite camp guide and a trainer for adult education. She has written numerous articles and given presentations on right-wing extremism and politics, commemoration and memorial culture in Austria and feminist and women's political issues. She has lectured at the universities of Klagenfurt/Celovec, Salzburg and Vienna, Austria.

Carina Klammer, sociologist. She is a PhD candidate at the University of Vienna. Areas of research interest are right-wing extremism, feminist theory and visual sociology. Her dissertation topic is: The Relationship between "Body" and "Mind" in the Ideology of the Extreme Right. Recent publication about the significance of anti-Muslim racism in the Freedom Party of Austria. Member of FIPU (research group ideologies and policies of inequality, www.fipu.at).

Oliver Kossack studied cultural and social sciences (BA) and European Studies (MA) at the European University Viadrina in Frankfurt (Oder), Germany and Roskilde University, Denmark. He works as a project coordinator at cultures interactive e.v. in the field of prevention of right-wing extremism and group-focused enmity in Germany and (Eastern) Europe. His PhD project focuses on the causes and effects of the government participation of East European radical right parties.

Eszter Kováts, is a PhD student in political science at University ELTE, Budapest. Since 2012 she has been responsible for the gender programme of the Friedrich-Ebert Foundation for East-Central Europe. She co-edited the volume *Gender as symbolic glue—The position and role of conservative and far right parties in the anti-gender mobilizations in Europe*, published by the FES and the Foundation for European Progressive Studies in May 2015.

Eeva Luhtakallio, PhD, is a lecturer in sociology at the University of Tampere. She is the author of *Practicing Democracy: Local Activism and Politics in France and Finland* (Palgrave Macmillan 2012) and has published widely in comparative political sociology and gender studies.

Diana Mulinari, PhD, is professor of gender studies at the Centre of Gender Studies, University of Lund, Sweden. She has written extensively on gender and development in Latin America and on the intersections of gender, race, ethnicity and class in the context of the Swedish welfare state.

Anders Neergaard, PhD, is associate professor at the Institute for Research on Migration, Ethnicity and Society (REMESO), ISV, Linköping University, Sweden. His research spans political sociology, third world studies, labour market studies and ethnic and migration studies, focussing on trade unions, labour market segmentation and cultural racism.

Kateryna Novikova, PhD in sociology at the John Paul II Catholic University of Lublin. She is an independent researcher and has conducted research on media discourses, networking and social movements, internet and identity, especially concerning imitation, knowledge sharing and self-creation, prejudices, ageism and ethnic stereotypes.

Mercedes Pöll is a sociologist with particular experience in the subjects of gender and sexuality studies. She holds a PhD in sociology and social policy (gender studies) from the University of Leeds, UK. With a focus on queer perspectives and analytical boundary work, Mercedes' research interests cover non-/normative intimacies (specifically relationships without sex), the culture(s) of compulsory sexuality, the concept of *sex*, intelligibility, as well as qualitative methodologies and research practice.

Anika Posselius, BA cultural and social sciences, MA European studies, studied at the European University Viadrina in Frankfurt (Oder), the University of Wrocław and the Adam Mickiewicz University Poznań. She is active as a volunteer, freelancer, trainer and project coordinator in the fields of educational, cultural and political work. Since 2007 she is working for the German NGO cultures interactive e.V. as project coordinator of national and international projects as well as trainer for adolescents and adults. Focuses: phenomenon of the radical and extreme right, group-focused hate, prevention, civil society, gender and human rights-based education.

Miquel Ramos, MA in sociology and anthropology of public policy from the University of València, Spain and graduate in information sciences from the Cardenal Herrera University (Valencia, Spain). Freelance journalist specializing in social movements and extreme right, hate crimes in Spain—monitoring, author of the hate crimes memory map crimenesdeodio.info and several reports on extreme right violence presented to the Valencian, Spanish and European parliaments.

Francesca Scrinzi, PhD, holds a position as senior lecturer in sociology at the University of Glasgow and is currently Marie Sklodowska-Curie Research Fellow at the European University Institute. She has researched migrant care workers, Evangelical migrants as well as gender relations in anti-immigration activism in Europe (European Research Council, 'Gendering activism in populist radical right parties. A comparative study of women's and men's participation in the Northern

League (Italy) and the National Front (France)', 2012–2014). Her publications include *Genre, migrations et emplois de care en France et en Italie* (Gender, Migration and Care Labour in France and Italy), 2013, Éditions Pétra, and *Migration, Masculinities and Reproductive Labour. Men of the Home*, Palgrave Macmillan (co-authored with Ester Gallo), 2016.

Kristian Steiner, PhD, is associate professor in peace and conflict studies at Malmö University, Sweden. His focus is on the construction of enemy images. In this context the empirical work deals with the images of Muslims and Islam in Swedish radical Christian newspapers. His current research involves radicalization, nationalism and globalization.

Marko Stojanovska Rupčić is a PhD candidate at the Central European University's department of Sociology and Social Anthropology in Budapest, Hungary. His interests include contemporary popular music in Central and Eastern Europe, as well as political landscapes in the region.

Alva Träbert, is a PhD candidate in sociology at the University of Edinburgh. Her research focuses on individual and collective queer identities in Scotland. She holds an MSc in gender history from Edinburgh and previously studied at the Ruhr University, Bochum. She teaches at Edinburgh University and abroad and is a co-organizer for the Edinburgh Gender History Network. She is a freelance trainer and delivers workshops on sexual consent and gender-based violence for charities.

Fabian Virchow, PhD, is professor in social theory and theories of political action at Dusseldorf University of Applied Sciences, Germany. He is Head of FORENA (Research Unit on Right-Wing Extremism). He has done scholarly work and published widely on worldview, history and praxeology of the extreme right in post-war Europe.

Tuukka Ylä-Anttila is a doctoral candidate with the Helsinki Research Group for Political Sociology at the University of Helsinki. His research deals with populist argumentation and political culture on- and off-line.

LIST OF FIGURES

LIST OF TABLES

Introduction

Michaela Köttig and Alice Blum

Europe is shifting to the right. Most recently, the national-conservative Prawo i Sprawiedliwość (PiS) party in Poland has shown that exclusionary and inhumane policies are the consequence of growing right-wing tendencies. With its call for a stricter abortion law, it is a symbol of the backward-looking politics that are on the rise in many European countries. Thus, Viktor Orbán, a nationalistic politician, has been Prime Minister of Hungary since 2010. Right-wing movements have arisen in various settings, whether in parliaments or as clandestine groups. Only a few years ago, members of the Golden Dawn movement in Greece killed the antifascist rapper, Pavlos, and in 2011 the National Socialist Underground (NSU) became public in Germany. In France, the National Front has been steadily winning voters for its agenda, and in the last European elections members of right-wing parties won more than 80[1] seats. The increasing numbers of asylum seekers in the European Union are being used by the extreme right in order to bring the European idea into discredit. Both women and men are involved in all these developments as active supporters or as victims of them.

These far-right developments are being registered and analysed in different ways in different European countries. In southern Europe,

M. Köttig (✉) • A. Blum
Frankfurt University of Applied Sciences, Frankfurt, Germany

© The Author(s) 2017
M. Köttig et al. (eds.), *Gender and Far Right Politics in Europe*,
DOI 10.1007/978-3-319-43533-6_1

1

research in this field has mostly dealt with the electoral successes of right-wing parties, such as the National Front in France, or the Golden Dawn Party in Greece. Researchers relate these successes to the economic crisis, which has disproportionately impacted southern European countries (Moffitt 2015). In northern Europe, researchers have investigated the causes of the electoral gains of right-wing parties, such as the populist Partij voor de Vrijheid in the Netherlands (see, e.g., Eissens and Bronkhorst 2011).

The European level was discussed by Beyme as long ago as 1988, and later studied in more detail by Mudde and Eatwell (2004). They examined the challenges posed by the extreme right for the Western democracies of Europe. Mudde then published a study of the East European countries in 2005, and a study of populist right-wing parties in 2007. In 2008, an encyclopaedia was published (Davis and Jackson 2008) which gives an overview of far-right politics in Europe and national traditions, together with discussions of specific topics. Later studies of particular countries follow this tradition, for instance, those in a comprehensive work published by the Bertelsmann Foundation in 2010 entitled Strategies for Combating Right-Wing Extremism in Europe. This book presents an overview of the radical right in Austria, Belgium, Denmark, France, Germany, Great Britain, Hungary, Italy, the Netherlands, Sweden and Switzerland. The book edited by Langenbacher and Schellenberg (2011) also shows the situation in different countries, and, more recently, the collection of articles edited by Melzer and Sarafin (2013) portrays the extreme right in Germany, Greece, Italy, Portugal, Poland, Romania, the Ukraine and Hungary.

In recent years, there have been various publications (such as Klandermans and Mayer 2006; Hainsworth 2008; Mammone et al. 2013; Mering and McCarty 2013) which provide more or less detailed accounts of extreme-right-wing phenomena in different countries and related issues. However, they hardly ever consider systematically to what extent women are involved, what their functions in right-wing groups are and what impact the social construction of gender has. There are some references to the results of investigations into attitudes (for instance in Beyme 1988), and Mudde (2007) refers to the European right-wing parties as 'men's parties' (*Männerparteien*).

The need for a Europe-wide debate on the significance of gender in the far right was the starting point for this book. The interdisciplinary research network 'Women and Right-Wing Extremism', which was founded in Germany in 2000, has taken on the task of collecting and systematising existing research on the significance of gender in the context of extreme-right tendencies. The 'Women and Right-Wing Extremism' network has established a gender-sensitive branch of research targeted at German right-wing extremism. Besides the general entanglement of right-wing extremism and gender (cf. Birsl 2011), scholars have analysed the lifeworlds and gender-specific strategies of female right-wing extremists (cf. Bitzan 1997; Köttig 2004; Roepke and Speit 2011), and also ideas of masculinity (Claus et al. 2010). The network, which was mainly concerned with Germany, wanted to extend its coverage to include other parts of Europe. In 2012, at a conference held in Nuremberg, scholars and journalists from many different European countries presented articles relating to their research on gender and right-wing extremism. This book is the result of that initiative, together with an online network and blog with the title 'Far Right Politics and Gender' (see: https://genderandfarright.wordpress.com).

Since these beginnings, there have been some important publications in the field of comparative research in Europe. Thus, Rydgren (2013) has made a transnational study of voting behaviour in working-class right-wing parties. Coffé (2013) examines the relationships among class belonging, gender and radical right voting in some Western European countries. Especially in the last two years, there have been further publications. A number of studies were published in 2015 in a special issue of the journal *Patterns of Prejudice* on gender and populist radical right politics. There has also been a recent publication on the subject of anti-gender mobilisation in Europe (Kováts and Põim 2015): on the basis of an initiative by Hungarian colleagues, it examines the connection between anti-gender movements and the positioning of conservative and extreme-right parties in five countries—Hungary, France, Germany, Poland and Slovakia. The results of this project are discussed in the article by Kováts in this book. Immerzeel, Coffé, and van der Lippe (2015) show that in 12 European countries more men than women vote for far-right parties. According to the authors, a 'gender gap' remains with big differences in the number of votes cast by women and men. However, at least in the case of France, this 'gender gap' is doubtful: Mayer (2015) shows that since 2012 Marine le Pen has been supported by almost equal numbers of men and women. Besides differences in voting behaviour, there have also been cross-border studies of other phenomena. For example, Akkermann (2015) examines gender issues in the family policies of six far-right parties in Europe. She comes to the conclusion that these parties largely follow traditional family policies. She interprets their acceptance of same-sex relationships and gender equality as rhetorical strategies. And comparative studies of participation by women in extreme-right contexts have been made in respect of Italy and France (Scrinzi 2014), and Hungary and Greece (Félix 2015).

In addition to these transnational gender perspectives, there have been some international publications devoted to specific topics in individual countries. For example, Mayer, Ajanovic, and Sauer (2014) analyse gender discourses in populist radical right parties in Austria. They come to the conclusion that not only traditional family values but also women's 'free choice', and LGBT-rights arguments play important roles in right-wing populist (re)framing processes of gender equality. However, the parties exploit these progressive arguments strategically in order to denigrate the (supposed) behaviour of Muslim men. A study of the situation in Germany has also been published (Dauber 2014).

The aim of this book is to make a systematic examination of the connection between the far right and the discourse on gender in different nation states. The authors have made it their task to analyse right-wing extremist tendencies in Europe from the specific perspective of gender. In all the countries considered, right-wing extremism is an important topic on the political agenda and cannot be ignored. Right-wing extremism has gained momentum, particularly in the countries of the former so-called Eastern Bloc and in the countries north of the Mediterranean, but also in the Netherlands, Sweden, Norway, Finland and the Federal Republic of Germany.

The book bundles existing findings regarding the quantitative dimension of activities carried out by men and women in different countries, and illuminates and juxtaposes gender ratios and the role of women in right-wing extremism. Besides their gender-specific approach to right-wing groups, the articles look at networks, organisational forms and specific strategies of female right-wing extremists, and their ideologies, especially regarding femininity and masculinity, hetero normativity and discourses on sexuality. Preventive and counter-strategies are also discussed, as well as media discourses and acknowledgement of this topic in public discourses. The book will contribute to expanding our knowledge of country-specific commonalities, achieving transparency with regard to international networking, and using this knowledge for multinational and comparative research.

For many of the authors, focusing on gender issues has a political motivation: commitment to gender equality, together with a critique of nationalist and racist exclusion. Their concern is to shed light on the activities of
women in the far right, and to show the significance for academic research
of gender-specific backgrounds in respect of the motivations and actions of
radical right-wing women and men, and the complex dynamics of gender-
related ideologies in the far right. Sensitivity to gender issues is a resource
which can make a constructive contribution to sound academic research
by helping to identify processes that otherwise remain hidden.

The chapters in this book were written independently of each other, and
reflect the individual research interests of the authors within the thematic
field of gender and the far right. Taken together, they present a picture
of the state of research on this topic in Europe, even if it is an incomplete
picture. On this basis, it should be possible to develop common research
questions and make systematic comparative studies in the future.

Part I presents an overview of the development of right-wing extremism and the current situation in various countries. Each study delves into
the gender discourse; particularly, the involvement and participation
of women in right-wing extremism in each country. In the first article,
Mulinari and Neergaard explore the specific Swedish situation. On the
basis of an empirical study, they show how women active in the Sweden
Democrats (SD) name and act upon their identities as members of what
many citizens and a growing number of scholars define as a racist or fascist party. In the second article, *Luhtakallio and Ylä-Anttila* present their
study of the male-dominated and conservative Finns Party. They focus on
gender equality and demonstrate that the Finns Party represents a backlash against gender equality politics in Finland; its electoral gains can be
seen in part as the victories of a new wave of masculinist politics. While
in Great Britain the right-wing movement is also male-dominated, British
women have founded several far-right organisations or parties, and there
is evidence that they have led to eruptions of street violence against certain immigrants, as *Dauber* shows in her contribution. *Bitzan* then gives
an overview of different phases in German research on women and/
or gender. The 'Forschungsnetzwerk Frauen und Rechtsextremismus'
(Research Network on Women and Right-Wing Extremism) is presented
as one of the central actors in the discourse and in research. *Klammer
and Goetz* introduce the Austrian situation. In their article, they discuss
the fundamental importance of gender as a category for analysing the
Freiheitliche Partei Österreichs (FPÖ) and its rearticulation of politics and

ideology. They take a look at the functions of female party members on the one hand, and the importance of male bonding on the other. Finally, they analyse the gender structure of anti-Muslim racism and antifeminism within the FPÖ and its political environment. *Anikó Félix's* article presents current research on women in radical right-wing political movements and organisations with special reference to the biggest radical right-wing party in Hungary: 'Jobbik, Movement for a better Hungary'. The article points out different types of women who join the radical right in Hungary. It shows what kind of motivations and ambitions women supporters have, how they connect to these movements and why they join. Looking to the south of Europe, *Ramos and Büttner* introduce women and gender ideologies in the far right in Spain. In their article, they focus on the public appearance of women and their role in programmes of right-wing organisations. Due to the fact that there are no investigations and sociological studies on gender, the aim is to get a first idea about the presence of women in extreme-right activities, and to examine the family concepts of three main ideological categories within the Spanish far right. A different perspective is offered by *Scrinzi* in her review of existing studies of women and gender relations in the National Front in France. She explores the relationships among gender, religion, secularism and recent ideological developments in the party by locating them in the specifics of the French political and cultural context. At the end of this chapter, *Alvanou* discusses the rise of the far right or nationalistic movement in Greece, leading to its dynamic presence in elections. The article presents the current scene and the period of the 4th August Regime as indicative examples of the far-right phenomenon in modern Greek history, highlighting gender issues relating to perceptions, roles, activities, stereotypes and how women participate in national politics.

Part II presents comparative research perspectives on European countries and beyond Europe. In the first article, *Dubslaff* compares the function, activities and political ideas of women's organisations within the National Democratic Party of Germany (NPD) and the French National Front (FN) between the 1980s and 2012. She examines the consequences of women's involvement in political processes—in terms of power sharing as well as political practice or ideological change—within both far-right parties. In the second article, *Kováts* analyses the genesis, the discourse and the structural factors of the anti-gender movements of different countries. She concludes that anti-gender movements need to be studied in a broader framework than country case studies, and that anti-gender fundamentalism and its success are symptoms and consequences of deeper socio-economic, political and cultural crises of liberal democracy. Finally, *Blee*—an American author with an established reputation in the field of research on the Ku Klux Klan and gender in the US—provides an outsider perspective on gender and right-wing extremism in Europe. Moreover, she compares commonalities and differences between the European and the American discourses.

Part III mainly presents the media discourse on gender and right-wing extremism. Using four countries as examples (Poland, Germany, Austria and Sweden), the authors examine the specific gender discourse regarding right-wing extremism in the media. *Novikova* analyses the media coverage of, and public discourses on, elderly ladies who are declared as, and declare themselves as, 'mohair berets' in Poland. Many of these women belong to the Catholic Church and have far-right views. These female activists are often represented as overly active and even threatening despite their age, health and appearance. On the basis of selected print media reports, *Köttig* shows in her contribution how the media construct gender stereotypes in dealing with the 'National Social Underground', a right-wing terror group in Germany. She then discusses the construction of offender personalities, which ignores or reinterprets the few known facts concerning the biographical backgrounds of the suspected perpetrators. *En, En and Pöll* explore the gender discourses in the Austrian far right in the book *MenschInnen: Gender Mainstreaming—Auf dem Weg zum geschlechtslosen Menschen* (Human/esses: Gender Mainstreaming—On the way to the genderless human) published by Barbara Rosenkranz in 2008. Their article shows that Rosenkranz' book and the discourses she draws on construct an elitist Other to the 'average citizen' and a threat to the continued survival of the Austrian nation and its people. The last article in this chapter is by *Steiner*. In his descriptive and comparative analysis, he researches the construction of Islam and Muslims, particularly Muslim women, in four Swedish newspapers in 2006 and 2007. He reveals a chasm between those media that accept the presence of Muslims and Islam in Sweden, and those that do not.

Part IV focuses on antifeminism and masculinity. Masculinities in the context of right-wing extremism have received little scholarly attention in studies or discourses in Europe. The discussion is based on four case studies. *Träbert* examines the antifeminist men's rights movement and its ideological connections with the political far right. Through the lens of online forums and networks, she explores antifeminist paradigms in

Germany, Switzerland and Austria and draws comparisons with the UK. In his article, *Stojanovska Rupčić* presents the latest work of the well-known Croatian singer Marko Perković Thompson. The spotlights of his research are on gender representations in the lyrics of Thompson's songs as well as in his public statements and Facebook activity. Furthermore, the author discusses in detail Thompson's ideas, which stem from the right-wing fringe of the Croatian political spectrum. After this, the far right's ideological constructions of 'deviant' male sexualities in Germany are analysed by *Claus and Virchow*. The authors show that the construction of normative male and female bodies, as well as a normative, child-producing family, dominates the picture of the far right, even though homosexuality and paedo-sexuality are also of great importance in far-right political thought and practice. Concluding the chapter, *Blum* deals with the construction of masculinity in the New-Right group 'Generation Identity', which originated in France. She focuses on the movement's history and ideological content, as well as the function and role of masculinity within the grouping.

Part V presents social-work approaches to finding gender-sensitive strategies for countering right-wing extremism. *Glaser* discusses projects which have worked with right-wing oriented and right-wing extremist women in Germany, and outlines certain demands for the further conceptual development of this specific kind of de-radicalisation work. Finally, based on the two-year WomEx project, with its European-wide linking of practitioners, *Baer, Kossack and Posselius* present some promising gender-reflective and gender-specific approaches and outline recommendations for prevention and intervention.

Thus, this book gives a good idea of current developments in the far right in Europe from a critical, emancipatory and gender-sensitive perspective. It is more than just a scientific analysis; it is a political statement, an attempt to counter radical right positions by means of sound research that exposes right-wing discursive strategies.

NOTE

1. See: http://www.europarl.europa.eu/aboutparliament/en/20150201
   PVL00010/Organisation-and-rules (accessed 21.03.2016).

REFERENCES

Akkerman, Tjitske. 2015. Gender and the Radical Right in Western Europe: A Comparative Analysis of Policy Agendas. *Patterns of Prejudice*, Special Issue on Gender and Populist Radical Right Politics, 49 (1–2).

Birsl, Ursula. 2011. *Rechtsextremismus und Gender*. Toronto/Berlin: Barbara Budrich Verlag.

Bitzan, Renate (ed). 1997. *Rechte Frauen*. Berlin: Elefanten Press.

Claus, Robert, Esther Lehnert, and Yves Müller (ed). 2010. *"Was ein rechter Mann ist...": Männlichkeiten im Rechtsextremismus*. Berlin: Dietz Verlag.

Coffé, Hilde. 2013. Gender, Class and Radical Right Voting. In *Class Politics and the Radical Right*, ed. Jens Rydgren, 138–155. London: Routledge.

Dauber, Andrea S. 2014. Not All Nazis Are Men: Women's Underestimated Potential for Violence in German Neo-Nazism. Continuation of the Past or Novel Phenomenon? In *Gendered Perspectives on Conflict and Violence*, vol 18(B), ed. Texler Segal Marcia, and Vasilikie Demos, 171–194.

Davies, Peter, and Paul Jackson. 2008. *The Far Right in Europe: An Encyclopedia*. Westport: Greenwood World Publishing.

Eissens, Ronald, and Suzette Bronkhorst. 2011. *Rechtsextremismus und -populismus in den Niederlanden: Nichts gelernt*. In Europa auf dem Rechten Weg, ed. Nora Langenbacher, and Britta Schellenberg, 131–151. Berlin: Friedrich-Ebert-Stiftung. Accessed 17 March 2016. http://library.fes.de/pdf-files/dialog/10031.pdf

Félix, Anikó. 2015. The Other Side of the Coin: Women's Participation in Far Right Parties and Movements in Greece and Hungary. *Intersections. East European Journal of Society and Politics* 1(1): 166–182.

Hainsworth, Paul. 2008. *The Extreme Right in Europe*. London: Routledge.

Immerzeel, Tim, Hilde Coffé, and Tanja van der Lippe. 2015. Explaining the Gender Gap in Radical Right Voting: A Cross-National Investigation in 12 Western European Countries. *Comparative European Politics* 13(2): 263–286.

Klandermans, Bert, and Nonna Mayer (ed). 2006. *Extreme Right Activists in Europe: Through the Magnifying Glass*. London: Routledge.

Köttig, Michaela. 2004. *Lebensgeschichten rechtsextrem orientierter Mädchen und junger Frauen—Biographische Verläufe im Kontext der Familien- und Gruppendynamik*. Gießen: Psychosozial-Verlag.

Kováts, Eszter, and Maari Põim. 2015. *Gender as Symbolic Glue. The Position and Role of Conservative and Far Right Parties in the Anti-gender Mobilisation in Europe*. Budapest: Foundation for European Progressive Studies and Friedrich-Ebert-Foundation. Accessed 16 March 2016. http://library.fes.de/pdf-files/bueros/budapest/11382.pdf

Langenbacher, Nora, and Britta Schellenberg (eds). 2011. *Europa auf dem Rechten Weg.* Berlin: Friedrich-Ebert-Stiftung. Accessed 17 March 2016. http:// library.fes.de/pdf-files/dialog/10031.pdf

Mammone, Andrea, Emmanuel Godin, and Brian Jenkins (ed). 2013. *Varieties of Right-Wing Extremism in Europe, Series: Extremism and Democracy.* London: Routledge.

Mayer, Nonna. 2015. The Closing of the Radical Right Gender Gap in France? *French Politics* 13(4): 391–414.

Mayer, Stefanie, Edma Ajanovic, and Birgit Sauer. 2014. Intersections and Inconsistencies. Framing Gender in Right-Wing Populist Discourses in Austria. *NORA—Nordic Journal of Feminist and Gender Research* 22(4). Accessed 29 October 2016. http://www.tandfonline.com/doi/abs/10.1080/08038740. 2014.964309

Melzer, Ralf, and Sebastian Serafin (ed). 2013. *Right-Wing Extremism in Europe: Country Analyses, Counter-Strategies and Labor-Market Oriented Exit Strategies.* Berlin: Friedrich-Ebert-Stiftung.

Moffitt, Benjamin. 2015. How to Perform Crisis: A Model for Understanding the Key Role of Crisis in Contemporary Populism. *Goverenment and Opposition* 50(02): 189–217.

Mudde, Caas (ed). 2005. *Racist Extremism in Central and Eastern Europe.* London: Routledge.

——— (ed). 2007. *Populist Radical Right Parties in Europe.* Cambridge: University Press Cambridge.

Mudde, Caas, and Roger Eatwell (ed). 2004. *Western Democracies and the New Extreme Right Challenge.* London: Routledge.

Roepke, Andrea, and Andreas Speit. 2011. *Mädelsache!: Frauen in der Neonazi-Szene.* Berlin: Ch. Links Verlag.

Rydgren, Jens (ed). 2013. *Class Politics and the Radical Right.* London: Routledge.

Sabine, von Mering, Timothy McCarty, and Abingdon Wyman. 2013. *Right-Wing Radicalism Today: Perspectives from Europe and the US.* Abingdon/Oxon: Routledge.

Scrinzi, Francesca. 2014. Gendering Activism in Populist Radical Right Parties. A Comparative Study of Women's and Men's Participation in the Northern League (Italy) and the National Front (France). Accessed 26 June 2016. http://www.gla.ac.uk/schools/socialpolitical/research/sociology/projects/ genderingactivisminpopulistradicalrightparties/publications/preliminary%20 report/

von Beyme, Klaus (ed). 1988. Right-Wing Extremism in Post-War Europe. *West European Politics* 11(2): 1–18. Accessed 17 March 2016. 10.1080/ 01402388808424678.

Country Reports

Doing Racism, Performing Femininity: Women in the Sweden Democrats

Diana Mulinari and Anders Neergaard

INTRODUCTION

During the past few decades, there has been an upsurge in research on Extreme Right Parties (ERP),[1] mirroring the political successes of these parties in Western Europe and to some extent in Eastern Europe. In the Swedish context this research, with a few exceptions, has been even more recent. However, these studies have so far rarely touched upon the theme of this book: gender. We would like to suggest that the marginalisation of gender analysis is linked to a certain extent with the exclusion of feminist, postcolonial (and critical) theory from mainstream academic studies on Erps.

This article has two aims. The first is to show the centrality of antiracist and postcolonial feminist scholarship for understanding these political parties. The second is to explore how women active in the Sweden Democrats (SD) name and act upon their identities as members of what many citizens, and a growing number of scholars, define as a racist (Hübinette and Lundström 2014; Berggren and Neergaard 2015) or as a fascist (Arnstad 2013) party. Methodologically, the research is a qualitative study based on

D. Mulinari (✉) • A. Neergaard
Lund University, Lund, Sweden
Linköping University, Norrköping, Sweden

© The Author(s) 2017   13
M. Köttig et al. (eds.), *Gender and Far Right Politics in Europe*,
DOI 10.1007/978-3-319-43533-6_2

text analysis, participant observation at municipal meetings and in-depth interviews with women in the SD.

TOWARDS AN ANTIRACIST FEMINIST THEORETICAL FRAMEWORK

We start by identifying two kinds of racist logics—exploitative and exclusionary. Exploitative racism is racism that through discursive and institutional practices produces a usable (exploitable) racialised labour force. Exclusionary racism, on the other hand, constructs the racialised as a threat that needs to be dealt with in a "civilised" manner by stopping immigration and by policies of repatriation, or, in a radicalised version, through annihilation. Exploitative and exclusionary racisms should be seen as ideal types that may co-exist but in different constellations and hierarchies.

While these two different racist logics may partially be understood as linked to class relations, we also contend that they are gendered. Whereas racialised men play an ambivalent role in exploitative racism, where they may form part of a highly educated labour force but at the same time be problematic in terms of employment, racialised women are moulded by colonial racist fantasies that see them as a subservient labour force in the expanding low-wage private service and care sector (Gavanas 2010). By contrast, exclusionary racism, with its focus on the racialised other as a threat to the nation, has a quite different gendered agenda. Aiming at the expulsion of the racialised other from the national body, male immigrants are portrayed, both metaphorically and literally, as rapists of the nation. Racialised women (often together with their small children) are conceptualised as parasites, reproducing the racialised other and annihilating the national body from within.[2]

SWEDISH EXCEPTIONALISM AND THE SUCCESS OF THE SDs

Sweden has often been admired, not only for its social-democratic welfare regime, with comparatively small class differences, which often includes Norway and Denmark (i.e. the Scandinavian model), but also for being (often together with Norway) a relatively gender-equal country, due to a political project of state feminism (Borchorst and Siim 2008). While the dismantling of Keynesian welfare state institutions began under social-democratic governments towards the end of the 1980s, the neoliberal assault against social insurance and welfare services started with the right-wing minority government in 1991–1994, with the (passive) support of New Democracy, a short-lived ERP with an increasingly racist rhetoric. However, neoliberalism was not fully institutionalised until the right-wing government of 2006, with serious impacts on the lives of women in their role as care-givers (Belfrage and Ryner 2009; Kuisma and Ryner 2012).

The Swedish racialisation regime is undergoing rapid changes. For a long time, Sweden has been known internationally as the model of a multicultural welfare state which extended substantial citizenship, welfare, and labour rights to all[3] within its borders (Schierup et al. 2006). However, under the twin pressures of neoliberalism and the EU's commitment to "managed migration", this Swedish exceptionalism has been, and continues to be, significantly eroded (Ålund et al. 2016).

This has gone hand in hand with politicians (especially from right-wing parties, but at times also from the Social Democratic party) arguing for policies aimed at connecting citizenship rights with assimilation; sometimes, linking immigrants with welfare "cheating", criminality and failing to identify with "Western values" (Hubinette and Lundström 2010). An important aspect of what have been named the "new assimilation" policies is a strong emphasis on gender equality as a national cultural symbol, an essential aspect of "Swedishness", which is portrayed as conflicting with immigrants, especially immigrants with a Muslim background (de los Reyes et al. 2002). Thus, when the chairman of the SD named Islam and the Muslims as the biggest threat to Sweden since World War II, it was in a context in which anti-Muslim racism (Listerborn 2002) had been present in varying degrees through mainstream public discourse, linking up to what is often symbolised by 9/11, but was well in place way before, a general Western demonisation of the Muslim Other (Morgan and Poynting 2012).

In 2010, the SD successfully entered the Swedish parliament with 5.7 % of the votes, and in 2014 more than doubled its support to 12.9 %. Research on the birth and growth of the SD combines two trajectories. The first trajectory links it to right-wing populism in a Scandinavian tradition, and the New Democracy of the early 1990s (Rydgren 2006), while the second and dominant understanding emphasises its background in the Neo-Nazi and racist social movements of the 1990s (Larsson and Ekman 2001; Deland and Westin 2007; Gardell 2015).

The official rhetoric and policies of the SD today are far from traditional vulgar and coarse racism (although individual representatives are repeatedly caught by the media using more or less obvious racist slurs); it is a nuanced, tactical, and strategically designed discourse that nevertheless fails (or does not want) to distance itself from fundamental ideas of race (mediated through concepts such as ethnic groups, natural residence, nationality, ethnicity and culture).

GENDER REPRESENTATION AND THE SWEDEN DEMOCRATS

While the SD has over 9000 members, only about 20 % are women, which is also the percentage in the Swedish parliament (22 % in 2014, a slight increase from the 2010 elections). The percentage of women representatives in municipal and regional councils is similar, substantially below the average of the other parties. The estimation (from exit and opinion polls) of the female votes is around a quarter to a third, and it is not increasing (see also Mulinari and Neergaard 2015).

When the SD doubled their number of votes in the 2014 national election, they did so in ways that repeated the campaign of 2010. Their central theme remained the Muslim threat and the welfare costs of immigration. However, in relation to gender there were some novelties compared to 2010. This included a more pronounced and developed political programme on gender issues, advocated by a new gender-equality representative of the party, who, following accusations of antifeminism, defined herself as "essentialist feminist". With the explicit aim of securing stronger support from women, the party announced some new policies, such as the right to full-time employment for women, who are often forced directly or indirectly to take part-time jobs, and parliamentary lists containing more women candidates (15 % to 22 %), which continues to be a low rate regarding female representation in Sweden.

In analysing the position of women as representatives of the SD, there is a clear pattern of strong male dominance. Following the elections in 2010, and partially as an effect of the entry of the SD into the national parliament, the percentage of female MPs decreased, which led a Swedish TV journalist to ask the SD chairman how it feels to have lower female parliamentary representation than in Muslim countries such as Afghanistan, Pakistan and the United Arab Emirates.[4] In so doing, the journalist played on the SD's racist propaganda against Muslims and its weakness on gender equality by pointing out that even conservative Muslim parliaments have better female representation than the SD.

AT THE MARGINS OF THE SWEDISH WELFARE MODEL

The women we interviewed differ from each other in terms of age (23–65), ethnic background (15 from the majority population, 5 with a migrant European background) and marital status (single, divorced, cohabitant, married). They also differ in their path to political involvement. While some have long experience in politics in other established political parties, others have been active in far-right populist parties at the municipal level or within extreme-right racist movements, and the third group has never been active in politics (Linden and Klandermans 2007).

What attracts women to far-right movements that appear to denigrate their rights? Claudia Koonz is a feminist historian whose work (1987) on Nazi women and on women's support of Nazism provides an interpretation focusing on the process of empowerment that their participation in these movements makes possible. Nazi womens' central role in the creation of the nation has opened up public/political spaces. The connection between empowerment and women's participation is also at the core of the explanation provided by sociologist Kathleen Blee (1996), based on her study of women in the Ku Klux Klan. She argues that women members of contemporary US racist groups reconcile the male-oriented agendas of organised racism with understandings of themselves and their gendered self-interests, situating the political action of women racists in rational (if deplorable) understandings of self and society (Blee 2007). Maarten Van Ginderachter (2005) develops a similar argument in his study of the extreme right and Flemish nationalist women's organisations in interwar Belgium. The author suggests, drawing on Karen Offen's distinction between "relational" and "individualist" feminism, that these movements were not uniformly antifeminist, citing a "relational" tradition to justify women's public and political participation. Women were attracted to these organisations, which appeared to denigrate their rights, because they were actively engaged in the production of a nationalist discourse of their own, feeling empowered with new opportunities for agency (see also Kevin 2003). While it would be a slight exaggeration to say that most of our informants saw themselves as empowered, political activism through the party did at least decrease their feeling of disempowerment and, as will be shown below, created a social embedding.

But why did these women feel disempowered? Mayer and Perrineau (1992), as researchers focussing on men, identify a process of neolib eral globalisation as the source of marginalisation. Our material shows that failure to respond to the demands that a gender order based on a social-democratic legacy imposes on its citizens in a period of neoliberal transformation is at the core of our informants' feeling of being outside the political norm. This marginalisation, or rather relative deprivation (Walker and Pettigrew 1984), is present in two ways: a workfare regime with demands for individual economic independence and a heteronormative gender regime that constructs women as both mothers and workers (Dahl 2004; Lundqvist 2011). With two exceptions (a young girl with a background in a neo-Nazi movement and a middle-aged woman with an academic career), the women we spoke to were employed irregularly and part-time, unemployed, on sick leave, or dependent on welfare because of their sporadic employment patterns. The following three quotes from women representing the SD illustrate this:

And it began with my husband—he joined from the beginning. And he thought, well, I needed something to do; because I'm on sick leave and can't really do anything but stay at home.   I needed to get out and meet people. No money. The Soc [she is referring to social assistance—author's comment] controlling what you eat. I've never been politically involved before. It's hard. I almost wouldn't have coped if I'd had a job. But as I'm unemployed, then it is easier.

In Sweden, a marginal position in the labour market not only has consequences for the household economy, but it creates a gap between these women and the professional identity of most Swedish women with a stable[5] position in the labour market. This pattern of weak professional identity and fragile link to the labour market dominates our material, with one exception: Annika, who works within welfare services in a multicultural district and whose professional identity is, according to her, a source of respect from other politicians. But in her deep identification with her work, the informant is in many ways a contrast to the SD's vision of women. The SD women's network argues that individualism has gone too far in society and has had negative effects on families and children, not least by a "depreciation of women's roles as mothers, the glorification of career and professional work that has been fed into the latest generation's consciousness".[6]

The marginal labour market position (Annika being an exception) is well illustrated by Maria, who tells the interviewer that she is hoping for a better tone in political life. She was not the only one of our informants to highlight the issue of how other politicians relate to SD representatives, but she captures the paradox that their position implies. The more they aim at providing classification systems that homogenise the phenomenon of immigration (the assumption being that immigrants live on welfare), the greater is the risk that the same classifications will be used against them in political debates:

> But I hope they understand. Because now we've had a course at the City Council (and that was yesterday) and they said—it was a lecturer from Sweden's municipalities and counties—and then she said that she was out lecturing about this, about this good tone in politics. About not allowing personal attacks, not violating anyone; everyone has the right to express their opinion in the council. But I can tell you that during the evening there were still some of them that crossed the line. And then you asked yourself, what had they learned from the course just a few hours ago?
> Interviewer: What—can you give some examples of that: because when you say 'crossed the line', what was that?
> Well, let's see.... That you address personal stuff, for example. It was when we requested this information on the costs of immigration to our municipality. And then the debate shifted to the personal, like: 'What about you? You've been a cost to the municipality too. You have been on sick leave for years. A lot of money for twelve years,' he said.... I felt so humiliated. We need a different tone in politics.

Female members of the SD, experience that they are attacked by what they themselves name as the "multicultural media" in articles targeting SD politicians, have often shown lifeforms where debts and forfeits, as well as interaction with the Enforcement Administration and with criminal justice are highly present.[7] These women represent a group that has difficulties in creating a life form that they are proud of in the context of the (neoliberal) transformation of the Swedish welfare state. This transformation has created a tougher labour market climate that embraces efficiency and requires employees to act competitively (Boreus 1997; Borchorst and Siim 2008; Gavanas 2010). Not only have their living conditions worsened, but the new ideological discourse criminalises poverty; citizens' rights to welfare are seen as a societal burden and they are described as cheaters. Many of the women we interviewed could be interpreted as having reacted against this stigmatisation by projecting it onto others, onto an entire category of people: immigrants.

SD women are representatives of a form of femininity (Martin 2001) that is difficult to locate in the Swedish discourse on gender equality, rooted as it is in women's equal participation in the labour market on the one hand and double-income households on the other. This discourse is central for women politicians in all Swedish parties whether left or right. Our empirical material shows that women react against a social-democratic model of gender equality, inspired to a certain extent by second-wave feminism (Bergqvist et al. 2007). Their marital status (many are divorced, single mothers or without children) may have decreased their identification with the Christian Democrats, the only party in parliament sharing at least some of their views about gender, although without the strong racist frame.

Women's activism must be understood as a strategy to mobilise the only capital (Adkins 2001) they have left: their Swedishness. We say "Swedishness", but should say "whiteness/Europeanness", as some of our informants have migrated from other European countries. But an understanding of whiteness that lacks a class analysis risks creating essentialised links between whiteness and privileges, privileges that this specific group often lack.[8] It is precisely their lack of privileges, their exclusion in terms of the national discourse on what a Swedish woman should be, that is fundamental to understanding their political involvement. In parallel to Beverly Skeggs' (1997) working-class women in search of respectability through traditional forms of femininity, this is a group in search of recognition; in Fraser's (2000) terminology, they locate misrecognition above ("elite") and below (racialised other) themselves.

In understanding the ideology of SD and other forms of racist organisations, Gidengil et al.'s (2005) emphasis on capturing racism and sexism through understanding white masculinity is central (Norocel 2013). However, for our focus on understanding the few women who join the SD as activists, the central debate among feminist historians on the location of women within Nazism as victims or co-perpetrators seems helpful (Bock 1998). Our study illustrates the significance of women's agency and, particularly, the experience of empowerment as a strong motivation to join the SD. While marginal within the male-dominated party structure, these women actively invest in discourses of "caring for their own" (Narayan 1995). In addition, they also develop a reasoning in which caring is extended to the "Other", but in the form of highlighting that "they" would feel better if they did not come to Sweden, or if they were repatriated, a partial form of caring racism (Mulinari and Neergaard 2014). Our study also shows that these investments in racist worldviews make them a serious threat to other women.

FEMINISM IS WRONG. BIOLOGY IS RIGHT. THE SD'S UNDERSTANDING OF GENDER EQUALITY

Gender equality is not given a specific place in the SD's key policy documents. Neither is gender given a separate section in its 2012 municipality programme. However, in their programme at the county level (regional issues concerning health, transport, etc.), the party argues in favour of what they define as a formal equality between men and women.[9] Yet, this is followed by three arguments that challenge Swedish social policy regarding gender equality. The first one is the statement that the SD does not consider it a problem that (despite formal equality) women and men do different things or do things at different levels. The second is the equalising shift that identifies men as also at risk of being discriminated against—a shift that is very similar to that regarding racism, which is acknowledged but also equalised through the notion of discrimination and racism against (true) Swedes. The third is SD's argument with respect to biological differences regarding health and illness—an argument which embraces a notion that gender equality (in the Swedish/feminist/hegemonic version) is about the denial of "real" differences between women and men.

Under the heading "Swedish gender equality equates woman with cattle", Margareta Sandstedt, at that time a member of the SD's party executive, declared: "How much money and suffering gender-equality ideology has consumed can be evaluated by looking at divorce rates, making visits to child and adult psychiatry wards, social services, schools, medical centres, and addiction care and law enforcement".[10]

For this party representative, gender equality is one of the roots of all societal conflicts. This quote shows that the SD is also a response to the successful Swedish women's movement, as well as to Social Democratic policies that provide not only public support for combining work and family, but equalise, accept and explicitly support different family forms (Lundqvist 2011). The SD often refers to science in order to legitimate its understanding of gender. Biological differences between women and men explain differences between them: it's all in the brain.[11]

Like cultural differences, gender is understood not only in terms of the "reality" of physical attributes but also in terms of specific (fixed, unchangeable) characteristics. In the following quote, Therese Borg, a leading female SD activist, develops this argument: "These policies do not offer, in our opinion, equal opportunities. On the contrary, they force equalising without any consideration taken that differences between men's and women's brains and hormones result in women and men generally having different qualities, or that from as early as newborn babies' differences between girls' and boys' attitudes may be traced. Policies take gender equality as a point of departure, and ignore the fact that, no matter how they may try to make women and men behave in the same way, they will not succeed because of biological makeup".[12]

However, gender equality is a difficult issue for the SD. On the one hand, the party's ideological core is suspicious of gender equality and its connection with feminism; on the other, gender equality, constructed as a Swedish national trait, is often the fundamental boundary between us and them. Swedishness in this context is gender equality as a national characteristic, which is used specifically to highlight the difference between Swedes and Muslims, as in the intervention by Jimmy Åkesson, the party leader, describing Muslims as the most serious threat to Sweden since the World War II.[13]

While it could be argued that the SD follows similar patterns to the way that anti-Muslim racism is articulated globally, we would like to suggest that the focus on gender at the core of the "cultural clash" is specific to the country's history of being a women-friendly welfare state (as in the case of Norway).[14] The argument that gender equality is a feature of Swedish culture, a point made by certain strands of Swedish mainstream feminism, has been increasingly used by the SD. While there is little evidence to suppose that, when feminists and the SD argue in similar ways against the oppression of Muslim women, this is based on similar ideological positions, there are some overlaps in both the framing of diasporic gender cultures and in their reading of gender equality as a Swedish quality.

CONCLUDING REMARKS

We have argued in these pages that the SD, despite its efforts to include women in the party, is confronted by two contending nationalist narratives: on the one hand that of a gender-equal Sweden, and on the other the need for traditional gender roles to be treated as vital for the maintenance of the nation. The SD's argument in support of gender equality is used only with reference to immigration, and is systematically criticised in all other contexts. To understand the strong antifeminist rhetoric of the SD in general, and SD women in particular, one has to grasp how feminism in Sweden plays out differently from the other countries mentioned above. Both academic feminism and the two strong feminist parties (the Left Party and the Feminist Initiative) have been the staunchest critics of the SD, calling it a racist party. Our analysis is in line with the few studies published to date. Towns et al. have argued that "[W]hile the Sweden Democrats claim to support gender equality in discussions of multiculturalism and immigration, the party is a fierce critic of gender equality in all other contexts" (2014, p. 237).

The more than doubling of the number of votes in the 2014 national election (12.9 % as compared to 5.7 % in 2010), shows that there is strong support for a cultural racist party in Sweden, resembling in many ways the three Nordic neighbours—Denmark and the Danish People's Party (21.1 %, 2015), Norway and the Progress Party (16.3 %, 2013), and Finland with the True Finns (17.6 %, 2015). While there are important differences between these parties, concerning for instance welfare, gender and racialised regimes, one could argue that a new version of the "Nordic Model" is linked to the presence of strong cultural racist parties. It is interesting to ask why the countries that came to represent social justice, aiming to produce a welfare regime that decreased class differences, and a gender regime abolishing forms of inequality between men and women, today form the region of Europe where cultural racist parties are most established and politically influential. What are the links between welfare and gender regimes in transformation, and the strength of cultural racist parties? This is an intellectual challenge for future research to pursue.

Finally, any feminist analysis that explains the participation of women in racist parties only as a product of their marginalisation is problematic. There is evidence that, while neoliberal policies have affected larger groups of women, few women transform their marginality into active support for a racist party. Furthermore, the crisis argument for explaining the growth of ERPs is not substantiated by Sweden or the Nordic region. Here, these parties have expanded (likewise, women's support for these parties, and in both Denmark and Norway there have been women party leaders) although these are countries with well-developed welfare regimes and with no serious economic crises in recent times. While our study emphasises that marginalisation is an important sociological concept for understanding women's participation in the SD, it is not enough. Women's investment in racist selves is located within an historical continuity of European colonialism in general, and the Swedish racialisation regime in particular.

Notes

1. We use extreme right parties as a general name for these parties; see also Table 7.1 in Berggren and Neergaard 2015, 194.
2. See the 2010 SD election film http://www.youtube.com/watch?v=5UiUdpYVubY (accessed 2016-03-10).
3. This has not been the case for undocumented/irregular immigrants in Sweden (Sager 2011).
4. http://www.youtube.com/watch?feature=player_detailpage&v=H--Q-atkZqg#t=346s (accessed 2011-05-23, no longer available).
5. Stable but with lower wages, higher degree of part-time and temporary employment.
6. See the interview with the chairperson of the SD's female network (http://nojesguiden.se/artiklar/lika-varda-men) (accessed 2016-03-10).
7. 'SD—One in ten with a criminal record—assault most common' http://expo.se/2006/val06-sd-a-var-tionde-kriminellt-belastad-a-misshandel-vanligast_1709.html (2006) (accessed 2016-03-10).
8. See the discussion on the use of the term "White trash" (Wray and Newitz 1997).
9. Sverigedemokraterna (2012) Generella riktlinjer för en sverigedemokratisk region-och landstingspolitik.
10. Sandstedt, M. (2007) http://www.sdkuriren.se/blog/index.php/margareta/2007/12/10/den_svenska_jamstalldheten_likstaller_kv (accessed 2009-10-27, no longer available).
11. One favourite reference here is Dahlström, A. (2007) Könet sitter i hjärnan. Göteborg: Corpus-Gullers.
12. Borg, T. (2011) (http://sdkvinnor.se/2011/10/08/fortryck-i-jamstalldhetens-namn/ (accessed 2016-03-10).
13. Åkesson, J. (2009) (http://www.aftonbladet.se/debatt/debattamnen/politik/article12049791.ab) (accessed 2016-03-10).
14. Björklund, P. http://www.sdkuriren.se/blog/index.php/bjorklund/2009/02/18/det_handlar_om_liv_och_dod, (accessed 2009-02-18, no longer available).

REFERENCES

Adkins, Lisa. 2001. Cultural Feminization: "Money, Sex and Power" for Women. *Signs. Journal of Women, Culture and Society* 26(3): 669–682.

Arnstad, Henrik. 2013. *Älskade fascism: De svartbruna rörelsernas ideologi och historia*. Stockholm: Norstedts.

Belfrage, Claes, and Magnus Ryner. 2009. Renegotiating the Swedish Social Democratic Settlement: From Pension Fund Socialism to Neoliberalization. *Politics & Society* 37(2): 257–287.

Berggren, Erik, and Anders Neergaard. 2015. Populism—Protest, Democratic Challenge and Right-Wing Extremism. In *International Migration and Ethnic Relations: Critical Perspectives*, ed. M. Dahlstedt, and A. Neergaard, 169–199. London: Routledge.

Bergqvist, Christina, Tania Blandy Olsson, and Diana Sainsbury. 2007. Swedish State Feminism: Continuity and Change. In *Changing State Feminism*, ed. J. Outshoorn, and J. Kantola, 224–245. Basingstoke: Palgrave Macmillan.

Blee, Kathleen. 1996. Becoming A Racist: Women in Contemporary Ku Klux Klan and Neo-Nazi Groups. *Gender & Society* 10(6): 680–702.

———. 2007. Ethnographies of the Far Right. *Journal of Contemporary Ethnography* 36(2): 119–128.

Bock, Gisela. 1998. Ordinary Women in Nazi Germany: Perpetrators, Victims, Followers, and Bystanders. In *Women in the Holocaust*, ed. D. Ofer, and L.J. Weitzman, 85–100. London: New Haven.

Borchorst, Ann, and Birte Siim. 2008. Woman-Friendly Policies and State Feminism Theorizing Scandinavian Gender Equality. *Feminist Theory* 9(2): 207–224.

Boreus, Kristina. 1997. The Shift to the Right. Neo-Liberalism in Argumentation and Language in the Swedish Public Debate Since 1969. *European Journal of Political Research* 31(3): 257–286.

Dahl, Ulrika. 2004. *Progressive Women, Traditional Men: The Politics of Knowledge and Gender Stories of 'Development' in the Northern Periphery of the EU*. Santa Cruz: University of California.

de los Reyes, Paulina, Irene Molina, and Diana Mulinari. 2002. *Maktens (o)lika förklädnader. Kön, Klass och etnicitet i det postkoloniala Sverige*. Stockholm: Atlas.

Deland, Mats, and Charles Westin. 2007. *Brunt. Nationalistisk och nazistisk mobilisering i vår närmaste omvärld under efterkrigstiden*. Atlas: Stockholm.

Fraser, Nancy. 2000. Rethinking Recognition. *New Left Review* 3: 107–120.

Gardell, Matias. 2015. *Raskrigaren: Seriemördaren Peter Mangs*. Stockholm: Leopard Förlag.

Gavanas, Anna. 2010. *Who Cleans the Welfare State? Migration, Informalization, Social Exclusion and Domestic Services in Stockholm*. Stockholm: Institute for Futures Studies.

Gidengil, Elisabeth, Matthew Hennigar, André Blais, and Neil Nevitte. 2005. Explaining the Gender Gap in Support for the New Right: The Case of Canada. *Comparative Political Studies* 38(10): 1171–1195.

Hubinette, Tobias, and Catrine Lundström. 2010. Sweden After the Recent Election: The Double-Binding Power of Swedish Whiteness Through the Mourning of the Loss of "Old Sweden" and the Passing of "Good Sweden". *NORA-Nordic Journal of Feminist and Gender Research* 19(1): 42–52.

Hübinette, T., and Catrine Lundström. 2014. Three Phases of Hegemonic Whiteness: Understanding Racial Temporalities in Sweden. *Social Identities* 20(6): 423–437.

Kevin, Passmore (ed). 2003. *Women, Gender and Fascism in Europe 1919–1945*. New Brunswick, NJ: Rutgers UP.

Koonz, Claudia. 1987. *Mothers in the Fatherland: Women, the Family, and Nazi Politics*, 1st edn. New York: St. Martin's Press.

Kuisma, Mikko, and Magnus Ryner. 2012. Third Way Decomposition and the Rightward Shift in Finnish and Swedish Politics. *Contemporary Politics* 18(3): 325–342.

Larsson, Stieg, and Mikael Ekman. 2001. *Sverigedemokraterna: Den nationella rörelsen*. Stockholm: Ordfront.

Linden, Annette, and Bert Klandermans. 2007. Revolutionaries, Wanderers, Converts, and Compliants Life Histories of Extreme Right Activists. *Journal of Contemporary Ethnography* 36(2): 184–201.

Listerborn, Carina. 2002. Understanding the Geography of Women's Fear: Toward a Reconceptualization of Fear and Space. In *Subjectivities, Knowledges, and Feminist Geographies: The Subjects and Ethics of Social Research*, ed. L. Bondi, 34–43. Lanham, Md: Rowman & Littlefield.

Lundqvist, Åsa. 2011. *Family Policy Paradoxes: Gender Equality and Labour Market Regulation in Sweden, 1930–2010*. Bristol: Policy.

Martin, Patricia. 2001. "Mobilizing Masculinities": Women's Experiences of Men at Work. *Organization* 8(November): 587–618.

Mayer, Nonna, and Pacal Perrineau. 1992. Why Do They Vote for Le Pen? *European Journal of Political Research* 22(July): 123–141.

Morgan, George, and Scott Poynting. 2012. *Global Islamophobia: Muslims and Moral Panic in the West*. London: Ashgate.

Mulinari, Diana, and Anders Neergaard. 2014. We Are Sweden Democrats Because We Care for Others: Exploring Racisms in the Swedish Extreme Right. *European Journal of Women's Studies* 21(2): 43–56.

Narayan, Uma. 1995. Colonialism and Its Others: Considerations On Rights and Care Discourses. *Hypatia* 10(2): 133–140.

Norocel, O. Cristian. 2013. "Give Us Back Sweden!" A Feminist Reading of the (Re)Interpretations of the Folkhem Conceptual Metaphor in Swedish Radical Right Populist Discourse. *NORA Nordic Journal of Feminist and Gender Studies* 21(1): 4–20.

Rydgren, Jens. 2006. *From Tax Populism to Ethnic Nationalism: Radical Right-Wing Populism in Sweden*. New York, NY: Berghahn Books.

Sager, Maja. 2011. *Everyday Clandestinity: Experiences on the Margins of Citizenship and Migration Policies*. Lund: Faculty of Social Sciences, Centre for Gender Studies, Lund University.

Schierup, Carl-Ullrik, Peo Hansen, and Stephen Castles. 2006. *Migration, Citizenship, and the European Welfare State: A European Dilemma*. Oxford: Oxford University Press.

Skeggs, Beverly. 1997. *Formations of Class and Gender. Becoming Respectable*. London and New York: Sage Publications.

Towns, Ann, Erika Karlsson, and Joshua Eyre. 2014. The Equality Conundrum: Gender and Nation in the Ideology of the Sweden Democrats. *Party Politics* 20(2): 237–247.

Walker, Iain, and Thomas Pettigrew. 1984. Relative Deprivation Theory: An Overview and Conceptual Critique. *British Journal of Social Psychology* 23: 301–316.

Wray, Matt, and Annalee Newitz. 1997. *White Trash: Race and Class in America*. London: Routledge.

Contesting Gender Equality Politics in Finland: The Finns Party Effect

Tuukka Ylä-Anttila and Eeva Luhtakallio

THE FINNS PARTY AND FINNISH EQUALITY POLITICS

What are the consequences of far-right electoral success in a country with a strong tradition of equality politics? In this chapter, we juxtapose the politics of gender advanced by the candidates and party publications of the Finns Party with Finnish equality politics.

The right-wing populist Finns Party[1] (*Perussuomalaiset* [PS]) broke through in the 2011 Finnish parliamentary elections, more than quadrupling its share of votes (19.1 %); it continued to do relatively well in the 2012 municipal elections (12.3 %), and entered government following the 2015 parliamentary elections with a strong result of 18.2 %. Men are over-represented in the party's electorate (Grönlund and Westinen 2012, 159), as is common with European radical right populist parties (Mudde 2007, 111–112). The gender repartition of candidates is also strongly

---

The authors have contributed equally to this work

T. Ylä-Anttila (✉)
Department of Social Research, University of Helsinki, Helsinki, Finland
School of Social Sciences and Humanities, University of Tampere, Tampere, Finland

E. Luhtakallio
School of Social Sciences, University of Tampere, Tampere, Finland

© The Author(s) 2017   29
M. Köttig et al. (eds.), *Gender and Far Right Politics in Europe*,
DOI 10.1007/978-3-319-43533-6_3

male-dominated: 66.8 % in the 2011 parliamentary elections, 76.7 % in the 2012 municipal elections, and 64.7 % in the 2015 parliamentary elections (Statistics Finland 2011, 2012, 2015). In the 2011 and 2012 elections, the overall percentage of female candidates dropped. For the municipal elections, this was the first time since the 1950s (Holli et al. 2007, 19–23). This is significant in the Finnish context, where a strong equality discourse has marked party politics since the 1970s. The Finns Party's linked discourses on nationalism and gender challenge the status quo on gender equality and create a counter-trend to recent developments in other parties, both quantitatively and qualitatively (see also Kantola and Saari 2012).

In this chapter, we first present an overview of the rise of the party and the context of the Finnish equality discourse. We then analyse two facets of the Finns Party's rise: the gender gap and the gender discourse. We compare the arguments of the party's male and female candidates on various policy issues, and present a view of the party's gender politics by analysing its publications. The comparative analysis finds that the party's left-populist elements—stressing social justice and poverty reduction—are more typical of female candidates, while the far-right candidates are mostly men. The analysis of the party's gender politics, in turn, indicates that the party strongly challenges prevailing Finnish conceptions of gender equality.

THE RISE OF THE FINNS PARTY

The Finns Party breakthrough in the 2011 elections was largely a protest against a stagnant political sphere, which had been dominated by three mainstream parties for decades. The euro crisis and a political corruption scandal fuelled the debate; these were served to the Finns Party as if on a silver platter right before the election (Arter 2010; Borg 2012; Mattila and Sundberg 2012; Pernaa 2012; Ylä-Anttila and Ylä-Anttila 2015). The growing support for the party also made it a credible alternative to voice objections to immigration, mobilized in particular by a lively online anti-immigration movement. The party was able to mobilize previous non-voters while also attracting voters away from mainstream parties. The Finns Party voters come from all societal classes, but especially from the working class. One of the most notable characteristics of their voter base, however, is its male dominance (Borg 2012; Ylä-Anttila 2012, 2014).

The argument that populism is a backlash against stagnant politics (Canovan 1999; Taggart 2004) fits the Finnish situation rather well. This is not to say that the PS vote could be brushed off as 'just a protest' without political content: it is undoubtedly ideological (Eatwell 2003, 51–52; Kestilä 2006). Anti-elitism and conservatism, frustration with politics in general, and anti-EU and anti-immigrant sentiments in particular were mobilized when the opportunity arose. One feature of the Finns Party's conservative ideology is that is represents an 'alternative' to the dominant gender equality politics. Yet, as our analysis will show, the relationship between the Finns Party and the 'hegemonic gender equality discourse' detected in Finnish politics (Holli 2003) is more complex than it may seem. We argue that the Finns Party is under strong pressure to include women, like many populist parties (see Niemi and Parkkinen 2012), while still emphasizing traditional gender roles. First, however, we will consider the context of Finnish equality politics.

GENDER AND EQUALITY IN FINNISH POLITICS

The Finnish party system and gender equality politics are historically intertwined; the two entered the public sphere nearly in step. Finland was the first European country to grant women the right to vote in parliamentary elections in 1906, followed by municipal elections in 1917. The parliamentary elections in 1907 made Finland the first country in the world to have women MPs (Ministry of Justice 2007, 13). Nevertheless, the early elections and parliaments were largely the domain of men. As late as 1954, only 15.2 % of candidates were women. This gradually increased to 41.2 % in 1991, but dropped slightly to 39.0 % in 2011, together with the rise of the Finns Party (Statistics Finland 2003a, b, 2007, 2011).

While the early developments of the 1900s did not render women's political representation equal to men's (Holli and Kantola 2005, 62), a programme for gender equality in political representation is inherent to the history of Finnish party politics. It has become customary to describe this feature through the concept of *state feminism*, meaning the plethora of policy issues specifically aimed at improving the gender equality that was included in the Finnish welfare state project, and the strong representation of the women's movement within party politics and state structures (see Kettunen 2008, 128–171; Holli and Kantola 2005, 2007), as illustrated by the importance of strong and independent women's associations within political parties. All major Finnish parties have a women's association, and these associations are all members of the umbrella organization 'Women's Associations in Cooperation' (Naisjärjestöt yhteistyössä ry [NYTKIS]).

NYTKIS is a good example of the wide cross-party cooperation between women's party associations and other civil society actors, characteristic of the Finnish field of gender equality politics, and leading to a certain level of consensus in major equality issues (Kantola and Saari 2012, 2, 7). This consensus has been effective in realizing several policies that were considered 'advanced' in terms of gender equality at the time, such as day care for children and a relatively long maternity leave as subjective rights. The consensual cooperation has also established a 'hegemonic' gender equality discourse, providing a means of 'equality education' for newcomers in the field (ibid.).

However, developments in recent decades have revealed that the Finnish style of equality politics is afflicted by an implementation problem: despite lengthy efforts and comprehensive legislation, essential equality indicators such as equal pay, gendered violence, or shared parental leave show stagnation rather than strong progress (Holli and Kantola 2007). The Finnish political sphere has a dual take on gender: on the one hand, gender equality has the status of a hegemonic discourse; on the other hand, implementation of equality policies falls short on multiple levels of governance. Gender discrimination is a difficult issue to discuss, as it tends to provoke deliberate underestimation or even hostile denial (Holli 2003, 2012; Holli et al. 2007; Luhtakallio 2012). This dualism also figures in the Finns Party discourse, as we will show.

The stagnation of contemporary equality politics is shown in women's political representation: the percentage of female electoral candidates began to stagnate in the 1990s and even drop slightly in the 2010s, coinciding with the electoral gains of the Finns Party. The party had more than doubled its number of candidates since the municipal elections of 2008, and 76.7 % of its candidates were men (Statistics Finland 2012). This overrepresentation of men marks a clear difference from other parties (Fig. 1), especially the Greens, who represent an opposition to the Finns Party on almost any issue (Grönlund and Westinen 2012, 183).

The elections of 2011 marked a step towards reversing the trend of women as more active voters due to an exceptionally strong mobilization of male voters, as Fig. 2 shows. This is partly explained by the Finns Party (Grönlund and Westinen 2012, 159), which was particularly successful in mobilizing men who did not previously vote (Borg 2012, 196).

Finnish equality policies and legislation are also facing recurrent problems. Studies on implementation of the gender quota law (Holli et al. 2006) show that attempts to circumvent the law are regular, and civil servants have a tendency to 'forget' to implement it (Holli et al. 2006;

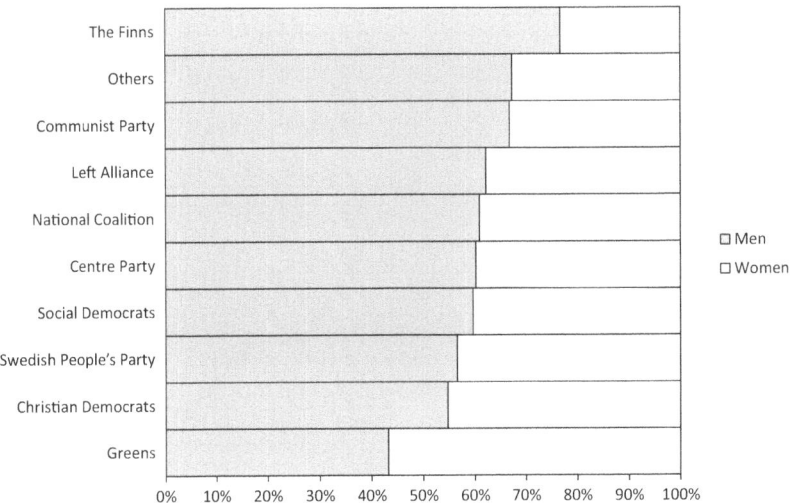

Fig. 1 Gender distribution of candidates by party in Finnish municipal elections 2012 (Statistics Finland 2012)

Holli 2011). A survey (Parviainen 2006, 300–302) found that 54 % of male respondents were ready to abolish the quota law, whereas 74 % of women felt it was a necessary measure. The resistance against quotas was particularly strong among male representatives of right-wing parties.

Nousiainen et al. (2013) suggest that a concept of equality that stresses quantitative 'factual' equality, and disregards more complex intersections of power and equality policies, creates conditions for calling into question the legitimacy of equality measures, regardless of their legal status. At least since the 1980s, Finnish equality struggles have been marked by recurrent attempts to deny the existence of gender discrimination (e.g. Holli et al. 2006, 2007; Holli 2011). Furthermore, Kantola and Saari (2012) argue that the emphasis on numerical claims regarding, for example, the representation of genders in the quota law, the 'women's euro is 80 cents' argument in equal pay debates, or the statistics of shelter visits and police intervention in gendered violence, enables problems underlying these phenomena to be concealed along with sources of gender discrimination in cultural practices and political power struggles. In their view, reducing equality to technical arguments about numbers and statistics is a sign of a recent turn towards conservative and right-wing thinking in the Finnish gender equality discourse (ibid.).

Fig. 2 Turnout (%) in Finnish parliamentary elections by gender, 1962–2011 (Statistics Finland 2007, 2011)

In sum, it seems that the new nationalist movement in Finnish politics is led by men and is connected with counter-arguments against the earlier gender equality politics. The hegemonic nature of the discourse on 'already achieved' gender equality, however, much of a fiction it may be, makes it a fruitful ground for 'fresh questioning' that undermines the legitimacy of equality policies. Next, we will examine how the Finns Party gender politics takes shape in this context.

THE FINNS PARTY GENDER GAP

What does the male dominance of the Finns Party mean for its politics? Does the political argumentation of Finns Party men differ from that of Finns Party women? We examine this by analysing male and female Finns Party candidates' arguments in the 2011 parliamentary elections. The dataset we use is the *Helsingin Sanomat* Voting Advice Application (HS VAA), a website set up by the largest daily newspaper in Finland, designed to facilitate voters' decisions by a political questionnaire. VAA's have become very popular among voters in Finland (Mykkänen 2011, 17).

The candidates who responded to the questionnaire also posted free-text comments on the questions, which were released, with the multiple-choice answers, as Open Data (Helsingin Sanomat (HS), 6 April 2011). This dataset offers a substantial body of non-moderated text produced by candidates, especially valuable for studying a populist party that typically accuses the media of misrepresenting their opinions. In this dataset, 202 (84.9 %) out of a total of 238 PS candidates posted written comments. Three questions were selected for analysis, representing left–right and liberal–conservative ideological cleavages. These were questions about income equality, immigration policy, and gay adoption rights, constituting a text dataset of roughly 15,000 words. These texts were qualitatively analysed, coded for recurring arguments and compared by gender.

LEFT-WING WOMEN, RIGHT-WING MEN

In the question on income equality—'Since the mid-1990s, income inequality has increased rapidly. How would you respond to this?'—Finns Party responses predominantly called for levelling income cleavages on the basis of social justice, an argument typical of the political left. Two populist subcategories of this argument were, first, appealing to the injustice experienced by disadvantaged people, and second, condemning the unjust position of elites. Some saw income equality as a matter of national unity, while others still argued, in right-wing fashion, that income cleavages are in fact necessary to encourage competition and reward achievement (Table 1).

Comparing respondents by gender, women argued more often for levelling of income cleavages to achieve social justice, but a difference is

Table 1 Arguments by gender for question on income equality[a]

	Women (N = 48)	Men (N = 98)	Difference (Women − Men)
Social justice	56 %	39 %	17 %*
Poverty reduction	42 %	19 %	22 %**
Anti-elitism	17 %	18 %	−2 %
Unity of the people	8 %	10 %	−2 %
Economic competition	0 %	13 %	13 %*

[a]Some respondents voiced several arguments, which is why the sum of percentages may be more or less than 100 %. **$p < 0.01$; *$p < 0.05$ based on a Pearson's chi-squared test (two-sided tests)

especially evident in those responses that specifically referenced the distress of the poor; this was more than twice as common among female respondents. 'The differences in income between the highest earners and the poorest, the "true underclass", are huge. [...] Income differences invoke despair and pessimism in the poorest part of the people. [...] the poor cannot afford anything but the most necessary of necessities' (F, 35).[2]

In the anti-elitist and the nationalist 'unity of the people' argument, there was no gender gap. However, only men used the right-wing argument that income cleavages have positive effects. 'I don't see differences in incomes as a signal of injustice as such. The problem is not that some earn plenty [...] I believe it is good that a person can get wealthy by honest work [...] This should not be prevented by unduly hard taxation' (M, 39).

The VAA also contained another question on economic redistribution: whether child benefits should be paid universally or according to income. Here, women again stressed poverty relief, while some men argued that child benefits are a 'reward' for mothers for rearing children to uphold the vitality of the nation.

MINORITY RIGHTS: MIXED MESSAGES OF (IN)TOLERANCE

The second question we analysed dealt with immigration policy: 'During the parliamentary term 2007–2011, immigration policy was tightened by several separate decisions. Do you feel that Finland's current immigration policy is too strict, agreeable, or too slack?' Here, the respondents most often argued in favour of selective immigration that would be economically beneficial for Finland, typically in the form of 'employment-based immigration', rating immigrants on the basis of job qualifications. Other recurring arguments included a discursive connection of immigration with crime, demanding the deportation of criminal immigrants. A simple 'Finns first' argument was that Finnish politics should focus on the interests of (ethnic) Finns, and an anti-multiculturalist argument was that while a diversity of cultural identities is positive in principle, cultures should be protected from mixing (see, e.g. Betz and Johnson 2004, 316–320) (Table 2).

Most notably, we observed the lack of any significant differences. All of the categories identified are uniformly supported by both genders. Male and female respondents are equally critical of Finnish immigration policy and often advocate selective immigration, where immigrants would

Table 2 Arguments by gender for question on immigration policy

	Women (N = 37)	Men (N = 86)	Difference (Women – Men)
Calculation of (economic) effects of immigration	35 %	33 %	2 %
Immigrant criminals	11 %	9 %	2 %
Finns first	11 %	7 %	4 %
Anti-multiculturalism	8 %	5 %	3 %

be evaluated for their potential contribution to the Finnish economy. 'Finland needs to be open to immigration that is neutral or beneficial in quality. We need to be strict when effects are negative [...] Finland cannot be the social office for the whole world [...] I would employ a citizenship test, a language test and a scoring system' (M, 24).

The final question analysed addressed adoption rights for gay couples: 'The Parliament legalized intra-family adoption for gay and lesbian couples in 2009. Should gay and lesbian couples have the right to adoption in general?' While the most common and repeated argument—'a child has a right to a mother and a father'—showed no gender gap, the argument of 'normality' of heterosexuality and the 'abnormality' of gay couples did. Men used this argument three times as often as women. 'Every child has a biological father and mother. According to my view, an adoption family should attempt to mimic this biologically "normal" arrangement, thus no one should have two mothers or two fathers' (M, 39).

Women, on the other hand, argued in favour of equal adoption rights for homo- and heterosexual couples roughly twice as often as men, often adding that gender or orientation does not matter as long as the child is cared for. 'A good father or mother is just that, even if the child is not their own. Being homosexual doesn't reduce the ability to be a parent. [...] Homosexuals have fought a difficult battle to become accepted: that's a school [that] undoubtedly gives one an outlook on things different from narrow-minded intolerance' (F, 43).

Finally, the conservative Christian 'homosexuality is sin' argument was mentioned by a handful of men (Table 3).

In sum, female Finns Party respondents expressed left-wing views on social justice, and poverty reduction in particular, more often than men. In contrast, only men used the right-wing argument that income

Table 3   Arguments by gender for question on homosexual adoption rights[a]

	Women (N = 40)	Men (N = 84)	Difference (Women–Men)
Child has a right to a mother and a father	25 %	26 %	−1 %
Homosexuality is abnormal	10 %	31 %	−21 %*
Equal rights	30 %	14 %	16 %*
Homosexuality is sin	0 %	6 %	−6 %*

[a]** $p < 0.01$; * $p < 0.05$ based on a Pearson's chi-squared test (two-sided tests)

cleavages enhance economic competition. The majority of both male and female candidates opposed immigration, and justified this with economic or cultural arguments or by connecting immigration with crime (see, e.g. Eatwell 2003; Hainsworth 2008; Mudde 2007). On the issue of gay adoption rights, the women of the party are more liberal. This shows that the connection between gender and far-right attitudes matters for the party: its hard-line right-wing policy seems partly to be a product of its male majority.

THE FINNS PARTY GENDER DISCOURSE

From the gender gap, we now turn to the gender discourse the party puts forward. We analysed how gender and equality politics figure in texts aimed both at supporters and at the wider public: the public material of the Finns Party women's organization, the party's electoral manifestos and the party magazine. To match the above analysis of the 2011 VAA, we chose the electoral manifesto of the 2011 parliamentary elections and volumes 2011 and 2012 of the party magazine *Perussuomalainen*.[3]

'WOMEN, NOT FEMINISTS'

The women's organizations of all Finnish mainstream parties (The National Coalition, the Social Democrats, the Centre Party, the Green League, the Left Alliance, the Swedish People's Party and the Christian Democrats) state their mission in very similar terms, being mainly concerned with advancing gender equality in politics and in society. On the websites of all organizations except the Finns Party, the first paragraph of the introduction contains the terms 'gender equality' or 'feminism'. The stated *raison d'être* of the Finns Party Women diverges from this: 'The goal of the women's organization is to gather together on a Christian social basis, and in cooperation with the party, those population groups whose interests and socially, economically and societally equal status have not been justly taken care of' (Finns Party Women 2012).

Only after listing seven population groups in need of 'more equality', including families, pensioners and the unemployed, none of which are specified in terms of gender, the website portrays five missions that aim at the aforementioned goal: 'creating a national network of women', 'promoting women's equality and general economic and social benefits', 'advancing the value of women's work in the contexts of society and the home as well as the changing labour environment', 'developing the maternity leave system and pension security', and 'defending the right of children to a safe and humane growing environment'.

Except for these missions that directly concern women, the organization's material stresses issues that are of general importance to the party. It highlights the significance of 'family values', and emphasizes equality between socio-economic and age groups rather than genders. In the party magazine, the chairwoman of the organization, Marja-Leena Leppänen, emphasizes that Finns Party women want to cooperate with men and be 'women, not feminists' (parliamentary elections issue 2011). The Finns Party Women's promotion leaflet strengthens this image, giving special emphasis to motherhood and caring, such as caring for elderly relatives, and associated social policies. In addition, women's entrepreneurship receives attention.

In the Finnish party subsidy system, around 10 % of the state subsidy is allocated to each party's women's organization (Ministry of Justice 2009; Finnish Government 2013). The party loses this share of the subsidy if it does not have a women's organization. The Finns Party Women's chairwoman admits in an interview in the party magazine (parliamentary elections issue 2011) that this is indeed the reason why the organization was founded and exists—to qualify for the subsidy. She adds that this is 'just like in all other parties', which is not the case: other women's party organizations were founded well before the subsidy came into effect—most of them decades ago. For instance, the history of the Social Democrats' women's organization (founded in 1900) dates back to the struggle for women's right to vote (Social Democratic Women 2013).

TRADITIONALISM MEETS HEGEMONIC GENDER EQUALITY?

Gender issues are few in the texts of the women's organization. Also, the 2011 electoral manifesto rarely addresses gender explicitly, even though it deals with diverse policy issues, including immigration, the EU, social and health issues, special needs of war veterans, the elderly, families, and so on. An exception is the question of parental leave, which the manifesto addresses by calling for an even division of the expenses between the employers of both parents.

Nevertheless, gender issues are important in the parts of the manifesto which deal with the party's vision of the role of the family in a society. They outline how the family should be connected to the notion of nationhood: 'The family is the basic unit of society and children are the future of the nation'. Initiatives to increase fertility are endorsed, and 'marriage is meant to unite a man and a woman'. It follows that the idea of gay marriage as an equality issue is turned down.

In the *Perussuomalainen* party magazine, gender equality does figure as a recurrent theme. The president of the organization has a column in several issues, and reports on the women's organization are frequent. Articles describe the organization's annual meetings and festivities, as well as events organized by its local subsections. Additionally, women in active campaign work for the party get publicity in the magazine. The tone is often 'empowering', and the general message suggests that women should be encouraged to join the party activities in greater numbers. The headlines are full of enthusiasm: 'The Finns Party Women Lapland: Power isn't given, it has to be taken!' (12/2011), 'Feminine energy on the road' (9/2012), or 'Women with an important cause: the Finns Party Women rolled up their sleeves and addressed societal problems in the Kemi spring meeting' (10/2012). The value of women's work for the party is emphasized, and the women themselves are described rather solemnly, for example: 'The Finns Party Women don't run wild at celebrities' parties, and no scandal headlines will be written [about] us. We are ordinary, or lone wolves, we are women, spouses, mothers and grandmothers. We are women who, year after year, work for the party for the sake of [the] common good along with running the everyday routines' (9/2012).

Equality is addressed in some stories, and the argument is in line with the typical hegemonic equality discourse we described previously, that is, equality is a national Finnish virtue that should be fostered and enhanced when it is in need of (small) amendments. However, mentions of gender equality *politics* are rare and often accompanied by 'pleasant' stories to 'soften' the topic, like in an article about the Lapland subsection's drive in which gender equality is discussed while distributing sweets: 'The Finns Women of Lapland delighted people on the slope of the Levi fell by distributing a thousand and one chocolate kisses on Women's Day, March 8th. With cheerful spirits and smiles, everybody got a kiss regardless of age, nationality, or gender. The theme of The Finns Party Women was a woman's life course. Sharing the expenses of parenthood, decrease in university intake, unemployment, entrepreneurship, and EU politics were discussed. Women's equality is in reality still unaccomplished. Domestic work and the burden of family responsibilities stop many women from being active, for example, in party politics' (5/2012).

The quotation repeats a recurrent feature of the Finnish political discourse on equality in general, that is, the idea of equality as a state of things that *can* be accomplished once and for all, instead of equality as a process or an ever-ongoing struggle (e.g. Holli et al. 2007). The examples given of the 'problems' that prevent equality from being realized are all directly related to motherhood. The emphasis on the joyfulness of the event and the humoristic allusions to kisses in the story are typical of articles reporting on women's organization activities—they serve to render the issues discussed sympathetic and perhaps less likely to trigger conflict within the party.

Such a discursive technique is in use when the magazine reports on the annual meeting of the women's organization, a rather undramatic proceeding described very matter-of-factly—the sitting president continues and a new board is elected—but at the end, the reporter describes how, during the evening's festivities, the women are invited to dance by 'willing, courteous local gentlemen' who are delighted to be cavaliers to Finns Party ladies (15/2012).

Women Are Welcome, But Gender Doesn't Matter

A recurrent theme in *Perussuomalainen* articles is the importance of women for the party and the good treatment they get, especially from party leader Timo Soini. He is portrayed as a (god)father figure who extends special protection to women party activists. As the president of the women's organization recounts in one of her columns, he welcomes a women's delegation to Brussels with a warm hug, encourages women to continue the good work, and 'also knows how to listen' (16/2011).

However, few women are in the party, the magazine highlights them with both words and images. The majority of these stories and pictures are not connected with gender equality issues, but create the impression that women have a front row seat in the party (see Niemi and Parkkinen 2012). 'Finns Party women improve the quality of politics' (3/2011), states the magazine, and then presents a variety of stories that repeat this message, without, however, going into further detail on how the party's politics may or may not be affected by the work of women activists.

On the one hand, the party's gender discourse builds on a repeated insistence that women are and should be welcome to be active in the party. On the other hand, it stresses that gender actually does not matter at all. The following story about women members of a local party association in eastern Finland captures the paradox: 'We have been accepted in the party with a lot of encouragement, and they have even made room so that women have been able to join the activities. I could say that womanhood has been a sheer benefit in this regard. [...] Men have quickly included women in the tasks of the party district. Women have been active themselves and have shown with their own work that they can take responsibility for things. [...] "Talking business and taking matters forward does not have to do with gender", says one of the party veterans. [...] The Finns Party Women of Etelä-Savo [...] find equality between genders in the party, both in the district and on the part of the party leaders, so self-evident that they have never even thought about the matter' (5/2011).

Women have been included, they feel welcome, men have happily 'made room' for them, and women have shown that they are worthy of the room given—and yet, gender 'does not matter', so much so that no one has ever given it a thought. The above quotation seems to portray the negotiation of a peaceful resolution of the 'gender issue' between the party activists: a male party veteran confirms that doing politics is gender neutral, and the women state that gender equality is not an issue of any importance. Furthermore, the story insinuates a critique of the 'traditional' conception of equality and positions gender equality as an old-fashioned concern.

MEN'S RIGHTS

Finally, *Perussuomalainen* magazine often treats gender and equality issues via discussions about child-care politics—and men. The debate on the Finnish child-care subsidy system gains plenty of attention. The coverage is univocal: the right to an allowance for home care of children gains unquestioned support, and strong appreciation of stay-at-home mothers is voiced. Home care is 'cost effective' (6/ 2012), and being a stay-at-home mother is 'a precious title' (13/ 2012).

Interestingly, discussions on fatherhood and child-care also get significant attention. These stories bring forward an important feature of the Finns Party equality politics. Whereas women's importance in the party is emphasized in multiple ways, as shown above, societal gender equality problems that particularly concern women, such as unequal pay or violence against women, are mainly ignored. In contrast, the question of fatherhood is directly linked to a discussion on men's rights in society and the need to promote *men's* equality. A story that reports on the founding of the Finns Party men's organization *Perusäijät,* 'Ordinary Blokes', depicts a man washing the bottom of a newborn baby: 'The ordinary bloke does not give in easily! The ordinary Finnish man sings at a karaoke night "I will never give in..." At home, it's a different story. Tough brute on the exterior, yet the ordinary bloke bends but does not break. In a tough spot, even a male may breed. A hardened shovel of a hand holds the newborn baby with tenderness. [...] "Everything works except breastfeeding", said a metal worker from Rauma, father of the newborn *Nuppu'* (15/2012).

The language the article uses to describe the man taking care of the baby is striking: the 'tough brute' and his 'hardened shovel of a hand' echo a 'good old' working class masculinity that is contrasted with the newborn baby girl *Nuppu* (Blossom). The story continues with an anti-feminist argument of equality 'gone too far' and claims that the party men's organization is needed to ensure that men are not discriminated against and women favoured 'in the name of equality'.

To recapitulate, gender equality issues are not addressed in the party manifesto, and it instead presents the traditional nuclear family as central to the vitality of the nation. In the party magazine, women feature strongly, and gender is often presented as the reason for writing about them; they are on display to show that there are active women in the party. The stories stress their activities *as women*, but womanhood often equals motherhood and other traditional caregiver roles. Gender equality politics is often labelled old-fashioned or in need of a 'new' perspective, that is, men's rights. Nevertheless, women's visibility in politics and men's right to stay at home with their children *are* topical questions of gender equality, and it is not without importance that the Finns Party magazine grants them space on its pages.

Conclusions

In this article, we have explored the Finns Party from a gender perspective and juxtaposed our findings with what previous studies have taught us about Finnish equality discourses and politics. The landslide electoral gains of a male-dominated and conservative Finns Party coincide with stagnating women's representation in Finland, and with a conservative turn in discourses on equality. We have shown how these developments resonate within the Finns Party by comparing the male and female candidates' opinions, and by analysing the gender discourses the party's publications portray.

There is indeed a gender gap in the party: women stress social justice and the rights of the disadvantaged in a left-wing vein. However, in terms of immigration politics, the Finns Party women and men follow the same line of thought, and opposition to immigration unites the party.

Our reading of party materials shows that Finns Party gender politics are conservative, if not outright anti-feminist. The prevailing conception of gender leans on traditional roles in representing women and men. The *Perussuomalainen* magazine does give women a special place in party publicity, but the role is mostly a supporting one: women confirm and prop the canon of the party. Gender equality is conceptualized either as society's support of motherhood, an accomplished fact, or, in some cases, through men's roles and rights as fathers.

In sum, we suggest, firstly, that populist right-wing politics and an anti-feminist political agenda are linked in several ways in Finland today. Despite men forming the majority of Finns Party candidates and voters, and being responsible for the most right-wing attitudes within the party, Finns Party women also refrain from supporting a feminist agenda in equality politics or politics that aim at dismantling power structures behind discriminatory practices, such as gendered violence or unequal pay. Secondly, the Finns Party equality discourse challenges Finnish state feminism by using features of the 'hegemonic' gender equality discourse. Conceiving equality as a matter of national pride, something already or nearly achieved, enables belittling gender discrimination and concealing power structures that cause gender inequality because they cannot possibly exist in a country that 'has gender equality'. In this regard, the Finns Party represents a backlash to gender equality politics in Finland, and its electoral gains can be seen in part as the victories of a new wave of masculinist politics.

Finally, while the Finns Party attempts to include more women to continue its electoral success, we can speculate on the effects of the potentially growing role of women in the party. On the one hand, the women's organization's participation in NYTKIS is likely to spread know-how on equality politics among the Finns Party women. This, combined with the Finns Party women's more left-wing opinions compared to men, indicates that an increase in the number of women could pull the party in a more liberal direction. On the other hand, there are signs that after electoral success, the party has rather moved even further towards the socially conservative far right (e.g. Ylä-Anttila and Ylä-Anttila 2015). Politicians with conservative gender agendas may further challenge Finnish state feminism by using a dualist equality discourse—where equality as a norm is taken as a given, while the existence of actual problems is denied. The Finns Party and its women may play an important role in this, as they emphasize 'already achieved' equality, the traditional conception of women as caregivers, the party's male leadership and men's rights.

Notes

1. Previously often translated as the True Finns, Ordinary Finns or Basic Finns, *Perussuomalaiset* adopted the official English name The Finns after receiving international media attention (Helsingin Sanomat (HS), 21 Aug. 2011). The word *perus* refers to fundamental 'down-to-earth' ordinariness as a virtue.
2. The gender and age of the candidates are portrayed.
3. Seventeen issues of *Perussuomalainen* magazine were published in 2011, and 16 issues in 2012. An average issue contains 24–28 pages and 42 articles, including feature stories, interviews, political columns, commentaries and opinions. We read through titles, introductions and subtitles in the 2011 and 2012 volumes. If any of these indicated that the story touched upon equality politics and/or gender-related issues, we included the article in our corpus. We found and analysed 47 gender and/or equality-related articles. We looked at the general themes these articles treated, as well as the recurrent discursive techniques used to address gender and equality. We will refer to the magazine by no. of issue/year of publication.

References

Arter, David. 2010. The Breakthrough of Another West European Populist Radical Right Party? The Case of the True Finns. *Government and Opposition* 45(4): 484–504.

Betz, Hans-Georg, and Carol Johnson. 2004. Against the Current—Stemming the Tide: The Nostalgic Ideology of the Contemporary Radical Populist Right. *Journal of Political Ideologies* 9(3): 311–327.

Borg, Sami. 2012. Perussuomalaiset. In *Muutosvaalit 2011*, ed. Sami Borg, 191–210. Oikeusministeriön selvityksiä ja ohjeita 16/2012. Oikeusministeriö (Ministry of Justice).

Canovan, Margaret. 1999. Trust the People! Populism and the Two Faces of Democracy. *Political Studies* 47(1): 2–16.

Eatwell, Roger. 2003. Ten Theories of the Extreme Right. In *Right-Wing Extremism in the Twenty-First Century*, ed. P. Merkl, and L. Weinberg, 47–73. London: Frank Cass.

Finnish Government. 2013. *Puoluetuet myönnetty*. Valtioneuvoston viestintäosaston tiedote 54/2013. Online. Accessed 7 March 2016. http://valtioneuvosto. fi/ajankohtaista/tiedotteet/tiedote/fi.jsp?oid=377140

Grönlund, Kimmo, and Westinen, Jussi. 2012. Puoluevalinta. In *Muutosvaalit 2011*, ed. Sami Borg, 156–188. Oikeusministeriön selvityksiä ja ohjeita 16/2012. Oikeusministeriö (Ministry of Justice).

Hainsworth, Paul. 2008. *The Extreme Right in Western Europe*. London: Routledge.

Holli, Anne Maria. 2003. *Discourse and Politics for Gender Equality in Late Twentieth Century Finland*. Acta Politica 23. Helsinki: Department of Political Science, University of Helsinki.

———. 2011. Transforming Local Politics? The Impact of Gender Quotas in Finland. Women and Representation. In *Local Government: International Case Studies*, ed. Barbara Pini and Paula McDonald, 142–158. Abingdon: Routledge.

———. 2012. Kriittisiä näkökulmia tasa-arvon tutkimukseen. In *Tasa-arvo toisin nähtynä*, ed. J. Kantola, K. Nousiainen, and M. Saari. Helsinki: Gaudeamus.

Holli, Anne Maria, Eeva Luhtakallio, and Eeva Raevaara. 2006. The Quota Trouble Talking about Gender Quotas in Finnish Local Politics. *International Feminist Journal of Politics* 8(2): 169–193.

———. 2007. *Sukupuolten valta/kunta. Politiikka, muutos ja vastarinta suomalaisissa kunnissa*. Tampere: Vastapaino.

Holli, Anne Maria, and Johanna Kantola. 2005. A Politics for Presence: State Feminism, Women's Movements and Political Representation in Finland. In *State Feminism and Political Representation*, ed. J. Lovenduski. Cambridge: Cambridge University Press.

———. 2007. State Feminism Finnish Style: Strong Policies Clash with Implementation Problems. In *Changing State Feminism*, ed. J. Kantola, and J. Outshoorn. Basingstoke: Palgrave Macmillan.

Helsingin Sanomat (HS). 2011a. *HS:n vaalikone on nyt avointa tietoa*, April 6. Online. Accessed 16 March 2012. http://blogit.hs.fi/hsnext/hsn-vaalikone-on-nyt-avointa-tietoa

———. 2011b. *Perussuomalaiset otti käyttöön englanninkielisen nimen*, August 21. Online. Accessed 16 March 2012. http://www.hs.fi/politiikka/artikkeli/1135268708128

Kantola, Johanna, and Milja Saari. 2012. *Conservative Women MPs' Constructions of Gender Equality in Finland*. Paper presented at the ECPR joint session of workshop *Consevratism, Conservative Parties and Women's Political Representation*. Antwerp, April 10–15.

Kestilä, Elina. 2006. Is there Demand for Radical Right Populism in the Finnish Electorate? *Scandinavian Political Studies* 29(3): 169–191.

Kettunen, Pauli. 2008. *Globalisaatio ja kansallinen me. Kansallisen katseen historiallinen kritiikki*. Tampere: Vastapaino.

Luhtakallio, Eeva. 2012. *Practicing Democracy Local Activism and Politics in France and Finland*. London: Palgrave MacMillan.

Mattila, Mikko, and Jan Sundberg. 2012. Vaalirahoitus ja vaalirahakohu. In *Muutosvaalit 2011*, ed. Sami Borg, 227–238. Oikeusministeriön selvityksiä ja ohjeita 16/2012. Oikeusministeriö (Ministry of Justice).

Ministry of Justice (Oikeusministeriö). 2007. *Eduskuntavaalit 1907*. Online. Accessed 16 January 2013. http://www.vaalit.fi/eduskuntavaalit1907/vaalit1907.pdf

———. 2009. *Puoluerahoituksen avoimuus. Vaali- ja puoluerahoitustoimikunnan mietintö*. Komiteanmietintö 3.

Mudde, Cas. 2007. *Populist Radical Right Parties in Europe*. Cambridge: Cambridge University Press.

Mykkänen, Juri. 2011. Kognitiivinen mobilisaatio ja vaalikoneiden käyttö. *Politiikka* 53(1): 16–29.

Niemi, Mari K., and Laura Parkkinen. 2012. Soinin enkelten siivin uuteen nousuun. *Kanava* 4: 4–8.

Nousiainen, Kevät, Anne Maria Holli, Johanna Kantola, Milja Saari, and Linda Hart. 2013. Theorizing Gender Equality: Perspectives on Power and Legitimacy. *Social Politics* 20(1): 41–64.

Parviainen, Mervi. 2006. *Tasa-arvo laskimella. Tutkimus tasa-arvolain kiintiösäännöksen vaikutuksista kunnallisten toimielintn jäsenvalinnoissa*. Helsinki: Edita.

Pernaa, Ville. 2012. Vaalikamppailu mediassa. In *Muutosvaalit 2011*, ed. Sami Borg, 29–42. Oikeusministeriön selvityksiä ja ohjeita 16/2012. Oikeusministeriö (Ministry of Justice).

Perussuomalainen. 15/2012. The Finns Party's Official Magazine. Archive online. http://www.perussuomalaiset.fi/perussuomalainen-lehti/lehtiarkisto

Statistics Finland (Tilastokeskus). 2003a. Women in Parliamentary Elections (*Naiset eduskuntavaaleissa*). Online. Accessed 15 January 2013. http://www.tilastokeskus.fi/til/evaa/2003/evaa_2003_2004-05-31_kat_004.html

———. 2003b. Percentage of Women Candidates by Party in Parliamentary Elections 1948–2003. (*Naisten osuus ehdokkaista puolueittain eduskuntavaaleissa 1948–2003*). Online. Accessed 16 January 2013. http://www.stat.fi/til/evaa/2003/evaa_2003_2004-05-31_tau_009.html

———. 2007. Parliamentary Elections 2007 (*Eduskuntavaalit 2007*). StatFin database. Online. Accessed 15 January 2013. http://tilastokeskus.fi/tup/statfin/index_en.html

―――. 2011. Parliamentary Elections 2011 (*Eduskuntavaalit 2011*). StatFin database. Online. Accessed 15 January 2013. http://tilastokeskus.fi/tup/statfin/index_en.html

―――. 2012. *Kunnallisvaalit 2012. Ehdokasasettelu ja ehdokkaiden taustaanalyysi.* Online. Accessed 16 January 2013. http://tilastokeskus.fi/kunnallisvaalit/

―――. 2015. Eduskuntavaaleissa 2015 yhteensä 2 146 ehdokasta. Online. Accessed 7 December 2015. http://tilastokeskus.fi/til/evaa/2015/01/evaa_2015_01_2015-04-10_tie_001_fi.html

Social Democratic Women. 2013. *Järjestö.* Online. Accessed 7 March 2013. http://www.demarinaiset.fi/jaerjestoe

Taggart, Paul. 2004. Populism and Representative Politics in Contemporary Europe. *Journal of Political Ideologies* 9(3): 269–288.

The Finns Party Women's Organization. 2011. *PS Naiset* 1: 1.

―――. 2012. *Annual Report 2011 (Toimintakertomus vuodelta 2011).* Online. Accessed 10 January 2013. http://ps-naiset.perussuomalaiset.fi/toimintakertomus2011

Ylä-Anttila, Tuukka. 2012. *What is Finnish about the Finns Party? Political Culture and Populism.* Master's thesis, University of Helsinki. Online. Accessed 7 December 2015. https://helda.helsinki.fi/handle/10138/42042

―――. 2014. Perussuomalaisten sisäiset poliittiset suuntaukset. Julkisen oikeuttamisen analyysi. *Politiikka* 56(3): 191–209.

Ylä-Anttila, Tuomas and Tuukka, Ylä-Anttila. 2015. Exploiting the Discursive Opportunity of the Euro Crisis: The Rise of the Finns Party. In *European Populism in the Shadow of the Great Recession*, ed. Hanspeter Kriesi, and Takis S. Pappas. Colchester: ECPR Press.

The Increasing Visibility of Right-Wing Extremist Women in Contemporary Europe: Is Great Britain an Exception?

Andrea S. Dauber

INTRODUCTION

The contemporary view on right-wing extremism in Great Britain holds that the far right is not anywhere near as established as in other European countries such as France or Germany (Goodwin 2012). Other countries in Western Europe show a higher level of far-right activities and political organisation and participation (Arzheimer and Carter 2006). Yet, to take this as evidence of a largely inactive British far-right scene would be to conceal some of the developments that have taken place in the past two decades. These developments are best observed on the micro- or meso-level and cannot be adequately contextualised in macro-level analyses. What macro-level analyses do show is that the British far-right political scene has had growing electoral success in recent years (Biggs and Knauss 2012).

The question of how gender is tied into British right-wing extremist developments has been similarly neglected. At the same time, theoretical grounds that would justify this negligence remain elusive. There is no acceptable reason why women should not be examined in the context of the far right. One would have to acknowledge that researchers themselves often reify traditional notions about gender roles, which, as has

A.S. Dauber (✉)
UC San Diego, Department of Sociology

© The Author(s) 2017
M. Köttig et al. (eds.), *Gender and Far Right Politics in Europe*,
DOI 10.1007/978-3-319-43533-6_4

been examined for Germany's Nazi past and Neo-Nazi present (Dauber 2014), could explain the lack of scholarly attention paid to women's roles in far-right political movements. Yet, even in its earliest stages, research has shown that right-wing extremist women play vital roles in other European countries, most notably Beate Zschäpe in Germany or Marine le Pen in France (cf. the articles in this book). It seems that research on British right-wing extremist women has not caught up yet. While researchers are becoming increasingly interested in the far-right's development in British society, the discussion remains confined to populations that are either male or not differentiated by gender (cf. Arzheimer and Carter 2006; Cockburn 2007; Ford and Goodwin 2010; Treadwell and Garland 2011). While gender differentiation in analyses might be a problem of accessibility of information, the consequence cannot be to explore men's attitudes and electoral behaviour, but to work towards establishing more effective tools for capturing gender-specific data.

Therefore, owing to a lack of adequate data, reports and research literature, this chapter presents an exploratory contribution to the gender gap in research on the British far right. I will examine signs of contemporary public right-wing extremism in Great Britain and extend the discussion to include women in contemporary far-right parties and movements. Moreover, I will draw an important distinction between right-wing extremist politics and underground, semi-public or public activism and discuss how gender is differentially tied into these two areas. With some notable exceptions, women are less visible in right-wing extremist party politics, which is most obvious when comparing the British context with French right-wing politician Marine le Pen and her niece Marion Maréchal-Le Pen, but women might play more of a role in underground activism. In this chapter, I will concentrate on the English Defence League (EDL) and the British National Party (BNP), the United Kingdom Independence Party (UKIP), and the British Freedom Party (BFP) which are at present the most well-known far-right parties and organisations in Great Britain. It must be stated that the status of the UKIP as a fascist party is not entirely clear, but Matthew J. Goodwin and Jocelyn Evans included it in their study of supporters of extreme right parties (Goodwin and Evans 2012).

To develop a more diversified picture of women in the far right, I will include information about how women organise themselves online and how they use modern technology and media to participate in the advancement of their political ideology.

RIGHT-WING EXTREMIST WOMEN IN GREAT BRITAIN: A POST-MODERN PHENOMENON?

British women have not made any noticeable appearance on the public stage yet. While Beate Zschäpe and Marine le Pen are names familiar to many Europeans, there are no well-known British right-wing extremist women whose names circulate beyond British borders, either as political representatives or leaders, or as violent right-wing extremist activists. While there are female political representatives of the far right who are visible in Great Britain, British right-wing extremist women have not appeared as fanatics who engage in violent forms of activism.[1] It would be wrong, however, to state that far-right violence is not a salient feature of British society, and it is quite possible that women's involvement has simply not been noticed on a national or international level. Just how acute the right-wing extremist danger is has recently been noted by government officials (Morris 2013).

Not surprisingly, the majority of scholarly contributions approach the issue of the far right in Great Britain from a political perspective. The development of parties such as the BNP, the National Front (NF), the UKIP and the BFP has not been sufficiently analysed from a sociological perspective even though their agendas are manifest expressions of perceived social inequalities, xenophobia, sexuality, prejudices and racial issues. Far-right parties and associations have slightly different agendas ranging from stressing British identity and cultural heritage in the context of European unification to openly promoting the deportation of immigrants, particularly Muslims.

As the author has argued elsewhere, it is essential to develop knowledge about fascist women's roles in the past before analysing the contemporary actions of fascist women (Dauber 2014). Research on far-right British women in the past is, however, not exhaustive. Notable exceptions are Vron Ware's examination of fascist women in the nineteenth and twentieth century Britain and Julie Gottlieb's *Feminine Fascism: Women in Britain's Fascist Movement 1923–1945* (Gottlieb 2003; Ware 1992). Gottlieb's analysis of women's incorporation into the fascist movement is helpful for understanding modern trends. Gottlieb examined how women could be drawn to a cause that represents two seemingly contradicting ideologies: women's rights and anti-democratic values. She argued that women's involvement was largely based on a rational decision. As followers of the fascist movement, women had access to the best of two worlds.

The fascist movement urged women to embrace motherhood while simultaneously demanding equal wages for men and women, thus trying to overcome the common practice of employing cheap female labour that left many men unemployed (Gottlieb 2003).

Gottlieb's research reveals an important link that could also further research on modern fascist women. The combination of tradition and modernity appealed to women prior to World War II; thus, it would make sense to investigate whether it continues to do so today. Recent developments in far-right parties point to this trend, as equality and women's rights are often made top priorities on far-right agendas, particularly in the context of a perceived "Islamification" of the country (Hill 2003). However, it seems as if researchers have not only neglected to examine contemporary forms of Nazism, they also have not taken a holistic look at the intersection of gender and political consciousness.

GENDER AND BRITISH FAR-RIGHT POLITICS

In my analysis, I propose to distinguish at least three dimensions of women's involvement with the far right. The most public and therefore most visible dimension is women's engagement in politics, including their voting behaviour. Perhaps unexpectedly, British women have assumed formative roles as founders, co-founders or directors in at least three British far-right parties and one organisation: the BNP, the BFP, the UKIP and the EDL. The second dimension is British women's participation and membership in semi-public associations and organisations such as the *Women's Division of the English Defence League* or *Stop Islamisation of Europe England*. I classify these as semi-public because members can choose to participate in anonymous ways, for example, by becoming a member and supporter of social network groups or by joining demonstrations. This dimension is also distinguished through the availability of information to outsiders, meaning that information about party officials can be accessed quite easily, while information about the identity of members of associations or organisations is not necessarily readily available. The third dimension, women's participation in underground operations and hate crimes, is the most difficult to analyse. This dimension has the greatest potential to disguise women's potentially violent involvement in far-right groups.

When considering gender in the context of British politics and the far right, it is important to understand some of the peculiarities of how women and men are involved in politics as voters. It is evident that this discussion of the development of British right-wing extremism largely, if not completely, fails to address gender in a differentiated analysis. This is in part owing to the difficulty of obtaining gender-differentiated data.

In 2009 the BNP had 2034 female members, roughly 17 per cent of the total of 11,811 members (Booth et al. 2009). If we take more recent figures into account, it appears that the percentage of women has risen. According to a survey by Goodwin and Evans, 72 per cent of UKIP, 70 per cent of BNP and 64 per cent of EDL supporters are men (Goodwin and Evans 2012). It thus follows that 28 per cent of UKIP, 30 per cent of BNP and 36 per cent of EDL supporters must be women. With women supporters representing around one-third of each group, it would be short-sighted to assume that women are unimportant. Yet, this ratio is not further investigated in Goodwin and Evans' study. Though the gap between 17 and 30 per cent is certainly not small, it is safe to say that women who vote for far-right parties are not a rare exception.

The EDL has received particular scholarly attention in recent years (Bartlett and Littler 2011; Richards 2011; Treadwell and Garland 2011). It has been reported that the EDL has three different groups of supporters (Richards 2011): The first group represents the socio-economically marginalised, mostly young males; the second group consists of violent football fans and supporters (hooligans); and the third group is made up of extremist ideologues with concerns that radical Islam is extending its influence in British society, traditional right-wing extremists, and racists. As Richards has noted, the first group is mainly composed of young males, but he does not specify who makes up the rest of the group (Richards 2011). While older men are certainly to be found in this group, women of lower and lowest SES (potentially single mothers since they are known to have the highest poverty risk) may be supporters of the EDL as well. With regard to the third group, British women have voiced concerns about the danger of Islamification in respect of women's rights and the protection of their children. To what degree they take on roles as ideologues is unclear; however, research has pointed out how right-wing extremist women exert indirect forms of violence such as aiding and abetting or mental instigation (Elverich 2007). What can be gathered from this typology is that women can potentially be found in all three groups from which the EDL draws its supporters and members, even if they are not very likely to be found among hooligans. However, because women fairly certainly do not represent the majority in any of the categories, there is a temptation to disregard their numbers, particularly when researchers are not sensitive to gender-differentiated issues.

Observable gender differences can be found in the political arena as well. A "gender gap" at election time can generally be observed across political contexts. In Great Britain, women have shown different tendencies over time. While they were once more likely to vote Conservative than men, they have demonstrated an inclination to vote left since the 1980s (Wolf 2010). With social class being much less influential in terms of voting behaviour nowadays, it may be assumed that owing to greater social mobility the younger generations in particular will consider their voting decision more carefully. This increases the chance they will vote for parties they would not have voted for at a time when social class was still very much a determinant of people's voting behaviour. Important issues that individuals care about, as well as the leaders of the respective parties, are two major influences on voting behaviour (Wolf 2010). There is a difference between women and men voters in respect of the issues they tend to place emphasis on (Campbell 2004). In a survey, women were nine per cent more likely than men to judge a policy based on how it would impact on their family and/or children, while men were seven per cent more likely to judge a policy based on how it would affect the country as a whole (Campbell 2007). These two emphases are not necessarily incompatible. Insofar as far-right parties manage to communicate both topics in their propaganda, which they often do, they address voters' concerns more comprehensively than some of the mainstream parties.

Understanding the different motivations of men and women is important when evaluating women's inclination to be a passive or active part of the far right. One unifying element can be seen in the UK's immigration pattern over the past decades. British immigration legislation, both past and present, is contributing greatly to anti-Muslim sentiments that are effectively instrumentalised by far-right parties to attract women voters, particularly in the context of women's rights, child protection and family support. Incidences of Muslim women being attacked by right-wingers give us an idea of how gender and religion's infringement on women's rights could play a role in British women's inclination to vote for right-wing extremist parties. Between March 2012 and June 2013, 632 anti-Muslim hate incidents were reported to the UK-based non-governmental organisation "Tell Mama," with 54 per cent of all incidents being linked to far-right supporters, such as members of the BNP (Nye 2013). The actual number of anti-Muslim hate crimes is potentially higher and there are no data that distinguish female and male perpetrators. Some far-right parties try to attract voters by focusing on these topics. Muslim immigration and the purported "Islamification" of Great Britain can be identified as a main theme of the British far right.

While a fairly good picture has been established of British women's voting behaviour (Campbell 2004, 2007, 2012; Campbell and Winters 2008), little is known about how gendered political attitudes develop. The Guardian reported at the beginning of 2013 that in the 2010 elections women showed a tendency to leave the Labour Party and turn to the Conservative Party, then headed by David Cameron (Topping 2013). Some women turned even further to the right, to one of the right-wing extremist parties. Cameron's cuts to the social welfare system after 2010 are likely to increase this tendency in elections to come.

WOMEN IN FAR-RIGHT PARTIES AND ORGANISATIONS

It has been argued that the process of increasing the share of women in British politics has come to a halt (Lovenduski 2012). Ford and Goodwin found that the BNP's effort at "'modernisation' has not succeeded in increasing the party's appeal among women" (Ford and Goodwin 2010). It is even more surprising, then, that women are fairly visible in far-right politics.

However, when examining women in the British far right, apart from the base of voters, it is noticeable that they have strategic roles and cannot readily be identified as being involved with the British criminal justice system. One of Great Britain's leading "counter-Jihadists," Ann Marchini, co-founded the self-proclaimed human rights organisation EDL, and has also been an activist for the BFP. Moreover, she has ties to the *International Civil Liberties Alliance*, an organisation whose chief executive is also a woman, Christine Brim. Marchini is thought to be wealthy, in her mid-fifties and believed to operate under at least two aliases (Gadher and Henry 2011). Interestingly, her role in the EDL seems to be a very important one. It has been reported that she has tried to turn the EDL into a credible political force (Gadher and Henry 2011).

Other women have prominent roles in the EDL as well. Leisha Brooks is a former leader of the EDL women's division; Roberta Moore was a leader of the EDL Jewish division, and Ruby Akhtar authors articles for the webpage and publishes on a regular basis. These women certainly do not have the popularity of Marine le Pen in France. Yet, the organisation does not try to conceal the fact that women hold important positions.

The BNP has been identified as the only right-wing party with any importance in the political scene at present (Husbands 2011), and women seem to have their share in it. In 2009, Cathy Duffy, who represented the village of East Goscote, was councillor on Charnwood borough council (Booth et al. 2009). Another female councillor, Tina Gentry, is a local politician who represents the BNP in Essex. According to *Unite against Fascism* (2013), the BNP had 14 women candidates in the 2013 local elections. In 2011, the BNP sent a woman to win the Barnsley Central by-election after the Labour Party's Member of Parliament, Eric Illsley, had resigned from his seat (BBC 2011). Enis Dalton, who finished ahead of the Liberal Democrats, based her political agenda on equal rights for women and the protection of women in the face of potential threats from alleged Muslim rape gangs (BNP n.d.). After equal rights, this perceived threat can be identified as the second main theme in nationalist parties' and organisations' propaganda that specifically aims at recruiting women for the far right. In the aforementioned 2013 elections, there was even a woman candidate for the NF. As far as this party is concerned, Tess Culnane is considered one of the key players. She has been committed to the fascist cause for quite some time and has had alternating affiliations with both the NF and the BNP (hopenothate.org n.d.).

The UKIP has several high-ranking women members as well. According to its homepage, the party director is actually a woman named Lisa Duffy, and she is not the only woman to have an important function in this party. There are also several women among the councillors of different local divisions, and a mother of two was proclaimed North West candidate in October 2013 for the 2014 European elections (UKIP 2013).

It is rather obvious that women do play important roles in the British far-right political scene. Therefore, it is important to note that Great Britain is home to a fairly large number of parties and organisations that can be classified as far-right or right-wing extremist, among them: 4 Freedoms Community, Casuals United, Combined Ex-Forces, England is Ours, English Nationalist Alliance, English Shieldwall, Infidels, March for England, Scottish Defence League, Stop Islamisation of Europe England, United British Alliance, to name but a few. Considering what has been shown above in respect of women's presence in the British far right, it is reasonable to assume that women are involved to a greater or lesser extent in some of these organisations as well. Moreover, there is a fair number of women's organisations such as Women for Aryan Unity or the National Women's Front. Gender is an important structural principle of far-right groups (Blee 2003). The most obvious reason why far-right parties and organisations seek to involve women as representatives or leading figures is to win as many women as possible, because women, once indoctrinated, are thought to pass ideological attitudes on to their children more success-fully than fathers. This idea is obviously derived from the strong connec-tion between womanhood and motherhood in far-right ideology.

A New Dimension of Women's Involvement: Online Presence

Women's involvement in far-right politics and activism, even if difficult to measure and analyse, can be better understood through the analysis of social media (Bartlett and Littler 2011).

While membership of a political party membership is a lesser form of ideological expression, membership in locally, regionally, nationally or internationally organised community forums is more important, especially because communication is facilitated by online channels. Participation in and support of far-right politics and agendas has been significantly extended by the internet, which is attractive to women because they can participate anonymously and do not risk discrimination by family members, friends and neighbours who do not support the far-right cause. There are several online groups of British women who express their opinions about contem-porary issues and openly, albeit anonymously, demonstrate their affiliation with the far right. The National Front, which issues the magazine "Blood and Honour," has a website on which the group promotes the idea of the "National Women's Front." The website carries the title "NF women launch own movement" (Blood and Honour Great Britain n.d.). The author of the website text describes the manifold roles of women in the National Front. It is clear that traditional notions of gender roles are being upheld in the distribution of tasks and assignments among National Front members. The proclaimed purpose of the National Women's Front is to recruit "strong and proud British women" and to "educate and inform women within the National Front" (Blood and Honour Great Britain n.d.). While the focus here is on recruitment and education, the author also addresses potential fields of public activity such as leafleting, anti-paedophile marches and Remembrance Day marches. At the same time, women are discouraged from participating in marches that could potentially turn violent. Instead, women in the movement should concentrate on educating their children in British history and culture, which is part of an expressed distrust of government, doctors, and foreigners as they could be paedophiles in disguise. It is obvious that women in the National Front have the traditionally feminised task of educating and shaping the next nationalist generation.

In their study of the EDL support network, Bartlett and Littler gathered data through social media to develop a more accurate picture of the group's demographics, involvement in EDL activity, political attitudes and social views (Bartlett and Littler 2011). The organisation claims to have "a significant number" of women supporters who are commonly referred to as the "EDL angels" (Bartlett and Littler 2011, 17). This group of women is rarely seen in large numbers at demonstrations; however, they, too, have created an online presence and use modern media technology (Bartlett and Littler 2011). For example, the EDL angels use the video hosting site YouTube to promote their visions and ideologies. In one of their videos, sexualised images of feminine angels are paired with photos of laughing, protesting and generally nice-looking women members of the division (YouTube 2011). The Facebook group for the North-East EDL angels was founded on April 29, 2012 and in 2012 had 304 "like me" supporters (Facebook n.d.). These are very recent trends which show that women continue to organise and use modern forms of communication to gather and disseminate information through the internet.

It is interesting to note that the message to women to join the white cause comes through different channels. YouTube hosts a wealth of videos that showcase women who explain why being nationalist is acceptable. The message is accessible from across the world, and women harbouring such sentiments can identify with women who show their face online and openly proclaim the nationalist cause. The overarching question to be considered in this context is what primary function the online presence of these groups has, and whether it will successfully recruit women as supporters and activists in the future.

Gender, the Far-Right, and Violence

Violence is as much an integral part of the British far right as it is of other European far-right groups. Certainly, there are differences in hate crime rates between men and women. However, where overlaps do exist, researchers should focus on them more than they have. Violent women are not completely invisible. As Jackie Oakley, editor of the White Nationalist Party's Valkyrie magazine and head of its women's division stated, "I head-butt, punch and kick just like a man. None of your poncey girly scratching for me; I'm up there with the men and so are all the other women in the group" (Hill 2003, 7).

If little is perceived about British far-right violence or activism, this does not mean that the far right is not a noticeable social and disruptive force in British society. Undoubtedly, British far-right parties and organisa-tions, even if to varying degrees, have the potential for violence. Goodwin and Evans provide a more detailed analysis of this potential for violence and argue that while only a few political parties openly advocate violence, narratives are cultivated among "more committed" followers that justify violence as a legitimate means to reach proclaimed goals (Goodwin and Evans 2012, 24). These narratives circulate within the party and are com-municated top-down through internal literature. The authors further find that there are differences between parties, for example, between the BNP and the UKIP. They specifically state, "Half of the BNP supporters in our sample expressing a view thought that preparing for conflict between dif-ferent groups is always or sometimes justifiable, while this figure among UKIP supporters was 31%" (Goodwin and Evans 2012, 24). Moreover, they found that almost 40 per cent of interviewed BNP supporters stated that armed conflict is always or sometimes justifiable. An even higher number—64 per cent—thought that violence might be necessary to defend their group from threats.

Insofar as gender serves as a mechanism to conceal support for, mem-bership in, and offences in the context of racist parties, organisations and protests or other forms of public demonstration, women's involvement in the British far right is likely to be underestimated. Offences by women are generally under-reported, as can be observed in cases of female perpetra-tors of domestic violence. The British Crime Survey has repeatedly found that men tend to not report abusive behaviour by their female partners (Hester 2013). The same can also be assumed for the public sphere. The chance that male victims will report violent behaviour by a woman to the police is lower than for female victims. Consequently, an underestima-tion of women's involvement in attacks motivated by far-right ideology might conceal the actual number of incidents. That far-right women do get involved in violent attacks can be seen in a recent case from Plymouth. Two women, aged 28 and 30, joined an EDL mob that "attacked and abused a terrified Kurdish family in a city centre takeaway" (Eve 2013). However, this article serves as an example of how female violence among right-wing extremists is perceived in the public sphere: as an exception. This explains the lengthy reporting about the women perpetrators while details about the male participants are not reported.

With regard to the EDL, it has been argued that there is a discrepancy between the organisation's official proclamation of being a liberal, pluralistic movement that fights Muslim extremism and the violence witnessed or the chants heard at demonstrations and other public events (Treadwell and Garland 2011). While violent activism among men remains a mystery, women's roles and involvement are even more mysterious.

Is Great Britain an Exception?

British women in the far right deserve more scholarly attention than they have been given. Even after reviewing existing data and research, we know painfully little about women in the British far right. The danger of underestimating British women's roles in extremist politics is high, in part because the public discourse of many far-right parties in respect of child, family and women's protection reinforces mental links to gender-specific roles. Simply put, it is easy to associate women on the far right with family- and equality-related values, which are to be found in the general population *per se*. Portraying women as family-oriented, home-based, passive followers contributes to camouflaging their actual activist involvement. In fact, as I have discussed, women of the far right have taken active roles in the movement as founders, co-founders, directors, board members, funders, electoral candidates, and even violent perpetrators.

Regarding the three dimensions of analysis, political involvement, underground or semi-public and public activism, it must be stated that information is difficult to gather and that this evaluation of women's roles is therefore premature. In terms of political participation, the review of existing data has shown that approximately one-third of British far-right party members are women. The BNP is currently the strongest right-wing extremist party, and it also has the largest share of women. British women have shown concern about political issues that affect their life situations, particularly family and child policies. Simultaneously, many right-wing extremist parties, such as the BNP, and also many organisations or associations, have these topics high up on their agendas which could lead to attracting more women over time, depending in part on how mainstream parties position themselves in these fields. The fact that the parties and organisations sometimes have local women leaders is also favourable. While they are not as popular as, for example, Marine le Pen in France, it would be inaccurate to state that women do not play a significant role in the British far right. As political leaders are known to influence voting behaviour, women leaders in the far right will play an important role in attracting women in the future.

Beyond the party landscape, women's involvement in underground, semi-public or public organisations is even more difficult to investigate. For example, estimating right-wing extremist women's involvement in the increasing number of attacks against Muslims would be an unmanageable task at present. A distinction between perpetrators and instigators would help to develop a more differentiated picture of women's participation. Obtaining a reliable picture of the likelihood of women carrying out violent attacks is contingent on many factors that are difficult to control, under-reporting of crimes by women being just one of them.

The mechanisms at work in women's involvement in far-right politics, commitment and activism could be inspired by a desire for state support for families paired with infringements on women's perceived liberal and self-determined status due to the influx of Muslim women. Since David Cameron's party formed a coalition with the Liberal Democrats in 2010, several spending cuts have impacted families. To the extent that British women continue to seek equality, improved family services and higher levels of protection, there is the danger of far-right parties wooing women with their agendas—whether or not they are realistic.

In the context of "Islamification," which British society is allegedly subjected to, Britons face a delicate situation: like any other European country, Great Britain has to manage a comprehensive welfare system in conjunction with economic globalisation and modern immigration trends. If women increasingly feel that their situations remain unaddressed, there is a potential danger that right-wing ideologies will appeal disproportionately to women from lower class backgrounds. It is difficult to judge at present whether Great Britain is an exception with regard to women's participation in right-wing extremism, but there is reason to believe that British women may be more involved than has commonly been assumed and that it is only a matter of time before they claim more attention, space and power in far-right politics and activism.

NOTE

1. The author was able to identify one case in British online media that will be discussed later in the chapter.

REFERENCES

Arzheimer, Kai, and Elisabeth Carter. 2006. Political Opportunity Structures and Right-Wing Extremist Party Success. *European Journal of Population Research* 45: 419–443.

Bartlett, Jamie, and Mark Littler. 2011, November. Inside the EDL. Populist Politics in a Digital Age. *Demos*. Accessed 20 December 2015. http://www.demos.co.uk/files/Inside_the_edl_WEB.pdf?1331035419

BBC News. 2011. Lib Dems Slump to Sixth as Labour Win Barnsley Poll, May 4. Accessed 1 January 2016. http://www.bbc.co.uk/news/uk-politics-12643639

Biggs, Michael, and Steven Knauss. 2012. Explaining Membership in the British National Party: A Multilevel Analysis of Contact and Threat. *European Sociological Review* 28(5): 633–646.

Blee, Kathleen M. 2003. *Inside Organized Racism: Women in the Hate Movement*. Berkeley, CA: University of California Press.

Blood & Honour Great Britain. n.d. National Womens Front. NF Women Launch Own Movement. An Introduction. Accessed 12 December 2015. http://www.bloodandhonourworldwide.co.uk/magazine/issue20/issue20p5.html

BNP. n.d. British National Party's Candidate in Barnsley Will Become "Voice" for Women. Accessed 21 December 2015. http://www.bnp.org.uk/news/british-national-party%E2%80%99s-candidate-barnsley-will-become-voice-women

Booth, Robert, Simon Rogers, and Paul Lewis. 2009, October 20. Analysis of a Party–What the BNP List Says About Its Members. *The Guardian*. Accessed 23 December 2015. http://www.theguardian.com/politics/2009/oct/20/bnp-membership-list-analysis

Campbell, Rosie. 2004. Gender, Ideology and Issue Preference: Is There Such a Thing as a Political Women's Interest in Britain? *British Journal of Politics and International Relations* 6(1): 20–46.

———. 2007. *Gender and Voting Behaviour in Britain: Non-Technical Summary (Research summary)*. ESRC End of Award Report, RES-000-22-1857. Swindon: ESRC.

———. 2012. What Do We *Really* Know about Women Voters? Gender, Elections and Public Opinion. *The Political Quarterly* 83(4): 703–710.

Campbell, Rosie, and Kristi Winters. 2008. Understanding Men's and Women's Political Interests: Evidence from a Study of Gendered Political Attitudes. *Journal of Elections, Public Opinion & Parties* 18(1): 53–74.

Cockburn, Tom. 2007. 'Performing' Racism: Engaging Young Supporters of the Far-Right in England. *British Journal of Sociology of Education* 28(5): 547–560.

Dauber, Andrea. 2014. Not All Nazis Are Men: Women's Underestimated Potential for Violence in German Neo-Nazism. Continuation of the Past or Novel Phenomenon? In *Advances in Gender Research*, vol B, ed. Marcia Segal, and Vasilikie Demos, 169–192. Bingley, UK: Emerald.

Elverich, Gabi. 2007. Rechtsextrem orientierte Frauen und Mädchen–eine besondere Zielgruppe? *Federal Agency for Civic Education (Bundeszentrale für Politische Bildung)*, October 15. Accessed 30 December 2015. http://www.bpb.de/politik/extremismus/rechtsextremismus/41506/rechtsextrem-orientierte-frauen-und-maedchen?p=all

Eve, Carl. 2013. Women Joined Racist EDL Mob Which Attacked Kurdish Family, Plymouth Crown Court Hears. *The Herald*, February 23. Accessed 20 December 2015. http://www.plymouthherald.co.uk/Women-joined-racist-EDL-mob-attacked-Kurdish/story-18232233-detail/story.html

Facebook. n.d. North East EDL Angels. Accessed 20 September 2013. https://www.facebook.com/NorthEastEDLAngels

Ford, Robert, and Matthew J. Goodwin. 2010. Angry White Men: Individual and Contextual Predictors of Support for the British National Party. *Political Studies* 58: 1–25.

Gadher, Dipesh, and Robin Henry. 2011. Unmasked: Wealthy Backers behind Far-Right League. *The Sunday Times*, December 11. Accessed 23 December 2015. http://www.thesundaytimes.co.uk/sto/news/uk_news/Society/article839700.ece

Goodwin, Matthew. 2012. United Kingdom. The History of Right-Wing Extremism: Three Distinct Waves. In *Preventing and Countering Far-Right Extremism: European Cooperation*, ed. Vidhya Ramalingam, Alex Glennie, and Sebastien Feve, 76–78. Swedish Ministry of Justice and Institute for Strategic Dialogue. Accessed 21 December 2015. http://www.strategicdialogue.org/FarRightEM.pdf

Goodwin, Matthew, and Jocelyn Evans. 2012. From Voting to Violence? Far-Right Extremism in Britain. *Searchlight Educational Trust*. Accessed 23 December 2015. http://www.channel4.com/media/c4-news/images/voting-to-violence%20%287%29.pdf

Gottlieb, Julie V. 2003. *Feminine Fascism: Women in Britain's Fascist Movement 1923–1945*. London: I. B. Tauris.

Hester, Marianne. 2013. Who Does What to Whom? Gender and Domestic Violence Perpetrators in English Police Records. *European Journal of Criminology* 10(5): 623–637.

Hill, Amelia. 2003. Far-Right Woos Women with Vows on Feminism and Family. *The Guardian*, September 21. Accessed 23 December 2015. http://www.theguardian.com/politics/2003/sep/21/uk.thefarright

HOPEnothate.org. n.d. National Front. Accessed 1 January 2016. http://www.hopenothate.org.uk/hate-groups/nf/

Husbands, Christopher T. 2011. The Situation of the Extreme Right in Great Britain. In *Is Europe on the "Right" Path? Right-Wing Extremism and Right-Wing Populism in Europe*, ed. Nora Langebacher, and Britta Schellenberg, 101–121. Bonn: Friedrich Ebert-Stiftung. Accessed 1 January 2016. http://library.fes.de/pdf-files/do/08338.pdf

Lovenduski, Joni. 2012. Feminising British Politics. *The Political Quarterly* 83(4): 697–702.

Morris, Nigel. 2013, March 13. UK 'Faces Threat of Murderous Attack from Far-Right Extremist'. *The Independent*. Accessed 19 December 2015. http://www.independent.co.uk/news/uk/politics/uk-faces-threat-of-murderous-attack-from-far-right-extremist-8533040.html

Nye, Catrin. 2013. 632 Anti-Muslim Hate Incidents Recorded by Tell Mama. *BBC News UK*, March 10. Accessed 30 November 2015. http://www.bbc.co.uk/news/uk-21712826

Richards, Julien. 2011. Globalization and the Rise of Far-Right Militancy in Europe: A UK Perspective. In *Confligo: Conflict in a Society in Transition*, ed. Borisz A. Szegál, and István András, 47–78. Dunaújváros, Hungary: Dunaújváros College Press.

Topping, Alexandra. 2013. Conservatives Worried about Diminishing Support by Women Voters. *The Guardian*, February 15. Accessed 23 December 2015. http://www.theguardian.com/politics/2013/feb/15/conservatives-worried-loss-of-women-voters

Treadwell, James, and Jon Garland. 2011. Masculinity, Marginalization, and Violence: A Case Study of the English Defence League. *British Journal of Criminology* 51(4): 621–634.

UKIP. 2013. UKIP NW Euro Candidates Announced, October 7. Accessed 1 January 2016. http://ukipnw.org.uk/ukip-nw-euro-candidates-announced/

Unite against Fascism. 2013. Elections. Accessed 1 January 2016. http://uaf.org.uk/wp-content/uploads/2013/04/nominations-2013-Elections-web-edit.pdf

Ware, Vron. 1992. *Beyond the Pale: White Women, Racism and History*. London and New York: Verso.

Wolf, Alison. 2010. Why Do Women Vote Differently from Men? *BBC News Magazine*, March 8. Accessed 23 December 2015. http://news.bbc.co.uk/2/hi/uk_news/magazine/8555358.stm

YouTube. 2011. EDL Angels, March 23. Accessed 1 January 2016. http://www.youtube.com/watch?v=NvHgwO5TV6k

Research on Gender and the Far Right in Germany Since 1990: Developments, Findings, and Future Prospects

Renate Bitzan

INTRODUCTION

This chapter gives an overview of different phases in German research on women and/or gender and the far right in recent decades. After some introductory remarks on the far right in Germany in general, the first and the second (on-going) phases of research on far-right women will be discussed under the headings "Making women visible" and "From assumptions to empirical findings". The "Forschungsnetzwerk Frauen und Rechtsextremismus" (Research Network on Women and Right Wing Extremism) will also be presented in this context. After this, light is thrown on the relatively new interest in constructions of masculinities within the far right, as a third phase of gender-sensitive research, before closing with a discussion of some future prospects.

REMARKS ON THE FAR RIGHT IN GERMANY

Germany is the country with the highest historical responsibility for the crimes of the national-socialist era, including World War II, concentration camps and the murder of millions of Jews, Sinti and Roma, homosexuals, political prisoners, so-called asocials and people from neighbouring coun-

R. Bitzan (✉)
Fakultät AMP, Technische Hochschule Nuremberg Georg Simon Ohm,
Nuremberg, Germany

© The Author(s) 2017
M. Köttig et al. (eds.), *Gender and Far Right Politics in Europe*,
DOI 10.1007/978-3-319-43533-6_5

65

tries. In the German post-war societies, we see ambivalent ways of dealing with this history. In East Germany (GDR) the state officially claimed to be both anti-capitalist and anti-fascist. But in fact, the regime displayed elements of an "authoritarian character" (Adorno). Additionally, there were recurring neo-fascist activities like propagandistic actions and violent attacks, and also attempts to found political organisations, but their existence was denied by the state. They were prevented from acting in public and from organising themselves officially and were referred to apolitically as "rowdies" (Wagner 2002; Stöss 2010, 106). In spite of de-nazification processes in both East and West Germany, in West Germany (FRG), which claimed to be liberal and democratic, it was not uncommon to find personal continuities from the nazi era in some professional and societal areas (such as the law and medicine). This was one reason for the radical criticism expressed by the 1968 student movement. Thereafter, historical research was intensified. Through all the decades, there has been a more or less strong far-right movement including old nazis and young neo-fascists—accompanied by a more or less strong anti-fascist movement.

The unification of East and West Germany led to a boom of "national" feeling in and after 1990. Especially in the early 1990s, there was a spate of racist pogroms and militant attacks against refugee hostels and the homes of immigrants. The political effect was that some neo-fascist groups were prohibited and a broad anti-fascist movement arose, while the right of political asylum was significantly restricted (AIB 2012). Also in the 1990s, the organisational structures of the far right expanded step by step from western Germany to eastern Germany.

Since then we can observe a parallel structure—with intersections—of far-right parties, especially the NPD (National Democratic Party of Germany), and so-called free comradeships. Some of the latter now call themselves "autonomous nationalists" (Schedler and Häusler 2011). Certain people, such as blacks, migrants, homosexuals, the homeless, punks, or anti-fascists, are under permanent threat of attack in specific districts or regions. Since 1990, more than 150 persons have been killed out of far-right motives, and many more injured in body and soul (Jansen 2013). There are many initiatives to counteract the far right (such as investigating local neo-fascist structures, or organising democratic training courses for young people, partly supported by government programmes), and broad public alliances against far-right demonstrations. But in the past few years a renaissance of the "totalitarianism" discourse, which speaks of "extremism" without differentiating between right and left, is also visible in a fraction of the scientific community and among policy makers. One thing is sure, and that is that everyday racism is widespread among parts of the population (Heitmeyer 2011).

Though there is no parliamentary representation of far-right parties on the national level, and only in a few federal states, they have succeeded in entering many local councils (mainly in the former GDR). In addition, there are attempts (in some regions successful attempts) to infiltrate civil society, social-service, and community structures, as advocates of the "ordinary people" (Virchow and Dornbusch 2008). These attempts correspond to the "*Kampf um die Köpfe*" (the struggle to win minds), part of the far right's strategy to win more sympathies in the so-called centre of society (ibid.). Since 2013/2014, new structures have become established uniting conservative and right-wing extremist people: the movement known as "PEGIDA" (Patriotic Europeans Against the Islamisation of the Occident) regularly holds local demonstrations that attract thousands of people in many towns. The main aim of PEGIDA is support for nationalist, anti-Muslim and anti-immigration policies, combined with massive propaganda against established politicians, and against the media, which is referred to as "*Lügenpresse*" (lying press). There is a new party with the name "Alternative für Deutschland" (Alternative for Germany, AfD), which first focused on opposing the idea of the European Union, and now seems to be catching a lot of votes with its anti-immigration arguments. In March of 2016, the AfD succeeded in entering three federal state parliaments with 12–25 per cent of the votes, making it the third strongest party there (and even second strongest in the case auf Saxony-Anhalt) (Spiegel 2016a). It cannot be said yet whether this is only a short-lived phenomenon due to the unsolved so-called refugee crisis, or whether these forces will be able to establish themselves more permanently as important political protagonists. Whatever the case, it is clear that at the present time there is a serious polarisation within German society: on the one hand a unique wave of solidarity and willingness to help the incoming refugees, and on the other hand a strong and aggressive articulation of anti-immigration feeling, accompanied by a new wave of violent attacks on immigrants and refugee hostels (Spiegel 2016b).

Making Women Visible: The First Phase of Gender-Sensitive Research on the Far Right

Until the end of the 1980s, gender was not an explicit issue in the discourse on contemporary far-right extremism, either in scientific research or in political anti-fascist groups. From the middle of the 1980s, feminist anti-fascist activists demanded that the role of women in the far right should be taken seriously, and they put a focus on patriarchal aspects (in the far right as well as in the academic community and in anti-fascist groups). First articles on far-right-oriented girls and women were published in the early 1990s. This can be seen as the starting point of the first phase of gender-sensitive research on the contemporary German far right.

The focal points of the discussion were the following: (a) The conventional ignorance of women's involvement could be due to gender-specific styles and spheres of political action. Men are more active in public arenas, women more in their social environment (Meyer 1994; Holzkamp and Rommelspacher 1991). (b) Far-right violence is supported by women and men in gender-specific ways, i.e. delegated vs. direct violence. Men strike out, women are more indirectly involved, often cheering the men on (Oltmans 1991). (c) Women have their own specific reasons for turning to the far right: the attractiveness of the traditional image of women (Siller 1991), or the externalisation of conflicts resulting from a so-called double socialisation (*doppelte Vergesellschaftung*) (Siller 1991; Birsl 1992; Birsl 1994), meaning that the anger caused by difficulties in combining employment and family roles is directed at vulnerable outsiders (such as immigrants). A similar mechanism involving externalisation of a conflict is seen in the concept of "ethnicisation of sexism" (Jäger 1996). Here, the background is sexual violence in families and neighbourhoods. But instead of an uncle or a neighbour, the "black man", the "foreign man" or historical "occupiers" are accused of being (potential) rapists. The concept of "culture of dominance" (Holzkamp and Rommelspacher 1991) is applied to societies which deal with differences between people in a hierarchic way, involving dominance and submission—learned firstly in the gender relationship, and afterwards adapted to other differences. Autochthonous women are subordinated under "their" men, but try to put themselves in the dominant role in their relationship with allochthonous people. Holzkamp and Rommelspacher also pointed out that the "borders of care" (ibid.) can lead to women's far-right orientations. The socialisation of women as considerate, "care-taking" and sensitive humans often goes hand in hand with a concentration on their own family. Beyond this emotional border, "strangers" are seen as a threat and as competitors for resources and chances.

From Assumptions to Empirical Findings: The Second and On-going Phase of Gender-Sensitive Research on the Far Right

The second phase of gender-sensitive research started with empirical research projects on girls and women and the far right in the early 1990s (such research is still being carried on). Different methodological approaches have been used: quantitative surveys of attitudes (Birsl 1992; Utzmann-Krombholz 1994; Polis 2001), qualitative guided interviews with female party members (Skrzydlo 1992; Büchner 1995; Roth 2006), qualitative biographical interviews with girls and women from the scene (Siller 1997; Köttig 1995; Köttig 2004; Sigl 2008), quantitative and qualitative analysis of documents and theoretical and ideological reconstructions (Bitzan 1994, 2000; Bitzan 2005; Sturhan 1994; Elverich 2000; Elverich 2005; Döhring and Feldmann 1999; Döring and Feldmann 2004; Bitzan et al. 2003; Welk 2008; Weber 2010; Lang 2011; Kemper 2014; Kaufhold 2015).

Due to the empirical findings from these studies, some feminist assumptions have been corrected, supplemented, or further specified. Thus, it has been shown that for most of the women the images of women propagated by the far right are *not* relevant as a motivation to join the movement. More important are nationalist and racist slogans (Skrzydlo 1992), or strong conventionalism (Büchner 1995). Reasons for turning to the far right are always a combination of discourses, opportunities and biographically important issues. It is not sufficient to focus on motivations that are specific to women: in this context, both gender-*specific* and gender-*unspecific* aspects are relevant (Köttig 2004).

The ideological images of women propagated by far-right female authors are heterogeneous and not exclusively "traditionalist". Even reminiscences of "emancipative" statements can be found (Bitzan 2000). The majority of these images are difference-oriented, while a minority is equality-oriented. For their own life, women may have liberal or modern visions and ways of life, and not a few take over various political functions. The age, educational background, and personal style of active far-right women differ considerably.

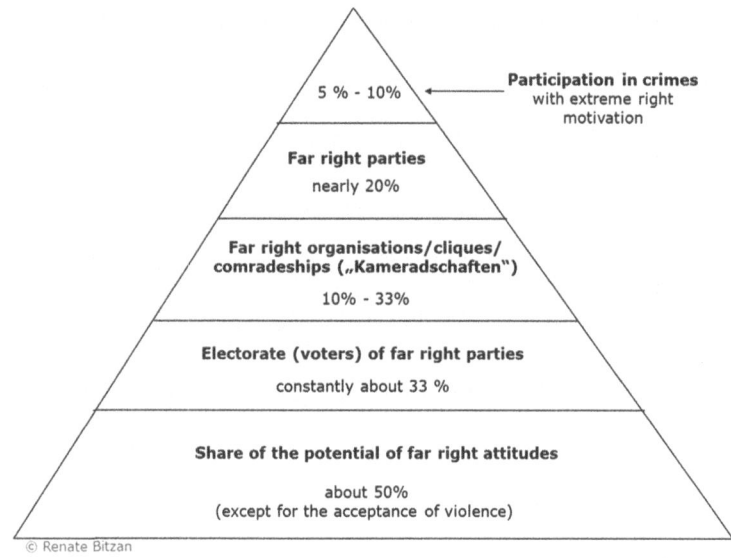

Participation in crimes
with extreme right
motivation

5 % - 10%

Far right parties
nearly 20%

Far right organisations/cliques/
comradeships („Kameradschaften")

10% - 33%

Electorate (voters) of far right parties
constantly about 33 %

Share of the potential of far right attitudes

about 50%
(except for the acceptance of violence)

© Renate Bitzan

Fig. 1   Quantitative proportion of women in diverse dimensions of the far right in Germany

Far-right women's organisations have noticeably increased in number since the end of the 1990s, but they differ in size and importance. The most important are the GDF ("Gemeinschaft deutscher Frauen", Union of German Women) and the RNF ("Ring nationaler Frauen", Circle of National Women).

The quantitative proportion of men and women in the far right in Germany differs depending on the dimension of participation we look at. Based partly on official statistics, partly on various empirical surveys, and partly on estimates by journalistic observers, women's participation in different types of activities can be visualised as a pyramid (Fig. 1).

THE "FORSCHUNGSNETZWERK FRAUEN UND RECHTSEXTREMISMUS"

The Research Network on Women and Right-Wing Extremism was founded in 2000 by six feminist scientists and journalists from different German cities to establish a continuous exchange of knowledge and cooperation on this topic. Today, it consists of 14 (female) members, who permanently exchange information and meet for two extended gatherings each year. To date, the members have held about 250 lectures and talks in the context of political education, information and discussions in civil society, social sciences and social work, mostly in Germany but also in Austria, Switzerland, Hungary, the USA, Canada, Israel, and Australia. The network has initiated three conferences (Hamburg 2001; Frankfurt a.M. 2010; Nuremberg 2012) and produced about 150 individual publications in the form of books and articles, a joint book in 2005 (Antifaschistisches Frauennetzwerk and Forschungsnetzwerk Frauen und Rechtsextremismus 2005), a joint manual in 2009 (revised edition 2014) (Forschungsnetzwerk Frauen und Rechtsextremismus 2009, 2014), a joint homepage (since 2011), and some joint public comments on the case of the so-called Nationalsozialistischer Untergrund and its terrorist suspect member, Beate Zschäpe (Forschungsnetzwerk Frauen und Rechtsextremismus 2011, 2013, 2015). Members of the network have given numerous interviews for the print media, radio and TV, have an advisory function for teachers, film-makers and students and researchers in the social sciences, support selected political projects, and cooperate with other scientists and journalists working on the topic. The expertise of the members of this network in the field of women and right-wing extremism is accepted by academics, as well as by the media and political initiatives (for more information, see http://www.frauen-und-rechtsextremismus.de).

All these activities have led to an increased sensitivity to, and more differentiated knowledge of, the relevance and roles of women in far-right politics—at least in the interested parts of the German public. As far as we know, there is no other country with such a well-established and well-structured, but nevertheless independent and non-institutionalised, research network on this specific topic. Current issues discussed by the research network include the role of women in the new populist movements or parties (PEGIDA, AfD), as simple participants, voters, speakers or leaders (e.g. Frauke Petry as head of the AfD), and the gender discourse of these and other more explicitly far-right forces: although they propagate anti-feminist ideas and traditionalist gender roles and family policies (Kemper 2014), they present women's emancipated status as a value of "German" or "Western civilisation", for instrumentalising this in the discourse against immigrants. The "ethnicisation of sexism" (see above) is reinforced by them and currently a widespread feature in public discourses. Critical and differentiated analyses and voices are necessary for future debates.

NEW RESEARCH FOCUS ON CONSTRUCTIONS OF MASCULINITY: THE THIRD PHASE OF GENDER-SENSITIVE RESEARCH ON THE FAR RIGHT

In the field of research on the contemporary far right in Germany, a new focus on masculinity started around 2003, and constitutes a third phase of gender-sensitive analysis (e.g. Geden 2004; Kohlstruck and Münch 2006; Lehnert 2008; Kenzo and Virchow 2008; Claus et al. 2010). Inspired by the critical masculinity studies which have developed in Germany since the end of the 1990s, this research relies mainly on the internationally used concepts of "hegemonic masculinity" (Connell 1999), "habitus", and "the serious games of masculinity" (Bourdieu 1997; Meuser 2008). In Connell's concept, the hierarchical relations between masculinity and femininity and between different forms of masculinity are central. The different masculinities are systematised as hegemonic, accomplice-like, subordinated, and marginalised. Which forms of masculinity are hegemonic, subordinated, and so on, can change in the course of history and in different societies or socio-cultural surroundings. Bourdieu's concept of "habitus" describes behaviours and incorporated attitudes, which mark persons as members of specific societal groups or classes. "The serious games of masculinity" are ritualised confrontations between boys or young men, in which they assume a male habitus by learning to see other boys or men as both antagonists and partners at the same time. This enables them to become competitive and to build male networks. The main results of research on masculinity within the far right are summarised below.

A central function of men in far-right ideology is to save the "pure race" by "protecting" white German women. This means controlling women's sexuality and reproductive abilities and fighting against "foreign" men as a "threat" to "our own" women (or better: to the "racial pureness" of the next generation).

The ways of "doing masculinity" in the far right and the attractiveness of this to men (especially young men) have been examined with the following results: being a "real man"—in sharp contrast to women and "softies"—is essential for those men who celebrate a "masculinity of soldiership" in the service of the "holy nation and race". The attractiveness of such an ideal can be seen against the background of changing gender norms within society. This can lead to uncertainty and therefore strengthen a longing for old school clearness in gender roles. Or—another interpretation—the so-called crisis of masculinity is not real, but a discourse intended to fight modernisation and defend male domination. The dominant "far-right masculinity" in its relationship to other masculinities can be described as "marginalised" due to the emphasis on physical force and out-dated gender norms. But from the point of view of different masculinities *within* the far-right scene, the "masculinity of soldiership" switches into the "hegemonic position" in relation, for example, to gay nazis who are in a "marginalised" position. The possibility of *diverse* "hegemonic masculinities" within the far right is also discussed: for example, "political soldier", "hedonistic street fighter", and "serious politician".

FUTURE PROSPECTS

The discussions on gender within the far right in and around the Research Network lead to the presumption that, in the long run, the presence of women will stabilise the far right (by educating the next generation) and open the door to influencing the middle of society (through a more "peaceful" image). The observable role models for women in the far-right spectrum (from white-pride mother to political office-holder) can attract women with various ambitions—as long as they share the ideological core of nationalist and racist beliefs.

"Real man" masculinities (perhaps in different variations) may be seen as one of the strongest—more or less hidden—motivations for young men to join the far-right scene. Campaigns against feminism and gender mainstreaming are issues which are building bridges between the far right, parts of the conservatives and parts of the men's rights movement—a coalition which may have serious effects on gender politics.

Even if the main far-right gender ideologies seem to be stable (like biology-based gender-specific tasks, pure race fantasies, heteronormativity), there are variations and on-going changes which must not be overlooked.

Issues for further gender-sensitive research on the far right in Germany should include the following: the involvement of men and women in violent attacks (in a comparative perspective) and how the police and the courts are dealing with it; the biographic development of people who grow up in families where both mother and father are active members of the far right; scientific evaluation of pedagogical projects with gender-sensitive concepts; relevance and strategies of far-right women (and men) as professionals in schools and social work, and as activists in civil society associations or parent's associations; the development of discursive and political coalitions against feminism and gender mainstreaming; the intersection of gender and anti-immigration discourses and movements. A historical and systematic comparison of gender discourses and gender positions in the former GDR and in the FRG, and their potential effects on the gender attitudes and types of activism of men and women in the far right today, would also be interesting. Finally, more international comparisons of gender discourses and practices in the far right in different countries would be welcome.

REFERENCES

Antifaschistisches Frauennetzwerk, and Forschungsnetzwerk Frauen und Rechtsextremismus (eds). 2005. *Braune Schwestern? Feministische Analysen zu Frauen in der extremen Rechten.* Münster/Hamburg: Unrast/rat.

AIB (Antifaschistisches Informationsblatt). 2012. *Das Pogrom von Rostock. Reaktionen, Rückblicke, Reflexionen,* vol 95, No. 2. AIB Berlin.

Birsl, Ursula. 1992. Frauen und Rechtsextremismus. *Aus Politik und Zeitgeschichte. Beilage zur Wochenzeitung das Parlament B* 3–4: 22–30.

———. 1994. *Rechtsextremismus: Weiblich—männlich? Eine Fallstudie.* Opladen: Leske+Budrich.

Bitzan, Renate. 1994. *Rechter Geist aus Frauenfedern. Zur Positionenvielfalt publizierender rechter Frauen insbesondere zum Geschlechterverhältnis und zu soziopolitischen ›Frauenfragen‹ (Zeitschriftenanalyse 1985–1993.* Unpublished Master's thesis in Sociology, University of Kassel, Department of Social Sciences.

———. 2000. *Selbstbilder rechter Frauen. Zwischen Antisexismus und völkischem Denken.* Tübingen: Edition Diskord.

———. 2005. Differenz und Gleichheit–Zur Geschlechterideologie rechter Frauen und ihren Anknüpfungspunkten zu feministischen Konzepten. In *Braune Schwestern? Feministische Analysen zu Frauen in der extremen Rechten,* ed. Antifaschistisches Frauennetzwerk and Forschungsnetzwerk Frauen und Rechtsextremismus, 75–90. Münster/Hamburg: Unrast/rat.

Bitzan, Renate, Michaela Köttig, and Berit Schröder. 2003. Vom Zusehen bis zum Mitmorden. Mediale Berichterstattung zur Beteiligung von Mädchen und Frauen an rechtsextrem motivierten Straftaten. *Zeitschrift für Frauenforschung und Geschlechterstudien* 21(2+3): 150–170.

Bourdieu, Pierre. 1997. Die männliche Herrschaft. In *Ein alltägliches Spiel. Geschlechterkonstruktion in der sozialen Praxis,* ed. Irene Dölling, and Beate Krais, 153–217. Frankfurt a.M.: Suhrkamp.

Büchner, Britta Ruth. 1995. *Rechte Frauen, Frauenrechte und Klischees der Normalität. Gespräche mit "Republikanerinnen".* Pfaffenweiler: Centaurus.

Claus, Robert, Esther Lehnert, and Yves Müller (ed). 2010. *Was ein rechter Mann ist .... Männlichkeiten im Rechtsextremismus.* Berlin: Karl Dietz Verlag.

Connell, Robert: W. (today Raewyn). 1999. *Der gemachte Mann. Konstruktion und Krise von Männlichkeiten.* Opladen: Leske+Budrich.

Döring, Kirsten, and Renate Feldmann. 1999. *Konstruktionen von Weiblichkeit in nationalsozialistischen und rechtsextremen Frauenzeitschriften.* Unpublished degree dissertation, Freie Universität Berlin.

———. 2004. *Von "N.S.-Frauenwarte" bis "Victory". Konstruktionen von Weiblichkeit in nationalsozialistischen und rechtsextremen Frauenzeitschriften.* Berlin: Logos-Verlag.

Elverich, Gabriele. 2000. *Der (modernisierte) Diskurs des Front National über die Stellung der Frau und seine Rezeption in der feministischen Kritik.* Unpublished degree dissertation, Göttingen University, Department of Social Sciences.

Elverich, Gabi. 2005. Zwischen Modernisierung und Retraditionalisierung. Extrem rechte Geschlechterpolitik am Beispiel des französischen Front National. In *Braune Schwestern? Feministische Analysen zu Frauen in der extremen Rechten,* ed. Antifaschistisches Frauennetzwerk, and Forschungsnetzwerk Frauen und Rechtsextremismus, 109–123. Münster/Hamburg: Unrast-Verlag/rat.

Forschungsnetzwerk Frauen und Rechtsextremismus. 2009 (revised edition 2014). *Handreichung zum Thema "Mädchen und Frauen in der extremen Rechten" für Multiplikatorinnen und Multiplikatoren zur Einführung in das Thema Frauen und Rechtsextremismus.* For more information see http://www.frauen-und-rechtsextremismus.de/cms/material

———. 2011. Und warum ist das Interessanteste an einer militanten Rechtsextremistin ihr Liebesleben?—Offener Brief des Forschungsnetzwerks Frauen und Rechtsextremismus zur Berichterstattung über die Rechtsextremistin Beate Zschäpe. www.frauen-und-rechtsextremismus.de

———. 2013. Unsere Stellungnahme zum NSU-Prozessbeginn—2. Offener Brief. www.frauen-und-rechtsextremismus.de

———. 2015. Statement des Forschungsnetzwerks Frauen und Rechtsextremismus zur Einlassung Beate Zschäpes im NSU-Prozess am December 9. www.frauen-und-rechtsextremismus.de

Geden, Oliver. 2004. *Männlichkeitskonstruktionen in der Freiheitlichen Partei Österreichs. Eine qualitativ-empirische Untersuchung.* Opladen: Leske+Budrich.

Heitmeyer, Wilhelm (ed). 2011. *Deutsche Zustände. Folge 10.* Frankfurt a.M.: Edition Suhrkamp.

Holzkamp, Christine, and Birgit Rommelspacher. 1991. Frauen und Rechtsextremismus. *Päd. Extra* 1/91: 33–39.

Jansen, Frank. 2013. Rechtsextreme Gewalt. Die Bundesregierung zählt 63 Todesopfer—es sind deutlich mehr. *Tagesspiegel,* March 20.

Jäger, Margret. 1996. *Fatale Effekte. Die Kritik am Patriarchat im Einwanderungsdiskurs.* Duisburg: DISS.

Kaufhold, Charlotte. 2015. *In guter Gesellschaft? Geschlecht, Schuld und Abwehr in der Berichterstattung über Beate Zschäpe.* Münster: Edition Assemblage.

Kemper, Andreas. 2014. *Keimzelle der Nation? Familien- und geschlechterpolitische Positionen der AfD—eine Expertise*, ed. Friedrich-Ebert-Stiftung. Berlin: Friedrich-Ebert-Stiftung.

Kenzo, Rena, and Fabian Virchow. 2008. Welches Männerbild vertritt die NPD? In *88 Fragen und Antworten zur NPD. Weltanschauung, Strategie und Auftreten einer Rechtspartei—und was Demokraten dagegen tun können*, ed. Fabian Virchow and Christian Dornbusch, 201–204. Schwalbach/Ts.: Wochenschau Verlag.

Köttig, Michaela. 1995. *... und da hat es angefangen, dass ich rechts geworden bin. Wahrnehmungen, Innenansichten und Selbstverortungen von Mädchen innerhalb der rechtsextremen Szene. Bedingungen und Prozesse des Hineinwachsens und der Distanzierung*. Unpublished degree dissertation, University of Kassel, Department Social Services.

———. 2004. *Lebensgeschichten rechtsextrem orientierter Mädchen und junger Frauen—Biographische Verläufe im Kontext der Familien- und Gruppendynamik*. Gießen: Psychosozial-Verlag.

Kohlstruck, Michael, and Anna-Verena Münch. 2006. Hypermaskuline Szenen und fremdenfeindliche Gewalt. Der Fall Schöberl. In *Moderner Rechtsextremismus in Deutschland*, ed. Andreas Klärner and Michael Kohlstruck, 302–336. Hamburg: Hamburger Edition.

Lang, Juliane. 2011. *Bedrohungsszenario "Gender"—der aktuelle Diskurs um Geschlecht im Rechtsextremismus*. Unpublished degree dissertation in Gender Studies, Humboldt-Universität zu Berlin, Zentrum für Transdisziplinäre Geschlechterstudien.

Lehnert, Esther. 2008. Geschlechtsreflektierende Ansätze in der pädagogischen Arbeit mit rechtsextrem orientierten Jugendlichen. Talk on the conference *Brave Mädels und echte Kerle? Theorie und Wirklichkeit von Geschlechtsrollen im Rechtsextremismus*. Berlin: Friedrich-Ebert-Stiftung, January 23. http://www.fes-gegen-rechtsextremismus.de/pdf_08/080123_lehnert.pdf

Meuser, Michael. 2008. Ernste Spiele. Zur Konstruktion von Männlichkeit im Wettbewerb der Männer. In *Die soziale Konstruktion von Männlichkeit. Hegemoniale und marginalisierte Männlichkeiten in Deutschland*, ed. Nina Baur, and Jens Luedtke, 33–44. Opladen and Farmington Hills: Verlag Barbara Budrich.

Meyer, Birgit. 1994. 'Wenn man so politisch aktiv ist, muß man sich ja noch lange nicht für Politik interessieren' Zum Politikverständnis von Mädchen. *Zeitschrift für Frauenforschung* 12 (1+2): 64–76.

Oltmans, Hilke. 1991. Siegen, kämpfen, durchgreifen lassen. Rechtsextremismus bei Mädchen. *Widersprüche* 35(June): 41–45.

Polis–Gesellschaft für Politik und Sozialforschung mbH. 2001. *Rechtsextremismus und Gewalt—Ergebnisse einer Repräsentativbefragung bei Jugendlichen*. Studie im Auftrag des Ministeriums für Frauen, Jugend, Familie und Gesundheit des Landes Nordrhein-Westfalen. Düsseldorf.

Roth, Silvia. 2006. *Motive rechtsextremen Engagements von Frauen. Eine Untersuchung über das politische Selbstverständnis von Frauen in rechtsextremen Parteien der Bundesrepublik Deutschland.* Unpublished degree dissertation, Freie Universität Berlin.

Schedler, Jan, and Alexander Häusler (ed). 2011. *Autonome Nationalisten. Neonazismus in Bewegung.* Wiesbaden: VS Verlag für Sozialwissenschaften.

Sigl, Johanna. 2008. *Lebensgeschichten von Aussteigerinnen aus der rechten Szene— eine biographieanalytische Studie.* Unpublished degree dissertation, Göttingen University, Department of Social Sciences.

Siller, Gertrud. 1991. Junge Frauen und Rechtsextremismus—Zum Zusammenhang von weiblicher Lebenserfahrung und rechtsextremistischem Gedankengut. *deutsche jugend* (1/91): 23–32.

———. 1997. *Rechtsextremismus bei Fraue.* Wiesbaden: Westdeutscher Verlag.

Skrzydlo, Annette. 1992. *Das Selbstverständnis von 'Republikanerinnen' und ihre Haltung zur Frauenpolitik.* Unpublished degree dissertation in the framework oft the empirical project „Frauen bei den ‚Republikanern' in Westberlin", Freie Universität Berlin, Department of Political Sciences.

Spiegel. 2016a. Abstimmungen in drei Ländern: Die Ergebnisse der Landtagswahlen im Überblick. *Spiegel Online*, March 14. http://www.spiegel.de/politik/deutschland/wahlen-2016-die-ergebnisse-der-landtagswahlen-im-ueberblick-a-1082093.html

———. 2016b. De Maizière zu Angriffen auf Asylheime: 'Gewalt kriecht bis in die Mitte der Gesellschaft'. *Spiegel Online*, February 5. http://www.spiegel.de/politik/deutschland/thomas-de-maiziere-gewalt-kriecht-bis-in-die-mitte-der-gesellschaft-a-1075863.html

Stöss, Richard. 2010. *Rechtsextremismus im Wandel.* Berlin: Friedrich-Ebert-Stiftung.

Sturhan, Kathrin. 1994. *Zur Stellung von Frauen in rechtsextremistischen Organisationen.* Unpublished degree dissertation, Göttingen University, Department of Socail Sciences.

Utzmann-Krombholz, Hilde. 1994. *Rechtsextremismus und Gewalt: Affinitäten und Resistenzen von Mädchen und jungen Frauen.* Studie im Auftrag des Ministeriums für die Gleichstellung von Frau und Mann des Landes Nordrhein-Westfalen ed. Düsseldorf.

Virchow, Fabian, and Christin Dornbusch eds. 2008. *88 Fragen und Antworten zur NPD. Weltanschauung, Strategie und Auftreten einer Rechtspartei—und was Demokraten dagegen tun können.* Schwalbach/Ts.: Wochenschau Verlag.

Wagner, Bernd. 2002. Kulturelle Subversion von rechts in Ost- und Westdeutschland: Zu rechtsextremen Entwicklungen und Strategien. In *Handbuch Rechtsradikalismus. Personen—Organisationen—Netzwerke. Vom Neonazismus bis in die Mitte der Gesellschaft*, ed. Thomas Grumke, and Bernd Wagner, 13–28. Opladen: Leske+Budrich.

Weber, Regina. 2010. *"Deutsche Kinder, deutsche Mütter—unseres Glückes Unterpfand" Rechtsextremistinnen: Von heterogenen Frauenbildern zur, deutschen Mutter' im Kampf für Familie und Volk?* Unpublished degree dissertation, University of Potsdam, Department of Business and Social Sciences.

Welk, Sarah. 2008. Ideologie versus Alltag. Kommunikationsstrategien neonazistischer Frauen im Internet, May 21. http://npd-blog.info/wp-content/uploads/2008/03/gdf_arbeit.pdf

Between German Nationalism and Anti-Muslim Racism: Representations of Gender in the Freedom Party of Austria (FPÖ)

Carina Klammer and Judith Goetz

INTRODUCTION

Until now, research on the Freedom Party of Austria (Freiheitliche Partei Österreichs, FPÖ)—and right-wing extremism in Austria in general—has paid very little attention to the construction of gender and the role of women as participants, voters or transporters of rightist opinions. Therefore, we will try to show how fundamental gender is as a category for analysing the FPÖ, and its rearticulations of policies and ideology, and why further research is necessary. First of all, we will focus on theories of right-wing extremism in Austria and what gaps emerge by ignoring or isolating gender issues. Then we will take a look at the functions of female party members on the one hand, and the importance of male bonding on the other. Finally, we will try to analyse the gender structure of anti-Muslim racism and anti-feminism within the FPÖ and its political environment.

C. Klammer (✉)
University of Vienna, Department of Political Science, Vienna, Austria

J. Goetz
University of Vienna, Vienna, Austria

© The Author(s) 2017
M. Köttig et al. (eds.), *Gender and Far Right Politics in Europe*,
DOI 10.1007/978-3-319-43533-6_6

GENDER-BLIND DEBATES ON EXTREMISM

Ignoring gender as a crucial category for analysing right-wing extremism starts with its very definition. In Germany, research on right-wing extremism criticises ideas of "extremism" which divide society into a supposedly neutral "centre" and its extremist "edges"—similar to a horseshoe (cf. Forum für kritische Rechtsextremismusforschung 2011; Falter 2013). The "centre" is defined as those who move within constitutional limits, while the "edges" are judged by the same criterion and fundamental differences between left and right are negated. Misanthropic attitudes are not explained as a by-product of the particular society, but are viewed as a "sickness", located outside of society. The hegemonic discourse on extremism, which is promoted and defended almost exclusively by male researchers, not only seems to propagate totalitarianism theories that try to equate two unequal ideologies as being equally "bad",[1] but it also has implications for political, governmental and scientific activity. Its attractiveness for post National-Socialist societies mainly lies in the "tendency to relativise National Socialism by equating it, at least implicitly, with Stalinism and Communism" (Falter 2011, 92, transl. JG). Therefore, interventions in these political and/or scientific discourses (often funded by state or EU institutions) are all the more important.

However, neither extremist theory itself, nor its critique, consider gender relations (or related questions of inclusion or exclusion) as fundamental issues. Among many other important aspects, however, there are differences in terms of equality (of all women),[2] self-determination and social analysis of capitalist socialisation and patriarchy among right-wing extremist activists and the so-called "Extremist Left".[3]

Despite the general need for critique, the common concept of "extremism" as propagated in Germany can only be applied to Austrian conditions to a limited extent. Among other things, Austria differs from Germany as far as the re-education process after the Second World War is concerned. Furthermore, in Austria the criminalisation of neo-Nazism is governed by the National Socialism prohibition law (*Verbotsgesetz*), whereas in Germany right-wing extremism is considered to be a criminal offence against the democratic order (*Demokratische Grundordnung*). Yet, a trend towards promoting the extremism debate in Austria can be noted as well. Worthy of mention in this context are the reports on the Protection of the Constitution (*Verfassungsschutzbericht*) since 2010.[4] Moreover, the FPÖ itself has an interest in encouraging the debates surrounding the equating of left-wing and right-wing extremism.

Thus, a different definition of "extremism" is necessary. According to Willibald Holzer (1993), right-wing extremism should be understood as an instrument for scientific description and analysis of political and social phenomena and to qualify ideological positions and/or patterns of organisation. It serves neither the vilification of parties, organisations or persons identified as right-wing extremist, nor is it to be understood as an accusation of criminal acts. The term is used as a critical concept and has to be differentiated from other ideas such as right-wing populism, which focuses on stylistic devices and propaganda techniques that are not only found in right-wing extremism, and the term neo-fascism, which is not able to describe the specifics of the Austrian-German history of National Socialism. According to Holzer (1993) the following characteristics (among others) describe right-wing extremism: the idea of "*Volk*" and "*Volksgemeinschaft*," ethnocentrism, ethnic pluralism, the exclusion of the so-called "other," anti-liberalism, anti-pluralism, anti-democratic opinions, constructions of the enemy, theories of scapegoats and a nationalising view of history. Following Holzer, Brigitte Bailer (1997, n.p.) highlights in her text entitled "Images of Women and Representation of Women in Austrian Right-Wing Extremism" (transl. JG) that extreme right-wing ideologies are "not a self-contained, logically structured construct of thoughts" and that three elements—the idea of "*Volksgemeinschaft*", an "essentialist belief" and a mostly racist connotation of (German) nationalism—have to be regarded as constitutive of right-wing extremism. The harmonised representation of the community of all members of the (German) "*Volk*", the biologistic reference to gender and "*Volk*", as well as their alleged "naturalness", and the connected "rejection" of the supposed "other" or "strangers" can be found in the party programme and the policies of the FPÖ. Therefore, the FPÖ may be classified as right-wing extremist (cf. Schiedel 2007).

Despite the usefulness of Holzer's explanation of right-wing extremism in order to counteract the discourse of extremism, a closer examination shows that the category of gender has little importance in Holzer's definition. Although he points out that the constitutive ideology of right-wing extremism focuses on the ideology of inequality based on the principle of "Nature", the biologism that is widespread in right-wing extremist circles, and which has a strong effect on gender relations, is largely omitted. The focus lies on the claimed natural inequality between the "races" or "nations". The construction of binary gender, separating "man" and "woman" into mutually opposing entities with certain essentials, which corresponds to the essentialist construction of "race", hardly finds mention in Holzer's considerations or in the works of other theorists of right-wing extremism. Despite the increasing fields of participation for extreme right-wing women in recent decades, a backlash in right-wing extremist circles can be seen, strongly focusing on traditional constructions of gender and pushing women once again into more limited roles. Although these trends are not necessarily associated with a decrease in the active political involvement of women, modern right-wing extremism, as we find it today, often draws on renaturalisation, the so-called "restoration" of a supposedly "natural" gender order. For this reason, we suggest that more attention should be given to these neglected topics, especially because this strictly binary gender model fulfils certain functions within right-wing extremism, such as keeping the supposed influence of "femininity" out of the sphere of politics, male bonding or society, and because the prevalence of the gender binary at the "centre" of society should be regarded as a common ground between it and the extreme right.

WOMEN AND RIGHT-WING EXTREMISM IN THE FPÖ

It cannot be denied that the political sphere of the extreme right in Austria is still dominated by men. Even the few exceptions, such as the existence of a few female German nationalist student associations[5] or the candidacy of Barbara Rosenkranz (FPÖ) for president, change little about this fact. Nevertheless, within the past few years, conservative parties in Austria have been more successful in supporting women in important political positions than the parties of the centre, such as the Social Democratic Party of Austria (Sozialdemokratische Partei Österreichs, SPÖ). Even in the FPÖ, women consistently occupy important political functions. Looking at the history of the party, Heide Schmidt, for example, was not only the first General Secretary of any party in Austria, but she was also candidate for the presidency in 1992. Furthermore, Susanne Riess-Passer, the former Federal Chairwoman of the party ("*Bundesparteiobfrau*"), was also the first female politician to be Vice Chancellor of Austria. In contrast to Rosenkranz, these two politicians are closer to the liberal wing of the FPÖ, and therefore they have also attracted less attention regarding their policies on women's issues. Further, important right-wing extremist women in Austria include Hemma Tiffner, before her death in 2014 publisher of the far-right periodical "Die Umwelt" ("The Environment", founded in

1972), which has little to do with environmental issues but rather with anti-Semitism and relativisation of National Socialism[6]; Kriemhild Trattnig, a former ideologist of the FPÖ, Jörg Haider's "political mother", and Lisbeth Grolitsch, former regional leader ("*Gau-Unterführerin*") of The Union of German Girls ("Bund deutscher Mädel", BDM) and co-founder of several right-wing extreme organisations. Apart from the women's organisation within the FPÖ, the IFF ("Initiative Freiheitlicher Frauen"), and the above-mentioned female German nationalist student associations, there are hardly any influential right-wing women-only organisations in Austria. Even though the proportion of women in the FPÖ has been increasing on various political levels within recent decades, the party continues to be male-dominated and no serious increase of political interest in women's issues or "feminisation" of the party can be observed. Women in leadership positions are supposed to be a signal of modernity and friendliness towards women. Furthermore, these women serve to encourage women voters and to substantiate the family policy interests of the FPÖ (cf. Rösselhumer 1999).

Male Bonding Between the FPÖ and German Nationalist Student Fraternities

Male bonding and gender segregation are actively practised by German nationalist student fraternities, which in Austria are anything but socially isolated, marginalised groups. On the contrary, these student fraternities tend to be the main link between organised neo-Nazism and the right-wing extremist parties in Parliament, especially the FPÖ. Even though different types such as national-liberal, German nationalist and openly right-wing fraternities exist, they share the same ideological background, based on nationalist, racist, anti-Semitic, homophobic, sexist and pan-German ideas. Pan-German means, for instance, that they consider themselves to be part of a racially constructed German cultural and ethnic community (*Volksgemeinschaft*) (cf. ÖH 2014; Schiedel 2007). There are also confessional, Catholic student fraternities, which differ from German nationalist ones in that they tend to be conservative (rather than extreme right), and they do not have to participate in academic fencing. Academic fencing (*Mensur*) fulfils certain (sexist, homophobic, anti-Semitic and racist) functions within German nationalist student fraternities. It serves as a barrier against the influence of women and the imagined threat of feminisation, assures membership of the community and is supposed to teach subordination and willingness to sacrifice oneself—characteristics which Jews or women are supposed not to possess. Furthermore, German nationalist student fraternities can be seen as elite unions, exclusively for (white, "German", middle or upper class) men who have influential political and economic connections. The common ground with the FPÖ can be found in the similar ideological background. To this day, not only the FPÖ recruits a major part of its personnel from student fraternities, but several leaders of Austrian neo-Nazi and right-wing extremist organisations are, or at least have been at some point in their lives, members of student fraternities, for instance, Otto Scrinzi, Gottfried Küssel, Andreas Thierry or Franz Radl. Although it would be wrong to consider every member of a German nationalist student fraternity a neo-Nazi, the intersections and overlappings between these student fraternities and neo-Nazi activities must be regarded as more than random coincidences or individual cases. Without exaggeration, members of these student fraternities have been involved in the majority of neo-Nazi activities in Austria after 1945. Together with neo-Nazis, members of German nationalist student fraternities participated in the first mass gathering of neo-Nazis and right-wing extremists in the Second Republic in Austria (1959), and in the "South Tyrol terror" between 1956 and 1988, in which 21 people were killed by neo-Nazis and right-wing extremists. As the FPÖ had become more liberal by the end of the 1960s, the members of student fraternities became discontent with this development. They began to found other right-wing extremist parties. In the 1990s, neo-Nazis and right-wing extremists used the houses of student fraternities as places of withdrawal in order to escape observation. This is because student fraternities had become the object of observations by the state and were mentioned in the report of the Federal Office for the Protection of the Constitution. But after the conservative ÖVP formed a government coalition with the FPÖ in 2000, the FPÖ succeeded in having the student fraternities removed from the report (cf. Gruppe AuA! 2009; Schiedel 2007).

The strong link between student fraternities and the neo-Nazi scene is indicated by their invitation policies. Neo-Nazis and right-wing extremists have frequently been invited to political or cultural events such as national "*Liederabende*". Moreover, members of student fraternities have been involved in anti-antifa activities. Together with others, Sebastian Ploner, a former parliamentary employee of Martin Graf, the former third President of the National Assembly, and a member of "aB! Olympia Wien", tried to attack an anti-fascist demonstration against the inauguration of Martin

Graf. Members of student fraternities have also been involved in the neo-Nazi website alpen-donau.info, as the operators not only boast about their contacts with fraternities, but the authorities have also discovered members of student fraternities among the users of the forum. Members of student fraternities can also be found in the "Identitäre" movement in Austria.

A common ideological denominator between the FPÖ and student fraternities is rejection of the idea of equality, which finds expression in racism, sexism and homophobia, as well as in counterpositions to the Left, emancipatory movements and policies such as those in favour of gender equality, or feminism in general. A further structural similarity between the FPÖ and the German nationalist student fraternities can be found in their androcentric ideology. Like other right-wing extremist or right-wing conservative parties, the FPÖ does not have a proper women's policy or party programme because women's topics are always subordinated to family issues, which in their understanding are inseparable from women's issues (Geden 2004). Furthermore, in the FPÖ as well as in German nationalist student fraternities, gender issues are frequently connected with racist agendas such as the promotion and protection of "our people" or "our families" against influence by immigrants. Policies in favour of gender equality can hardly be found. On the contrary, such policies are regarded as "gender madness" (Klement 2008)[7] or a conspiracy to abolish the difference between men and women (Rosenkranz 2008).

NEW ENEMY: OLD PATTERNS? THE GENDER STRUCTURE OF ANTI-MUSLIM RACISM

Since discussions about Islam and Islamism have become an important issue within European politics,[8] the new Strache FPÖ (like many other right-wing organisations) has started to include the historical narrative of Muslims as a "threat to the Christian Occident" in their policies against foreigners. Although the majority of German nationalists are influenced by an anti-clerical tradition, the founding myth of Europe having been shaped by Christianity (as a homogeneous cultural unit) has a specific historical background within right-wing ideologies. The idea of a sovereign "Occident" built an ideological bridge between different political forces which believed in common "enemies" like the Ottoman Empire, the Jews or the Soviet Union (cf. Faber 2000). After the First World War, the term was frequently used to express the longing for a new European supremacy. After the Second World War, the defeated Germany in particular used

references to a common "Christian Occident" to claim its right to participate in the reform of Europe. Furthermore, old and new Nazis used the
term as a synonym for "Pan-Germany" or the German "*Reich*"—terms
which have (at least in the public discourse) become taboo (cf. Conze
2005). The discourse of the "Occident" lost its significance and was partly
forgotten when democratic images of Europe became established, while
well-established images of "the Orient" (characterised as uncivilised,
hypersexual and martial) did not simply disappear but were incorporated
into the discourse of "Islamisation".

It is significant that the FPÖ in particular uses gendered issues such
as the instrumentalisation of women's rights (the freedom not to have
to wear a headscarf, the prohibition of the burka, the condemnation
of "harmful traditions" like forced marriage) to get attention and to
strengthen right-wing positions within the public discourse. In 2008, the
former FPÖ politician Susanne Winter, who has been excluded from the
FPÖ because of anti-Semitic Facebook postings in 2015, gained media
attention because of her speech at the FPÖ New Year meeting. Winter
called Prophet Mohammed a "child molester".[9] It is certainly no coincidence that such discourses have been introduced by female members of
the party. As women and "mothers" themselves, they try to instrumen-
talise gender issues to propagate and legitimise racist and anti-minority
(anti-immigration) policies.

The fact that in 2010 the FPÖ quoted a statement against Islamism
by the famous feminist Alice Schwarzer on an election poster is symp-
tomatic of a strategy which tries to monopolise women's issues for racist propaganda against immigrants.[10] Furthermore, gender images play a
crucial role not only in the context of political strategies, but also on an
ideological level. Specific concepts of masculinity and femininity are perceived in terms of the so-called "clash of civilisations". The generalised
view of Muslims as an anti-modern collective that still honours the traditional heterosexual family therefore becomes a major threat. Especially
pregnancy in Muslim women is pictured as an underhand demographic
method or "weapon" to conquer Europe. While the duty of women is to
reproduce the nation ("*Volkskörper*"), it is regarded as the duty of men to
defend it. To emphasise the male position as "protector of the nation",
Austrian women are proclaimed as the "first victims of Islamisation".
When a Muslim immigrant refers to Austrian women as "impure", this is
perceived as an attack against the absolute position of the Austrian male
and the racialised order in general.

The characterisation of Muslims as separatist and willing to sacrifice themselves for "their own cause" evokes admiration as well as defensive reactions. The nationalist longing for a homogeneous collective and the wish to re-establish the traditional gender order is projected onto "the Muslim".[11] The fact that the FPÖ has an indifferent or even positive attitude towards Islam in general does not affect its propaganda against Muslim immigrants, but suggests that there is a field of tension between various far-right groups concerning the role of Muslims in the global world order and as exterior alliance partners.[12] In consequence, the progress of "Islamisation" is not blamed on the immigrants themselves but on the "*Vaterlandsverräter*" (traitors to the homeland). In particular, the impact of feminism as well as the "spreading" of homosexuality (seen as symptoms of modern "decadency") are accused of "weakening" the nation by "decomposing" its *natural* gender order.[13]

ANTI-FEMINISM AS CONSTITUTIVE IDEOLOGY OF AUSTRIAN RIGHT-WING EXTREMISM AND THE FPÖ

Holzer identifies anti-egalitarianism as a major ideological moment of right-wing extremism, but pays little attention to the widespread anti-feminism in right-wing extremist circles and to the patriarchal, hierarchical structure of the imagined "*Volksgemeinschaft*". Anti-feminists try to influence and obstruct debates about equality and attempt to revoke the feminist achievements of recent decades. They imagine a feminist domination in society, which would benefit women and girls, so that boys and men are seen as the disadvantaged victims. One major effort of the movement is to place this alleged male victim role in a broad public discourse (cf. Kemper 2011, 2012).

Anti-feminism has a long tradition as a political strategy against gender equality. Since the beginning of women's movements, there have been men fighting them. Frequently, an anti-feminist ideology is mixed with other sexist, homophobic, racist and anti-Semitic ways of thinking, and therefore must be seen as a key element of extreme right ideology. With the increasing occurrence of right-wing extremist anti-feminist groups, it is clearly important to consider the ideological aspects of anti-feminism in right wing extremism.

An example from the Austrian far-right discussion illustrates this phenomenon. In 2008, Barbara Rosenkranz (FPÖ) published the anti-feminist book "MenschInnen. Gender Mainstreaming on the way to a sexless society". According to Rosenkranz, the concept of gender main-streaming poses a "scary" threat to Western culture by changing human nature. She claims that the recognition of different life styles, gender iden-tities and sexual orientations is a more important objective than equality between men and women. In her view, the "chief ideologists" of gender theories have infiltrated both the universities and the EU. Rosenkranz concludes that the interests of the experts are opposed to those of the mothers, and that the real motivation of gender mainstreaming is getting women back to work after childbirth. This goes against the "true wishes" of mothers and reflects only economic interests. Rosenkranz thinks that "mothers" are in danger of becoming sexless workers, the "victims" of an economic and childless elite who relentlessly seek to implement gender mainstreaming in coalition with feminism and Marxism, their major allies. Her anti-feminist and homophobic work is not an ideological novelty, as the FPÖ has attracted attention with similar ideas for a long time. The FPÖ also sees gender mainstreaming as an EU re-education programme for the abolition of the family and reduction of the number of children.[14] Rosenkranz is therefore supported by the FPÖ and frequently invited as lecturer for gender issues.

ANTI-FEMINIST ALLIANCES

Anti-feminism is an issue which often leads to (strategic) alliances among not always clearly identifiable right-wing (extremist) groups, organ-isations and parties. Thus, for example, the FPÖ functions as the main coalition partner of so-called fathers' rights groups. The fathers' rights movement in Austria as we know it today is only a few years old. The so-called men's rights activists started to become organised in the 1970s in the USA. Initially, there were different groups, including pro-feminist ones. However, increasing institutionalisation, de-politicisation and the question of how to behave towards masculinists led to a strengthening of German-speaking men's rights activists and masculinists, from which also fathers' rights activists emerged in the 1990s. In Austria, today there is an increasing network of fathers' rights organisations. Some of them have joined forces in an Austrian "fathers' platform" which, according to their self-description, focuses on "family-related human rights, in particular, the right to family life". The concerns of fathers' rights groups appear harm-less at first glance, but a closer look shows that, for example, behind the request for "true equality" there is often the hidden idea of a supposedly "natural" distribution of power between the sexes. This means nothing more than a classic role distribution, based on a biologistic understanding of the supposed natural functions of men and women in this society. According to these groups, the state interferes far too much in the content and the distribution of tasks between men and women (cf. Goetz 2013). The forms of cooperation with the FPÖ are manifold. For example, some FPÖ politicians bring the concerns of the Austrian fathers' rights movement into (public and parliamentary) political debates, not least because the FPÖ image of the family consistently agrees with the ideas of fathers' rights activists. Thus, in the course of debates on child custody, fathers' rights activists have been nominated by the FPÖ as experts in the relevant working groups. In addition, the parliamentary club of the FPÖ operated a supposedly "independent" platform called "divorce victims" (www.trennungsopfer.at) for some years. The website was launched by the third President of the National Assembly, Norbert Hofer. In 2012, a dossier on "The network of child abusers" caused a scandal because it was spread by Thomas Tayenthal, who used to work for the FPÖ parliamentary club, and it associated famous personalities such as Austrian President Heinz Fischer with convicted sex offenders. Tayenthal himself was the operator of the "divorce victims" website and repeatedly lectured at fathers' rights events. Fathers' rights activists also collaborated several times with Karlheinz Klement, who was noticed, for example, because of notorious statements like "Homosexuality is a culture of death". Klement has been excluded from the FPÖ more than once.

Norbert Hofer (FPÖ) voluntarily submitted charges against himself during an investigation on § 278b (terrorist organisations) against fathers' right activists. Herwig B., who was convicted for other offences in the course of this investigation, has also been the operator of the forum www.genderwahn.com, which as a result of repeated violation of existing laws is no longer online, but was known for its perpetual right-wing extremist, misogynist contents posted by users with names like "Women's Shelter Hunter" ("Frauenhausjäger") or "Volk". The threats, slander and defamation are now continuing on the website www.justiz-debakel.com, where profoundly anti-democratic, misogynist content is being published, such as a list of the addresses of all battered women's shelters in Vienna (cf. Goetz 2013).

The debate is important because the Austrian fathers' rights activists are not a socially marginalised phenomenon. Members of this movement have influence on political processes and thus introduce and boost anti-feminist thinking and misogynistic contents in political discourse through different strategies. And they can be sure of the support of right-wing extremist and right-wing conservative parties. The common denominator of all involved groups is primarily anti-feminism established out of a concern to uphold certain concepts of masculinity and male dominance.

CONCLUSION

Dominant academic approaches to right-wing extremism in Austria clearly have conceptual blind spots with regard to gender and gender relations. According to Brigitte Bailer (1997, n.p.), research tends to ignore "the essential question of gender relations in right-wing extremism and the ideological codification of women's role in this spectrum" (transl. JG). This does not seem to have changed much. A gender-reflected theory of right-wing extremism could therefore have a significant impact on research in this field. Similar arguments to those already published in the German context would also be desirable for Austria.

NOTES

1. The main criticism focuses on Uwe Backes and Eckhard Jesse because they have created the scientific and theoretical underpinnings of this model.
2. Women's issues can also be found in the debates and policies of the extreme right. Liliane Crips (1990) speaks of "national feminism" and Renate Bitzan (of "anti-sexist racists" and "sexism-critical nationalists"). These differ from progressive feminists primarily by their neglect of other factors of discrimination based on origin, sex, class, and notions of equality of "our" women with "our" men (cf. Bitzan 2005).
3. Therefore, we prefer to speak of the radical left instead of using the term "extreme left".
4. Cf. APA/red, derStandard.at. 2010. "Verfassungsschutz: 'Gewaltige Zunahme linksextremer Delikte." Der Standard, April 26. http://derstandard.at/1271375264810/Verfassungsschutzbericht-Verfassungsschutz-Gewaltige-Zunahme-linksextremer-Delikte.
5. The female equivalent of German nationalist student fraternities are so-called Mädelschaften or Damenverbindungen. Despite the fact that they have little political influence in Austria, their ideological opinions do not differ from those of their male comrades.

6. DÖW. Die Umwelt. Accessed March 18, 2015. http://www. doew.at/erkennen/rechtsextremismus/rechtsextreme-organisationen/die-umwelt.
7. Parlament, 2008. Genderfragen als brisantes Thema. Accessed March 18, 2014. http://www.parlament.gv.at/PAKT/PR/JAHR_2008/PK0552/.
8. The construction of Muslimness is not simply reducible to a prejudice or biased perception. Furthermore, it is embedded within general social structures, like current state policies in respect of migration and integration. Within this process, restrictions on the labour market (aimed at excluding unskilled immigrants from non-EU countries or those who are not useful for the national economy) and questions of (national) security play a crucial role.
9. Höfler, Klaus. 2008. "Grazer FPÖ-Obfrau Winter: „Kinderschänder Mohammed". Die Presse, January 13. http://diepresse.com/home/politik/innenpolitik/355243/Grazer-FPOObfrau-Winter_Kinderschaender-Mohammed.
10. Especially male party members accept women's rights issues only as a strategy for spreading *the real* issue in the public discourse. The instrumentalisation of further topics, such as the protection of animals in respect of the "Halal-Frage" ([Halal question, author's note] Höferl 2012: 12 quoted by Klammer 2013, 89) is considered similarly. At the same time, the ethnicisation of sexism can function as an outlet for female right-wing extremists. It enables them to pay attention to issues of gender inequality without getting into conflict with the ideological principles or sexism of male party members.
11. The desire for military masculinity is often expressed by references to historical figures like Prince Eugene or Charles Martel, who helped to defeat the Ottoman Empire.
12. Especially nationalists from Arab countries are seen as an ally against the USA, "the Jews" and/or Israel as well as the modern age in general.
13. Even if the anti-Muslim enemy image has incited a dispute about the role of Israel within the far right, anti-Muslim racism does not replace anti-Semitism because anti-Semites still imagine that phenomena of *disintegration* and *decay* (like multiculturalism, leftism, homosexuality, feminism, etc.) are caused by "the Jew".
14. Cf. f.e. FPÖ Amstetten. 2009. Gender-Mainstreaming. Accessed March 18, 2014. http://www.fpoe-amstetten.at/2009/12/03/gender-mainstreaming/.

REFERENCES

Bailer, Brigitte. 1997, January 22. *Frauenbild und Frauenrepräsentanz im österreichischen Rechtsextremismus.* *DÖW.* Accessed 13 August 2013. http://doewweb01.doew.at/thema/thema_alt/rechts/refrauen/frauenbildre.html

Bitzan, Renate. 2005. Differenz und Gleichheit. Zur Geschlechterideologie rechter Frauen und ihren Anknüpfungspunkten zu feministischen Konzepten. In *Braune Schwestern? Feministische Analyse zu Frauen in der extremen Rechten,* ed. Antifaschistisches Frauennetzwerk, Forschungsnetzwerk Frauen und Rechtsextremismus, 67–83. Münster: Unrast Verlag.

Conze, Vanessa. 2005. *Das Europa der Deutschen: Ideen von Europa in Deutschland zwischen Reichstradition und Westorientierung (1920–1970).* Oldenbourg: Wissenschaftsverlag.

Crips, Liliane. 1990. Nationalfeministische Utopien. *Feministische Studien* 1: 128–136.

Faber, Richard. 2000. *Abendland. Ein politischer Kampfbegriff.* Berlin, Wien: Philo.

Falter, Matthias. 2011. Critical Thinking Beyond Hufeisen. "Extremismus" und seine politische Funktionalität. In *Ordnung. Macht. Extremismus. Effekte und Alternativen des Extremismusmodells,* ed. Forum für kritische Rechtsextremismusforschung, 85–101. Wiesbaden: Verlag für Sozialwissenschaften.

———. 2013. Grundlagen und Konsequenzen des Extremismuskonzepts. In *NSU-Terror. Ermittlungen am rechten Abgrund. Ereignis, Kontexte, Diskurse,* ed. Imke Schmincke, and Jasmin Siri, 117–124. Bielefeld: Transcript Verlag.

Forum für kritische Rechtsextremismusforschung (ed). 2011. *Ordnung. Macht. Extremismus. Effekte und Alternativen des Extremismusmodells.* Wiesbaden: Verlag für Sozialwissenschaften.

Geden, Oliver. 2004. *Männlichkeitskonstruktionen in der Freiheitlichen Partei Österreichs. Eine qualitativ-empirische Untersuchung.* Opladen: Leske + Budrich.

Goetz, Judith. 2013. *Vom Trennungsopfer bis zum Frauenhausjäger—Die österreichische Väterrechtsbewegung macht mobil.* AEP-Informationen, feministische Zeitschrift für Politik und Gesellschaft 2.

———. 2014. (Re)Naturalisierungen der Geschlechterordnung. Anmerkungen zur Geschlechtsblindheit der (österreichischen) Rechtsextremismusforschung. In *Rechtsextremismus. Entwicklungen und Analysen—Band 1,* ed. Forschungsgruppe Ideologien und Politiken der Ungleichheit. Wien: Mandelbaum-Verlag.

Gruppe AuA! 2009. Braune Burschen. Die Geschichte des österreichischen Rechtsextremismus und Neonazismus ist nicht zuletzt auch eine Geschichte der völkischen Korporationen. In *Völkische Verbindungen. Beiträge zum deutschen Korporationsunwesen in Österreich,* ed. ÖH. Wien: Eigenverlag.

Holzer, Willibald. 1993. Rechtsextremismus. Konturen, Definitionsmerkmale und Erklärungsansätze. In *Handbuch des österreichischen Rechtsextremismus*, ed. D.Ö.W. Stiftung, 11–96. Wien: Deuticke.

Kemper, Andreas. 2011. *(R)echte Kerle. Zur Kumpanei der MännerRECHTSbewegung*. Münster: Unrast Verlag.

——— (ed). 2012. *Die Maskulisten. Organisierter Antifeminismus im deutschsprachigen Raum*. Münster: Unrast Verlag.

Klammer, Carina. 2013. *Imaginationen des Untergangs. Zur Konstruktion antimuslimischer Fremdbilder im Rahmen der Identitätspolitik der FPÖ*. Wien et al.: LIT.

Klement, Karlheinz. 2008. Speech on "Gender-Madness" in the Austrian Parlament. Accessed 22 October 2016. https://www.youtube.com/watch?v=tAQ1D_unnrE

Mattl, Siegfried, and Karl Stuhlpfarrer. 2000. Abwehr und Inszenierung im Labyrinth der Zweiten Republik. In *NS-Herrschaft in Österreich*, ed. Emerich Tálos et al., 902–934. Wien: öbv & Hpt.

ÖH (ed). 2014. *Völkische Verbindungen. Beiträge zum deutschen Korporationsunwesen in Österreich*. Wien: Eigenverlag.

Rosenkranz, Barbara. 2008. *MenschInnen. Gendermainstreaming–Auf dem Weg zur geschlechtslosen Gesellschaft*. Graz: Ares-Verlag.

Rösslhumer, Maria. 1999. *Die FPÖ und die Frauen*. Wien: Döcker Verlag.

Schiedel, Heribert. 2007. *Der Rechte Rand. Extremistische Gesinnungen in unserer Gesellschaft*. Wien: Edition Steinbauer.

Stiefel, Dieter. 1981. *Entnazifizierung in Österreich*. Wien-München-Zürich: Europaverlag.

Towards an Alternative Emancipation? The New Way(s) of Women's Mobilisation in the Hungarian Radical Right Subculture

Anikó Félix

INTRODUCTION

At the beginning of the 2000s, a new radical right force started to rise, namely Jobbik founded in 2003. Experts argue that its success was due to many factors, such as the global and domestic economic crises, governmental crises, the effects of growing tension between Roma and non-Roma, and strong anti-Romani attitudes in the host society (Karácsony and Róna 2010). Another factor was the creation of a wide offline and online network around the party (Jeskó et al. 2012). The aggregate result was that Jobbik managed to gain 16.7 % in the Hungarian Parliamentary election in 2010 (OVI 2010).

The party is popular not only with 'typical' right-wing supporters such as under-educated middle-aged men, but also with young people irrespective of their socio-economic status or gender. Therefore, one of the dimensions in which we can scrutinise the radical right is gender, including an examination of women voters, which is what I am going to focus on.

A. Félix (✉)
Department of Sociology, University/ELTE, MTA-ELTE Research Group,
Budapest, Hungary

© The Author(s) 2017
M. Köttig et al. (eds.), *Gender and Far Right Politics in Europe*,
DOI 10.1007/978-3-319-43533-6_7

TERMINOLOGY AND DEFINITIONS

There are different types of radical right groups, but they share a common ground, namely nationalistic, racist, xenophobic and anti-democratic attitudes, and they all support the idea of a strong state (Mudde 2000). Many academics highlight the radical right's anti-establishment face, which is a challenge for democratic states (Givens 2005). I prefer to use the term 'radical right' as I agree that the main feature of these parties is their anti-establishment character. Furthermore, the term 'radical right' is less judgemental than, for instance, the term 'extreme right'.

Regarding the role of women in the radical right, there are researchers who investigate the so-called radical right gender gap (Givens 2005), in other words, the under-representation of women in these movements and parties, while others focus on women activists, voters and members. As I am interested in what types of women participate in the Hungarian radical right, this study is of the second kind. Like Kathleen M. Blee, who argues that women joined the Ku Klux Klan because they saw promise and hope in it (Blee 1996), my original hypothesis was that female supporters of the current Hungarian radical right also get some benefits from joining. I presumed that they join the movements in large numbers because they consider its activities to be worthwhile for themselves. Jobbik has been trying to grow bigger since 2006, and has therefore tried to appeal to different social-demographic groups: it has made efforts to attract highly skilled young people, and also female supporters. Although women do not appear as a clearly 'targeted group' in the Jobbik rhetoric, they feature in the discourse concerning motherhood and heterosexual normativity (Pető 2012, 133). As a consequence, my assumption was that the presence of women around Jobbik is important for the party and brings benefits for the women who join.

METHODOLOGY AND DIMENSIONS

The aim of this chapter is to uncover and understand women's motivations and types of participation in the current Hungarian radical right. It unfolds how the movement places women and on the other hand, how women see their role and place inside the movement. In order to examine both sides efficiently, I used more than one method, following the principle of *methodological triangulation* (Guion et al. 2013), which increases validity and reliability. In the beginning, I was a real outsider without any contact and simply observed how women appear as part of the group during their social activities, how they participate. Then through the interviews I tried to understand their own self-representations, their motivations and paths of engagement. Finally, I compared the two: what an outsider sees and their own narratives. I started my research in August 2011 at a radical right festival called National Assembly of Hungarians, where I did participant observation. After this, I made participant observations at other events, demonstrations and so-called women's assemblies organised by the radical right subculture. The radical right subculture is a wide network that includes many different organisations, from bands to paramilitary groups, and involves different events from national festivals to Jobbik rallies. But they have all been connected together by Jobbik, which is at the centre of this network (Jeskó et al. 2012). I was able to observe that these events have different characteristics and women's participation varies greatly. After each event I started to build contacts, inviting interviewees from each kind of event. Then, I applied the snowball method to gain new interviewees. Overall, I conducted 17 semi-structured interviews with women supporters, activists and members of Jobbik from different age groups and socio-cultural backgrounds (Newton 2010). My youngest interviewee was 22 years old, a student, who was a Jobbik activist, while the oldest was 69 years old, someone who was working on the cultural field of this subculture. Regarding their social status, they ranged from middle class to upper middle class, and from low skilled to well educated (see list of interviewees below). A content analysis of blogs and websites was the third method (Mayring 2000) through which I examined women's ways of virtual participation. In this online research, I used the snowball method again, meaning that I was led by the principle of 'who suggests who' as a 'virtual snowball'. Here, I was able to observe different forms of women's activity, from simple online member status to active organiser. In analysing the results, my leading questions were how women represent themselves in the movement, how they get involved and how they participate. The diversity of women in the current Hungarian radical right led me to identify three types of women with different socio-economic backgrounds and levels of engagement. My typology is based on Andrea Pető's book on conservative and right-wing women in Hungary (Pető 2003).

MORAL AND ETHICAL DIMENSIONS OF THE RESEARCH

Examining radical right groups with qualitative methods has special moral and ethical dimensions for researchers. I experienced a moral challenge when my interviewees thanked me for sharing their worldview and agreeing with their arguments, or when they wanted to convince me. I was consciously trying to find the proper distance, showing enough empathy but not being too close or too friendly. In order to solve my dilemma, I tried during the interviews to be neutral and passive, positioning myself as a listener rather than as a real partner, and I did not reveal my own view of the topics we talked about. During the analysis, I also tried to keep a proper distance, avoid judgements, and refrain from applying my own values and ideological preferences.

ALTERNATIVE EMANCIPATION AND THE THREE TYPES OF WOMEN

I have studied how women can connect to, engage with and act as members of the radical right movement, and what kinds of motivation and positions they have in it. My proposal is that the radical right with its multifaceted characteristics can give women opportunities to be seen and possibilities to make their voice heard in the subculture. They can raise their self-esteem, enjoy equality with men, or even make a career in the radical right subculture. This connects to Durham's theory concerning the "rational calculation" of Nazi movements, according to which such parties—*Jobbik* in the case of Hungary—must be open to female supporters (Durham 1998).

The common ground of the three types of women is that a form of alternative emancipation occurs in each case, which is linked to the ideology, current profile and characteristics of the radical right subculture. I call the first type the 'Culture keeper', someone whose main agenda is biological and cultural reproduction. She has some characteristics that connect her to the strong radical right subculture and to growing consumer ethnocentrism. This type may be a businesswoman, and even have a spectacular career in the subculture. The second type is the 'Fighter', someone who joins military or paramilitary organisations like the Hungarian Guard or National Guard.[1] These absolutely masculine movements let women join, and in some sense they may be able to feel equal with men, as women are allowed to participate in 'fights' and represent the movements. The third type is the 'Spiritual woman', a woman who uses the radical right ideology to create a feeling of superiority for herself. Women can do this in the public sphere only to a limited extent, and find alternative opportunities in the frame of the radical right subculture.

The Culture Keeper, the First Type

The first type is similar to the one we are already familiar with. The Culture keeper's primary role is reproduction of the nation, both culturally and biologically, as is usual in nationalist movements (Yuval-Davis 1999). This means that she produces members of the young generation physically and also teaches them. This 'well-known' type of radical woman usually raises children, works in education and teaches cultural traditions. Besides the traditional roles of this type, there is a new phenomenon emerging which is strongly associated with increasing consumer ethnocentrism. This means consumer attitudes that prefer national products by all means, regardless of their quality or price (Shimp and Sharma 1987). Consumer ethnocentrism has developed along with the growth of the radical right and has created a strong subculture. In this subculture, 'truly Hungarian' products are very important, and there are many shops whose profile is 'truly Hungarian', offering not only everyday products like food and other daily items, but also intellectual products.

Within this virulent market, Culture keepers can find opportunities and can work actively in these businesses; in addition to fulfilling their traditional roles. Their activity is legitimated and supported by men, because it reproduces and strengthens the subculture. Men are able to maintain their dominant position, and at the same time women can go out to work in the public sphere or between the public and the private spheres.

As far as their demographic characteristics are concerned, these women belong to the middle or upper middle classes, and have a middle-level education. They have husbands and children, or even grandchildren. Their husbands, or other close relatives, are often prominent in the radical right subculture, writers or politicians. This fact is important because men support the women's activities or their businesses. One of my interviewees provided an example illustrating this point: "I have always been close to book publishing. My husband, as well as my father-in-law, were writers. In the family I had helped a lot with this activity, so it was logical that book publishing would be my vocation" "Ingrid" (b. 1951).

Culture keepers are usually religious, but their religion covers a wide spectrum, ranging from Hungarian paganism to Christianity. Their political activity can be described as average, which also symbolises their middle position between the two other types. They usually appear at major radical right protests, but they do not stand in the front line the way the Fighter does, whom I will present below. In her virtual activity, the Culture keeper is in the middle between the two others. She writes blogs and websites, shares her thoughts, and is slightly more active than the Fighter, but does not create virtual communities the way the Spiritual woman does.

In my research, I have distinguished two 'subtypes' of Culture keeper: one who tends to work on cultural reproduction and the other who is more interested in material and biological reproduction. The first subtype appears not only in the educational system, as was the case in earlier periods, but also in the propagation of culture. Because of their mission, they often work as editors or writers for book publishing companies, newspapers or radio stations of the subculture. They might work in their own shops or companies with a 'truly Hungarian' profile, or may be engaged in some other cultural or intellectual activities concerned with folk customs or folk attire. Besides their job, they organise other cultural events like exhibitions or performances. This subtype organises and leads cultural programmes for the subculture, and circulates information about the events, for example, in leaflets. By applying their social skills, they continue their educational 'mission' in the new area; thus, reaching younger generations: "There are youngsters who come back every time, who are growing up here. (...) There are students in colleges who moved to the city, and they were coming back again and again" "Krisztina" (b. 1969).

The other subtype works on the reproduction of material goods: they work in food markets, which are also influenced by strong consumer ethnocentrism. As they told me, their goal is to preserve and protect Hungarian products. In this activity, they can also build highly successful businesses.

This subtype often argues that products turned out by the Hungarian economy are of a better quality and are healthier than foreign ones. Their activity remains in the biological reproduction category, as their mission is to preserve the nation's health by offering healthy, organic Hungarian foods. On the other hand, by using this frame they can reach people who are interested in organic products without having any particular ideological background. In the course of selling them these 'healthy' products, *Jobbik* businesswomen are able to recruit potentially new supporters and thus to strengthen the subculture.

The Culture keeper shows us how a strong subculture can help women to develop their potential in the field of trade. While they preserve their typical role, they move one step closer to the public sphere. Their activity is legitimised by men because it helps to strengthen the subculture.

THE FIGHTER, THE SECOND TYPE

I call the second archetype the Fighter. We suggest that groups which openly support violence are always the hardest to reach. As Blee argues, researchers have paid less attention to groups whose political agenda they find "unsavoury, dangerous, or deliberately deceptive" (Blee 1993, 322). Nonetheless, during my research I succeeded in maintaining a normal working relationship with these women, and did not feel myself to be in danger at any point. By adopting a neutral manner, it is possible to make a meaningful study of such groups.

The Fighters' most important characteristic is their extremely bold political activity. This means that they are always in the front line at protests and events organised by the radical right, and if necessary, they will engage in a fight. They are often members of the Hungarian Guard or Youth Movements of the radical right. Due to their explicitly violent agenda, women are generally very rare in these military or paramilitary movements. It is therefore interesting to try and understand their motivations.

Their socio-economic status is lower than that of the other two types, and typically they are less educated, which is related to the fact that in this group the younger generation is over-represented. As I have observed, many of them are single mothers or young women without children. The young girls would like to be mothers, and the women who already have children practise cultural reproduction with their own children.

The first question is why they join movements of such a clearly masculine nature. Paradoxically, the Fighter uses the movement as a tool for alternative emancipation.

For young Fighter women or single mothers, these organisations primarily provide a strong community, in which they can feel at home, make friends or even find a partner. These women are often truly active members of the groups. They told me that when they joined the groups, one of their motivations was that they wanted to be equal to men. In answer to my question, the interviewees said that they feel this equality after joining, and on the surface it seems that equality is really achieved in the movements. The organisations let them join and they can regard themselves as full members. In their own eyes, this means that in the groups they must behave in the same way as men. If they can meet all the conditions, they may join the groups. So they can be members of the Guard if they satisfy the requirements. About these requirements, one of them told me: "For women who join the Guard, there is no more whining and crying. They must run the circles in the same way, and must face the police if necessary" "Mónika" (b. 1987). Nevertheless, I found that equality is not complete for this type. My interviewees told me that there is still some distinction or discrimination between men and women within the groups, as for example in the front line during the so-called fights: "When big shit happens, like a police attack, children and women go to the back, if the commander says so... but I think it is discrimination, as we can also protect ourselves" "Gabriella" (b. 1967). Women's roles within the Guard are a sign that they do not have full equality. During my participant observations, I could see these differentiations. At first glance, it seemed that the women were mixed with the men without any discrimination. However, I found that women were over-represented in the so-called media sector and in the health service of these movements.

Their online activity presented the same picture: they appear in the movement's websites and blogs, but most of them only as members and not as private bloggers. This suggests that they are controlled in the virtual sphere, their thoughts appearing only in interviews in answer to specific questions. In these cases, they try to hide their gender, and highlight their equality. "Now I should say that I am a sensitive young girl (...) but other people as well as me see that I'm not thinking and doing the things a 22-year old girl does. (...) First of all, I am a Guardist. That is the line that leads me."[2]

There are some violent and masculine movements that intend to give the impression that they are gender-blind and that it does not matter if you are a woman. If you can 'run the circles' in the same way as men, you will be equal. In some cases, this kind of emancipation actually happens, even though it is not complete. Fighters can join these movements and become active members, but only with limitations. They will always be discriminated against as 'second line' members, particularly in 'fights' or in particular sectors like the media or health service.

THE SPIRITUAL WOMAN, THE THIRD TYPE

The third type of woman that I have identified in the Hungarian radical right is the so-called Spiritual woman. We can find a prefiguration of this type in the past, educated women who joined the right when they recognised a chance to represent themselves as healers of the nation (Pető 2008). Having studied these women, Andrea Pető argues that they were the first women to receive a doctoral degree; they were self-confident and wanted to build their own career (Pető 2008).

The typical Spiritual women is well educated, coming mainly from the field of medicine and health care, most of them being doctors. In addition to a doctoral degree, they often have some other qualification from the field of alternative medicine. They have a higher socio-economic status than the other two types; most of them are married with children. They are religious, but their religiosity is a mixture of occultism, Christianity and Hungarian pagan church dogmas. Their direct political activity is quite low; they do not participate in protests, and even if they get involved, they do not stand in the front line the way the Fighters do.

In the case of the Spiritual woman, the tool for emancipation is the hybrid ideology of the radical right. If we wish to understand it, first we should know a bit about this ideology. It talks about the supremacy of 'Us' (Hungarians), about alternative historical narratives which are combined with some part of 'real history'. In this hybrid ideology, there are many narratives besides the 'common ground', which may occasionally even contradict each other. One of the most important characteristics is that the boundaries are not very strict; therefore, everyone can find his or her own ideological frame. The Spiritual woman also builds her own ideology, creating the 'Hungarian women's superiority' discourse and thus a quasi-power position.

THE WAY OF ALTERNATIVE EMANCIPATION IN THE CASE OF SPIRITUAL WOMEN

One fundamental point of this hybrid ideology is the anti-Semitic theory, which denies the Jewish roots of Christianity. It argues that Jesus and his mother were not Jews, but Hungarians. In this way, they posit a continuity between the Virgin Mary and the supposed ancient Hungarian pagan goddess called 'Babba Mary'. It is also convenient for the Spiritual woman to create a goddess cult and thus increase the importance of the role of women. If we went along with this theory, we could reach the conclusion that God is a Hungarian woman. "I am a Hungarian pagan. My view is that God was also a woman, because everything that was ever born came from women, and that is why the world also came from a woman (...). This woman is Babba Mary. I don't believe in Judeo-Christianity; it's based on manipulation" "Borbála" (b. 1977).

The ideological frame argues that the Hungarian nation is one of the oldest, and it was a matriarchal society. Spiritual women create a powerful position for themselves, highlighting the importance of women leaders in the past and today. According to their narrative, these female leaders, called 'Golden women', were scientists, healers and had a shaman's skills. Besides their healing activity, their role was to lead the community and educate young ladies and women. Spiritual women create continuity between their own activity and that of these quasi-historical figures in order to justify their power demands.

The last point in the Spiritual women's ideological framework comes from the well-known Jobbik phrase: demand for radical change.[3] The meaning of this phrase is not always clear, as it refers to a vague new era when the world will change and Hungary will achieve justice. According to the Spiritual women, this change will be carried out by Hungarian women in particular. Therefore, they build an ideological pyramid, the high point of which is this argument: "In creating a new world women have the leading role. Where we used to live for a thousand years was the opposite side of the world. Women have the rational leading role" "Ágota" (b. 1949).

They create their own ideological framework by selecting certain parts of the whole ideology which is legitimised by the whole subculture. This ideology makes an explicit power demand because in the radical right subculture women cannot explicitly exercise power. Therefore, they must find alternative grounds or areas within the subculture where they can show their power.

Alternative Grounds

The first ground where Spiritual women can demonstrate their power is the so-called women's assemblies. These assemblies are open to anyone, but are usually attended by women who would like to know more about their femininity and are interested in spirituality. Thus, they can reach women who would not otherwise be interested in the ideology of the radical right, but who are certainly influenced by it here, because Spiritual women hide their radical right views and communicate them to the participants in a covert way.

In the assemblies, participants talk about femininity and the power of women, sing spiritual and pagan songs, play musical instruments, and carry out some ritual practices. During the events, the leaders wear 'shaman clothes' or 'truly Hungarian clothes'. When the Spiritual women talk about the power of women, they often refer to the 'Golden women' and the great past of the Hungarian women leaders. They also sneak explicitly racist and anti-Semitic thoughts into their speeches. In this network, someone who has participated once can be an organiser next time, so that the assemblies can spread all over the country.

The other alternative ground is the virtual assemblies. The online activity of Spiritual women is the highest among the three types. The internet is a powerful medium for them, where they can express themselves, spread propaganda, share their thoughts and lead the online and offline communities. In their blogs and websites, they associate their spiritual, religious and radical ideologies and quasi-historical stories with anti-Semitism and racism. They are in intensive contact with users, help them with their physical and psychological problems and answer their questions, using their healing skills online. In their texts, they often introduce themselves as Babba Mary's mediators in order to demonstrate their spiritual skills, as well as to legitimate their ideas. The following quote from a blog talks about the radical change that women will bring to Hungary: "As I see it, the new women's nature is the key to the Hungarian uprising. The future belongs to women's power."[4]

In the virtual ground, the online arena is organised in just the same way as the offline arena, creating the same assemblies, sharing thoughts and spreading the radical right ideology both overly and covertly.

Conclusion

In this chapter, I have distinguished three types of women's behaviour in the current Hungarian radical right. These types are different in respect of the women's socio-economic status, their thoughts about femininity, their motivations and the ways they reach the community. However, the common feature is that all of them connect somehow to the activities and the ideology of Jobbik and the growth of its supporter group.

The first type that I have identified is the Culture keeper who takes advantage of the growing popularity of the radical right subculture, which has been revitalised by Jobbik. Women of this type can found their own businesses selling 'truly Hungarian products', thereby reproducing the (sub)culture in both material and symbolic ways. Their activity is legitimised by the community and makes the supporter group bigger and stronger.

The second type is the Fighter. These women are often members of paramilitary organisations. They stand in the front line during protests and do not refrain from using violence. These paramilitary organisations have been connected to Jobbik from their foundation. Therefore, even if women's equality in these very masculine movements is not complete, the fact that they can join these movements and the movements let them be active members is a means of participation for women in the subculture around Jobbik.

The third type is the Spiritual woman. For their alternative emancipation, they use one of the main characteristics of the ideology of Jobbik, the belief in the superiority and ancient origin of Hungarians, which links with a racialised spiritualism and paganism to establish women's superiority. Since they cannot make their power demands in the public sphere of the radical right, they try to find alternative grounds, such as online and offline women's assemblies. Through their activities, they are able to recruit new women supporters. These types are not exhaustive, and their analysis could be more nuanced. Also, it would be useful to test the results on a more substantial sample. The gender perspective is one key to grasping a deeper understanding of the radical right than is offered by the current literature on this topic.

Acknowledgement I would like to express my deep appreciation to Andrea Pető and Anikó Gregor, who helped me a lot through their work on the topic and their suggestions. Without their support and encouragement, this research would not have been possible.

Notes

1. The Hungarian Guard has been banned since 2007, but post-Guard organisations were still working across the country in 2014. (See more at: http://www.athenainstitute.eu/en/map/olvas/42).
2. http://vasihazafi.hu/index.php?option=com_content&view=article&id=53:vasi-gardista-lany-az-interju-folytatodik&catid=7:militaria&Itemid=10 (Download: 24.09.2011).
3. See more at: http://alapszerv.jobbikhosting.com/Jobbik-program 2010OGY.pdf, accessed 22.03.2016.
4. http://www.csillagtitkok.hu/cikkek/uj-fejezet-nyitanya.html, accessed 22.03.2016.

REFERENCES

Blee, Kathleen M. 1993. Evidence, Empathy, and Ethics: Lessons from Oral Histories of the Klan. *The Journal of American History* 80(2): 596–606.
———. 1996. Becoming a Racist: Women in Contemporary Ku Klux Klan and Neo-Nazi Groups. *Gender & Society* 10(6): 680–702.
Durham, Martin. 1998. *Women and Fascism*. London/New York: Routledge.
Givens, Terri E. 2005. *Voting Radical Right in Western Europe*. Hardback: University of Texas, Austin.
Guion, L.A., D. C. Diehl, and D. McDonald. 2013. *Triangulation: Establishing the Validity of Qualitative Studies*, FCS6014, one of a series of the Department of Family, Youth and Community Sciences, Florida Cooperative Extension Service, Institute of Food and Agricultural Sciences, University of Florida. Original publication date September 2002. Revised August 2011. Original written by Lisa A. Guion, former faculty member; revised by David C. Diehl and Debra McDonald. Accessed 15 January 2014. http://edis.ifas.ufl.edu
Jeskó, József, Judit Bakó, and Zoltán Tóth. 2012. A radikális jobboldal webes hálózatai. *Politikatudományi Szemle* 21(1): 81–101.
Mayring, Philipp. 2000, June. Qualitative Content Analysis. *Forum Qualitative Sozialforschung/Forum: Qualitative Social Research* 1(2). ISSN 1438–5627. Accessed 21 March 2016. http://www.qualitative-research.net/index.php/fqs/article/view/1089/2385
Mudde, Cas. 2000. *The Ideology of the Extreme Right*. Manchester: University Press.
Newton, Nigel. 2010. *The Use of Semi-Structured Interviews in Qualitative Research: Strengths and Weaknesses*. Paper Submitted in Part Completion of the Requirements of the Degree of Doctor of Philosophy, University of Bristol. 2010. Accessed 15 January 2014. http://www.academia.edu/1561689/The_use_of_semistructured_interviews_in_qualitative_research_strengths_and_weaknesses
OVI. 2010. Országos Választási Iroda 2010. évi Országgyűlési Képviselő Választás. Accessed 12 December 2012. http://www.valasztas.hu/hu/parval2010/354/354_0_index.html
Pető, Andrea. 2003. *Napasszonyok és holdkisasszonyok—A mai magyar konzervatív női politizálás alaktana*. Budapest: Balassi Kiadó.
Yuval-Davis, Nira. 1999. *Gender and Nation*. London: Sage Publications.

OVERVIEW OF THE (ANONYMISED) INTERVIEWEES

1. "Ágota" 1949. Natural healing therapist, August 2011, Bösztörpuszta.
2. "Borbála" 1977. Dula, natural health therapist, August 2011, Bösztörpuszta.
3. "Cecil" 1976. Trainer in women's assemblies, August 2011, Bösztörpuszta.

4. "Dóra" 1952. Teacher, culture programme coordinator, August 2011, Bösztörpuszta.
5. "Erika" 1962. Seller, August 2011, Budapest.
6. "Flóra" 1949. Pensioner, September 2011, Budapest.
7. "Gabriella" 1967. Nurse, September 2011, Budapest.
8. "Hella" 1978. Shop owner and seller, editor and reporter for a radio station, September 2011, Budapest.
9. "Ingrid" 1951. Owner of a book publishing company, programme coordinator, September 2011, Budapest.
10. "Jolán" 1950. Shop owner, leader of handmade product sessions, September 2011, Budapest.
11. "Krisztina" 1969. Shop assistant, February 2012, Budapest.
12. "Laura" 1988. Confectioner, February 2012, Budapest.
13. "Mónika" 1987. Student, February 2012, Budapest.
14. "Nóra" 1975. Yoga teacher, February 2012, Budapest.
15. "Orsolya" 1946. Radio editor, February 2012, Budapest.
16. "Petra" 1943. Folktale collector, storybook writer, March 2012, Budapest.
17. "Renáta" 1990. Student, March 2012, Budapest.

PLACES OF PARTICIPANT OBSERVATIONS

Women's assemblies
Service in the Homecoming Church
A lecture in the House of Hungarians
An open market in Óbuda
Jobbik and Hungarian National Guard demonstrations

LIST OF ANALYSED BLOGS AND WEBSITES

http://lelekgardrob.blog.hu/
http://www.liliomkert.blogol.hu/
http://www.magyargarda.hu
http://www.ifjusagitagozat.eoldal.hu/cikkek/ifjusagi-tagozat/zilahi-amalia bemutatkozasa.html   http://www.minalunk.hu/rakosmente/hirek/2174/307/Beszelgetes_Szogi_Zsuzsannaval__a_Jobbik_Ifjusagi_Tagozatanak_elnokevel
http://vasihazafi.hu/
http://www.temesvarigabi.eoldal.hu/
http://aranyasszony.gportal.hu/
http://www.rimalany.eoldal.hu
http://www.hangado.eoldal.hu/
http://lendvaykati.gportal.hu/

http://www.csillagtitkok.hu/
http://www.aranyasszonyok.eoldal.hu/
http://www.omah.extra.hu/index.php?id=4&

Women and Gender Ideologies in the Far Right in Spain

Miquel Ramos and Frauke Büttner

Introduction

The presence and influence of women in the Spanish far right is not widely known. There are no analyses or sociological studies on gender aspects within the spectrum of political extreme-right activities. There are several publications on the Spanish extreme right, where the structures and ideological background of the main organisations and parties are analysed (Cantarero 2007; Casals i Meseguer 2009; Hernández-Carr 2011; Ibarra 2011). For this study, we have examined a large number of primary sources to try to find everything related to gender issues. The proportion of women within the far right is at an outside estimate about 20 % (Büttner 2011, 182), but there is no statistical investigation to back this figure up. There is no systematically gathered data on the number of women within right-wing organisations in Spain. In view of this initial situation, our analysis will focus on the gender approach that some of these associations—we have chosen organisations representing different tendencies within the far right—include in their programmes, propaganda

M. Ramos (✉)
València, Spain

F. Büttner
Free University of Berlin, Berlin, Germany

© The Author(s) 2017   111
M. Köttig et al. (eds.), *Gender and Far Right Politics in Europe*,
DOI 10.1007/978-3-319-43533-6_8

and texts that are publicly available on the World Wide Web, as well as the positions women occupy within such organisations.

Our aim is to obtain a first idea about the way in which right-wing organisations in Spain see the role of women. This analysis may serve as a basis for a further research on gender roles and masculinity in the future, as well as a comparative study of the situation in other countries.

THE FAR RIGHT IN SPAIN

General Francisco Franco ruled Spain between 1939 and 1975, after his coup against the Spanish Republic in 1936, supported by Hitler and Mussolini. After dictator Franco's death (1975), the only extreme-right party represented in parliament was "Fuerza Nueva" (FN) with a single seat in 1979. Since then right-wing parties have not been represented in the Spanish Parliament, but only on the municipal level. Far-right parties received about 0.27 % of the votes (67,009 votes) in the general election in 2015 (Antifeixistes Pais Valencià 2015). There are several reasons why the extreme right has been unable to become a real political power and influence in the post-Franquist era. The beneficiary was ultimately the right-wing conservative alliance "Alianza Popular" (Büttner 2011, 198), the antecessor of the party Partido Popular. Within the ideological spectrum of the far right, we can distinguish three categories:

- **Falangists and nostalgic Franquist organisations**: Their target group is the conservative, nationalist and ultra-Catholic spectrum, as well as parts of the working class. Traditional values have a great importance and the Franco regime is often glorified. The main fascist organisation during the Franco regime was the Spanish "Falange". Born in Spain in 1931, this was the organisation that accompanied the regime; it was fascist-inspired, anti-democratic and opposed to the political parties. It defended a totalitarian state and corporatism based on a single vertical union of employers and employees. Defined as anti-capitalist and anti-communist, and noted for its extreme nationalism and defence of Catholicism, its members contemplated revolutionary means to achieve their political goals. After Franco's death, the far-right organisations held a nostalgic position of return to Franco's fascism, until the late 1980s, when they began to look to Europe and tried to modernise their language. On February 20, 2016, the Ministry of the Interior listed on its website 12 different

Falangist splinter groups. Furthermore, there are a few nostalgic far-right groups, such as "Confederación Nacional de Excombatientes" or "Fundación Nacional Francisco Franco".

- **Populists and neo-fascists**: These are characterised by a populist and nationalist discourse, which uses no fascist or neo-Nazi symbols, but they are sometimes formed by former fascist leaders. In this category, we can find neo-fascist and populist parties such as "España (2000)" and the right-wing populist party "Pataforma per Catalunya" (PxC). Both formations were created by former Francoist militants in the same year, 2002: José Luís Roberto (España 2000) and Josep Anglada (PxC) who decided to formalise nominations locally: "España 2000" in Valencia and PxC in Vic. The political career of PxC must be understood as "an attempt to distinguish itself from the extreme right stigmatised Spanish and approach successful radical right populist formations in Europe. The organisation, led by a person from the traditional extreme right, Josep Anglada, has tried to outrun those elements of their political tradition that can weigh down their chances of electoral success and focus exclusively on the discourses and forms of mobilisation that have electorally effective result for the new European extreme right" (Hernández-Carr 2011).
- **Neo-Nazis and free spectrum**: With a markedly nationalist xenophobic, anti-capitalist and anti-communist discourse, this group includes most young neo-Nazi skinheads, hooligans and independent activists who do not renounce the Nazi and fascist symbols. In this spectrum appear neo-Nazi organisations such as "Democracia Nacional" (DN), "Movimiento Social Republicano" (MSR) and "Alianza Nacional" (AN) and some organisations of what we define as free spectrum. This category covers "the wide spectrum of non-aligned far-right forces in Spain, ranging from nationalist revolutionary and patriotic organisations to extreme right-wing skinheads and cultural-political groups and their networks" (Büttner 2011, 186). Many of their activities are closely linked to the DN, MSR and AN parties, as well as to far-right football fans. Movements that belong to this free spectrum include, for example, the "Autonomous Nationalists" who act in "Bases Autónomas", a neo-Nazi organisation that was active in the 1990s (Ibarra 2011). One important organisation within this free spectrum is "Hogar Social Madrid".

Women's role within the contemporary Spanish extreme-right movement is strongly related to their proposed role during Spanish fascism, which was founded on a patriarchal, ultraconservative and Catholic vision. In this context, it seems important to mention that a "Sección Feminina" (SF) (Female Section) inside the traditional Falange was founded in 1934 and dissolved in 1977. The mass organisation with up to 680,000 members was headed by Pilar Primo de Rivera, sister of the founder of Falangism, José Antonio Primo de Rivera (*1903–1936) (Constenla 2009). Its goal was to instruct young women to become good patriots, Christians and wives. In June 1934, she organised the Women's Section, and was its leader, which is a national delegate position, for 42 years. Pilar Primo de Rivera makes it obvious that she and her organisation always paid attention to the principle of male supremacy, saying, as an example: "Women can never discover anything. They lack creative talent, which God reserves for masculine brightness"[1] (Constenla 2009).

Because of great fragmentation within the Falangist organisations and their strong reference to Franquism, we will focus our analysis on the organisations mentioned in Sects. 2 and 3. These organisations are also more comparable to the main right-wing and populist organisations which are active nowadays in other European countries.

RIGHT-WING POPULISTS AND NEO-FASCISTS

España 2000

Another neo-fascist and populist party with a spectrum of members ranging from nostalgic followers of the late General Franco to neo-Nazis is "España 2000" ("Spain 2000"). Observations of their public events in Valencia clearly show that women are hardly present in their activities and demonstrations.

The party has parliament representation with four councillors in the local assemblies in Silla (Valencia) and in five towns around Madrid. The organisation's leader is a rich businessman from Valencia, José Luis Roberto, who has strong connections to private security businesses, martial arts and prostitution.[2] Due to his economic interests, Roberto has even publicly called for the legalisation of prostitution in clubs. This has brought him much criticism from other right-wing extremists, who see a contradiction in his political speeches against immigration and his involvement in the prostitution business, where 90 % of workers are immigrants.

In 2014, the political programme of "España 2000" referred to women in only one section, which is called "In defence of life" (España 2000a, n.d.). In this programme, the party defends the heterosexual family and mentions women only as mothers: "The abolishment of all differences between the roles of men and women denies biological and cultural reality that gives women a special responsibility in procreation and in the education of children. (…) It is absurd to pitch mother at home and employed mother against one another, because the nation needs children of both classes. So we must create favorable conditions for unemployed mothers and for working mothers" (España 2000a, n.d.). In the current political programme of "España 2000", women are mentioned only in two short parts of the text: first, complaining about the low birth-rate among Spanish women in view of "massive immigration". And secondly, under the heading "Massive immigration creates tensions in society" in the context of "cultures and ways of life foreign to Europe", which condemn women to wear a burqa or treat them as sexual objects (España 2000b). "España 2000" deals with gender issues most notably when it comes to Muslims. Here, women's rights turn into a major issue to support the party's anti-Islam discourse, as we can see in one of their posters, showing a stoned woman beneath the heading: "For women's rights—against the requirements of Islam".[3]

While women within the party are not very numerous, we can single out two of them as prominent members. One is Ana Martín, vice-president of "España 2000" from its founding in 2002 until the third National Congress of the party in 2011 (España 2011). In an interview, she said that she was the first affiliated woman to "España 2000" (Ana Martín, Interview 2009). In a speech by Martín in Valencia on October 12, 2009, at a protest march of "España 2000", she declared; "We have a lack of work, and too many immigrants. (…) We must defend conventions and traditions. Family, religion, life (…)" (España 2000c).

Plataforma per Catalunya

A similar stance has been taken by another right-wing populist party, "Plataforma per Catalunya" (PxC)–"Platform for Catalonia". PxC was founded in April 2002 from a local party called "Plataforma Vigatana" in the Catalan town of Vic (Barcelona), and was led for many years by Josep Anglada, former leader of FN. With its critical discourse on immigration, yet constituting itself within the democratic system, the party has been able to reach new elector circles (Erra and Serra 2008, 22). In 2011, with a very anti-Islamic discourse, the party (Casals 2011) became the most successful extreme-right party since the dissolution of FN, with 67 councillors between 2011 and 2015, when they lost 59 seats and kept just 8. The party's main focus is to fight against Islam, and it often heavily underlines women's rights as a method to attack this religion, as in its electoral declarations under the heading "Immigration and Islam. For another immigration policy and against the Islamic violation of women's rights" (Plataforma per Catalunya, n.d.).

In their programme, they do not specifically mention women's rights, they just promise general support for families. But we find arguments against discrimination closely linked to the anti-Islamic discourse. In Sects. 6.14–9 of their programme, they argue that "habits such as covering the face of women with veils, proclaiming holy war, polygamy, clitoris ablations, arranged marriages and promoting or maintaining any type of discrimination against women simply because of being so must be condemned, prosecuted and typified in the Penal Code. We will not accept any culture that fosters discrimination against women. Prohibition of the burqa" (Plataforma per Catalunya, n.d.).

In a photo on its website accessed in September 2012, we could see that around one-quarter of the members with party functions were women. As of March 25, 2016, Plataforma per Catalunya posted on its website that in the municipal councils where they had political representation, 8 out of 47 councillors were women.

NEO-NAZI ORGANISATIONS AND THE FREE SPECTRUM

Democracia Nacional

Democracia Nacional was founded in 1995 by former neo-Nazi militants from the CEDADE ("Círculo Español de Amigos de Europa") organisation and Spanish Juntas. CEDADE was an important neo-Nazi organisation in Spain (Ramos 2013), active between 1966 and 1993. Spanish Juntas was created in 1983 to reorganise the Spanish far right after the loss of the last member of parliament of the FN, trying to copy the French "National Front" (Casals 2009). DN has no public female representatives. Although they avoid demanding that women should be exclusively responsible for domestic tasks, they clarify that nature has predetermined a different function and responsibility for women.

"We don't say that home and the children are the exclusive responsibilities of women, neither do we pretend to minimalise the importance
of fatherhood; we don't propose a return to this old-fashioned and rigid
sexual separation of duties. We limit ourselves to showing that it's obvious
that nature has assigned women a decisive function in human reproduction
which men cannot assume themselves, so that's the reason why women
must be socially recognised and protected" (Democracia Nacional n.d., 49).

However, DN does not take a clear stand on the right of women to
choose. "To improve the situation of women, to improve family life, the
demographic situation of the nation and the future of social protection,
it is necessary to provide women with possibilities that have been systematically denied to them; especially, we want to add to the integration of
women in the labour market the possibility to choose an option that is
currently not available for the majority of Spanish women for economic
reasons: to choose as a measure of self-realisation the care of their children
and housekeeping, and the possibility to recognise and honour it because
it constitutes a social function of such great importance to social stability,
family and self care" (Democracia Nacional n.d., 49).

DN rejects any concepts of partnership that are not aligned to a
heterosexually-defined family concept and thus fully rejects all "lesbian,
gay, bisexual and transgender" (LGBT) people: "People of the same sex
will not be permitted to marry, according to the idea that such relationships are not constitutive of a real family" (Democracia Nacional n.d., 50).

Women are very present in activities of the DN, especially in the youth
section. Nonetheless, we find hardly any women in leadership roles. On
the electoral list for the European Elections 2014, there were 11 female
candidates out of a total of 26, as the party indicated on its website
[Democracia Nacional (a)].

Movimiento Social Republicano

"Movimiento Social Republicano" (Republican and Social Movement,
MSR) is mostly rooted in Catalonia and Aragon and is a part of the "Alliance
of European National Movements" (AENM), the main European alliance
of far-right parties, such as the Hungarian "Jobbik" and "British National
Party" BNP. MSR presents itself as a radical social and profound national
party (Movimiento Social Republicano, n.d.).

One of the visible faces of this party, Carmen Martin Padial, was one
of the few prominent women within the extreme right in Spain. She was

the party's candidate for the last European elections in 2009 and in the third position in the next 2014 European elections. In the fourth position, there was another female candidate, Sara Valentín Melchor (Rius Sant 2014a). Therefore, two out of five MSR candidates for the European Parliament were women. Padial left the party in July 2014, together with the former leader of MSR, Juan Antonio Llopart, and other neo-Nazi cadres (Rius Sant 2014b).

In the MSR electoral programme accessible on the internet, we find demands to integrate women into the labour market, and statements against women's exploitation as sex workers and against domestic violence. MSR stresses that they will never accept abortion as women's right. The party claims the same rights for women and men in all areas, not going further into gender roles within the family (Movimiento Social Republicano, n.d.).

A few years ago, Carmen Maria Padial, as one of the leading women within MSR, opposed equalising men and women, but defended the right of women to free choice. On the other hand, she strongly criticised feminism. For example, at a conference called "Primavera Valenciana" in May 2012, in her presentation on "the situation of women in contemporary society", she said: "The struggle for women's rights is not based on working outside the home; it is possible to choose a career or to take care of your children at home, because it makes you proud. (…) Today we look stupid if we decide to take care of our little children (…) We want to be free, we do not want to be oppressed by sexist or Taliban feminists. These Taliban women do not care about the fact that the minimum male wage is 128 % of the female wage. It has no importance, they only pay attention to abortion and lesbians (…). For the Talibans those women who have decided to take care of their children or elders are retrograde, we are the ones who struggle for women's liberation (…) I'm proud to have left my job twice to dedicate myself to motherhood (…) (Primavera Valenciana 2012, min. 41:00–43:15).

The way she uses the terms "sexist" and "Taliban feminists" suggests that a feminist in her reading is a person who dogmatically impedes women's choice of motherhood. The freedom of choice that Padial claims gives a strong weight to the decision for children; at least, she points out that in her opinion it is an either/or decision, namely either a career or taking care of children. There is no serious intent of campaigning for the equal rights and responsibilities of women and men, even mentioning the unequal pay between men and women. Padial demands freedom of choice for women, albeit with a prioritisation for the choice in favour of the family.

Alianza Nacional

Within the spectrum of the radical Spanish right-wing movement, there is also a small neo-Nazi party called "Alianza Nacional" (AN) (National Alliance), whose members consider themselves as "national and revolutionaries" (Alianza Nacional, n.d.-a). This party has no more than 100 members, mostly in Málaga (Andalucía) and Madrid. AN was founded in 2005, with the motto "Nation, Race, Socialism" (Plataforma Zaragoza Antifascista, n.d., 4).

AN is the only party within the Spanish far right that openly argues with the term "race". The party has a very traditional and conservative family concept. In an area of their homepage called "ministry of family" they emphasise that "the family has to become the principal core of society again", promising support to all "national families" with more than two children and to all "women who want to have children" (Alianza Nacional, n.d.-b). In their so-called "national programme", available on their website, they reject the right to abortion and other "anti-natural" operations, such as sex reassignment surgery (Alianza Nacional, n.d.-c).

In 2015, AN created a "female front" named Genus, emphasising the natural role of women with reference to the "traditional family", as they explain on their website: "Aware of the special idiosyncrasies of European women, their way of thinking, feeling or being, we have taken the step of creating a female front (…) another example of woman, healthy and proud able to break the chains and gags with which the system has chained her true nature. A system that not only seeks class confrontation to ruin the community, but also gender confrontation to destroy the family" (Alianza Nacional, n.d.-d). They announce "activities that emphasise the status of women and others who seek the restoration of traditional family ties", such as "craft workshops" and "charity markets" (Alianza Nacional, n.d.-d).

Despite the lack of women in important positions, in 2013 a woman linked to the Madrid Nazi skinhead movement, Ana Pavon, was responsible for reading a speech at several events, including a march against "usury and financial terrorism" in Madrid (Marcha frente la usura y el terrorismo finaciero 2013). Moreover, some women are present at demonstrations, marches and party activities, all of which are organised and dominated by men. Many of the women attending public demonstrations and marches are dressed in Nazi skinhead fashions.

The Free Spectrum

The free spectrum consists of autonomous neo-Nazi organisations without any party affiliation. Autonomous neo-Nazi groups are mainly organised on a local level and have no regional or national structures. Most of their activists are also members of extreme-right parties.

Hogar Social Madrid (HSM)

In 2014, a group of neo-Nazi activists occupied an abandoned building in Madrid. They announced this place as "Hogar Social Madrid", a self-managed space dedicated to housing and feeding destitute Spaniards, in order to denounce alleged discrimination against these families in the matter of social assistance, which they claim is given only to immigrants.

This is the same initiative as those of "CasaPound" in Italy and "Golden Dawn" in Greece, two organisations with which they have close cooperation (Hidalgo 2015); they are neo-Nazis who give help only to white families. The discourse of Hogar Social Madrid (HSM) is based on xenophobia and racism; they deny being neo-Nazis, calling themselves "patriots". They collect food at the doors of supermarkets and take it to Spanish families. The media have paid much attention to these activities and to spokeswoman, Melissa Dominguez Ruiz, who has been invited several times to take part in TV debates. Dominguez Ruiz is a philosophy student and mother of a child.

The Youth Front ("Frente Juvenil") of this organisation carried out a campaign in Madrid in March 2016 "against radical feminism". They used banners with the slogan "If they open the door for you it's education, not sexism", or, as on the photo below: "If they call you pretty it's praise, not sexism.".[4]

Militant Neo-Nazi Groups and the Music Scene

It is probably not coincidental that 50 men, but only one woman, were charged following the three most important police operations against neo-Nazi groups in Spain in 2005. The groups involved were "Blood & Honour", "Front Hammerskin" and "Frente Antisistema".

Only two out of about 60 bands in the Spanish neo-Nazi music scene have female members: "Invictos" and "FeminaSS". Both have a song dedicated to Nazi girls: Femina SS sings about the "Skingirl Oi!" (Feminass

2013) and "Invictos" about the "Skingirl", affirming the action on the street and the fight together with the men: "Skingirl (…) fight till the end (…). Stay by your side, coming out to fight" (Invictos 2013).

WOMEN'S ORGANISATIONS WITHIN THE FREE SPECTRUM

Since 2013, two new anti-feminist women's organisations formed by Nazi and fascist militants have appeared in Spain. The first of these is the "Athena Circle", led by one of the ex-MSR party leaders, Carmen Martín Padial, which is defined as an "association of women against feminism" (Circulo atena n.d.), and does not belong to any party or organisation. In an interview on the neo-Nazi website "Zentropa Iberia", a representative of Athena Circle states that "CA women are fighting politically in different groups but CA is independent" (Zentropa Iberia, n.d.).

In the same interview, the organisation explains its view on gender and gender roles: "We feel that the voice of millions of women is silenced or ignored by a certain sector, sexist or *hembrist*. The sector is the current *hembrist* feminism, progressive is totally removed from the real and just demands of women. We extol the feminine, we are female. We do not conceive a society in which one half attacks the other half all the time, we are not against the men, we walk with them, we do not feel superior to them and of course not inferior, we feel ourselves different. We are not sexist, we do not think in terms of gender, we can think in terms of actions, attitudes, but not by the gender of a person" (Zentropa Iberia, n.d.).

The interviewed women stress that they see themselves side by side with men, pointing out the difference between men and women based upon natural circumstances. They categorise feminism as "*hembrist*", a neologism in the Spanish language used to refer to *misandria* or contempt for men. The term has been popularised and defined as authoritarianism against men, gender biases that hurt men in actions or opinions, or interested use of political respectability gained by the older feminism that demands equal rights in order to advance a repressive ideology against men. This provocative over-statement of social reality seems to have the function of discrediting feminism and emphasising the right of women to be "real" and "female" women.

The second organisation created in 2013 is "Alianza Edelweiss". In their blog, its members describe themselves as "0 % feminist, 100 % feminine", and agitate for motherhood and against abortion (Alianza Edelweiss 2015). On the website of the "Democracia Nacional Joven"

(Young Democracia Nacional Party), they are advertised as claiming "true values, putting femininity into feminism, defending the lives of children rather than their murder. The role of woman as a complement to man, not his enemy, both with different qualities, but proud to walk hand in hand to form a perfect social unit (…) is proud of its white race and its preservation (…) aims to promote values that evoke the image of a contemporary yet traditional woman, a female warrior, entrepreneurial, supportive and healthy" (Democracia Nacional Joven n.d.).

CONCLUSIONS

In Spain, the participation of women in public activities is visible, but much lower than the presence of men. In some organisations like "Democracia Nacional" and their youth organisation, women are visible at demonstrations, but not in political functions. Only a few women are political functionaries or speakers of organisations. There are a few women members of RAC (Rock against Communism) groups.

Although the parties are located in different parts of the ideological spectrum, from populist to neo-Nazis, they have similar ideas about the family and the role of women. Almost all stress the importance of free choice between job and family, but with a clear priority: working outside of the home should not prevent a woman from taking care of her family. The organisations analysed leave no doubt that they demand that women should be allowed to dedicate their life to family and motherhood, without restrictions. In a few cases, the unequal pay for male and female workers is criticised, but without elaborating a concrete demand from this, with the exception of MSR. This party mentions free choice in their programmatic statements concerning work, but the statements by one of their female protagonists show that in the case of a conflict, it should be possible to decide in favour of the family.

The demand for equal rights for women is mostly linked to propaganda against Islam. In the neo-Nazi sector and within the free spectrum, female roles vary and can include contradictory positions in respect of feminism, as shown in the case of Padial/MSR, although this discourse is closely linked to her as a person. On the other hand, there are very conservative approaches stressing the imperative union of femininity with motherhood and family. Often, the right of women to behave in a "female" way is stressed.

The ideological foundation in the gender approach of all the organisations analysed is the assumption of a natural difference between man and woman, understood as equal but not the same. Both new women's organisations deal with this topic. This way of thinking parts from a fixed, conservative and traditional understanding of gender roles, based on a biological point of view. In some programmes, this biological view of gender goes hand in hand with emphasising the importance of support just for "Spanish" families. This family concept ends with the racist exclusion of immigrants and other "non-Spanish" people.

We can assert that the vision of today's extreme right is defined by a traditional and conservative gender interpretation, preserving some central elements of the Franquist ideology and showing the strong influence of the Catholic Church in Spain. Nevertheless, gender roles have changed and become more varied under the influence of democracy and an ideological modernisation within the extreme right. We find ambiguous positions concerning women's rights in the modern neo-Nazi groups. In most party programmes, the topic does not have great importance; the arguments are focused on the concept of the family as opposed to women's rights.

Although the organised extreme right currently has no representation in parliament, as we have shown, the main conservative party (now in government) uses much of the extreme-right discourse, preventing the growth of a strong party further to the right. The lack of reliable data and analyses regarding the members of far-right groups, and gender aspects in particular, makes a clear analysis difficult, and hinders the development of effective counter-strategies to prevent girls and women from joining far-right groups and to impede the extension of far-right ideologies in society. It is therefore essential to carry out more detailed investigations and research on this issue.

Notes

1. All quotes have been translated by Frauke Büttner and Miquel Ramos.
2. Jose Luis Roberto has served as a spokesman for the "business association of prostitution" (ANELA—Asociación Nacional de Empresarios de Locales de Alterne) in Spain. The book "Lords of prostitution in Spain" by the journalist Joan Cantarero describes the role of this association and José Luis Roberto's part in it. It denounces the regime of control and exploitation from which the sex workers suffer.

3. Picture: http://espana2000.org/wp-content/uploads/2012/11/ contra-las-imposiciones-del-islam-218x300.jpg, accessed February 2, 2016.
4. https://twitter.com/FrenteJuvenil_/status/703138332671225 856, accessed March 18, 2016.

REFERENCES

Alianza Edelweiss. 2015. Blog. Accessed 10 March 2016. http://mujeresporeuropa.blogspot.com.es
Alianza Nacional. n.d.-a. Ideario. Accessed 27 April 2014. anlostuyos.wordpress.com/nosotros/ideario
Alianza Nacional. n.d.-b. Ministerio de Familia. Accessed 2 February 2016. https://anlostuyos.wordpress.com/ministerio-familia
Alianza Nacional. n.d.-c. Programa. Accessed 2 February 2016. https://anlostuyos.wordpress.com/programa/
Alianza Nacional. n.d.-d. Genus. Accessed 2 February 2016. https://anlostuyos.wordpress.com/genus/
Ana Martín presenta Oradores. 2009, Octubre 12. Published October 16, 2009. Accessed 11 March 2016. https://www.youtube.com/watch?v=RukbBFyJpvs
Antifeixistes Pais Valencia. 2015. ELECCIONS 2015: Menys candidatures ultres i els pitjors resultats de la història, December 22. Accessed 6 February 2015. www.antifeixistes.org/9952_eleccions-2015-menys-candidatures-ultres-i-els-pitjors-resultats-de-la-historia.htm
Büttner, Frauke. 2011. Right-Wing Extremism in Spain: Between Parliamentary Insignificance, Far-Right Populism and Racist Violence. In *Is Europe on the 'Right'Path? Right-Wing Extremism and Right-Wing Populism in Europe*, ed. Nora Langenbacher, and Britta Schellenberg, 181–197. Berlin: Friedrich-Ebert-Foundation.
Cantarero, Joan. 2007. *Los amos de la prostitución en España*. Barcelona, Spain: Grupo Z Ediciones B.
Casals I Meseguer, Xavier. 2009. La renovación de la ultraderecha española: Una historia generacional (1966–2008). *Historia y Política 22* (July–December), 233–258. Universidad Complutense de Madrid.
———. 2011. El Populismo que viene (120) Paisaje político después de la batalla electoral del 20-N (I), November 28. Accessed 27 April 2014. http://xaviercasals.wordpress.com/2011/11/28/el-populismo-que-viene-120-paisaje-politico-despues-de-la-batalla-electoral-del-20-n-i/
Circulo Atenea. n.d. Website. Accessed 2 February 2016. circuloatenea.com
Constenla, Tereixa. 2009. Con un pequeño gemido, basta. El Pais, May 20. Accessed 3 March 2014. http://elpais.com/diario/2009/05/10/cultura/1241906403_850215.html

Democracia Nacional n.d. Documentos Ideológicos y Programaticos de Democracia National. Accessed 11 March 2016. http://democracianacional. org/dn/wp-content/uploads/2014/06/programa_dn.pdf

Democracia Nacional (a). Conoce a nuestros candidatos. Elecciones Europeas 2014. Accessed 11 March 2016. http://democracianacional.org/dn3/modules.php?name=News&file=article&sid=4494

Democracia Nacional Joven n.d. Alianza Edelweiss. Accessed 2 February 2016. http://www.dnj.democracianacional.org/modules.php?name=News&file=article&sid=963

Erra, Miquel, and Joan Serra Carné. 2008. Tota la veritat sobre Plataforma per Catalunya. Ara Llibres, Badalona.

España. 2000a. Programa. Una Política para los Españoles. Accessed 24 April 2014. www.archiburgos.org/sembrar/elecciones2008/Programas%20elecciones%202008/E-2000.pdf

———. 2000b. Programa Político. Accessed 2 February 2016. http:// espana2000.org/?page_id=3226

———. 2000c. Vicepresidenta E2000. Manifestación España 2000 'Falta trabajo, sobra inmigración' Zapatero Diimisión!, Published October 10, 2009. Accessed 11 March 2016. http://www.youtube.com/watch?v=RukbBFyJpvs

———. 2011. Vídeo Resumen III Congreso Nacional España 2000, Valencia, 8 de Octubre 2011. Accessed 27 April 2014. https://www.youtube.com/ watch?v=5vNHDAKms3g

Feminass—Skingirl Oi. 2013, February 27. Accessed 24 April 2014. www.youtube.com/watch?v=5aL_Kh2R1Hc

Hernández-Carr, Aitor. 2011. El largo ciclo electoral de Plataforma per Catalunya: Del ámbito local a la implantación nacional (2003–2011), Working Paper 300, Institut de Ciènciès Politiques y Socials, Barcelona.

Hidalgo, Carlos. 2015. Los neonazis del Hogar Social trabajan con Amanecer Dorado y los fascistas italianos, ABC, September 30. Accessed 21 March 2016. http://www.abc.es/madrid/20150930/abci-neonazis-hogar-social-trabajan-201509292029.html

Ibarra, Esteban. 2011. La España racista: La lucha en defensa de las víctimas del odio (Temas de Hoy)

Invictos—Skingirl. 2013, February 28. Accessed 5 May 2014. www.youtube.com/watch?v=3Lx0ZeVDJ3w

Marcha frente la usura y el terrorismo finaciero (Alocución Ana Pavón). 2013, April 27. Accessed 28 April 2014. http://www.youtube.com/watch?v=Dqfp9v0xXck

Martín, Ana. 2008. Interview, October 1. Accessed 24 April 2014. https://www.youtube.com/watch?v=yA_iPuxX1EU

Movimiento Social Republicano (a). n.d. Programa Político. Accessed 2 February 2016. http://msr.org.es/nosotros/programa-politico

Movimiento Social Republicano. n.d. *MSR. La Alternativa para el siglo XXI*, printed in Spain, Ediciones Nueva República S.L.

Plataforma per Catalunya. n.d. Immigració i Islam: Per una altra política migratòria i contra la vulneració islàmica dels drets de la dona. Accessed 2 February 2016. www.pxcatalunya.com/pagines/declaracio-programatica6.html

Plataforma Zaragoza Antifascista. n.d. Dossier sobra Alianza Nacional. Accessed 11 March 2016. www.antifeixistes.org/pdfs/dossier_AN.pdf

Primavera Valenciana. 2012. La lucha de la mujer hoy, May 15, 2012, min. 41:00–43:15. Accessed 24 April 2014. http://www.youtube.com/watch?v= 3D2YgipHw58

Ramos, Miquel. 2013. El legado de la neonazi CEDADE persiste 20 años después, La Marea, November 11. Accessed 20 March 2016. http://www.lamarea. com/2013/11/11/cedade/

Rius Sant, Xavier. 2014a. El MSR se Presenta a Las Europeas. (…), February 5. Accessed 11 March 2016. xavier-rius.blogspot.de/2014/02/el-msr-se-presenta-las-europeas-tras.html

———. 2014b. Juan A. Llopart, Martínez Cayuela, Carmen M Padial y otros dirigentes del MSR abandonan el partido, July 29. Accessed 2 February 2016. http://xavier-rius.blogspot.com.es/2014/07/j-llopart-martinez-cayuela-carmen-m.html

Zentropa Iberia, Blog. n.d. Accessed 27 April 2014. http://zentropaiberia.tumblr.com/post/53948544504/1-lo-primero-agradeceros-vuestra-amabilidad

A 'New' National Front? Gender, Religion, Secularism and the French Populist Radical Right

Francesca Scrinzi

INTRODUCTION

In 2011, Jean-Marie Le Pen's daughter, Marine, succeeded her father as leader of the French National Front party (*Front national*, henceforth NF). With the declared objective of transforming the NF into a large mainstream party with a vocation to govern, she engaged in an enterprise of 'modernisation' and 'de-demonisation' (*dédiabolisation*) of the party's public image, attracting a great deal of attention in the media. This strategy proved to be effective, as in the first round of the 2012 presidential elections, she won a record 17.9 % of the vote. In the 2014 European elections, it was the most voted-for political formation, before the conservative party. Survey data indicate that the traditional 'gender gap' between the number of men and women voting for the NF is narrowing (Mayer 2013). Various scholarly interventions have addressed the question of whether the NF has changed and, if so, to what extent, by analysing the party's ideology, political communication, electoral base, organisation and its relationship with the conservative right[1] (Mayer 2013; Dézé 2012; Crépon 2012; Shields 2013).

F. Scrinzi (✉)
University of Glasgow, Glasgow, UK

© The Author(s) 2017   127
M. Köttig et al. (eds.), *Gender and Far Right Politics in Europe*,
DOI 10.1007/978-3-319-43533-6_9

Some authors note that the 'de-demonisation' strategy implemented by Marine Le Pen, while constituting a novelty in the context of the French populist radical right[2] (PRR), clearly locates the NF in current dynamics affecting this family of parties in other European countries. Indeed, as the political scientist Nonna Mayer (2013, 161) suggests, the NF can be analysed as a 'magnifying glass of the far right's evolution in Western Europe' to apprehend contemporary developments in the ideology and electoral support of these parties. Gender and religion hold a key position in the current changes affecting 'anti-immigration' politics across Europe, in the context of a rising hostility towards Muslim migrants (Betz 2004; Mudde 2007).

This chapter[3] reviews the recent literature on the 'new' NF as well as existing studies of women and gender relations in the NF and explores the relationship among gender, religion, secularism and recent developments in the party, by locating them in the specifics of the French political and cultural context. Firstly, this chapter sets the scene for Marine Le Pen's 'de-demonisation' strategy by presenting the heated and highly gendered public debates on multiculturalism, religion and secularism which have taken place in France in recent decades. Secondly, it explores the gendered dimension of the NF ideology and its transformation, based on the mobilisation of the theme of secularism by Marine Le Pen. The conclusion points to changes and continuities which can be observed in the NF ideology in relation to women and gender.

PUBLIC DEBATES ON IMMIGRATION, SECULARISM AND GENDER IN FRANCE

According to the dominant discourse on the so-called 'republican' model of integration of migrants, citizenship in France is based on principles of universalism and individualism: integration into the nation is supposed to be based on a direct relationship between the individual and the State, to the exclusion of all intermediary groups. Citizenship also relies on a gendered prescriptive distinction between the public political sphere, which is seen as neutral, and the private sphere, where the display of religious and cultural specificities is tolerated (Lemière 2008). Secularism (*laïcité*), intended as the separation and independence of the State from all religious organisations, is a central element of this French 'republican' model of integration: it requires that citizens avoid displaying their cultural and religious specificities in the public political arena, by confining them to the private sphere of the family. This 'universalistic' discourse is associated with suspicion vis-à-vis the potential '*communautarisme*' (sectarianism) of ethnic minorities, which would threaten national integrity.

This dominant discourse on integration is highly gendered. It was established in the 1980s, under a left-wing government, at a time when some of the political goals of the women's movement were being realised. At that time, with the progressive feminisation of the migrant population in France, State-funded programmes and agencies aiming to promote the integration of migrants were informed by normative representations of feminine migration in terms of a move from tradition to modernity, including gender modernity (Morokvasic 2008). Inclusion in the labour market, specifically in flexible and non-skilled jobs where migrant women are over-represented (Chaïb 2008), is supposed to be emancipatory: female migrants tend to be seen as passive and subaltern women with no previous experience of employment. Conversely, migrant men tend to be stigmatised as patriarchal and oppressive. Today issues of gender have remained central to the dominant discourse on the integration of migrants. Over the past decade, conservative politicians and representatives of right-wing governments have declared gender equality as a defining value of the French national identity, as opposed to the patriarchal 'cultures' attributed to the migrants. This use of feminist claims by right-wing parties to attack immigration can be observed during the presidency of Nicolas Sarkozy and under the Raffarin government. The defence of women's rights was used to support the argument that immigration must be controlled and limited, and that immigration constitutes a threat to French republican values (Cette France là 2009). The same period was characterised by the intense mediatisation of acts of sexual violence committed in the suburbs inhabited by working-class racialised French and migrants (*banlieues*). According to feminist and antiracist intellectuals and activists, this 'State feminism' (Tissot 2008) is instrumental in countering immigration and legitimising its association with issues of 'law and order'. Further, it serves to make gender inequalities in France invisible while being unaccompanied by policies aiming to redress these inequalities. Some academic interventions denounced the media focus on the figure of the '*garçon arabe*', the young male of immigrant origin, as racialised men of the suburbs tend to be depicted as potential rapists (Guénif Souilamas and Macé 2006). This constitutes the stigmatised *alter ego* of the '*beurette emancipée*' (emancipated young woman of immigrant origin), who epitomises the republican model of integration and is seen as its typical beneficiary. According to these studies, through these representations sexism is racialised and attributed to migrants, while sexism in French society is made invisible (Hamel 2005). The idea of 'sexual democracy' (with regard to women's and gay rights) is thus associated with French society and is used to draw a distinction between the city and the *banlieues* (Fassin 2006).

This right-wing 'State feminism' (Tissot 2008) was particularly visible at the time of the law passed in 2004, banning the wearing of 'conspicuous signs' of religious affiliation in public schools. In public debates around this law, profound divisions emerged among, on the one hand, French activists claiming to defend women's rights, and, on the other, antiracist activists (Scott 2007). While some have argued that the law reflects a 'neo-colonialist' approach and targets Muslim girls wearing headscarves, others have supported it as a means to promote republican values of secular liberalism and to achieve greater gender equality for all women. These different positions are exemplified by two feminist organisations: MIR (*Mouvement des Indigènes de la République*, Movement of the Indigenous of the Republic), which opposed the law, and NPNS (*Ni Putes Ni Soumises*, Neither Whores Nor Subaltern), which was in favour of the law and received support from the right-wing government in office at the time. Unlike other feminist groups which mobilised around the law, both these organisations claim to defend not only the interests of racialised women, who are made invisible in the 'universalistic' definition of French citizenship, but also those of—at least some—racialised men, who are stigmatised by dominant gendered representations of immigration. NPNS, however, makes a distinction between those men who adopt sexist behaviours or are oriented towards religious fundamentalism as a reaction to their stigmatisation and those who are the agents of sexist violence in the *banlieues*, while MIR claims to defend all racialised men, whatever their relationship to women (Garcia 2012). From the point of view of feminist and antiracist activists, these debates raise the issue of how to combine the antiracist and feminist struggles. Further, they exemplify the difficulties faced by migrant and racialised women in expressing their issues without fuelling further racism in a context where the defence of women's rights in public discourse is closely articulated with the stigmatisation of migrant (and particularly Muslim) men.[4]

The diverse and ambivalent political uses which can be made of the issue of secularism in the French context have been exposed even more sharply in recent years. In 2010, some rightist mobilisations took place in the name of secularism and against the 'Islamisation' of French society.[5]

These involved participants belonging to both the far right and the left wing, including some feminists. In turn this has led to reaction from other feminist activists, who have criticised the essentialistic representation of Islam which is inherent in these mobilisations, and the shift from 'universalistic secularism' to 'identity secularism' which characterises them (Lesselier 2010). According to these critiques, the paradoxical convergence of the rightist forces with some feminists is a consequence of the attitudes of left-wing and feminist organisations, which tend to shy away from the matter of religion and the fundamentalist religious practices of racialised groups.[6]

SECULARISM AND GENDER IN THE NF 'IDEOLOGICAL TURN'

Religion is considered as a strategic site for the analysis of recent changes in PRR ideology across Europe (Betz 2004; Mudde 2007), which, since 2001, has increasingly targeted Muslims. Several PRR parties have denounced immigration from Muslim countries, claiming to be defending Europe's 'Christian civilisation' against the threat of Islam. This tends to be conflated with Islamic fundamentalism. At the same time, in many cases the rejection of migrants, especially Muslims, is justified on the basis of arguments such as the defence of women's and/or gay rights, as migrants are associated with conservatism with respect to gender and sexuality. The theme of gender equality is being used by PRR parties as a new way to frame 'anti-immigration' claims in contexts as different as France, the UK, Italy, Germany, the Netherlands and Scandinavian countries, and to legitimate themselves in the political arena (Meret and Siim 2013; Scrinzi 2014a; Scrinzi 2014b). This argument adds to those traditionally used by these parties, which define immigration as the direct cause of unemployment, the reduction of welfare state provision, criminality, and as a threat to the national culture and identity. Thus, the changes in the ideology of the Western European PRR rely on the coexistence of contradictory elements. These parties claim to be against immigration from Muslim countries in order to preserve liberal values. At the same time, they base their claims on religion, with Christianity considered to be the essence of the European civilisation.

While the enterprise of 'modernisation' of the NF implemented by Marine Le Pen highlights some specificities of the French context—in which the idea of secularism as a republican value has a long history—it can be inscribed within this international trend. Marine Le Pen draws imagery from the left-wing, presenting herself as the defender of secularism and the 'republican model of integration' (Baubérot 2012). For instance, she has compared public Muslim prayers to the Nazi occupation of France and made references to a 'new French resistance' against this 'new occupation'. The NF leader has even mobilised the legacy of the French revolution, traditionally unpopular with the French PRR and far right. Marine Le Pen started this strategy of 'republicanisation' of the party ideology (Shields 2013) in 2002, under the leadership of her father whose electoral campaigns she coordinated. In 2007 two NF posters displayed women, one of whom was a young woman of African origin, with the words 'nationality', 'assimilation', 'social mobility' in one case and 'secularism', 'security', 'public service', 'purchasing power' and 'equality' in the other, indicating that the party was attempting to appeal to young, female and racialised voters. Paradoxically, this 'republicanisation' of the NF coexists with a call for the defence of Catholicism. Marine Le Pen has defined freedom, equality and solidarity (*liberté, égalité et fraternité*) as 'Christian values' which have been corrupted by the French revolution, declaring that 'one must make a distinction between the principle of secularism and the way in which it has been distorted' (quoted in Ivaldi 2012). She considers the defence of all these values as an opportunity to restore the Christian roots of French society. Her statements on the matter of women's rights are equally paradoxical, alternating between defending women's liberation and defending the traditional family, the latter viewed as the basis of the nation's welfare. On the one hand, for example, Le Pen has declared that she will not attempt to abrogate the right to abortion; on the other, she has stated that the right to abortion may undermine French demographics; and that women are not given a 'real choice' when it comes to abortion so that measures must be taken to leave them free to choose to keep their child. Further, the NF has supported the ban on wearing the burqa in the name of women's rights[7] and makes an explicit association between sexual violence and migrant/racialised men.[8] Sociological analyses of this 'rhetoric turn' of Marine Le Pen claim that the NF instrumentally mobilises pseudo-feminist claims to raise electoral support and to legitimate 'anti-immigration' politics (Larzillière and Sal 2011). In this perspective, feminism is used as a 'metaphor of racism' (Tevanian 2007). I call this discourse the *racialisation of sexism* (Scrinzi 2014a). The issue of women's rights is appropriated to re-frame the anti-immigration agenda in the context of the crisis of multiculturalism and hostility towards Muslims: as other PRR parties, the NF, treat gender equality as a standard against which a superior national self can be measured against inferior foreign others. Thus, ethno-pluralism is applied to define women's rights as a cultural trait which is specific to Europe as opposed to other 'cultures'.

Because of these declarations, Marine Le Pen, who is a twice-divorced single mother of three children, has had to confront the Catholic traditionalist faction of the NF, which is highly critical of her attempt to appropriate secularism, and more specifically of her positions on abortion. Bernard Antony, who acted as an intermediary between Jean-Marie Le Pen and the Catholic traditionalist as well as Catholic fundamentalist milieus, quit the party after overt criticism of the positions of the new leader. However, it must be noted that while Le Pen's secularist claims target Muslim migrants, they do not address Catholic fundamentalism. Analyses of the relationship between Catholicism and the party before the advent of the new leader indicate that this is traditionally contradictory. Jean-Marie Le Pen has paid homage to the Catholic Church and mobilised Catholicism as the source of French identity, through the use of religious symbols and references (Lecoeur 2003), but the NF has traditionally not appealed to practising Catholic voters (Mayer 2002). As a matter of fact, the Catholic Church has on various occasions criticised the party's positions on immigration (Costes 1988); and in recent debates on the law banning the display of religious signs in public schools, representatives of the Catholic Church have argued that religious signs, including crucifixes and Muslim headscarves, should be tolerated. Instead of appealing to those voters who hold a strong Catholic faith, with the exception of a minority of Catholic traditionalists and fundamentalists, the NF seems to attract voters who are in search of a religious or political identity which can guarantee some moral values and a certain idea of the world. Indeed Catholicism is widely mobilised as a symbol of national belonging by NF party members, including those who declare themselves atheists (Crépon 2006). Studies in social psychology indicate that the Catholic religion offers NF voters and members a symbolic framework sustaining a representation of the 'natural' social order with which they can identify (Orfali 2005). Nonetheless, it should be noted that recent studies suggest that the growing stigmatisation of the Muslim population is modifying the relationship observed in the past between Catholicism and the NF electoral support (Mayer 2013).

Despite these changes in the political communication and public image of the NF, there is consensus among scholars on the continuity of the party's core ideology. It is argued that the traditional 'nativism' (Mudde 2007) of the NF ideology is masked by the reference to republican values, but remains powerfully expressed by the traditional principle of the 'national preference' in access to the labour market and the welfare state (Ivaldi 2012). This principle exemplifies the connection, established in NF ideology, between 'anti-immigration' politics and the defence of the nation on the one hand, and, on the other, the defence of the traditional family. Indeed, this connection has characterised the party since its origins: the 'national preference', it is claimed, serves to preserve the integrity of the traditional family, while the latter provides the fundamental base of the 'natural' social order (Lesselier 1997b). Women and the family are represented as potential victims of immigration, which is associated with crime, insecurity and violence, and it is the women in the family who are assigned the responsibility of reproducing the 'natural' social order. This ideology relies on the naturalisation of the public/private divide and is heavily influenced by socio-biology, through the legacy of the PRR 'think tank' of the New Right. This analysis of the gendered dimension of the NF ideology echoes feminist studies pointing out that the right-wing discourse is a discourse of social order grounded in nature (Guillaumin 1988), based on the naturalisation of social relations, where sexism and racism—intended as ideologies which naturalise unequal social relations—are closely linked. Women are mobilised by nationalist projects as biological reproducers of the nation, in eugenist and pro-natality initiatives, and as social reproducers of the nation, via claims that women are the repositories of national culture and identity through their role as mothers (Yuval-Davis 1997). Analyses of Jean-Marie Le Pen's discourse (Lallemand 1997) have indicated that the metaphor of the family is used to legitimate the principle of 'national preference', as the national society is likened to a family and contractual links are likened to blood ties. The nation is compared to a domestic community threatened by invaders, on the basis of dualisms opposing Us (the inside, the private) to the Other looming large on the outside: this assimilation of the national society to a domestic community serves to naturalise xenophobia (Stolcke 2000). The party itself, claiming to represent and defend the family, tends to be constructed as a family (Orfali 1990), thus legitimating the internal hierarchies between the leader, constructed as a benevolent father, and the base, as well as between men and women. Sexual, medical and martial metaphors are also used to sustain this representation of society and to distinguish Us from the racialised Other, those who can be integrated into the nation from those who must be excluded from it. For instance, Jean-Marie Le Pen tended to associate immigration with disease and contagion, as well as with the enemy and the invader (Lallemand 1997). As today, under the leadership of Marine Le Pen, migrants are not only represented as a threat to the family and as a sexual threat to female citizens but also as a threat to gender equality, the connection between the essentialistic construction of gender and the family on the one hand and of cultural difference and the nation on the other is maintained at the heart of the NF ideology today. This backs up feminist analyses of the right-wing discourse and symbolic organisation, which argue that the defining characteristic of the right is its reliance on essentialist constructions of the Other to forge and reproduce hierarchical differences, variously based on gender, sexuality, culture, class or religion (Bacchetta and Power 2002). Thus, the inclusion of new ideological elements, such as the 'republicanisation' of the NF discourse and the mobilisation of the theme the of gender equality, does not seem to invalidate existing scholarly analyses which associate the NF ideology with the naturalisation of social relations of gender and ethnicity.

CONCLUSION

Is there a 'new' NF? Is the party becoming less radical and more democratic? Is it on the way to becoming a mainstream party with wide electoral support? The new leadership is undoubtedly accompanied by certain changes affecting the party's public image and ideology, as well as its constituency. Sociologists and political scientists, however, refer to the changes in the ideology, political communication and policy of the NF as a 'repackaging exercise' (Shields 2013, 193). They stress the rhetorical ability of past and present NF leaders, their linguistic strategies, such as the use of different discourses in addressing different audiences, and the importance of testing the party's discourse and its evolution on the basis of a systematic analysis of its practices and policy (Sédov 2011). These scholars emphasise the thread of continuity with the past and define the changes in terms of a tactical reformulation of the NF discourse and policy, which is associated with generational changes in terms of members' and leaders' recruitment. The advent of younger party representatives such as Marine Le Pen, replacing senior activists and politicians whose vision and ideas were defined by the history of the 1930s and 1940s (WW2 and Vichy France, French colonial history and the Algerian war) completes the shift of the NF. From modern racism, focusing on issues of blood and biology (Guillaumin 1972), it has moved to a discourse focusing on the issue of cultural differences, which has developed since the 1970s.

This chapter has addressed the gendered dimension of changes in the NF ideology and has exposed the tensions inherent in the appropriation of issues of secularism and gender equality—two traditionally left-wing ideological markers—by the French PRR, as the left appears to be divided on these issues. In addition to the erosion of the electoral 'gender gap' among supporters of the NF, the mobilisation of the theme of gender equality as an 'anti-immigration' argument and the shift to more moderate positions on issues of reproductive rights indicate that gender is an important dimension of the party ideology's current evolution. The chapter has also pointed to the dominant representations and recent public debates on multiculturalism, religion and secularism within which these ideological changes are located, addressing the issue of how the party has mobilised existing repertoires to construct its 'new' gendered claims.

If, following existing feminist analyses of nationalist and rightist political projects, we maintain that the naturalisation of social relations is key to the ideology of these movements, then we observe a remarkable continuity between the past and the present ideology of the NF: this is still based on a close linkage between defence of the family on the one hand, and the struggle against immigration on the other. Conversely, there is also an element of novelty in the essentialist representation of gender and cultural difference which continues to characterise the NF. In the past, the racialised Other in the party discourse was rarely female (Lesselier 1997a). The importance of the linkage between family and nation in the NF ideology required the hypervisibility of the racialised man, represented as a sexual and cultural threat to female citizens. Today, while the stigmatisation of racialised men is still central to NF the propaganda, racialised women have acquired a new visibility, being exposed—by a female leader—as symbols of feminine oppression in debates on the burqa, the Muslim headscarf, and sexual violence (Cette France là 2009). In Europe, the opposition of PRR parties to 'Islam', which these parties identify with Islamic fundamentalism, 'has brought [them] to the struggle for women's rights, sometimes even criticizing feminists for doing too little for immigrant women' (Mudde 2007, 96). The figure of the female Other thus seems to epitomise the paradoxes in Marine Le

Pen's propaganda. On the one hand, migrant women are represented as victims of patriarchal practices, which are condemned by the party. On the other, Marine Le Pen's discourse and policy proposals on women and the family echo findings on rightist organisations across the world, where female activists claim rights for the women of their own 'community' (variously defined on the basis of nationality, culture, religion, class...), while opposing the same rights for female Others (Bacchetta and Power 2002).

NOTES

1. On this ongoing academic debate see also the panel organised by Nonna Mayer and Alexandre Dézé titled Le 'nouveau' Front national en question (Questioning the 'new' French National Front), 12th Conference of the AFSP–Association Française de Science Politique (French Association of Political Science) Paris, July 2013.
2. There is a lack of consensus among scholars on the categories to be used to indicate these parties, variously defined by using the notions of 'far right', 'populism', 'radicalism', 'extremism', etc. For the purpose of this chapter, I follow Cas Mudde's (2007) indication to use the category of 'populist radical right' (PRR), based on nativism, populism and authoritarianism as the core elements of the ideology of these parties.
3. This chapter is based on the project 'Gendering activism in populist radical right parties. A comparative study of women's and men's participation in the Northern League (Italy) and the National Front, France', European Research Council, Starting grant, 2012–2014, http://www.gla.ac.uk/schools/socialpolitical/research/sociology/projects/genderingactivisminpopulistradicalrightparties/
4. On this issue see (Ho 2007) on the Australian context.
5. Such as the *Assises internationales sur l'islamisation de nos pays* (International forum on the islamisation of our nations) organised by the online magazine *Riposte Laïque* and the party *Bloc identitaire*.
6. On this issue in the USA, see (Blee 2012).
7. http://www.frontnational.com/?tag=burqa
8. http://www.frontnational.com/?p=5911

REFERENCES

Bacchetta, Paola, and Margaret Power (ed). 2002. *Right-Wing Women: From Conservatives to Extremists Around the World*. New York: Routledge.

Baubérot, Jean. 2012. *La laïcité falsifiée*. Paris: La Découverte.

Betz, Hans-Georg. 2004. *La droite populiste en Europe. Extrême et démocrate?* Paris: CEVIPOF/Autrement.

Blee, Kathleen. 2012. Bolstering Feminist Politics in a Time of Conservative Ascendancy. *Queries* 1(7): 112–119.

Cette France là. 2009. Le sexe de l'immigration. *Cette France là*. 06/05/2007–20/06/2008. http://www.cettefrancela.net/volume-1/descriptions/article/le-sexe-de-l-immigration?artpage=2-2

Chaïb, Sabah. 2008. Femmes immigrées et travail salarié. *Cahiers du Cedref* 16: 209–229.

Costes, André. 1988. L'Eglise catholique dans le débat sur l'immigration. *Revue européenne de migrations internationales* 4(1–2): 29–48.

Crépon, Sylvain. 2006. *La nouvelle extrême droite Enquête sur les jeunes militants du Front National*. Paris: Harmattan.

———. 2012. *Enquête au cœur du nouveau Front national*. Paris: Editions du Nouveau monde.

Dézé, Alexandre. 2012. *Le Front national: À la conquête du pouvoir?* Paris: Armand Colin.

Fassin, Éric. 2006. Questions Sexuelles, Questions Raciales. Parallèles, Tensions, Articulations. In *De la question sociale à la question raciale ? Représenter la société française*, ed. Didier Fassin, and Éric Fassin, 230–248. Paris: La Découverte.

Garcia, Marie-Carmen. 2012. Des féminismes aux prises avec l'"intersectionnalité: Le mouvement Ni Putes Ni Soumises et le Collectif féministe du Mouvement des Indigènes de la République. *Cahiers du genre* 52: 145–161.

Guillaumin, Colette. 1972. *L'idéologie raciste. Genèse et langage actuel*. Paris: La Haye, Mouton.

———. 1988. Sexism, a Right-Wing Constant of Any Discourse: A Theoretical Note. In *The Nature of the Right. A Feminist Analysis of Order Patterns*, ed. Gill Seidel, 21–26. Amsterdam: John Benjamins.

Guénif Souilamas, Nacira, and Éric Macé. 2006. *Les Féministes et le garçon arabe*. Paris: Editions de l'Aube.

Hamel, Christelle. 2005. De la racialisation du sexisme au sexisme identitaire. *Migrations Société* 17(99–100): 91–104.

Ho, Christina. 2007. Muslim Women's New Defenders: Women's Rights, Nationalism and Islamophobia in Contemporary Australia. *Women's Studies International Forum* 30: 290–298.

Ivaldi, Gilles. 2012. Permanences et évolutions de l'idéologie frontiste. In *Le Front national. Mutations de l'extreme droite française*, ed. Pierre Delwit, 95–112. Bruxelles: Editions de l'université de Bruxelles.

Lallemand, Michel. 1997. La métaphore sexuelle de Jean-Marie Le Pen. In *L'extrême droite et les femmes. Enjeux et actualité*, ed. Claudie Lesselier, and Fiammetta Venner, 71–103. Villeurbanne: Éditions Golias.

Larzillière, Capucine, and Lisbeth Sal. 2011. Comprendre l'instrumentalisation du féminisme à des fins racistes pour resister. *Contretemps*, September 15. http://www.contretemps.eu/interventions/comprendre-instrumentalisation-f%C3%A9minisme-fins-racistes-r%C3%A9sister

Lecoeur, Erwin. 2003. *Un néo-populisme à la française Trente ans de Front national*. Paris: La Découverte.

Lemière, Jacques. 2008. De la continuité entre deux prescriptions: De l'intégration à l'identité nationale. *Journal des anthropologues*, hors série. http://www.reseau-terra.eu/article702.html

Lesselier, Claudie. 1997a. De la Vierge Marie à Jeanne d'Arc. L'extrême droite frontiste et catholique et les femmes (1984–1990). In *L'extrême droite et les femmes. Enjeux et actualité*, ed. Claudie Lesselier, and Fiammetta Venner, 41–70. Villeurbanne: Éditions Golias.

———. 1997b. 'Préférence familiale' et 'préférence nationale': Le programme du Front national. In *L'extrême droite et les femmes. Enjeux et actualité*, ed. Claudie Lesselier, and Fiammetta Venner, 105–110. Villeurbanne: Éditions Golias.

———. 2010. Assises de la haine ? *Prochoix* 54: 31–41.

Mayer, Nonna. 2002. *Ces français qui votent FN*. Paris: Flammarion.

———. 2013. From Jean-Marie to Marine Le Pen: Electoral Change on the Far Right. *Parliamentary Affairs* 66: 160–178.

Meret, Susi, and Birte Siim. 2013. Gender, Populism and Politics of Belonging. In *Negotiating Diversity in an Emergent European Public Sphere*, ed. Birte Siim, and Monika Mokre, 78–96. Basingstoke: Palgrave.

Morokvasic, Mirjana. 2008. Femmes et genre dans l'étude des migrations: Un regard rétrospectif. *Cahiers du CEDREF* 16: 33–56.

Mudde, Cas. 2007. *Populist Radical Right Parties in Europe*. Cambridge: Cambridge University Press.

Orfali, Brigitte. 1990. Le FN ou le parti-famille. *Esprit* 164: 15–24.

———. 2005. *Sociologie de l'adhésion. Rêver, militer, changer le monde*. Paris: Zagros.

Scott, Joan Wallach. 2007. *The Politics of Veil*. Princeton: Princeton University Press.

Scrinzi, Francesca. 2014a. *Caring for the Nation. Men and Women Activists in Radical Right Populist Parties* 2012–2014. Final Research Report. European Research Council, Starting Grant. http://www.gla.ac.uk/media/media_383799_en.pdf

———. 2014b. Rapporti di genere e militanza nella Lega nord. In *Attraverso la Lega. La costruzione del consenso sul territorio e le trasformazioni della società italiana*, ed. Anna Curcio, and Lorenza Perini, 163–184. Bologna: Il Mulino.

Sédov, Yannick. 2011. Portes ouvertes. Entretien avec Annie Collovald. *Vacarme* 55. http://www.vacarme.org/article2011.html

Shields, James. 2013. Marine Le Pen and the 'New' FN: A Change of Style or of Substance? *Parliamentary Affairs* 66: 179–196.

Stolcke, Verena. 2000. Le nuove frontiere e le nuove retoriche culturali dell'esclusione in Europa. In *I confini della globalizzazione. Lavoro, culture, cittadinanza*, ed. Sandro Mezzadra, and Antonello Petrillo, 157–182. Roma: Manifestolibri.

Tevanian, Pierre. 2007. *La République du mépris Les métamorphoses du racisme dans la France des années Sarkozy*. Paris: La Découverte.

Tissot, Sylvie. 2008. Bilan d'un féminisme d'Etat. De Ni putes ni soumises aux lois anti-voile, February 1. http://lmsi.net/Bilan-d-un-feminisme-d-Etat

Yuval-Davis, Nira. 1997. *Gender and Nation*. London: Sage Publications.

Nationalism and Women in Greece During 1936–1941 and Today: Indicative Historical and Sociological Notes

Maria Chr. Alvanou

INTRODUCTION

Nationalism has once again become a subject of discussion among media and political analysts in Europe. The present article highlights two important expressions of nationalism in modern Greek history and the respective role of Greek women: the crucial and controversial political period 1936–1941 and today. It is a scholarly approach to an issue that needs more public attention, discussion and research.

The definition of nationalism is a difficult task as it has to do with the much debated and sensitive notion of nation.[1] The concept of nation, according to different standpoints, has to do with (or can have to do with) race (another very difficult concept to define, where there is not even agreement on its existence), origin, religion, culture, land, language, law (international and domestic), collective memory, personal and group identity, to name but a few of the elements that need to be considered. What constitutes a nation has not been a matter of consensus among academics, people or political parties in the course of history, especially in relation to the form of the nation-state. Nevertheless, for the purpose of this article, the following aspects and characteristics of the concept of nationalism are taken into account: it is a political ideology and phenomenon according

M.C. Alvanou (✉)
Thessaloniki, Greece

© The Author(s) 2017
M. Köttig et al. (eds.), *Gender and Far Right Politics in Europe*,
DOI 10.1007/978-3-319-43533-6_10

to which the fatherland constitutes the ultimate value that stands beyond time and collective identity and is built on a perception of the "other" which can lead to animosity against other nations (Panagiotides 2005, 232–234). But nationalism is more than theoretical aspects and definitions; it has political and real consequences in history and society that also have to do with gender. Gender is another concept that offers a fertile ground for debate. In sociological research, there are many arguments, especially concerning whether it is a real or "natural" notion or a "socially constructed label".[2] Yet, the fact is that, despite various explanations and theories, women differ from men in their involvement in political history. Men have been the apparent actors writing political history; with their decisions they have affected the way women find their place in political developments. Certain stereotypes have long affected women's lives and there are political ideologies that accept or even promote such stereotypes. Thus, questions arise about the relationship between nationalism and women: How do nationalist movements view female gender and its role in the state or in society? How and why are women motivated to support such movements? In this paper, answers to the above questions will be given with respect to Greek manifestations of nationalism, by exploring two chronological periods in Greek history with reference to women. The values and principles of two aspects of nationalism will shed light on how women were viewed in the past, and how they are viewed today.

NATIONALISM AND FEMALE GENDER ISSUES DURING THE "4TH OF AUGUST REGIME"

A monumental expression of Greek modern nationalism is the chronological period 1936–1941, widely known as the "4th of August Regime". It was formed on August 4th, 1936, by General Ioannis Metaxas, a prominent Greek military figure who entered politics and assumed power during troublesome national and parliamentary times (Linardatos 1988a, b). He established a regime that was authoritarian and remained in popular perception as a fascist one and a dictatorship.[3] Scholars argue about the complex political identity and ideology of the regime, linking it with several aspects of fascism.[4]

The regime promoted nationalistic ideals and a strong cultural connection to the historic heritage provided by the ancient Greek classical period (Sarantis 1993, 3). This is common for nationalism, because the past serves as a cultural reason for national pride and an alibi for a sense of superiority over other nations. A glorious past is supposed to feed the present, a very useful role, especially if the present is lacking in glory. The same connection to the past can be seen in the case of the Nazis who made historic connections to the Vikings and Nordic mythology, and in the case of the Fascists of Mussolini who made connections to ancient Rome (Hitchens and Brun 2013, 26).

Yet, there are important differences between the "4th of August Regime" and the regimes of Hitler and Mussolini. There was a lack of coherent and systematic ideology, as well as different and less sophisticated rhetoric (Sarantis, 11) propaganda, recruitment methods, engagement of art and absence of commissioned scholarly and scientific research.[5] Also, Metaxas did not achieve being adored as a cult, a "godlike" figure, in the way Hitler was (although he was presented as the nation's "saviour").

Ironically, Metaxas is remembered today, among other reasons, for his short and negative reply to Mussolini's request to allow the Italian army to cross Greece at the beginning of the Second World War. This may also explain why the "4th of August Regime" has been used as the historical cradle for Greek nationalism, connecting Metaxas' response to the glorious resistance of the Greeks and national-religious-patriotic ideals.[6]

The head of the regime promoted protection of the Orthodox Christian religion (though his relationship with religion and the Orthodox Church is not very clear) (Sarantis, 9) and family (ibid.; Ploumidis, 9),[7] both perceived as vital for the nation's unity and strength. Ioannis Metaxas saw ideals such as the King, Fatherland, Religion and the Regeneration of Greece as indisputable (Sarantis 8; Papathanassiou 2011, 106). These ideals were seen as uniting Greeks, serving as political, patriotic, religious-cultural, social and financial points of reference, and their enemies should be fought. Thus, a fierce anti-communist campaign took place. Those perceived as communists, leftists and opposing the regime were denied not only freedom of political expression, but also the opportunity to work and live like the rest of Greek citizens. They were sent into exile and suffered intolerable torture.[8]

In the quest for regeneration, the institution of the family was viewed as existential and fundamental (Sarantis, 9). The glorious "Greek race" was a central notion and Greeks the chosen people among the nations, destined to civilize all others (ibid., 3). Nationalistic pride was connected with a perceived superiority over the rest of the world. In such a vision, the role of women as mothers was pivotal (Papathanassiou 95). Through birth, women were helping the constant rebirth of the nation, both in real and cultural terms. After all the word "nation" comes from the Latin terms *nasci* and *natio*, both related to birth (Vincent 2010, 226). Through the task of giving birth, women were connected to the nation and were instruments of its existence and growth. Greek women married to Greek men would produce Greek children and make the nation bigger, greater and stronger. Furthermore, mothers safeguarded national and patriotic ideals by passing on all the traditional, patriotic and religious value, vital to the nation (Toktas 2002, 29).

The model of Spartan strong patriotic women, giving birth to good, brave, patriotic Spartan men was promoted.[9] During the regime, Greek women, like Spartan women, were made aware that their offspring belonged to the country and not to themselves. Spartan women have remained famous in history for saying, as their husbands or sons went off to war: *"ἤ ταν ἤ επί τας"*, meaning *"return either carrying the shield or on the shield"*. Spartan men should return from war either as brave fighters who did not abandon the fight (the shield) or dead (carried by their fellow soldiers on the shield). During the "4th of August Regime", the same principle of readiness to sacrifice one's children to the Fatherland applied to parents (Sarantis, 9), as children belonged to the country (ibid.). This is not something strange, as in nationalism, the family and its members are the functional property of the nation.

In the above context, sexual promiscuity for women was discouraged,[10] as it could endanger the foundations of the Greek family and was viewed as a communist trait leading to the destruction of social fibre. When the female body and its reproductive ability are the foundations of nation-building, then the freedom of sexuality and the quest for pleasure outside the bonds of family become dangerous. Patriotic values and nationhood dictate moral rules that are necessary for the survival of the nation. These restrict women, because female sexuality belongs first to the nation and is supposed to play a strategic role in the nation's future. A nation that wants to be powerful must control this power and direct it for its own benefit.

In terms of active involvement, girls and women had their own place in the organizations founded by the regime. There were female members in *"Εθνική Οργάνωση Νέων"* (*"EON"*, *"National Youth Organization"*) and girls in the equivalent organization for children. While the training of boys in the regime's organizations was inspired by military ideals (Ploumidis 4), the training of girls focused on more "feminine" topics. This was due to the above-mentioned role of the Greek woman as a mother in the family and in the nation, while Greek men were to serve the nation mainly with their military capabilities and spirit. Girls were trained in practical skills valuable in everyday life and in the household (Papathanassiou 102), but above all they were to become disciplined women with a high patriotic morale in the service of the nation. Depending on their age, the female members of the organizations were divided into *"σκαπάνισσες"* (*"ska-panisses"*) for little girls, *"φαλαγγίτισσες Β"* (*"falagitisses Β"*) for teenage girls and *"φαλαγγίτισσες Α"* (*"falagitisses Α"*) for young women, and they wore a dark blue military-type uniform (Ploumidis, 2). Though women were not perceived as actively contributing to the military defence of the country, they had a military-type uniform, and the terms *"skapanisses"* and *"falagitisses"* are also military.[11] The organizational character and discipline, as well as the fighting spirit and morale that exist in military formations, led to a "militarization" of the girls' and women's organizations.

Participating in the regime's organizations (under the supervision of the state) gave women the opportunity to be active outside the home (Ploumidis, 4). Yet, this "freedom" should not be seen as part of an emancipation policy or a feminist orientation on the part of the regime. Opportunities were given to women to socialize, and even to contribute to the public sphere, but only in ways that complied with the traditional role of Greek women and in no way contested gender barriers. The popular assumption that women are emancipated by nationalism (and sometimes even during national liberation struggles, when female fighters take an active role) is far from true. Such an impression may be given, but the reality is that women are only as active as the patriarchal authorities allow them to be within the scope of nationalism.

It is dangerous to draw conclusions about the participation of women in the regime's policies. Being a member of the organizations founded and promoted by the regime did not automatically mean embracing its principles and ideology. Some women may have been convinced nationalists, but we cannot presume this was the case for all of them. It was more of a social obligation, a necessity in order to be able to survive and function inside society and the state. People who were not communists—or did not want to be considered as such—had to be part of these organizations; it was expected of them. The regime issued *"πιστοποιητικά κοινωνικών φρονημάτων"* (*"certificates of social convictions"*), official documents essentially testifying that citizens were not communists (or communist sympathizers), dangerous to the law and order of the country. These certificates were necessary for vital transactions between citizens and the state, and essential for the social and economic survival of people living during those times. A female EON member was not automatically a woman engaged in nationalist politics, or embracing the principles of the regime. She could just be one of the Greek citizens trying to survive in a regime that directly or indirectly imposed participation in its organizations.[12] We cannot expect defiance or heroic resistance from every woman (or man for that matter).

Additionally, one should take into account another aspect: during that time, the disastrous negative results of nationalism in political power were not known to the extent that we know and acknowledge them today. Before the Second World War, few people in Greece could understand the hazards posed by nationalist ideologies. Greek women, many without proper or full education, did not know much about political theories. Their position in society was formed by the "ideology" of being good mothers and wives, living a peaceful life, looking after the household and staying out of trouble. Participating in the regime's organizations meant ensuring an untroubled everyday life with no exiles, no torture and no social exclusion. It meant being a good and law-abiding citizen, a respectable and honourable woman, fit to be a good wife and mother. What more could a woman of that period ask for?

NATIONALISM AND WOMEN IN PRESENT TIMES: THE "GOLDEN DAWN" MODEL

Many underline the economic conditions of the period when the "4th of August Regime" was established. There was the global financial crisis of 1929 and Greece was deeply in debt, facing serious economic hazards.[13] Moreover, there were feelings of national humiliation, as in 1922 Greece had suffered a catastrophic military defeat in Asia Minor that resulted in a refugee problem (Payne 1995, 317). The country was still struggling with the many social and economic effects of this loss (Xifaras 1995). The whole situation resembled what is happening today (Chouliarakis and Lazaretou 2014). A serious debt crisis has led to financial "memoranda", international loans and several types of severe austerity measures. In addition, there are other institutional and political weaknesses, including a general pathogenic situation due to unpunished political scandals, government problems and issues concerning the function of justice, general corruption, anachronistic education and unsatisfactory quality of life and citizens' rights (Alvanou 2008). The ground has become fertile for social unrest, violent extremism and even a new wave of terror (Alvanou 2009).

These are the settings in which the political party *«Χρυσή Αυγή»* (*"Golden Dawn"*) managed to score significant electoral gains during national and European elections.[14] "Golden Dawn" does not accept the political adjective "far right"[15] attributed to it by many, and the party presents itself on its website as "the only nationalist movement in Greece". It rejects the current political establishment and system, considering them corrupt and responsible for the failure and current situation of the country.[16] A lot has been discussed and written on the electoral achievements of this party; yet there is no concrete, absolute explanation, although the situation the country has been facing must be taken into account.

To map the party's ideology, one must go to the source.[17] "Golden Dawn" describes itself in its charter as a people's movement, struggling for a Greece that belongs to the Greeks, fighting in the front line against the "nation-killer Memorandum" and the "sinful status quo of the parties of the political establishment. Against the alteration of the population, with the millions of illegal immigrants and the dissolution of the Greek society…".[18]

The above principles, and the whole content of the online rhetoric presented in this article, make it evident that "Golden Dawn" promotes the nationalist ideal rooted in Greek history and is working for the "good of the nation" (as perceived by "Golden Dawn"). Its political rhetoric is characterized by "ethnocentrism" (Tzogopoulos 2013). Accordingly, one must see the role of women as preserving the Greek nation. For "Golden Dawn", one is born Greek and this is strictly a natural procedure, not just a legal status.[19] "Greekness" cannot come out of socialization, education, or any legal process that grants citizenship. It is the womb of the Greek mother where the creation of Greeks takes place. This turns women into precious agents of the Greek nation with reference to "racial ecology", as the Greek race must be preserved.[20] According to the party's rhetoric, the "true" and "genuine" Greeks are the "authentic continuation of the Ancient Greeks", as proved by history and science. The party is opposed to attempts by "internationalists", "liberals" and "Marxists" to give Greek citizenship to immigrants, to "make them Greek" and so "break the racial continuity" of the nation".[21]

The party is open to women[22] and there are female members in its parliamentary team.[23] The wife of the leader is a prominent parliamentary member and their daughter is an active member, too. The *"Μέτωπο*

Γυναικών" (*"Women's Front"*) is dedicated to female members, running a blog especially for women, where views on female gender and its role are evident. The blog is also titled "Women's Front"[24]: *Για του Λαό και την Πατρίδα"* (*"for the People and Fatherland"*),[25] and it provides links to websites of local "Golden Dawn" groups, as well as to the official web page of *"Golden Dawn".*[26] The banner shows the graphic image of a braided little girl aiming with a sling, and the motto: *"Πάντα έτοιμη"* (*"always ready"*). The image of the little girl and the whole blog content call for an active, non-passive female position in the movement. The blog includes the image of a cover of the magazine *"Νεολαία"* (*"Youth"*) that was published during the "4th of August Regime", showing Greek women and the Greek flag.[27] The admiration for the regime period is evident, and there are links to several covers of that magazine.

There are a vast number of activities for women. "Women's Front" organizes events such as self-defence classes[28] and handcraft workshops,[29] breast cancer awareness seminars,[30] ideological discussions and so on.[31] Furthermore, the blog offers news from the women's clubs, and it has an art section showing works of architecture, sculpture, painting and photography.[32] The different thematic sections include cooking and beauty.[33]

Publications on the "Women's Front" blog help us to understand how women are perceived, their position in the party and in a nationalist state.[34] A woman is believed to be more favoured by nature than man, because motherhood is the greatest honour.[35] Furthermore, women have a responsibility for bringing children up and how they turn out.[36] Feminism should not be aimed at equality with men, because this is against nature and natural laws.[37] In addition, *"the presumed liberation of woman disorientates her from the real essence of her highest role, Motherhood..."*[38] Feminism and the quest for equality between the two sexes are viewed as incompatible with the nationalist vision. The role of woman as a mother is linked with the survival of the Greek nation[39] and is promoted as a healthy model with higher values than the mainstream model.[40] The respect of women by men derives from the view that a woman is "the natural and only completion" of man, the one who takes care of him. The woman makes the man a father and *"continuer of the Race".*[41] Bright examples for Greek women are the ancient Spartan women, the heroines of the 1821 revolution against the Ottomans, the Greek teachers and mothers during the Macedonian Struggle, or the women of Epirus in the epic of Pindos.[42]

For "Golden Dawn", the maternal identity is truly celebrated as important for the nation. Hence, there seems to be little place for women who, whether by choice or due to biological circumstances, "fail" to fulfil their reproductive duty, taking into account the issue of a declining population (major and vital for the survival of the Greek race). This is why the party proposes protection of the unmarried mother, financial support for motherhood, support for women who give birth to many children, and the banning of abortions.[43] Among the political positions of "Golden Dawn" is also female military service (with the exception of mothers) at the age of 18 for the duration of 14 months.[44] Women should serve in urban areas and non-combat squads. This type of military duty is clearly a supportive one, and does not contradict "femininity" or obstruct maternal duties (which are a priority for the nation).[45] Woman is connected to defence of the country by motherhood and by participating in the army.

The historical model of the Spartan woman (see above) is repeated as a positive one to be imitated.[46] Yet, the Spartan model is only superficially liberal or "feminist" in comparison to the classical Athenian one. With the exception of the famous Aspasia (and other notable "*hetaerae*", who could enter the public sphere as the educated lovers and companions of men), the Athenian female population led a very secluded and restricted life. Spartan women were able to live a life outside the home, to participate in training and athletics. Yet, these activities were preparing them to become strong mothers, in order to give birth to strong, healthy Spartan fighters. Sparta was a military camp-like establishment and the role of women was defined in such terms. War and defending the fatherland was the essence of the existence of Spartans. The Spartan woman was the mother of the fighter, the mother of the soldier who was responsible for this great duty. Spartan women enjoyed no real freedom, but played the role of a breeder. They did not even enjoy raising their sons, as they had to turn them over to the responsibility and harsh upbringing programme of the Spartan community. Hence, the ideal of the Spartan woman is far from the liberties and the individual role a modern woman would wish.

Concluding Remarks

Nationalism has as its basis the notion of nationhood, constructed in ways that link women's contribution to nation-building with motherhood, reproduction and family as the initial cell of the nation. This is why the two expressions of nationalism presented in this paper focus on the role of Greek women as mothers. The construction of nation and national identity are mainly a male privilege. It is not accidental that the word "homeland" is translated in Greek as "fatherland" *("πατρίδα")*. Though the natural process of giving birth is a function of the female body, and though motherhood is central to the existence of the nation, it is nevertheless men who are regarded as the continuers of the nation. Women's social existence takes place in a very restricted space. They can be active in many ways, participate in organizations and events. They can and should be strong, but always because they were meant to become mothers. Motherhood is building material for the nation. Of course, this is a utilitarian approach to women's value in society, but hardly a Greek novelty; it has to do with the very character of nationalism and how it perceives the strength of the nation in relation to the function of gender.

This has been an initial attempt to shed light on a vast and complex topic, like Greek political history in general and the issue of Greek women participating in political developments. Nationalism is again knocking on Europe's door, and it is crucial to examine how much, why and in what ways it can attract female sympathizers, voters and members, taking into account the parameters and cultural environment of each country. In Greece, a deeper look at the Greek woman in society is necessary: What are her dreams and goals? What possibilities does she have to achieve them in contemporary Greece and Europe? How does she participate in the political reality of her country? What are the problems or insecurities she faces and what can be adequate solutions? Are gaps left by other political trends exploited by nationalism? There are many questions to be answered. It is time to start searching for answers as the phenomenon of nationalism in the country is developing. A first, small step, yet an important step, has been made.

NOTES

1. On the problems surrounding the definition of nation, see Smith (2010, 10) and the Nationalism Project, http://www.nationalismproject.org/what.htm, accessed March 17, 2016.
2. Regarding this issue, see Hubbard (1990) and Gergen (2001).
3. For popular perceptions on how the regime is considered a dictatorship and how it has served as an inspiration for the Colonels' dictatorship, see Michailides (2012).
4. For example, see *"the closest approach Greece ever made to fascism"*, Sarandis (1993, 2).

5. Himmler had created a whole group of scholars, taking advantage of their findings in order to legitimize Nazi plans and especially the Holocaust, Pringle (2006).

6. For example, see the glorifications of the regime's era on the official Golden Dawn webpage, http://www.xryshaygh.com/index.php/enimerosi/view/to-ethniko-kathestws-ths-4hs-augoustou-kai-o-iwannhs-metajas-binteo-fwtogra, accessed March 11, 2016.

7. Ibid. See also Ploumidis, 9.

8. Regarding torture, see Linardatos (1988).

9. Promoted also in school texts, Papathanassiou, 107–108.

10. The strict law on the sexual exploitation of women was enacted in 1936. On the values of female virtue, Papathanassiou, 97.

11. "*Skapanisses*" is the female version of "*skapaneas*" which is an army rank and "*falaggitisses*" refers to "*falagga*" which is an army formation.

12. By 1939 membership of EON had become practically compulsory, Sarantis 8.

13. On the debt of the country, the temporary moratorium of debts and the measures taken by Metaxas and his predecessors, see online project "The Economic History of the Greek Interwar Period by Prof. Thanos Veremis, accessed March 17, 2016, http://www.ime.gr/projects/interwar_economy/index.html

14. The party scored 6.99 % during the 2015 national elections, 6.92 % during the 2012 national elections (in June), 6.97 during the 2012 national elections (in May) and 9.39 % during the 2014 European Elections. Data from the Greek Ministry of Interior webpage, http://ekloges.ypes.gr

15. The party strongly denies any link with "fascism" (a pejorative term in the political vocabulary), or with "Nazism". From the official website of the party, http://www.xryshaygh.com/index.php/kinima/ideologia, accessed March 11, 2016.

16. For an analysis of the position of Golden Dawn on this, as well as the current political situation in Greece, see Vasilopoulou and Halikiopoulou (2015).

17. On the official party website the complete identity of the party and what a member should accept is described in detail, http://www.xryshaygh.com/index.php/kinima, accessed March 11, 2016.

18. Ibid.

19. In the blog of "Women's Front" there is a poster showing a photo of a beautiful ancient Greek statue of a Greek woman (classical period) and next to it the sketch of an ill-formed, pregnant woman with the caption: You are born Greek, you do not become one. No citizenship for *allogenus* (note: meaning foreigners in the nation), http://whitewomenfront.blogspot.gr/search/label/BANNERS, accessed March 11, 2016.

20. On racial purity and the dangers of racial mixing: http://whitewomenfront.blogspot.gr/2010/04/blog-post_06.html, accessed March 11, 2016.

21. Official website of the party, http://www.xryshaygh.com/index.php/kinima/ideologia, accessed March 11, 2016.

22. Ibid., one can see the call both to men and women, http://www.xryshaygh.com/index.php/kinima/ideologia

23. http://whitewomenfront.blogspot.gr/2013/02/blog-post_25.html, accessed March 11, 2016.

24. The blog has links to the pages of "Golden Dawn" as well as to the ideology and political position section of the official website of "Golden Dawn".

25. http://whitewomenfront.blogspot.gr/, accessed March 11, 2016.

26. http://www.xryshaygh.com/, accessed March 11, 2016.

27. http://whitewomenfront.blogspot.gr/, accessed March 11, 2016.

28. Only for Greek women, http://whitewomenfront.blogspot.gr/2012/10/blog-post_9.html. Accessed March 11, 2016.

29. http://whitewomenfront.blogspot.gr/2012/12/blog-post_7.html, accessed March 11, 2016.

30. http://whitewomenfront.blogspot.gr/2011/04/134.html, accessed March 11, 2016.

31. Golden Dawn International News, http://golden-dawn-international-newsroom.blogspot.gr/p/the-truth-about-golden-dawn.html, accessed March 11, 2016.

32. http://whitewomenfront-art.blogspot.gr/, accessed March 11, 2016.

33. http://whitewomenfront-cooking.blogspot.gr/, accessed March 11, 2016.

34. The archives of the blog and the online ideological library of the "Women's Front" are vast. Here just excerpts from indicative articles are presented. A research project solely on the online communication strategy and literature of the "Women's Front" would be

required to analyse all the texts. Access to the ideological online library/blog section is restricted only to invited members; public access and viewing is denied, https://www.blogger.com/blogin.g?blogspotURL=http://ideology-studies.blogspot.gr/, accessed March 11, 2016.

35. http://whitewomenfront.blogspot.gr/2008/09/blog-post_15.html, http://whitewomenfront.blogspot.gr/2007/05/blog-post_26.html, accessed March 11, 2016.

36. http://whitewomenfront.blogspot.gr/2008/09/blog-post_15.html, accessed March 11, 2016.

37. Ibid.

38. http://whitewomenfront.blogspot.gr/2007/05/blog-post_26.html, accessed March 11, 2016.

39. Ibid.

40. http://whitewomenfront.blogspot.gr/2012/04/blog-post_29.html, accessed March 11, 2016.

41. http://whitewomenfront.blogspot.gr/2010/02/blog-post_17.html, accessed March 11, 2016.

42. http://whitewomenfront.blogspot.gr/2007/05/blog-post_26.html, accessed March 11, 2016.

43. Official party website http://www.xryshaygh.com/index.php/kinima/thesis (accessed March 11, 2016). For the hot issue of entanglements between gender, sexuality and nationalism, female body, contraception and abortion, see Halkias (2004).

44. Ibid.

45. Unlike the Israeli Army, since Israeli women can carry guns and enter combat units.

46. http://whitewomenfront.blogspot.gr/2007/07/blog-post_11.html, accessed March 11, 2016.

REFERENCES

Alvanou, Maria. 2008. Riots in Greece: Law, Order and the Police. *Jurist*, December 15. Accessed 11 March 2016. http://jurist.org/forum/2008/12/riots-in-greece-law-order-and-police.php

———. 2009. Fighting Terrorism in Greece: Prevent Attacks but Respect Rights. *Jurist*, July 17. Accessed 11 March 2016. http://jurist.org/forum/2009/07/fighting-terrorism-in-greece-prevent.php

Chouliarakis, George, and Sophia Lazaretou. 2014. *Deja vu? The Greek Crisis Experience, the 2010s versus the 1930s. Lessons from History.* Working papers 176, Bank of Greece.

Gergen, Mary M. 2001. *Feminist Reconstructions in Psychology: Narrative, Gender, and Performance.* Thousand Oaks, CA: Sage Publications, Inc.

Golden Dawn International News. Accessed 11 March 2016. http://golden-dawn-international-newsroom.blogspot.gr/p/the-truth-about-golden-dawn.html [in Greek].

Golden Dawn Official Website. Accessed 11 March 2016. http://www.xryshaygh.com/ [in Greek].

——— 11 March 2016. http://www.xryshaygh.com/index.php/enimerosi/view/to-ethniko-kathestws-ths-4hs-augoustou-kai-o-iwannhs-metajas-binteo-fwtogra [in Greek].

——— 11 March 2016. http://www.xryshaygh.com/index.php/kinima [in Greek].

——— 11 March 2016. http://www.xryshaygh.com/index.php/kinima/ideologia [in Greek].

——— 11 March 2016. http://www.xryshaygh.com/index.php/kinima/thesis [in Greek].

Greek Ministry of Interior Webpage. Accessed 11 March 2016. http://ekloges.ypes.gr [in Greek].

Halkias, Alexandra. 2004. *The Empty Cradle of Democracy: Sex, Abortion, and Nationalism in Modern Greece.* Durham and London: Duke University Press.

Hubbard, Ruth. 1990. *The Politics of Women's Biology.* New Jersey: Rutgers University Press.

Ideology-Studies Blog. Attempted Access-Access Denied March 11 2016. http://ideology-studies.blogspot.com/; https://www.blogger.com/blogin.g?blogspotURL=http://ideology-studies.blogspot.gr/ [in Greek].

Linardatos, Spyros. 1988a. *The Regime of August 4th.* Athens: Themelio. [in Greek].

———. 1988b. *How We Reached to August 4th.* Athens: Themelio. [in Greek].

Meleagrou-Hitchens, Alexander, and Hans Brun. 2013. *A Neo-Nationalist Network: The English Defence League and Europe's Counter-Jihad Movement.* London: ICSR. Accessed 11 March 2016. http://icsr.info/wp-content/uploads/2013/03/ICSR-ECJM-Report_Online.pdf

Michailides, Giorgos. 2012. The Dictatorship of Metaxas: The Ideological "Forefather" of the Junta and Golden Dawn. *Iefimerida: Stories, August 4.* Accessed 17 March 2016. http://www.iefimerida.gr/news/62186/%CE%B7-%CE%B4%CE%B9%CE%BA%CF%84%CE%B1%CF%84%CE%BF%CF%81%CE%AF%CE%B1-%CF%84%CE%BF%CF%85-%CE%BC%CE%B5%CF%84%CE%B1%CE%BE%CE%AC-%CE%BF-%CE%B9%CE%B4%CE%B5%CE%BF%CE%BB%CE%BF%CE%B3%CE%B9%CE%BA%CF%8C%CF%82-%C2%AB%CF%80%C

F%81%CF%8C%CE%B3%CE%BF%CE%BD%CE%BF%CF%82%C2%BB-
%CF%84%CE%B7%CF%82-%CF%87%CE%BF%CF%8D%CE%BD%CF%84%CE
%B1%CF%82-%CE%BA%CE%B1%CE%B9-%CF%84%CE%B7%CF%82-
%CF%87%CF%81%CF%85%CF%83%CE%AE%CF%82-%CE%B1%CF%85%CE%
B3%CE%AE%CF%82?utm_campaign=shareaholic&utm_medium=google_
mail&utm_source=email%20%28sent%20via%20%29 [in Greek].

Panagiotides, Nathaniel M. 2005. *Rights and Minorities.* Alexandroupolis [in Greek].

Papathanassiou, Christos. 2011. The Reading School Texts of the 4th of August Regime, 1939–1941. Master thesis, University of Ioannina. Accessed 11 March 2016. http://edu.pep.uoi.gr/history/images/ergasies/papa8a.pdf [in Greek].

Payne, Stanley G. 1995. *A History of Fascism 1914–1945.* The University of Wisconsin Press.

Ploumidis, Spyridon. n.d. *The Fascist Youth EON of I. Metaxas.* Accessed 11 March 2016. http://www.arch.uoa.gr/fileadmin/arch.uoa.gr/uploads/drast_hist/fasismos_ekpaid/ploumidisspiros.pdf [in Greek].

Pringle, Heather. 2006. *The Master Plan: Himmler's Scholars and the Holocaust.* New York: Hyperion Books.

Sarandis, Constantine. 1993. The Ideology and Character of the Metaxas Regime. In *The Metaxas Dictatorship: Aspects of Greece 1936–1940,* ed. Robin Higham, and Thanos Veremis, 147–178. Athens: The Hellenic Foundation for Defense and Foreign Policy. Accessed 11 March 2016. http://www.arts.yorku.ca/hist/tgallant/documents/sarandismetaxas_001.pdf

Smith, Anthony D. 2010. *Nationalism.* Cambridge-Malten: Polity.

The Nationalism Project. Accessed 17 March 2016. http://www.nationalismproject.org/what.htm

Toktas, Sule. 2002. Nationalism, Militarism and Gender Politics: Women in the Military. *Minerva Quarterly Report on Women and the Military* 20(2): 29–44.

Tzogopoulos, George N. 2013. Grim Times Mean Bonanza for Greek's Far Right as Golden Dawn Shines. *Global Times,* March 23. Accessed 11 March 2016. http://www.globaltimes.cn/content/765400.shtml

Vasilopoulou, Sophia, and Daphne Halikiopoulou. 2015. Greek Politics: Economic Crisis or Crisis of Democracy? *World Affairs,* September. Accessed 17 March 2016. http://www.worldaffairsjournal.org/article/greek-politics-economic-crisis-or-crisis-democracy

Veremis, Thanos. 2009. The Economic History of the Greek Interwar Period Project, Foundation of the Hellenic World. Accessed 17 March 2016. http://www.ime.gr/projects/interwar_economy/index.html

Vincent, Andrew. 2010. *Modern Political Ideologies.* West Sussex: John Wiley & Sons Ltd.

Women's Front Blog. Accessed 11 March 2016. http://whitewomenfront-art. blogspot.gr/ [in Greek].

———— 11 March 2016. http://whitewomenfront-cooking.blogspot.gr/ [in Greek].

———— 11 March 2016. http://whitewomenfront.blogspot.gr/search/label/ BANNERS [in Greek].

———— 11 March 2016. http://whitewomenfront.blogspot.gr/2007/07/blog-post_11.html [in Greek].

———— 11 March 2016. http://whitewomenfront.blogspot.gr/2008/09/blog-post_15.html [in Greek].

———— 11 March 2016. http://whitewomenfront.blogspot.gr/2010/04/blog-post_06.html [in Greek].

———— 11 March 2016. http://whitewomenfront.blogspot.gr/2010/02/blog-post_17.html [in Greek].

———— 11 March 2016. http://whitewomenfront.blogspot.gr/2011/04/134. html [in Greek].

———— 11 March 2016. http://whitewomenfront.blogspot.gr/2012/12/blog-post_7.html [in Greek].

———— 11 March 2016. http://whitewomenfront.blogspot.gr/2012/10/blog-post_9.html [in Greek].

———— 11 March 2016, http://whitewomenfront.blogspot.gr/2012/04/blog-post_29.html [in Greek].

———— 11 March 2016. http://whitewomenfront.blogspot.gr/2013/02/blog-post_25.html [in Greek].

Xifaras, Dimitris Chr. 1995. The Greek Nationalistic Ideology in the Interwar Period. *Theseis* 53, October–December. Accessed 17 March 2016. http:// www.theseis.com/index.php?option=com_content&task=view&id=516&Ite mid=29 [in Greek].

PART II

Comparative Perspectives in Europe and the US

Women on the Fast Track: Gender Issues in the National Democratic Party of Germany and the French National Front (1980s–2012)

Valérie Dubslaff

INTRODUCTION

In the 1990s, the starting point seemed to be similar for the National Front (*Front National*, FN) in France and the National Democratic Party of Germany (*Nationaldemokratische Partei Deutschlands*, NPD), for they were both politically insignificant in their countries. While the FN was bogged down by a deep leadership crisis, which led to the split between its founder Jean-Marie Le Pen and Bruno Mégret in 1998 and weakened the far right for a long time, the German NPD had to face fierce rivalry with other far-right parties like the German People's Union (*Deutsche Volksunion*, DVU) or the Republicans (*Die Republikaner*, REP). The discrepancy between their evolution in the past two decades is striking, for the German party—with a few exceptions—has since then been caught in a steady downward trend while the French one has progressively risen and prevailed in politics. After the 2012 elections, the National Front became the third political force in France and thus is not only tolerated, but also courted. By contrast, the revelations of terrorist crimes by the extremist National Socialist Underground (*Nationalsozialistischer Untergrund*,

V. Dubslaff (✉)
Université de Caen Normandie, Caen, France

© The Author(s) 2017
M. Köttig et al. (eds.), *Gender and Far Right Politics in Europe*,
DOI 10.1007/978-3-319-43533-6_11

NSU) in Germany have led to public demands to ban the extremist NPD and accelerated its political disintegration. This asymmetrical evolution of the far right in France and in Germany may result from specific political cultures and dynamics, more or less favourable contexts and strategic innovations within the extreme right-wing parties. The aim of this article is to compare these developments and to examine the present situation of the French and German extremist parties through the prism of gender that gives a particular meaning to political transition.

THE FEMINISATION OF RIGHT-WING EXTREMISM

Gender and Structural Changes Inside the NPD and the FN

The NPD is commonly qualified as a masculine organisation for its sex ratio is unfavourable to women. In recent years, the party has had to face fluctuation in terms of membership, which has declined steadily, from 7200 members in 2008 to about 5900 in 2012, of whom less than one third are women. Beyond its radicalisation, the strategic turn of the NPD led to rejuvenation and proletarianisation of the party's basis: most NPD women were born between 1960 and 1990, and have a low average level of academic education. They mainly come from the middle and lower social classes and often are employed in the service sector (Priester 2009, 77–94). By contrast, the National Front, which has been enjoying an upward trend and can count on tens of thousands of supporters (officially 58,000 in 2012), has undergone a stronger feminisation in the last few years. While in the 1980s, more than 80 % of the party members were men (Ysmal 1996, 107–118), the women's proportion had increased to 45 % by 2012. Since Marine Le Pen took over the leadership of the FN in 2011, she has largely opened the party—especially to women—to recruit sympathisers from beyond the formerly targeted audience, working hard on the party's credibility and respectability (Perrineau 2014). Thus, the FN was more successful in attracting French voters than the NPD was in winning Germans, although its former leader, Holger Apfel, pursued a similar strategy by invoking a "respectable radicalism" (*seriöse Radikalität*), which has not been very convincing (Iost 2012, 60).

This observation of gender asymmetry can be made with regard to women's participation in the power structures of both extreme right-wing parties. Barely exceeding 11 % in 2012, women were clearly under-represented in the NPD's federal executive committee, which remained far behind the average gender ratio of other German parties: the conservative Christian Democratic Union (CDU) and the Social Democratic Party of Germany (SPD) had 34 % and 41 % women, respectively, in their executive committees.[1] Conversely, with 35 % women in its executive committee, the National Front approached the conservative French Union for a Popular Movement (UMP, 38 %) and the Socialist Party (PS, 42 %).[2] Even if women were still under-represented in the FN, the party provided some women with access to political key positions and therefore granted them a certain empowerment: in 2012, the party leader (Marine Le Pen), one deputy party leader (Marie-Christine Arnautu) and the leader of the FN's youth organisation (Nathalie Pigeot) were women. Although the proportion of women has slightly increased in the past few years in the German NPD, they still remain a marginalised minority that is not involved in political decision-making.

The NPD's persistence at the political periphery in Germany is due to the fact that on the federal level the party has never attained the 5 % of votes necessary to enter Parliament, scoring only 1.5 % at the federal elections in 2009, while the French National Front has achieved remarkable results in several elections since 1986. In 2012, Marine Le Pen scored the best results ever obtained by an extreme right-wing party in France by gathering 17.9 % of the votes in the first round of the presidential election. It even achieved the first position in the European elections in 2014 with the votes of 25.4 % of the electorate. Through its electoral potential, the FN has risen to be the third political force in the country and presents itself as a serious challenger of the socialist government. Its growing participation in the democratic and public debate in France facilitates and trivialises the commitment of men and women on the far right, while the NPD continues to be isolated organisationally and ideologically from federal politics in Germany, its sympathisers being exposed to the risk of social and professional exclusion. The fundamental difference between the German NPD and the French FN is that the latter has undergone a normalisation process the German party is far from achieving, because of its obvious ideological continuity of historical National Socialism, which is not politically acceptable in Germany. The FN became a part of the French political mainstream which accepts the formal rules of liberal democracy (Camus 2011, 153–156), whereas the NPD has been facing proceedings since 2013 which could lead to its banning because of its anti-constitutional nature.

The new self-confidence of the National Front, which is due to a special political culture in France, has also had an impact on French voting habits. In 2012, women gave their vote to the FN more easily than in the past, considerably reducing the gender gap: in 2007, 12 % of men and only 9 % of women voted for Jean-Marie Le Pen (Mayer 2007), whereas in 2012 as many women as men voted for his daughter (almost 18 %).[3] mainly encouraged by the fact that Marine Le Pen, who explicitly appealed to the female electorate during her campaign, is herself a woman they could identify with. In Germany, on the contrary, where barely 30 % of all NPD voters are women, the gender gap remains unchanged on the federal level.

The German party's male dominance is also reflected in the low number of female representatives in the regional parliaments of this federal state, given that since 2004 only one NPD woman, Gitta Schüssler, has been able to gain a parliamentary seat in Saxony. By contrast, the French legislative election in 2012 was marked by a return of the National Front to Parliament after more than two decades. By gaining a seat in the National Assembly for Marion Maréchal-Le Pen and Gilbert Collard, the far-right party was able to enhance its integration in French political institutions. Maréchal-Le Pen was born in 1989 and is currently the youngest Member of Parliament in France. She is—this is no accident—a niece of Marine Le Pen and a grandchild of the FN founder Jean-Marie Le Pen. Her political breakthrough is not surprising, as it is originally due to Le Pen and his clan's nepotism rather than to the encouragement of a political offspring.

Since 2011, the FN has experienced an upward trend as far as gender is concerned: the more the party feminises its political profile, the more it recruits women who agree to officially carry the FN torch, to run for elections and to take political responsibilities. So, by seemingly granting women more autonomy and political participation, the French extremist party seems to succeed in overcoming women's reticence, which still persists in Germany.

Women Organise Themselves: The French CNFE and the German RNF

The FN has a certain advance in matters of female organisation since the National Circle of European Women (*Cercle National des Femmes d'Europe*, CNFE) was founded by Martine Lehideux in 1985 as a think-tank intending "*to enlighten women on social, educational, cultural and political problems and family issues they are daily confronted with and to remind them that Europe only may flourish through their support*" (Laroche 1997, 153). This organisation, advocating the need to lead "*women and families back to their right position, the position of honour*", was, in fact, an anti-feminist reaction to the women's movement, born in the aftermath of May 1968. Designed as a mixed-gender association with a 70 % majority of women, the CNFE remained structurally insignificant (albeit ideologically important). In 1987, the number of members exceeded 3000 women and men but it decreased steadily afterwards. Although the CNFE was never officially disbanded, its activity came to a halt and the organisation disappeared even before Lehideux left the FN to join Carl Lang's extremist Party of France in 2009.

The founding of a female organisation within the NPD in Germany in 2006 was triggered by the awareness that the nationalist camp lagged far behind the major German democratic parties. Since its appearance, the Circle of Nationalist Women (*Ring Nationaler Frauen*, RNF) has remained a small structure that never really exceeded 100 members. Its viability has largely depended on its leaders' activism: having gone through several crises in the past few years under the leadership of Gitta Schüssler (2006–2009), Edda Schmidt (2009–2012) and Sigrid Schüssler (2012–2014), the RNF seems to have found a new, maybe more consensual leader with Ricarda Riefling who is endeavouring to invigorate its structures. Thus, this organisation plays a rather minor role within the NPD, which is more interested in encouraging youth and popularising the Young National Democrats (*Junge Nationaldemokraten*, JN), a suborganisation which functions as an important motor of political mobilisation for the party.

Even if the French CNFE and the German RNF emerged at different times, their constitution, function and mission are similar. Despite the fact that their political influence remains rather weak, their symbolic value both for the parties and for extremist women is considerable, for they are proof that women are increasingly accepted and evidence of their—at least symbolic—empowerment within the far right. These organisations aim at the political professionalisation of women and encourage them to assume political responsibilities. By doing so, they represent women's political interests and aim to enhance their solidarity in a far-right context.

Extremist women's organisations focus on media coverage and public attention to disseminate their political message, so they devote an important part of their time to supporting the political events of their parties and those of the whole far-right movement. In the late 1990s, the CNFE always participated in the FN's Joan of Arc celebration on the 1st of May, pushing empty prams to demonstrate against depopulation in France. Similarly, the RNF supports almost all major public appearances of the NPD, like the annual "funeral march" (*Trauermarsch*) in February to denounce what they cynically call the Allies' "Bomb Holocaust" of Dresden. The French extremists have launched some striking actions in order to achieve a greater public impact: as part of the campaign against abortion in the early 1990s, women and men of the CNFE supported Catholic attacks on hospitals and women's clinics offering legal abortions (Renaud 1995). In Germany, by contrast, the RNF undertakes rather unspectacular activities like cultural excursions, cleaning missions in forests and wreath-laying ceremonies in cemeteries. By means of such female organisations, the far-right parties are able to recruit and politicise women and to use them as a vehicle for propaganda.

EXTREMIST GENDER POLICIES IN FRANCE AND IN GERMANY: NATION, FAMILY AND WOMEN'S RIGHTS

In its 2001 programme, the National Front explains its conception of an abstract and homogeneous "French Nation", legitimised by the tradition of historical counter-revolution and a thousand-year-old Christian civilisation shaped by its "heroic and divine history". This religious view is put into perspective 10 years later in the 2012 programme, when the FN relies on the secular tradition of the French Republic and on 1905, the symbolic date which saw the separation of Church and State in France. The ideological edifice of the NPD, and *a fortiori* of the RNF, derives from a similar ethnocentric conception of an unchanging transcendent national order, from the *Volksgemeinschaft* which is supposed to be welded together by its descent, language, culture, history and consciousness, and which has developed organically over the centuries (NPD 1996). These national myths function as projection surfaces for gender stereotypes.

Both the CNFE and the RNF propagate essentialist gender stereotypes, pretending that "nature" has provided men and women with special genetic characteristics, faculties and duties, but they use different, if not contrary, explanations to legitimise their gender ideology. According to the CNFE in the 1990s, the Holy Bible stipulates a polarised and hierarchical gender order, embodied by Adam and Eve. The RNF, on the other hand, bases its values on pagan Nordic and Germanic myths derived from the

Edda sagas and tales, which describe how man and woman were formed simultaneously by three gods and are consequently of equal importance (*gleichwertig*), but different in kind (*ungleichartig*) (RNF 2009).

Nevertheless, both gender conceptions are alike in their political interpretation. They aim at preserving traditional gender roles and at protecting them against "modernity" and cultural globalisation. That is why feminism—considered by the NPD and the FN as the key to moral decay in western societies—is an important point of attack. Jean-Marie Le Pen used indirect ways to disqualify the historical importance of feminism by proposing an alternative religious and nationalist definition of it: according to him the Virgin Mary and Joan of Arc, who in extremist narratives symbolise purity, faith and the struggle for national liberation, are the only true representatives of women's emancipation.

Moreover, family, considered as the "main pillar of society" by the French FN and "as germ cell of the nation" by the German NPD has always been firmly defended by their female organisations, which seek to support a patriarchal and heterosexual family order against the creeping destruction of traditional values. Lifelong marriage serves as a protective frame for moral norms and for racial continuity: "*lifelong marriage sublimates purely biological gender relations by extending them to emotional and spiritual areas*", wrote the NPD in 2007 (NPD 2007). The NPD rejects alternative family arrangements (such as patchwork families and same-sex parents). The FN is more ambiguous here: Marine Le Pen herself is divorced and often talks about her past experience as a single mother. The party fought against the "civil solidarity pact" (PACS), which was established in France in 1999 as an alternative to marriage. In 2012, the National Front accepted the PACS as a legal framework, even for homosexual partnership, but called on the French to resist "marriage for everyone", which has been debated in the National Assembly in France in 2012/2013, in order to preserve biological filiation and to fight "other perversions" (polygamy, incest, zoophilia). Many FN activists, but not Marine Le Pen, participated in the large-scale reactionary "Demonstration for everyone", organised in several French cities in 2013 to protest against equal rights for homosexuals. In the past, the CNFE used to consider homosexuality as blasphemy and Jean-Marie Le Pen himself is known for his homophobic diatribes against HIV-positive people in the 1980s. His daughter distances herself from the homophobic party line: she describes homosexuality as a private matter that should remain untroubled by politics. By doing so, she implicitly defends the inequality between heterosexuals and homosexuals. The

NPD remains intransigent towards sexual minorities which are accused of not defending the "State's interest" and consequently should not be "tolerated" inside the *Volksgemeinschaft* (RNF 2009).

The second line of attack for both the NPD and the FN is the propagation of motherhood. The RNF mostly agitates against childless women, feminists, lesbians or academics, who are pilloried for *"refusing to have children"* (RNF 2010). In the 1990s, the CNFE and the FN called on politicians to intensify moral pressure on women and consequently fought for the repeal of the legislation on abortion ("Loi Veil", 1975). The FN progressively passed over to a more flexible pro-life orientation, anchoring the principle of "sacred nature of life" in its 2001 programme. During the 2012 campaign, Marine Le Pen repeated in the media that she is personally in favour of the existing rights, but at the same time argued in favour of free choice for women not to abort. She argued that the costs of abortion should no longer be covered by the normal health insurance, and demanded a referendum to decide on this matter (FN 2012).

In Germany, the RNF joins the sexist line of its party and combines racist or anti-Semitic positions with pro-natalist demands. It adopts long-standing NPD positions by considering abortion and contraception as murder. In 2007, Gitta Schüssler, Member of the Saxon Parliament and former RNF leader, called it an attempted *"Holocaust of German Children"* (NPD 2007, 39). This analogy trivialises the historical genocide perpetrated by National Socialism during the Third *Reich* by victimising aborted foetuses and glorifying born children as "survivors". One principal demand is the reintroduction of penal action and thus a reform of § 218 of the German penal code, which up to the mid-1970s prohibited abortion.

At the time of its foundation in the early 1970s, the National Front asked for a "mothers' salary" (*revenu maternel*) to compensate for the education and upbringing of French children. Today, the party extends this to both mother and father ("parents' salary"), who may choose who is going to raise the children. The NPD has proposed a "mothers' salary" since 1996, considering that a mother is still irreplaceable for her child. Claiming to provide German women with the possibility of choosing their way of life, this alternative salary is meant to "liberate" them from the "obligation" to work: *"women are not expected to work outside their home for financial reasons"* says the 2010 programme (NPD 2010). In fact, it aims at repatriating them to the domestic sphere and at creating jobs for German men on the labour market. Besides, like the French CNFE did in the 1980s, the RNF currently fights against external childcare, which is compared to genital mutilation (RNF 2008). By contrast, Marine Le Pen is in favour of expanding childcare and developing nurseries in order to allow women to conciliate work and private life.

This seemingly gender-equitable family model conforms in reality to the FN's principle of "national preference" or "national priority", which combines racism and a fierce criticism of globalisation and immigration. The 2001 FN programme intended to reveal a conspiracy fomented on purpose by governments in power: "*the policies pursued against families for three decades have an unacknowledged but deliberate goal: the will to eliminate France by limiting births of French children and by calling for an increasing number of immigrants on our soil*" (FN 2001). His whole life, Jean-Marie Le Pen, who is a veteran of the Algerian war, has fought against immigrants from former French colonies (such as Algeria and Morocco), whom he criminalises and blames for French grievances. And since 1972, by basing his political doctrine on the ideological tandem of "immigration and insecurity", he has tried to reverse the trend by pursuing a pro-birth policy and the deportation of foreigners, thus giving a sexist dimension to a racist programme.

Since 2011, Marine Le Pen has tied in with her father's anti-multicultural offensive but intensified the anti-Islam crusade. She exploited the "Arab spring" to represent herself as the herald of Islamophobia, conjuring up the vision of millions of North Africans invading France to impose their values. Her words were underlined by symbolic acts: in 2011 she went to Lampedusa, an Italian island in the Mediterranean, to "support" the local population in its fight against clandestine immigration. Muslims, considered as reactionary forces, are set up against the French who embody the ideals of progress, laicism and liberty in extremist narratives. Families, women and minorities need to be protected by law. To her, the French suburbs represent the greatest menace of Muslim domination: "*More and more I hear testimonies about the fact that in some parts of town it is not good to be a woman or a homosexual, a Jew, let alone a French or a White*".[4] By the victimisation of minorities, the National Front has never defended before, Marine Le Pen constructs the image of a sexist, homophobic, anti-Semitic and anti-French Muslim enemy, who only she and her party can contain.

For the German RNF, Islamophobia is the most important aspect of its racism. In its "social nationalism", the NPD combines racist ideas with anti-capitalist ones, arguing that "*high finance, government and labour unions have smuggled millions of foreigners into Germany against the will of the German People*" (NPD 2010, 12). Integration policies are qualified as "genocide", and "multicultural madness" is considered as a threat to civil peace. The struggle against globalisation was also a major axis of Marine Le Pen's electoral campaign in 2012: she opposed her own political camp, the "nationals", to the "globalisers" embodied by the conservative UMP and the socialist PS (ironically named "UMPS" by the FN), which were accused of being corrupted by immigrants who abuse the welfare system and by the European Union, capitalist companies and banks that seek to dispossess the French. Thus, the FN in France and the NPD in Germany pretend to defend the social interests of ordinary people and protect them against poverty and precariousness.

Consequently, one can say that the NPD has intransigent positions in gender matters and seems nowadays to be more reactionary than the FN. Indeed, the French party has progressively distanced itself from the ultra-Catholic camp and overcome the rigid gender conceptions formerly disseminated by Lehideux's CNFE. The present-day National Front blurs its gender policies in order to court conservative as well as more liberal milieus.

GENDER RELEVANCE TO THE POLITICAL STYLE: THE EXAMPLE OF THE FN

Since its creation in 1972, the National Front has always been considered as a "Le Pen party". By prevailing over Bruno Gollnisch, a long-time extremist activist, during the internal party election in January 2011, Marine Le Pen took her father's place and proposed a new political battle plan in order to conquer France. But what was presented as a break was in fact ambiguous. For the first time in France, a woman became a leader of a far-right party, but she owed her election to her father who designated her as his successor in 2002 rather than to her gender. However, the break was real in 2015: at the end of an unprecedented crisis due to Le Pen's anti-Semitic remarks, she politically and personally broke with her father who was excluded from the party he had founded.

Moreover, Marine Le Pen seems to embody a new kind of extremism that ideologically breaks away from her father's. Jean-Marie Le Pen is known as a political hardliner: he is a traditionalist who has always defended the French Empire and taken up virulent anti-Semitic positions, as in 1987 when he openly negated the existence of Nazi gas chambers.[5] On the contrary, Marine Le Pen, who intends to convert the FN into a populist and republican parliamentary party, officially rejects violence and radicalism as political means and has performed a shift of the party's image towards trivialisation: in the name of respectability and moderation, she has excluded troublemakers like avowed neo-Nazis and negationists: "*I refuse to accept the return of radical, caricatural and anachronistic groups inside the National Front. The crossover between Catholic fundamentalists, Petainists and Holocaust-possessed persons is not coherent. The National Front must not serve as a resonance chamber for their delusions*".[6] Unlike her father, who always had a certain sympathy for collaborationists, she qualifies the Holocaust as the greatest barbarism in history. By putting anti-Muslim racism in the place of anti-Semitism, Marine Le Pen has officially broken away from old ideological demons of the French far right, which nonetheless remain well rooted within the party. She is seeking to tie in with widespread anti-Muslim resentment and to conquer the Jewish electorate. This ideological trivialisation is combined with the domestication of the political style of the Le Pens. Jean-Marie Le Pen is well known for his sulphurous character and his openly demonstrated maleness, which is part of his personality cult. He has often attracted attention by his verbal abuses, trials for incitement to racial hatred, and physical attacks: in 1997 he even slapped the face of a female socialist Member of Parliament. Certainly, Marine Le Pen accentuates her moderate and non-violent femininity. But on the other hand, she constantly transgresses the "natural" borders of her gender. She uses sexual imagery to defame her political opponents and deny them any kind of masculinity. For her, the former French president, Sarkozy, embodied "hectic impotence" (*impuissance agitée*) and the new president, Hollande, "flabby impotence" (*impuissance molle*).[7] Indirectly, she represents herself as a potent masculine leader, who is able to precipitate a political change in the country. Her deep rough voice, as well as her stature and threatening behaviour, are accessories she can capitalise on politically. Because of this gendered ambiguity, she is celebrated as a homo-icon in certain circles.

It appears that the apparent political rupture is in reality contrived, for trivialisation is synonymous with ambiguity: until 2015, the double leadership of Jean-Marie Le Pen (honorary chairman) and his daughter (president) facilitated a balancing act within the party. The former clientele (ultra-Catholics, traditionalists, neo-Nazis and anti-Semites) remained loyal to him, while Marine Le Pen attracted new voters and sympathisers. This guaranteed greater possibilities of political and personal identification (Crépon 2012).

Without any doubt, Marine Le Pen's greatest achievement in the past few years has been her ability to attract and keep new clienteles. Even if the idea of a real political modernisation of the party remains questionable, its so-called de-demonisation is undeniable. Membership of the party and voting for it is no longer taboo, even for social groups one would not expect. On the one hand, Marine Le Pen attracts men by embodying an intransigent political leader who, like her father, dares to address tough "masculine" topics like immigration, insecurity and economics. But, on the other hand, the most important new clientele of the National Front is women. They more easily identify with Marine Le Pen, who refers to her female experience as a central political theme (Fourest and Venner 2011). Using the leitmotif of victimisation, she has repeatedly underlined the political discrimination she had to face because she is a "Le Pen" and often stresses her past struggle to be accepted as a serious female politician in a masculinist political environment. Her demands are often unambiguously feminist: when demanding the reintroduction of the French franc, she argues that the new banknotes should feature the portraits of Joan of Arc and of the illustrious feminist Olympe de Gouges, who wrote the "Declaration of the Rights of Woman and the Female Citizen" in 1791 during the French Revolution.

She also addresses left-wing sympathisers as well as ethnic, religious or sexual minorities whom she purposely integrates in a vague definition of nationalism, explaining that *"no matter if you are a man or a woman, heterosexual or homosexual, Christian, Jewish or Muslim, you are French first!"*.[8] But the "emancipation" she proposes is in fact ambivalent: even if her positions seem to be progressive, she has never really intended to leave behind the basic ideology of her party. She takes off the edge and thus makes it easier to accept. The normalisation process of Marine Le Pen's National Front is best shown by the fact that during the 2012 electoral campaign, the French conservatives recognised the constitutional conformity of the extremist party, explaining that the FN was "compatible with the values of the French Republic". Though the FN has adapted itself to the mainstream in some respects, it has also provoked a shift to the right of large parts of French society.

CONCLUSION

The evolution of the far right in the past 20 years shows the impact of gender on general political processes and *a fortiori* on sociological, strategic and ideological shifts within the right-wing formations. The disclosure of complex gender arrangements within the National Front and the National Democratic Party of Germany makes it possible to evaluate and give a concrete meaning to women's increased involvement in those parties. Like in other European extremist parties, the FN and the NPD have both registered a stronger influx of women in recent years, even if female integration—numerically and symbolically—has progressed far more in the French party, where women are more directly involved in the power structures and in the political praxis. Even though "feminisation" does not mean "emancipation", it signifies a greater autonomy and thus a greater female self-confidence within the far right. It also implies a valorisation of gender policies within the parties' ideology: while they remained reactionary in the case of the French CNFE in the 1990s and the German RNF, Marine Le Pen's FN appears to be more versatile because she makes concessions, especially in gender politics. But her pseudo-progressive statements in defence of the achievements of historical feminism are in fact ambivalent, for they are used xenophobically against so-called outsiders (Muslims, immigrants…) and so reveal the extremist ideological core of the FN party line. Nevertheless, she managed to succeed in something her father would never have dreamt of: she overcame the party's bad image and trivialised it. While the National Front is nowadays treated as a "normal" democratic party, the NPD is doomed to a shadowy existence in public and in politics because of its political rigidity and its National-Socialist demons. Even the RNF women have not succeeded in using their feminine "nature" to cover up and change the violent and terrorist image of far-right extremism in Germany.

NOTES

1. Bundeswahlleiter. "Parteien". Accessed July 15, 2012. http://www.bundeswahlleiter.de/de/parteien
2. Front National. "Bureau politique". Accessed September 22, 2012. http://www.frontnational.com/fonctions/bureau-politique; Parti Socialiste. "L'équipe". Accessed September 22, 2012. http://www.parti-socialiste.fr/l-equipe; Union pour un Mouvement Populaire. "Equipe dirigeante". Accessed June 12, 2012. http://www.u-m-p.org/notre-equipe/ump/equipe-dirigeante

3. Consumer Science and Analytics. "Le vote des femmes au 1er tour de l'élection présidentielle". Accessed September 12, 2012. http://csa.eu/elections2012/Type/10/Sondage/Etude/1971/Le-vote-des-femmes-au-1er-tour-de-l-election-presidentielle.aspx

4. Speech delivered by Marine Le Pen in Lyon on December 10, 2010.

5. Interview with Jean-Marie Le Pen by Grand Jury RTL-Le Monde, on September 13, 1987.

6. Agence France Presse. "Press release by Marine Le Pen". Accessed October 5, 2011. http://www.afp.fr

7. Interview with Marine Le Pen by La Chaîne Info on September 11, 2012. Accessed September 11, 2012. http://www.lci.fr

8. Speech delivered by Marine Le Pen in Paris on May 1, 2011.

REFERENCES

Camus, Jean-Yves. 2011. Le processus de normalisation des droites radicales en. *Europe Cités* 45(1): 153–156.

Crépon, Sylvain. 2012. *Enquête au cœur du nouveau Front National*. Paris: Nouveau Monde.

Fourest, Caroline, and Fiametta Venner. 2011. *Marine Le Pen*. Paris: Grasset.

Front National. 2001. *Pour un Avenir Français*. Saint-Cloud: Godefroy de Bouillon.

Front National. 2012. *La Voix du Peuple, l'Esprit de la France*. Accessed 12 August 2012. http://www.frontnational.com/le-projet-de-marine-le-pen

Iost, Delphine. 2012. L'extrême droite allemande: Une stratégie de communication moderne. *Hérodote* 144(1): 60–76.

Laroche, Françoise. 1997. Maréchale nous voilà! Le Cercle National des Femmes d'Europe. In *L'extrême droite et les femmes*, ed. C. Lesselier, and F. Venner, 153–164. Villeurbanne: Golias.

Mayer, Nonna. 2007. Les votes Le Pen du 21 avril 2002 au 22 avril 2007. Accessed 12 August 2012. http://www.cevipof.com/PEF/2007/V1/rapports/VotesLePen_NM.pdf

Nationaldemokatische Partei Deutschlands. 1996. Grundsatzprogramm der NPD. Accessed 16 March 2009. http://www.npd.net/html/240/artikel/detail/209

Nationaldemokratische Partei Deutschlands. 2002. Aktionsprogramm für ein besseres Deutschland. Accessed 16 March 2009. http://www.npd.net/html/240/artikel/detail/209

Nationaldemokratische Partei Deutschlands. 2010. Arbeit. Familie. Vaterland. Accessed 27 December 2010. http://www.npd.de/html/240

Nationaldemokratische Partei Deutschlands. 2007. Die demographische Katastrophe stoppen! Der bevölkerungspolitische Notstand des deutschen Volks und die familienpolitischen Initiativen der NPD-Fraktion im sächsischen Landtag. Accessed 7 March 2009. http://npd-fraktion-sachsen.de/pdf/veroeffentlichungen/broschuere_demographie_komprimiert.pdf

Perrineau, Pascal. 2014. *La France au front*. Paris: Fayard.

Priester, Karin. 2009. Female involvement in extreme rightism Women running for offices in extreme right-wing parties and electoral movements in Germany between 1998 and 2008. *Leviathan* 37(1): 77–94.

Renaud, Dely. 1995. Les liaisons du FN avec les anti-IVG. *Libération*, July 20. Accessed 13 July 2012. http://www.liberation.fr/france-archive/1995/07/20/les-liaisons-du-fn-avec-les-anti-ivg-depuis-les-annees-80-l-extreme-droite-intensifie-sa-campagne-an_140175

Ring Nationaler Frauen. 2008. Wieviel Krippe will der Staat? Accessed 17 January 2011. http://www.ring-nationaler-frauen.de

Ring Nationaler Frauen. 2009. Internationaler Tag gegen Gewalt an Frauen. Accessed 17 January 2011. http://www.ring-nationaler-frauen.de

Ring Nationaler Frauen. 2009. Homosexuelle bleiben für uns eine nicht staatstragende Minderheit. Accessed 17 January 2011. http://www.ring-nationaler-frauen.de

Ring Nationaler Frauen. 2010. Gesetze (nur) für Ausländer in Deutschland. Accessed 17 January 2011. http://www.ring-nationaler-frauen.de

Ring Nationaler Frauen. 2010. Landesweite Aktionen des RNF-Sachsens: Ist der internationale Frauentag noch zeitgemäß? Accessed 17 January 2011. http://www.ring-nationaler-frauen.de

Ysmal, Colette. 1996. Sociologie des élites du FN. In *Le Front National à découvert*, ed. N. Mayer, and P. Perrineau, 107–118. Paris: Presses de Sciences Po.

The Emergence of Powerful Anti-Gender Movements in Europe and the Crisis of Liberal Democracy

Eszter Kováts

Introduction

In recent years several European countries have witnessed the emergence of powerful social movements mobilizing against the enemy they call "gender ideology", "gender theory" or "genderism". Under these labels various issues are united and attacked by conservative, partly fundamentalist groups of society, including satellite organizations of the Roman Catholic Church: certain women's rights (e.g. reproductive rights in Spain), certain LGBT issues (e.g. same-sex marriage in Croatia, France and Slovenia; human rights strategy of the government in Slovakia), government gender policies (e.g. ratifying the Istanbul Convention in Poland, gender-sensitive education in schools in France), gender mainstreaming as an administrative policy tool (e.g. in Austria, Germany, Poland), progressive sexual education programmes (in Croatia, Germany and Poland), or gender studies departments and their financing (in Germany and Poland). These movements have become a real challenge for the progressive actors interested in gender issues or LGBT rights, partly because they were unprepared for the attacks, and partly because they follow unrelated (and sometimes

---

E. Kováts (✉)
Budapest, Hungary

© The Author(s) 2017   175
M. Köttig et al. (eds.), *Gender and Far Right Politics in Europe*,
DOI 10.1007/978-3-319-43533-6_12

conflicting) agendas. So liberal, green or leftist politicians, women's rights activists, LGBT activists, gender policy officers of public administrations, and gender studies scholars have found themselves put into the same "gender ideologist" or "genderist" box by these movements.[1]

The level and quality of involvement of conservative and far-right parties in these movements is different. While in Poland and Germany, for instance, these parties and movements mobilizing against gender show many personal overlaps, and the parties adopt a concrete position in the debates, in France, for instance, the situation is more ambiguous (see Kováts and Põim 2015). I will first summarize some key elements of previous research findings relevant to this paper and conceptualize the challenge these movements pose to liberal democracy. The second section is a reflection on the different interpretations so far elaborated for understanding the mobilizational potential of the enemy image "gender ideology". In the third section, I will briefly elaborate my preliminary argument for discussion, namely, that anti-gender activism points to societal crisis phenomena going beyond gender equality and LGBT rights, which also connect, at least partially, the understanding of these movements to that of the rise of the far right all over Europe.

"Gender Ideology" as an Enemy Image in Europe

How we refer to these movements is theoretically relevant and is not an unproblematic question (see, for instance, Hark and Villa 2015, 7–8; Kuhar 2014). However, exploring this in depth lies outside the scope of this paper. While being aware of its limits, I will use the term "anti-gender movements" in this paper, meaning by it all those movements mobilizing against what they mean by "gender" and "gender ideology", or, in a broader sense, intimate citizenship or sexual citizenship (Kuhar 2014). This does not necessarily mean that these movements are explicitly antifeminist or anti-LGBT, even though their fight is fought with the enemy constructed by the term and the alleged contents of gender, and even if their struggle may have detrimental consequences for gender equality and sexual rights.

In most affected countries, the concerns of the movements are connected to accusations of imperialism. Omnipresent is the discourse of foreign forces (like EU, UN, WHO) imposing something on our countries in order to weaken them as nations and destroy traditions or even mankind (See e.g. Félix 2015; Grzebalska 2015; and specifically on the anti-colonial frame Korolczuk 2015). This is often strengthened by the impossibility of translating, or reluctance to translate, the term gender and gender mainstreaming into the national languages. The other recurrent element of the discourse is the figure of the "child in danger", which is based on fear and has proved successful for the mobilization of masses, especially parents (Chetcuti 2014; Graff 2014). The connection of these two: gender as an intrigue of lobbies which have infiltrated transnational organizations, and as an ideology that threatens our children, makes of "gender" an enemy, an illegitimate claim which needs to be eradicated.

In order to conceptualize the challenge posed by this enemy image, I use Chantal Mouffe's well-known theory of antagonism and agonism.[2] To grasp the *political*, she distances herself from Carl Schmitt's idea of the impossibility of pluralism, as well as from the technocratic-liberal belief in consensuses based on rational debates. She argues that "*[p]roperly political questions always involve decisions which require us to make a choice between conflicting alternatives*", and that liberalism has a central deficiency, namely that it negates "*the ineradicable character of antagonism (...), the conflicts that pluralism entails; conflicts for which no rational solution could ever exist*" (Mouffe 2005, 10). In her understanding of liberal democracy, it is important to find a way to reconcile the political (which inherently contains antagonism) with democratic pluralism (which cannot be based on rational, anti-political deliberation). "*The crucial point here is to show how antagonism can be transformed so as to make available a form of we/they opposition compatible with pluralist democracy*" (Mouffe 2005, 19). For this purpose she introduces the concept of agonism:

> *Conflict, in order to be accepted as legitimate, needs to take a form that does not destroy the political association. This means that some kind of common bond must exist between the parties in conflict, so that they will not treat their opponents as enemies to be eradicated, seeing their demands as illegitimate, which is precisely what happens with the antagonistic friend/enemy relation. (...) If we want to acknowledge on one side the permanence of the antagonistic dimension of the conflict, while on the other side allowing for the possibility of its 'taming', we need to envisage a third type of relation. This is the type of relation which I have proposed to call 'agonism'. While antagonism is a we/they relation in which the two sides are enemies who do not share any common ground, agonism is a we/they relation where the conflicting parties, although acknowledging that there is no rational solution to their conflict, nevertheless recognize the legitimacy of their opponents. They are 'adversaries', not enemies. This means*

that, while in conflict, they see themselves as belonging to the same political association, as sharing a common symbolic space within which the conflict takes place. We could say that the task of democracy is to transform antagonism into agonism. (Mouffe 2005, 20)

In the case of the anti-gender discourse, the concept of "gender ideology" proved to be a tool to create a them/us divide in the sense of antagonism and through it delegitimize different groups in society and politics: in this understanding "gender ideology" and those who are perceived as its lobbyists are not acknowledged as legitimate opponents and are blamed for not sharing any common ground and the same political association. Anti-gender movements in this sense are similar to far-right movements in that they acknowledge the political but negate pluralism. Therefore they pose a challenge to liberal democracy and to the actors committed to it: how to acknowledge rationally insoluble antagonisms while transforming them into agonisms.

When it comes to the analysis of anti-gender movements, the origin of the discourse has been the issue which has so far received the most scientific interest (e.g. Buss 1998; Carnac 2014; Fillod 2014; Paternotte 2015; Robcis 2015), as well as the distortions which the figure of "gender theory" or "gender ideology" has caused in respect of the concepts used in gender studies and in gender policy (e.g. Garbagnoli 2014; Frey et al. 2014).

The research carried out on the origins of the anti-gender discourse and the term "gender ideology" itself (summarized, for instance, in Paternotte 2015) points to the Vatican. Following the 1995 UN Fourth Conference on Women which took place in Beijing (and formulated among others the strategy of gender mainstreaming), the Holy See included in its documents terms like "gender feminists" and "gender agenda" (e.g. Buss 1998). In 2003 the Pontifical Council for Family published the Family Lexicon,[3] first in Italian and subsequently in various languages, which systematically expounded the Vatican's position on what it called "gender theory" and "gender ideology" (Fillod 2014).

The relevant entries in the lexicon refer to John Paul II's writings, mainly his "Theology of the Body" (1979), "Mulieris Dignitatem" (On the Dignity and Vocation of Women, 1988) and "Letter to Women" (1995) (Fillod 2014; Robcis 2015), which can be regarded as founding the anthropology of women. In formulating theses about women's nature, these writings show a shift from earlier ideas of the subordination of women to men, towards the complementarity of men and women (as Mary Anne Case argues, "far from being longstanding Catholic orthodoxy, complementarity is a mid-twentieth century innovation imported into Catholicism", Case 2016, 2) and towards the relationality of human nature (the man exists in relation to the woman, the woman exists in relation to the man) (Garbagnoli 2014, 153–155). These essentialist ideas build the foundation for all argumentations against the critical and constructivist contents of the concept of gender, whether gender equality issues or homosexuality. In this understanding, the term "gender theory" or "gender ideology" serves to represent what is against Catholic teaching on the ontological difference and complementarity of the sexes (Carnac 2014). Several lay people and members of clergy, as national experts, have contributed to spreading these ideas. Among the most influential, as they reach beyond their national borders, are Michel Schooyans, Tony Anatrella, Gabriele Kuby and Marguerite Peeters (Paternotte 2015, 140–141).

Apart from research on the origins of the discourse, and national case studies, studies of these movements have focused on the complicated relations the anti-gender discourse maintains to science and scientificity (Hark and Villa 2015; Fillod 2014; Frey et al. 2014; Kuhar 2014); the role of the Catholic Church not only in the production of the discourse but also in the mobilization (Fassin 2014; Kuhar 2014; Kuhar and Paternotte forthcoming; Marschütz 2014; Paternotte 2015; Perintfalvi 2015), and the role of the conservative and far-right parties in shaping the discourse and the mobilizations (Kováts and Põim 2015).

Research on anti-gender movements is currently being developed. The transnational connections have just started to be explored (Kováts and Põim 2015; Paternotte et al. 2015; Kuhar and Paternotte forthcoming). This research can contribute to situating this phenomenon in a broader context, and can answer questions like: How can we explain the emergence of these movements in some countries and their non-emergence in others? Are there specific structural circumstances which enabled successful mobilization in one country and failure in another? What do we know about the people committed to the goals of these movements as far as their socio-economic status, general attitudes, political ideologies and motivations for mobilization are concerned? Addressing these questions will help to overcome treating these movements in and for themselves and to grasp something of the broader societal and political framework that provides fertile ground for them.

INTERPRETATIVE FRAMEWORKS

In this section I attempt to critically analyse the different conceptualizations in which the Europe-wide anti-gender movements have so far been understood.

The most naive interpretation is that anti-genderism is a misunderstanding by ignorant people, and that if the concept of gender and gender equality is explained in an understandable way, they will know that there is nothing to fear. This interpretation proved wrong when "let's explain it to them" strategies failed (Grzebalska and Soós 2016; Kováts 2015). Therefore this framework will not be further explored.

National Circumstances

Especially in the initial phase of the movements, when research had not yet revealed the simultaneity of the movements in different countries and the transnational connections (in respect of the discourse and the travelling practices), scholars trying to understand what was going on explained the movements in terms of the particular national circumstances, for instance, from the national historical perspective of the right or far right, or the relation between State and Catholic Church, and so on (e.g. Brustier 2014; Grabowska 2015). David Paternotte also points to this fact: "Despite some exceptions (…) recent mobilisation is explained by social science scholars through national factors—providing us with an iconic case of methodological nationalism" (Paternotte 2015, 130).

Concentrating on the national circumstances proved useful to understanding the national and local contexts as grounds for mobilization, and for instance why a certain issue could become a trigger in a certain country, and which organizational form contributed to the success or failure of the movement. Also, for understanding the construction of the enemy (or even the need for an enemy, see Félix 2015; Kováts and Pető 2017) in the specific context, the national approach could provide useful insights.

However, the simultaneity of the movements, different triggers in countries with various political landscape and gender/LGBT policies, and travelling practices (Kováts and Põim 2015; Paternotte 2015) point clearly to the fact that this national approach is insufficient to fully understand what is at stake.

A variant of the national interpretation is the regional one: Agnieszka Graff develops the idea of a historical East-West divide for the Polish and

Slovak anti-gender movements: "The relative instability of our democracies, the enormous frustrations and resentments about the economic situation, the weakness of women's and LGBT movements, the strength of nationalist movements—all this has made the anti-gender campaign possible" (Graff 2014, 434). The author operates here within the problematic framework of "East-Central Europe's lagging behind compared to the West", which, among other things, does not account for the fact that anti-gender movements have emerged in countries with various political landscapes and gender/LGBT policies, including countries in Western Europe, despite presumably strong women's rights and LGBT movements and strong democracies. Further exploration is needed to establish whether the specificities of the movements reflect, at least partially, the former East-West divide. Certainly the research project by Kuhar and Paternotte (eds. Kuhar and Paternotte forthcoming), aiming at depicting the transnational connections, will provide answers to that question.

Strategy of the Roman Catholic Church

As shown in the previous section, the role of the Roman Catholic Church in shaping the discourse and in the mobilizations cannot be overlooked. However, several scholars hold the view that understanding the actors behind the discourse and the mobilizations is equal to understanding the movements. According to this view, the thousands and millions of people joining the movements are manipulated, and used in an evil plan of the Catholic Church.

In this framework, anti-gender mobilization is a mere invention and strategy of the Church, to consolidate its role, regain power and clericalize society by new means (Fillod 2014; Kuhar 2014; Paternotte 2015; Robcis 2015). It must be noted, however, that even these authors emphasize that the Catholic Church must not be seen as a monolithic bloc, and scholars and activists should not interpret anti-gender movements as a Catholic conspiracy. This is evidenced by the various voices (e.g. Marschütz 2014; Perintfalvi 2015) and materials distributed by those Catholics who defend different views on the issue.[4]

Still, scholars who know not only the teachings of the Church, but also the internal debates over teachings and power struggles, acknowledge the Church's undeniably decisive role and critically reflect on the role played in spreading hatred and exclusion by this discourse (Marschütz 2014; Perintfalvi 2015).

This is a broader framework than the national one, and grasps essential features which go beyond national specificities and (seemingly) national policy debates. It not only helps to explain the discourse, but also to identify the actors, their connections and strategies. But this approach reduces Church politics to a fierce battle of ideologies, and anti-gender mobilization to a conscious manipulation strategy. This does not account for the scope of the phenomenon, for its popularity among the masses and for the reasons behind this popularity.

Conservative Backlash

The movements are frequently understood as a conservative backlash against achieved levels of equality between women and men and/or LGBT rights.

In their Preface entitled "Gender/Backlash. In the Wake of yet Another Conservative Revolution", the editors of the volume "Anti-Gender Movements on the Rise?" state: "The concept of 'backlash' refers to perceived setbacks and deteriorations in the relations between (and among) men and women. Its proponents assume that gender equality and LGBT rights are on the decline all over the developed world, or that there is at least a significant increase in rabid attacks against them" (Anti-Gender Movements on the Rise 2015, 7).

This perspective of "the patriarchy/heteronormativity fighting back" seems as tempting as it is simplifying. The activists on the field, especially those subjected to aggressive attacks, can often see only the attack on their work and achievements. It can easily be perceived as, and reduced to, a backlash. They are often stigmatized and pushed into a defensive position which in turn seems to justify their views and increases their urgent demands for reinforcement of EU and UN norms. This is also a morally comfortable position. It would be a capitulation to revise their own positions, language, or agenda on the grounds of unjust, often *ad hominem* attacks. The gender concept of the opponents is so obviously distorted compared to those in gender studies or gender policy, and this leads to the fact that activists often adhere uncritically to the framework of pro-contra proposed by these movements (pro-gender against anti-gender, see Grzebalska and Soós 2016; Kováts 2015).

In itself, the fact that these movements appear simultaneously, partly co-ordinated, and show transnational ties, points to the fact that they are something more than patriarchy or heteronormativity fighting back.

Though these movements are not necessarily anti-feminist and homophobic *per se*, they undoubtedly fight the terms in which equality is defined by progressive actors (anti-discrimination language, human rights paradigm, statistical equality, individualizing identity politics). This position is even more challenging as the above-mentioned essentialist Catholic teaching on complementarity and relationality, being the ideological background of these movements, contests the possibility of articulating certain questions of gender inequality and the equality of loves.

On the basis of the above-mentioned regional argument, the framing of anti-gender movements as solely a backlash is problematic. As Elżbieta Korolczuk argues, "in countries such as Poland, Ukraine, and Russia the process of women's empowerment and the emancipation of the LGBT community has been uneven, fragile, and far from revolutionary. (…) Thus, 'backlash' understood as an adverse reaction to something that has gained popularity, prominence, or influence does not seem to be a very productive model" (Korolczuk 2015, 52). Though I don't share her view on the East-West divide having an explanatory value, the argument against the backlash framing seems to be reasonable.

Gender as Symbolic Glue

In the previous section, I have presented the most current interpretative frameworks which, in my view, have contributed to understanding one aspect of this complex phenomenon in depth. However, in and for themselves none of them can alone account for the complexity of the anti-gender phenomenon. In this limited space, and at this stage of the research on transnational connections, I cannot pretend to fill this gap, but I will attempt to describe the direction in which the existing results lead, for further elaboration and discussion.

Based on the English, French, German and Hungarian literature, it seems that more and more scholars are seeing a link between these movements and the crisis of the socio-economic order.

Chetcuti argues that this nationalist neoconservatism is a sort of answer to the neoliberal consensus (Chetcuti 2014, 253). Wimbauer and her colleagues argue, based on an impressive literature of feminist economics and feminist critics of the neoliberal order, that discourses against gender equality and gender studies are an explicit or implicit attempt to get experiences of precarity and precarization under control (Wimbauer et al. 2015, 43) and that the feminist and LGBT struggles have found a comfortable place in the neoliberal order and are therefore made co-responsible for the damage it causes by the anti-gender actors (ibid., 50–52). Solty echoes this latter thesis (Solty 2015, 37) and goes even further. In his comparison of the movement against an LGBT-friendly curriculum in Baden-Württemberg and protests against a school reform in the US, he speaks about "culturalization of the social question" by the right wing. He argues that the rage over socio-economic deep structures is shifted to the cultural surface structure (ibid., 36), and concludes his analysis by arguing that the left must find another vision rather than adhering to neoliberal ideas, and re-invent its emancipatory programme.

Andrea Pető (Pető 2015a, 2015b) argues that it is indispensable for scholars seeking to understand anti-gender movements, and for activists and politicians on the progressive side seeking to counteract them, to reflect on the content of progressive politics (questioning neoliberalism), on the language of equality (statistical equality, human rights, EU as a neoliberal project while being sold as norm owner of gender equality and human rights) and on the language of politics (technocratic, policy-based). She pleads for a re-enchantment of politics and of the language of (gender) politics (Pető 2015b). This is all the more necessary because what remains of the post-World War II consensus is becoming more and more challenged by the growing fundamentalism represented by the far right and now by anti-gender movements (Kováts et al. 2015).

There is no simple identification between anti-gender movements and the far right: far-right parties are not on the side of anti-gender struggles in all countries and contexts; anti-gender mobilizations reach out far more, and labelling these movements as fundamentalist does not help to better understand them, on the contrary. Still one can argue that the understanding of anti-gender movements and understanding the rise of the far right can, at least partially, follow similar patterns. Weronika Grzebalska makes this argument when she connects these movements with the failure of progressive politics:

> [W]aging a war against the rise of political extremism and religious fundamentalism can only bring us so far as mitigating the symptoms of a disease instead of curing its root causes. So what are these root causes and why do masses of people become radicalized against liberal democracy in its current form? (…) [T]hanks to a growing literature dealing with the social consequences of the current economic system we know for sure that a large part of the answer

to this question is that the neoliberal, market-driven democracy that we currently see in Europe, structurally excludes a huge number of people (...) It is in this context that conservative protest movements create a space for these people to vent their fears and insecurities, voice their anger and dissatisfaction with politics and claim a sense of agency and empowerment that European liberals and social democrats once promised—but failed to deliver.

She then describes some examples, one of them being how the massive immigration of Polish women resulted in a moral panic on the right that proposed a return to traditional family values as a solution.

By all means, members of the European feminist and LGBT+ movements as well as progressive politicians have been right in opposing anti-gender mobilizations, and criticizing the solutions offered by them as threatening human rights and destructive to democratic society. But as they were calling for the need to protect women's and minority rights and other liberal values from right-wing attacks, what they so often ignored is the fact that the liberal democratic system in its current form has become an empty slogan to the vast masses of people to whom it has very little to offer, among them rural mothers forced to migrate to support their families (...) Therefore, the task that stands before European political leaders and decision makers is to acknowledge the connection between anti-genderism and other forms of right-wing radicalisation on the one hand, and the broader crisis of democracy stemming from the failure of the current globalised, capitalist order on the other." (Grzebalska 2016)

Conclusion

In this paper I have tried to demonstrate that the emergence of powerful anti-gender movements points to social crisis phenomena going beyond gender equality and LGBT rights. These movements and their success in identifying gender as an enemy are rather symptoms and consequences of deeper socio-economic, political and cultural crises of liberal democracy which need further scientific investigation. These crises need to be acknowledged and tackled, while new common grounds for transforming antagonisms into agonistic struggles (Mouffe 2005) need to be established; otherwise, the ongoing "process of dedemocratization of capitalism through the de-economization of democracy" (Streeck 2013, 28) will lead to further crises in Europe.

NOTES

1. Grzebalska and Soós (2016) provide a comprehensive analysis of the strategies used so far by progressive actors Europe-wide to counter these movements.
2. She elaborates these concepts in *The Democratic Paradox* (2000). I quote her from *On the political* (Mouffe 2005).
3. "Lexicon for Ambiguous and Controversial Terms on the Family, Life and Ethical Questions."
4. See for instance a leaflet spread in the German-speaking countries: http://www.dbk.de/fileadmin/redaktion/diverse_downloads/presse_2015/2015-187a-Flyer-Gender.pdf, accessed 30.03.2016.

REFERENCES

Anti-Gender Movements on the Rise? 2015. *Strategising for Gender Equality in Central and Eastern Europe.* Heinrich-Böll-Stiftung.

Brustier, Gaël. 2014. *Le Mai 68 conservateur. Que restera-t-il de La Manif pour Tous?* Les éditions du cerf, Paris.

Buss, Doris E. 1998. Robes, Relics and Rights: The Vatican and the Beijing Conference on Women. *Social and Legal Studies* 7(3): 339–363.

Carnac, Romain. 2014/2010. L'Église catholique contre „la théorie du genre": Construction d'un objet polémique dans le débat public français contemporain. In *Synergies Italie. Les discours intitutionnels au prisme du „genre": Perspectives italo-françaises.* 125–143.

Case, Mary Anne. 2016. The Role of the Popes in the Invention of Complementarity and the Vatican's Anathematization of Gender. In *Forthcoming Religion and Gender Habemus Gender Special Issue 2016,* University of Chicago, Public Law Working Paper No. 565.

Chetcuti, Natacha. 2014/2012. Quand les questions de genre et d'homosexualités deviennent un enjeu républicain. *Les Temps Modernes* 678, 241–253.

Fassin, Eric. 2014. Same-Sex Marriage, Nation and Race: French Political Logics and Rhetorics. *Contemporary French Civilization* 32: 281–301.

Félix, Anikó. 2015. The Hungarian Case. In *Gender as Symbolic Glue. The Position and Role of Conservative and Far Right Parties in the Anti-gender Mobilizations in Europe,* ed. Eszter Kováts, and Maari Põim, 62–82. Foundation for European Progressive Studies and Friedrich-Ebert-Stiftung, Brussels and Budapest.

Fillod, Odile. 2014/2013. L'invention de la „théorie du genre": Le mariage blanc du Vatican et de la science. *Contemporary French Civilization* 32: 321–333.

Frey, Regine, Marc Gärtner, Manfred Köhnen, and Sebastian Scheele. 2014. *Gender, Wissenschaftlichkeit und Ideologie. Argumente im Streit um Geschlechterverhältnisse.* Heinrich-Böll-Stiftung, Gunda-Werner-Institut.

Garbagnoli, Sara. 2014/2010. Le Vatican contre la dénaturalisation de l'ordre sexuel. Enjeux d'un discours institutionnel réactionnaire. In *Synergies Italie. Les discours intitutionnels au prisme du "genre": Perspectives italo-françaises.* 145–167.

Grabowska, Magdalena. 2015. Cultural War or "Business as Usual"? Recent Instances, and the Historical Origins of a "Backlash" Against Women's and Sexual Rights in Poland. In *Anti-Gender Movements on the Rise? Strategising for Gender Equality in Central and Eastern Europe,* 54–64. Heinrich-Böll-Stiftung.

Graff, Agnieszka. 2014. Report from the Gender Trenches: War Against 'Genderism' in Poland. *European Journal of Women's Studies* 21: 431–442.

Graff, Agnieszka, and Elżbieta Korolczuk. forthcoming. *Gender as "Ebola from Brussels": The Anti-Colonial Frame and Transnational Right-Wing Populism.*

Grzebalska, Weronika. 2015. The Polish Case. In *Gender as Symbolic Glue. The Position and Role of Conservative and Far Right Parties in the Anti-gender Mobilizations in Europe,* ed. Eszter Kováts, and Maari Põim, 83–103. Foundation for European Progressive Studies and Friedrich-Ebert-Stiftung, Brussels and Budapest.

———. 2016. *Why the War on "Gender Ideology" Matters—And not Just to Feminists. Anti-genderism and the Crisis of Neoliberal Democracy.* Accessed 30 March 2016. http://visegradinsight.eu/why-the-war-on-gender-ideology-matters-and-not-just-to-feminists/

Grzebalska, Weronika, and Eszter Petronella Soós. 2016. *Conservatives vs. the "Culture of Death". How Progressives Handled the War on "Gender".* Foundation for European Progressive Studies, Brussels. Accessed 30 March 2016. http://www.feps-europe.eu/assets/17de2a21-4e6f-4fad-a5b3-c75f009c177e/wg-anti-gender-movements-feps-formatcompressedpdf.pdf

Hark, Sabine, and Paula-Irene Villa. 2015. *Anti-genderismus. Sexualität und Geschlecht als Schauplätze aktueller politischer Auseinandersetzungen.* Transcript Verlag.

Korolczuk, Elżbieta. 2015. "The War on Gender" from a Transnational Perspective—Lessons for a Feminist Strategising. In: *Anti-Gender Movements on the Rise? Strategising for Gender Equality in Central and Eastern Europe,* 43–53. Heinrich-Böll-Stiftung.

Kováts, Eszter. 2015. A "Gender" Mint ellenségkép Európában: Kihívások és lehetőségek a feminista és az LMBT+ mozgalmak számára. ["Gender" as Enemy Image in Europe: Challenges and Possibilities for the Feminist and LGBT+ Movements]. In *Az LMBTQ+ mozgalom helyzete—Társadalmi attitűdök és politikai környezet.* 68–87. ed. Mikecz, Dániel and Tóth, Csaba. Republikon Intézet, Friedrich Naumann Stiftung für die Freiheit.

Kováts, Eszter, and Andrea Pető. 2017. Anti-Gender Discourse in Hungary: A Discourse Without a Movement? In. *Anti-Gender Campaigns in Europe: Religious and Political Mobilizations Against Equality,* ed. Roman Kuhar and David Paternotte. Rowman & Littlefield. (forthcoming).

Kováts, Eszter, and Maari Põim (ed). 2015. *Gender as Symbolic Glue. The Position and Role of Conservative and far Right Parties in the Anti-gender Mobilizations in Europe*. Foundation for European Progressive Studies and Friedrich-Ebert-Stiftung, Brussels and Budapest. Accessed 30 March 2016. http://library.fes. de/pdf-files/bueros/budapest/11382.pdf

Kováts, Eszter, Maari Põim, and Judit Tánczos. 2015. *Beyond Gender? Anti-gender Mobilization and the Lessons for Progressives*. Foundation for European Progressive Studies and Friedrich-Ebert-Stiftung. Accessed 30 March 2016. http://www.fesbp.hu/common/pdf/FEPS_FES_Policy_Brief_2015.pdf

Kuhar, Roman. 2014. Playing with Science: Sexual Citizenship and the Roman Catholic Church Counter-Narratives in Slovenia and Croatia. In *Women's Studies International Forum*.

Kuhar, Roman and David Paternotte (eds.). 2017: *Anti-Gender Campaigns in Europe: Religious and Political Mobilizations against Equality*. Rowman & Littlefield (forthcoming).

Marschütz, Gerhard. 2014. Zur Kritik an der vermeintlichen Gender-Ideologie: Wachstumspotenzial für die eigene Lehre. In *Herder Korrespondenz*, September. Accessed 30 March 2016. https://www.herder-korrespondenz.de/heftarchiv/68-jahrgang-2014/heft-9-2014/zur-kritik-an-der-vermeintlichen-gender-ideologie-wachstumspotenzial-fuer-die-eigene-lehre

Mouffe, Chantal. 2005. *On the Political (Thinking in Action)*. London and New York: Routledge.

Paternotte, David. 2015. Blessing the Crowds. Catholic Mobilisations against Gender in Europe. In *Anti-Genderismus. Sexualität und Geschlecht als Schauplätze aktueller politischer Auseinandersetzungen*. ed. Sabine Hark, and Paula-Irene Villa, 129–148. Transcript Verlag.

Paternotte, David, Valérie Piette, and Van Der Sophie Dussen (ed). 2015. *Habemus gender! Déconstruction d'une riposte religieuse*. Sextant, Bruxelles.

Perintfalvi, Rita. 2015. *The Real Face of the Anti-Gender Kulturkampf. The Rise of a New Kind of Political and Religious Fundamentalism in Europe?* Accessed 30 March 2016. http://www.icmica-miic.org/home-eng/361-themes/men-and-women/11731-the-real-face-of-the-anti-gender-kulturkampf.html

Pető, Andrea. 2015a. "Anti-gender" Mobilisational Discourse of Conservative and Far Right Parties as a Challenge for Progressive Politics. In *Gender as Symbolic Glue. The Position and Role of Conservative and far Right Parties in the Anti-gender Mobilizations in Europe*, ed. Eszter Kováts, and Maari Põim, 62–82. Foundation for European Progressive Studies and Friedrich-Ebert-Stiftung, Brussels and Budapest.

———. 2015b. Gender Equality as Re-enchantment: Political Mobilisation in Times of "Neo-Patriarchal Neoliberalism" and Possibilities of Bipartisan Dialogue. In *Woman Up! 2. A Transatlantic Dialogue*. 139–145. Foundation for European Progressive Studies. Accessed 30 March 2016. http://www.feps-europe.eu/en/publications/details/298

Robcis, Camille. 2015. A New Dreyus Affair? Catholics, the "Theory of gender", and the Turn to the Human in France. *The Journal of Modern History* 87(4): 892–923.

Solty, Ingar. 2015. Öffentliche Schulbildung, Sexualerziehung und rechter Widerstand gegen kulturelle Liberalisierung. Lassen sich die Bewegung gegen den Bildungsplan 2015 in Baden-Württemberg und die Bewegung gegen die "Common Core State Standards Initiative" in den USA vergleichen? In *Unheilige Allianz. Das Geflecht von christlichen Fundamentalisten und politisch Rechten am Beispiel des Widerstands gegen den Bildungsplan in Baden-Württemberg*, ed. Lucie Rosa Billmann, 30–37. Luxemburg-Stiftung.

Streeck, Wolfgang. 2013. *Gekaufte Zeit. Die vertagte Krise des demokratischen Kapitalismus*. Berlin: Suhrkamp Verlag.

Wimbauer, Christine, Mona Motakef, and Julia Teschlade. 2015. Prekäre Selbstverständlichkeiten. Neun prekarisierungstheoretische Thesen zu Diskursen gegen Gleichstellungspolitik und Geschlechterforschung. In *Anti-Genderismus. Sexualität und Geschlecht als Schauplätze aktueller politischer Auseinandersetzungen*, ed. Sabine Hark, and Paula-Irene Villa, 41–58. Transcript Verlag.

Similarities/Differences in Gender and Far-Right Politics in Europe and the USA

Kathleen Blee

INTRODUCTION

Scholars of gender and the far right are engaged in complex tasks of generalizing and specifying. These tasks pull the analytic eye in different directions. To see the general, we must look broadly, across time and space, across social and political contexts, across cultures, languages, and histories. We find the general by studying across social settings of great differences to find threads of similarity. By contrast, to see the specific we must look narrowly, within individual countries, cities, groups, subgroups, and in narrow slices of time. We find the specific by studying more homogeneous social settings to find the paths of social action that exist in unique times and places.

Understanding the place of gender in the far right requires that we study both the general and the specific. Generalizing is needed to understand *if* gender matters in far-right political movements. Looking at the general pushes us to consider commonalities across nations and times and places in why women (or men) join the far right, the characteristics of how they participate, and how far-right leaders wield ideas about gender in the service of national, racial, religious, or class-based political agendas. Specifying is needed to understand *how* gender matters in far-

K. Blee (✉)
University of Pittsburgh, Pittsburgh, PA, USA

© The Author(s) 2017   191
M. Köttig et al. (eds.), *Gender and Far Right Politics in Europe*,
DOI 10.1007/978-3-319-43533-6_13

right politics in individual places and times. Searching for the specific requires us to examine how different national, historical, and regional contexts shape the mobilization and actions of women and men in far-right politics.

This chapter examines the general and specific aspects of women in the far right by comparing the situation in the USA with the information on Europe in the chapters of this volume. My goal is to add another comparative lens on gender and the far right, extending the intra-European comparisons that the preceding essays provide. To focus on the general, I highlight commonalities across various countries of Europe as well as across the USA. Of course, Europe and the USA are quite heterogeneous regions, with vast differences across areas. My comparison thus emphasizes general tendencies and patterns within the USA and within Europe, while recognizing that these do not apply evenly within these regions. To focus on the specific, I describe a number of significant differences between the European and the US experience of gender in the far right. The chapter concludes with suggestions for future research in this very understudied area of scholarship.

THE FAR RIGHT IN THE USA

Throughout history, the far right in the USA has been largely organized around issues of race (Blee and Creasap 2010). Extreme-right groups consider race to be the central fault line of society, dividing whites from non-whites. Hostility toward Jews is also widespread in the USA far right, even as anti-Semitic attitudes among the general population have declined significantly over time (King and Weiner 2007). Racist groups regard Jews as masters of a world-wide conspiracy that is aimed at curbing the rights of white and Aryan people. They argue that Jews control the international economy, the media, and the government. Indeed, many in the far right refer to the US government, especially at the national level, as a Zionist Occupation Government or ZOG (Zeskind 2009). A particularly vicious racist ideology known as Christian Identity has been influential in the USA (Barkun 1994). Despite its name, Christian Identity adherents do not affiliate with any conventional Christian theology, church, or denomination. On the contrary, Christian Identity philosophy teaches that Christianity has been polluted by its connection to Judaism in the US tradition of Judeo-Christianity. Christian Identity adherents proclaim that non-whites are descended from beings that preceded the Biblical Adam, so they are essentially non-humans in a human form. In contrast, Jews are described as the literal descendants of the Biblical Satan, so they are essentially the devil in a human form. This depiction of Jews is particularly dangerous because it positions racial believers as needing to kill Jews to rid the earth of Satan.

The main racist groups in the USA now are white supremacists and associated neo-Nazis (Dobratz and Shanks-Meile 1997, 2004). The Ku Klux Klan is the oldest far-right movement, with its origins in the states of the defeated South after the Civil War and the abolition of slavery (Blee 1991; Cunningham 2013). Today, however, the Klan has become small, fragmented, and largely ineffectual. In its place, a myriad of white supremacist and neo-Nazi groups, including neo-Nazi skinheads, have emerged (Durham 2007; Futrell et al. 2006; Simi and Futrell 2010; Zeskind 2009). These now constitute the most vibrant sectors of the modern far right in the USA.

Today's far right is quite diverse. Some groups are highly organized, with a firm sense of membership and identifiable leaders and spokespersons. Others are fluid and only minimally organized, so it is difficult to determine who constitutes members or leaders. A few US far-right groups recruit openly and seek to influence the public through the internet and print propaganda. Other groups exist virtually underground to hide themselves from the authorities, with propaganda limited to internet sites and postings that hide the identities of group members and their locations. Some groups post explicit and virulent racism on their websites, in graffiti tags on public and private property, and on flyers or newsletters they distribute to outsiders and potential recruits; others present a more moderate face to the public and reserve their vicious ideas about racial minorities for confirmed members (Bhatia 2004; Bonilla-Silva 2006; Cooter 2006; Daniels 2009; Rogers and Litt 2004). There are no extreme-right political parties in the USA.

Networks among extreme-right groups in the past century have generally been fragile, but they have been particularly loose in recent years as many racists have adopted the strategy they term "leaderless resistance," along with a structure of small unconnected racist cells modeled after militant jihadist movements, to avoid detection and prosecution (Dobratz and Waldner 2012; Kaplan 1997). Because of this structure, it is extremely difficult to estimate the number of members or supporters of the extreme right although the Southern Poverty Law Center, a respected racist monitoring group, has identified 784 currently operating hate groups.

Violence is key to the agendas of most US extreme-right groups. Not all groups practice violence, but most advocate or acknowledge its necessity to preserve the white race against threats posed by Jews and other non-whites. Some far-right groups create elaborate plans for terrorist violence. Others use violence more opportunistically, by attacking members of enemy groups when they have a chance. In most extreme-right groups, violence is also part of the group culture. Far-rightists listen to aggressive, violent music and inflict violence on each other and themselves as well as their perceived enemies. Moreover, a significant amount of racist violence in recent years has been committed by "lone wolf" white supremacists who have no connection to racist groups except as readers of their propaganda and internet sites.

One belief that fuels racist violence is fear of an upcoming race war. Sometimes known as RaHoWa! (Racial Holy War), this is a prediction of an upcoming apocalyptic racial version of the Protestant prophecy of a Biblical end time in which forces of good struggle to the death with forces of evil (Michael 2006; also Barkun 1994; Blee 1999). Racist groups constantly note evidence that a race war is around the corner as justification for their actions and urge whites to prepare to defend themselves by any means necessary. A second belief among racists that propels them to violent action is the notion that whites are imperiled by immigration and a higher birthrate of non-whites, especially African Americans and Latino/as. Whites face, in the language of racist extremists, the peril of "race suicide" (Perry 2004).

Gender

Women are a significant and perhaps growing part of the far right in the USA today (Ferber 2004). Giving precise numbers is impossible, but it is likely that women constitute about 25 % of all racist activists today. Women are found across the landscape of the racist movement, although they are more prominent in some neo-Nazi and white power skinhead groups than in the more gender-traditional Ku Klux Klans or Christian Identity groups. In gender-traditional racist groups, women are likely to be the wives and daughters of male members, but other racist groups recruit women directly (Blee 2016). Far-right groups generally recruit women to expand their size, but some target women to bring men into the group (Blazak 2004; Blee 2002). Other racist leaders regard women as safer recruits than men. They assume that women are less likely to commit petty crimes and attract the attention of the police. And many racist leaders think that women are central to the task of establishing an intergenerational racist movement by raising children in the tenets of the far right.

Few far-right groups have women in any official leadership positions. In many, however, women play unofficial roles as leaders in the sense of promoting group solidarity, socializing recruits into the expectations of the groups, and developing goals and strategies. For the most part, women are expected to handle traditional female tasks within racist groups. They are assigned to bear large numbers of white babies to combat the threat of white racial suicide. Women are expected to rear white warrior children by homeschooling them to shield them from the influences of multiculturalism in the schools and by providing a racist home in which the values of white supremacy are evident and nourished. In a few groups, particularly some neo-Nazi groups, women are also expected to play more active and public roles as female racial warriors. These women participate in street violence against target groups, as well as the ritualized violence of brutal initiations in groups and aggressive interactions at white supremacist cultural events, such as white power music festivals. Even as female racial warriors, however, women's roles are generally subordinate. Women are typically assigned to provide emergency medical care to wounded (male) racial warriors, assemble supplies for and keep up correspondence with imprisoned racial POWs, and be cheerleaders for the aggressive actions of their male counterparts (Blee 2002, 2012; also Ferber 1998).

COMPARING THE USA AND EUROPE

There are significant similarities between the gendered nature of the far right in European nations and the USA. One is the growing importance of—and the related emergence of tensions around—women's place in far-right politics. In the USA, women's long-time marginality in racist movements is being eroded by the growing numbers of women in the far right. The women recruited into these groups, however, often expect to be regarded as full and serious comrades in the struggle for white supremacism. It is not uncommon for these U.S. women to challenge the men who oppose their presence in racist movements or who try to consign them to marginal roles. Some parts of the European far right show similar patterns of gender diversity and tension. Valerie Dubslaff in this volume argues that both German and French far-right parties have seen an influx of women in recent years, with variable changes in women's integration and gender politics in the two countries. In both US and European far-right parties and groups, women are rarely in official leadership positions, although some far-right parties, like Golden Dawn in Greece, described by Maria Alvanou in this volume, have a strong female presence. Moreover, the media and electoral popularity of Marine Le Pen in the French National Front may change the pattern of female marginality in the European far right in the future. The few women leaders in the far right—and here Marine Le Pen is no exception—have been depicted as less marginal, scary, and dangerous than the typical image of right-wing extremists, a handy portrayal for far-right parties that seek support from the political mainstream.

A second commonality is the complicated link between womanhood and religion in the far right. In both Europe and the USA, far-right leaders have attacked religious communities they oppose by proclaiming that they are protecting women's rights by doing so. The US far right has consistently regarded Jews as a primary enemy, in part by claiming that Jewish businessmen sexually prey on their non-Jewish white women employees. Attacking Jews is thus a way to protect the sexual integrity of white women. [A similar argument is made about African American men who are considered sexual predators in all spheres of life.] Modern European far-right groups similarly attack European Muslims as importing anti-women practices like veiling and subordination. In this interpretation, curbing the power of Islam becomes a way of protecting white European-descent women. Miquel Ramos and Frauke Büttner describe in this volume how Spanish rightists link equal rights for women (implicitly, non-Islam women) to the battle against Islam in modern Spain. Similarly, the rightist Freedom Party in Austria, as Carina Klammer and Judith Goetz show in this volume, employs gender as a propaganda tool by arguing that the party can protect non-Islamic women from being forced to adopt Muslim practices like veiling and forced marriage. White women are not necessarily portrayed in opposition to religion, however. Some far-right movements have historically had significant links to Christian churches, especially in Spain. And, recently, far-right movements on both continents have promulgated various forms of spirituality, including ancient Nordic religions, with associations to rightist womanhood. A particularly striking example is Anikó Félix's study in this volume of the Hungarian radical right's construction of the racist spiritual woman who traces her ancestry to a national pagan goddess and to a Hungarian (not Jewish) version of Jesus's mother Mary.

A third similarity is the complex role of sexuality in the far right. For the most part, far-right movements are decidedly heterosexual and consider lesbians, gay men, transgendered persons, and others with minority sexual expressions to be abhorrent, sick, and deviant. Groups that trace their ideological heritage to World War II-era German Nazism, for example, commonly express venomous hatred toward sexual minorities that they regard as a degenerate group that is holding back the full exercise of supremacy by white Aryans. Among a few far-right groups in both the USA and Europe, however, the presence of gay persons is tolerated within limits (Waldner et al. 2006). One rightist group in England, for example, allows gay contingents at their anti-Muslim rallies, insisting that gay groups are strategic allies against the threat of unchecked immigration of fundamentalist Muslims (Goodwin 2013; Southern Poverty Law Center 2000; Treadwell and Garland 2011). A commonality across many far-right groups, however, is an explicit or implied link between enemy women (Jewish, Muslim, non-white) and dangerous sexuality. Enemy women are commonly regarded as temptresses who seek to pollute the nation (or the race) by seducing far-right men.

Just as interesting as their similarities are the significant differences between European far-right groups and those in the USA. One difference is structural. The nations of Europe have a great variety of far-right groups, from loosely organized skinheads to electoral parties, while the USA today has no real far-right political party. Indeed, the US far right generally stays away from electoral politics in all forms. There are several implications of this difference. In European nations with far-right parties, it is easier to estimate the strength of this political tendency by examining membership and electoral votes. And becoming a member of a far-right party involves a clear decision in which a person must commit to the explicit platform and goals of the party. In the non-electoral far right in the USA, by contrast, membership is quite vague and difficult to estimate. People rarely join far-right movements in any official way. Rather, they drift into such affiliations by hanging around with current affiliates. As a result, participation in US far-right groups is often quite erratic and people can be associated with a group for a considerable time before they become fully aware of its ideology or agenda. Another implication is that far-right parties in Europe have networks that link them to similar parties in other countries, as well as established opportunities to interact with parties with similar political ideas through parliament and media events. There are no similarly established networks among the far-right groups in the USA. Rather, their contacts with like-minded comrades in other groups happen at occasional gatherings, rallies, and meetings, although these are also opportunities for conflict and betrayal among leaders of these groups. Research is quite fragmentary; it may be the case that less organized groups are more receptive to women members than official far-right parties, but further study is needed.

A second difference is the face that the far right presents to the public. In the USA, most far-right groups have little interest in making themselves attractive to the general public. Most groups do not openly recruit strangers, but rather bring people into the group through personal contacts, in an effort to ensure that new members are trustworthy and not affiliated with the police. US groups thus use their public messages largely to spread ideas of white supremacism to new sectors of the white population and to create fear among non-whites. Their messages are thus generally raw, provocative, and angry. In Europe, the presence of far-right parties means that there is a public face of the far right in some (but certainly not all) nations that is less threatening and seemingly more mainstream. And these public messages can be associated with women, linking women's responsibility for family care to the far right's effort to care for the European population.

A third difference is the nature of the perceived enemy. In the USA, it is Jews and non-whites. In Europe, the enemy is increasingly framed as Islam, but also immigrants from Asia and Africa. European far-right groups thus have a greater ability to call for broad coalitions across gender, race, religions (except Islam), class, and even sexuality in opposition to the threat of unchecked immigration and militant Islam. In the USA, the pool of potential allies is much smaller, generally only like-minded heterosexual, working, or lower-middle-class whites of European descent.

Finally, the broader political context is very different in Europe and the USA. Many nations of Europe have significant histories and current formations of progressive politics and broad acceptance of gender equality. Far-right parties thus need to operate within those political parameters. Eeva Luhtakallio and Tuukka Ylä-Anttila in this volume show that a significant minority of women in the radical right populist Finn Party support policies such as state-provided social benefits and gay adoption rights (far more than Finns Party men), reflecting the larger national support for gender equality in Finland. However, Diana Mulinari and Anders Neergaard in this volume find a different pattern in Sweden where the rightist Swedish Democrats hold a strictly antifeminist stance in a nation with a widespread belief in gender equality (also Kimmel 2007). The USA has a much more politically conservative population than those of northern Europe, and acceptance of gender equality is uneven across the country. A decades-long effort to enshrine women's equality in the US Constitution failed when it failed to attract sufficient support from the states, and women's rights to abortion, birth control, equal pay, and a workplace free of harassment have found mixed support in the courts and legislatures of US states and the federal government (Schreiber 2012). Thus, in contrast to those in the Scandinavian countries, far-right groups in the USA do not necessarily counter the social norms of their audiences when they support gender traditionalism or suggest the desirability of racial separation or hierarchies.

FUTURE RESEARCH

Studies of gender and the far right have followed a similar trajectory in Europe and the USA. Before 1990, almost no scholars considered women a significant part of the far right in either region. Studies of women in politics focused almost exclusively on women's participation in progressive and feminist politics, such as suffrage, anti-war, lesbian/gay, socialist, anti-racist/antifascist, and anti-colonial movements. Correspondingly, studies of the far right focused almost exclusively on men in these movements. Occasionally, such studies made brief mention of the existence of women in far-right politics, but these women were generally regarded as ancillary actors or auxiliaries to the real movement. Men were considered the only important political actors in the far right, an assumption that seemed to be confirmed by the near monopoly of official leadership positions by rightist men.

The first wave of feminist work changed the picture of women on the far right. Scholars in Germany, Italy, Great Britain, and the USA, among other places, showed that women were involved in a variety of far-right groups, from fascist parties to right-wing terrorist groups. This initial set of feminist studies moved beyond simply rectifying the earlier omission of women from scholarship on the right. Rather, these studies charted the ways in which extreme-right parties and movements were themselves gendered. Scholars documented how the far-right marginalized and excluded women from positions of significant power and how these groups built on and refined an ideology of white womanhood that promoted both subservience to white men and superiority over non-white men and women.

These studies also showed that some far-right groups had used proto-feminist or women's rights rhetoric to bring women into their movements by promising that agendas of white supremacy, anti-immigration, or fascism could be empowering for them.

The next wave of feminist work expanded the geographic scope of early feminist scholars of the far right beyond the global North. These studies looked at women's participation in rightist movements in the Middle East, Africa, Asia, and Latin America. These also expanded research on right-wing women beyond single nations to compare the place of women on the far right across national borders, time, and variants of rightist philosophy. Broadly, this wave of research confirmed the general association of far-right politics with ideologies of gender essentialism and a stark divide between the public world (mostly men's) and the private world (mostly women's). The increasing scope of these works also introduced important complications. They showed the difficulty of comparing right-wing movements across borders since the very concept of far-right politics is a Western notion that assumes the existence of such political features as a relatively stable state, democratic structures against which the far right battles, and some separation of state and religion. Without these characteristics, defining the far right is difficult. As Fallon and Moreau (2012) point out in their study of women in Sub-Saharan Africa, it is difficult to decide whether to consider as right wing those African situations in which women join dictatorial, state-supporting organizations in military states in which women have little or no opportunity to avoid participating. Similarly, it is unclear whether scholars should consider as far right those women's organizations that support fundamentalist, authoritarian, and theocratic statist goals of militant Islamic movements.

Today, work on women in the far right has moved in new directions as the chapters in this volume so nicely illustrate. First, important work in the USA, Europe, and elsewhere is examining how far-right ideas, practices, and plans circulate across national borders and the extent to which women are agents of that circulation. This volume shows how ideas in the far right have moved extensively across national borders within Europe. Other research has studied the increasing transnationalism of some segments of the far right, from the spread of Pan-Aryan ideologies on the internet to the transmission of weapons and money through international networks of white supremacists or extreme rightists. Second, scholars are studying fissures and breakdowns in the public/private dichotomy that has traditionally established women as lesser members of far-right groups.

New work is exploring how far-right movements use private concerns, such as family or femininity, to advance political agendas. This work also examines how far-right movements wrestle with the contradictions of being hostile to the existing state while advocating state action. Examples of this are European far-right efforts to convince the government to curb immigration or the birthrate of immigrants, or US racist movements that advocate freedom for individuals on the topic of gun ownership but sharp constraints on individual freedom in matters of sexual preference. Third, there is significant attention paid to the political complications of many far-right movements, such as the simultaneous rightist and leftist politics of both pro- and anti-militant Islamic movements in Europe or the simultaneous feminist and antifeminist politics of both racist and antiracist movements in the USA.

There is much that needs further study on gender and the far right. Certainly, studies with a broader spatial scope and more rigorous comparison of far-right movements across borders and over time would be welcome. Closer-up studies of the far right, using observational, ethnographic, and direct interviewing methods, are also essential. Many studies of the far right draw exclusively on evidence found in the writings or speeches of these activists, but such information can be distorted for public consumption and highly misleading. Additional work on men and masculinity is needed as well, in order to fully understand the gendered nature of the far right. There is a set of studies that point out the masculinist quality of much of the extreme right, noting the common expressions of conventional masculinity through anger, aggression, domination of women, other men, and nature, assertions of leadership, and violence. Yet, masculinity exists in other forms in some parts of the far right, in the form of male expressions of close bonding with other men, fear, performative displays, and submission. Scholars should also explore emerging forms of far-right organization and affiliation, such as on-line networks and lone wolf operatives who develop far-right beliefs and sometimes commit acts of violence without actual contact with far-right groups (Blee 2014; Southern Poverty Law Center 2015). Andrea Dauber's examination of the far right in Great Britain in this volume shows the importance of the on-line presence of women supporters to promote the movement through such internet platforms as YouTube and the social media site Facebook. And finally, scholarship in the future should consider more deeply the limits and boundaries of gender in far-right politics, not simply its existence. As Renate Bitzan argues in this volume, scholars need to understand both "gender-*specific* [and] gender-*unspecific* aspects" of the far right (also Ware 1992). Feminist scholars have established that gender is important in the far right, but have not yet determined what aspects of the far right are the most affected by gendered ideas and relationships and in which aspects gender is less important. It is possible, for example, that gender matters a lot for recruitment, but less for maintaining affiliation over time. Or that gender is significant in far-right political parties but less significant in far-right movements. This is a new frontier for future scholars.

REFERENCES

Barkun, Michael. 1994. *Religion and the Racist Right: The Origins of the Christian Identity Movement.* Chapel Hill: University of North Carolina Press.

Bhatia, Rajani. 2004. Green or Brown? White Nativist Environmental Movements. In *Home-Grown Hate: Gender and Organized Racism*, ed. Abby Ferber, 205–225. New York: Routledge.

Blazak, Randy. 2004. 'Getting It': The Role of Women in Male Desistance from Hate Groups. In *Home-Grown Hate: Gender and Organized Racism*, ed. Abby Ferber, 154–171. New York: Routledge.

Blee, Kathleen. 1991. *Women of the Klan: Racism and Gender in the 1920s.* Berkeley: University of California Press.

———. 1999. Racist Activism and Apocalyptic/Millennial Thinking. *Journal of Millennial Studies* 2(1). http://www.mille.org/publications/journal.html

———. 2002. *Inside Organized Racism: Women in the Hate Movement.* Berkeley: University of California Press.

———. 2012. Does Gender Matter in the United States Far-Right? *Politics, Religion & Ideology* 13(2): 253–265.

———. 2014. Why Do Racists and Anti-Semites Kill? Op-ed at CNN.com, April 15.

———. 2016. Personal Effects from Far-Right Activism. In *The Consequences of Social Movements: People, Policies, and Institutions*, ed. Lorenzo Bosi, Marco Giugni, and Katrin Uba, 66–84. New York: Oxford University Press.

Blee, Kathleen, and Kimberly A. Creasap. 2010. Conservative and Right-Wing Movements. *Annual Review of Sociology* 36: 269–286.

Bonilla-Silva, Eduardo. 2006. *Racism Without Racists: Color-Blind Racism and the Persistence of Racial Inequality in the United States.* Lanham, MD: Rowman and Littlefield.

Cooter, Amy Beth. 2006. Neo-Nazi Normalization: The Skinhead Movement and Integration into Normative Structures. *Sociological Inquiry* 76(2): 145–165.

Cunningham, David. 2013. *Klansville, U.S.A.: The Rise and Fall of the Civil Rights Era Ku Klux Klan.* New York: Oxford University Press.

Daniels, Jessie. 2009. *Cyber Racism: White Supremacy Online and the New Attack on Civil Rights*. Lanham, MD: Rowman & Littlefield Publishers.

Dobratz, Betty A., and Stephanie Shanks-Meile. 1997. *"White Power, White Pride!": The White Separatist Movement in the United States*. Independence, KY: Twayne Publishers.

———. 2004. The White Separatist Movement: Worldviews on Gender, Feminism, Nature, and Change. In *Home-Grown Hate: Gender and Organized Racism*, ed. Abby Ferber, 108–137. New York: Routledge.

Dobratz, Betty, and Lisa Waldner. 2012. Repertoires of Contention: White Separatist Views on the Use of Violence and Leaderless Resistance. *Mobilization: An International Quarterly* 17(1): 49–66.

Durham, Martin. 2007. *White Rage: The Extreme Right and American Politics*. New York: Taylor & Francis.

Fallon, Kathleen, and Julie Moreau. 2012. Righting Africa? Contextualizing Notons of Women's Right-Wing Activism in Sub-Saharan Africa. In *Women of the Right: Comparisons and Interplay Across Borders*, ed. Kathleen M. Blee, and Sandra McGee Deutsch, 68–80. University Park: Pennsylvania State University Press.

Ferber, Abby. 1998. *White Man Falling: Race, Gender, and White Supremacy*. Oxford, UK: Rowman and Littlefield.

———. 2004. Introduction. In *Home-Grown Hate: Gender and Organized Racism*, ed. Abby Ferber, 1–18. New York: Routledge.

Futrell, Robert, Pete Simi, and Simon Gottschalk. 2006. Understanding Music in Movements: The White Power Music Scene. *The Sociological Quarterly* 47(2): 275–304.

Goodwin, Matthew. 2013. The Roots of Extremism: The English Defence League and the Counter-Jihad Challenge. Chatham House. http://www.openbriefing.org/docs/rootsofextremism.pdf

Kaplan, Jeffrey. 1997. Leaderless Resistance. *Terrorism and Political Violence* 9(3): 80–95.

Kimmel, Michael. 2007. Racism as Adolescent Male Rite of Passage: Ex-Nazis in Scandinavia. *Journal of Contemporary Ethnography* 36(2): 202–218.

King, R.D., and M.F. Weiner. 2007. Group Position, Collective Threat, and American Anti-Semitism. *Social Problems* 54(1): 47–77.

Michael, George. 2006. RAHOWA! A History of the World Church of the Creator. *Terrorism and Political Violence* 18(4): 561–583.

Perry, Barbara. 2004. White Genocide: White Supremacists and the Politics of Reproduction. In *Home-Grown Hate: Gender and Organized Racism*, ed. Abby Ferber, 75–95. New York: Routledge.

Rogers, JoAnn, and Jacquelyn Litt. 2004. Normalizing Racism: A Case Study of Motherhood in White Supremacy. In *Home-Grown Hate: Gender and Organized Racism*, ed. Abby Ferber, 97–112. New York: Routledge.

Schreiber, Ronnee. 2012. *Righting Feminism: Conservative Women and American Politics*. New York: Oxford University Press.

Simi, Pete, and Robert Futrell. 2010. *American Swastika: Inside the White Power Movement's Hidden Spaces of Hate*. New York: Rowman & Littlefield.

Southern Poverty Law Center. 2000. Gay Aryan Nations Members Are the Fringe of the Fringe. *Intelligence Report* 100(Fall).

———. 2015. *The Age of the Wolf: A Study of the Rise of Lone Wolf and Leaderless Resistance Terrorism*. Montgomery, AL: SPLC.

Treadwell, James, and Jon Garland. 2011. Masculinity, Marginalization and Violence: A Case Study of the English Defence League. *British Journal of Criminology* 51(4): 621–634.

Waldner, Lisa K., Heather Martin, and Lyndsay Capeder. 2006. Ideology of Gay Racialist Skinheads and Stigma Management Techniques. *Journal of Political and Military Sociology* 34(1): 165–184.

Ware, Vron. 1992. *Beyond the Pale: White Women, Racism, and History*. London: Verso Books.

Zeskind, Leonard. 2009. *Blood and Politics: The History of the White Nationalist Movement from the Margins to the Mainstream*. New York: Macmillan.

PART III

Media Discourse on Gender

"Mohair Berets": Media Representations of Elderly Right-Wing Women and Aestheticization of Age in Poland

Kateryna Novikova

INTRODUCTION

Ageing is inevitable. More or less inevitably, there are various biased inter-pretations of ageing and its influence on social life; both ageism and anti-ageist discourses use ageing processes and actors in a way they cannot resist (e.g. Coupland and Coupland 1999). There are certain socially con-structed age norms, closely connected with other identifications, especially gender and religion, as well as political views. Even if it is not only age that determines political views, elderly people are considered to be more conservative, following the stereotype that "older people are set in their ways". Yet the so-called ageing-conservatism hypothesis has been proved false in several studies (Morgan and Kunkel 2011, 229–230). The full story is obviously more complex, especially in terms of its popular percep-tion and representation in the public discourse. The media representations of elderly women in Poland that suggest conservative, right-wing or even fundamentalist Catholic political views are reproduced widely in popular discourses, especially thanks to the internet and new media. The intention of this chapter is to present and analyse the main discursive strategies con-cerning right-wing elderly female activists and their engagement in various

K. Novikova (✉)
Alcide de Gasperi University of Euroregional Economy, Jozefow/Warsaw, Poland

© The Author(s) 2017
M. Köttig et al. (eds.), *Gender and Far Right Politics in Europe*,
DOI 10.1007/978-3-319-43533-6_14

fields. The study of age and gender factors is enhanced by a consideration of other factors, such as religiosity, sense of belonging, national identity and especially appearance and dress, which emerge as key signifiers in the discursive construction of the image of elderly right-wing female activists.

THE CONTEXT

The post-socialist transformation period, and later Polish accession to and development within the EU, define the socio-cultural and political context of the issue studied here. There are other important factors, such as a difficult historical legacy, disturbing political controversies or the specific role of the Catholic Church. Nevertheless, an extensive analysis of the background situation is not our goal. The luminous works of Kopecky and Mudde (2012), Pańkowski (2010), Porter-Szucs (2011), Staniszkis (2001) and others are full of valuable analyses of transformation, politics and the relations of the state and the Church with the extreme right wing of the Polish political scene and its voters.

The discursive construction of the power of elderly female far-right followers and activists started within the mass media discourse. It was later followed by political declarations by both adversaries and representatives of the radical right-wing segment of the Polish political scene. Among the sources for analysis there are popular dailies (*Gazeta Wyborcza, Rzeczpospolita, Dziennik Gazeta Prawna, Polska The Times*, etc.) and their internet information and blogging mirrors that have presented various sides of the "mohair" phenomenon from an ironic or even critical viewpoint. However, the term "mohair berets" became popular not only because of this professional media coverage. Its popularity also grew thanks to the mindful internet users who have warned about the negative features of the phenomenon on internet forums and personal blogs. The few academic studies of the phenomenon of "mohair berets" that have been conducted in Poland also take both the popular media and the internet as their sources (e.g. Szarota 2008, Koscianska 2008). The role of popular culture is also crucial here. There are certain popular songs and artistic performances that can be regarded as an artistic battle against these new enemies.

MOHEROWE BERETY

In the Polish popular discourse, the elderly ladies whose political views are defined as conservative right, frequently nationalist and with a strong Catholic component have been metonymically named "mohair berets"

(Thel 2011). The mohair beret is a warm winter headwear typical for elderly women, especially women from poorer social backgrounds in Poland (Marciniak 2011, 137). Porter-Szucs refers to the newspaper article from 2004 where the term was used for the first time: "the expression *moherowe berety* (mohair berets)" was used "as an insulting term for poor, elderly, devout women" (Porter-Szucs 2011, 446). In English the term appeared a year later, also in a newspaper and on its internet page (Kohn 2005). The Polish use of this ironic term starts from the *Rzeczpospolita* newspaper article "Labyrinths of the Parish Priest" by Maja Narbutt, who coined this expression to describe "old ladies" that "have their eyes fixed on Father Jankowski—an outstanding Church dignitary connected with *Solidarność* from the 1980 ties, and they hang on his every word. Rumour has it that the prelate has his own legion of *mohair berets* in Gdańsk" (Narbutt 2004).[1] Legion is a term suggesting if not yet dangerous, still powerful women, similar to the British or specifically Scottish conservative *blue rinse brigades* that represent a "homogeneous group of elderly women with white or bluish-white hair" (Bednarek 2012, 159). It is important to emphasize that these elderly women are seen as a threatening social power only when they come together as part of "a voting bloc"; one individual elderly woman who listens to Radio Maryja is harmless, but hundreds of such women are dangerous (Robbins-Ruszkowski 2015, 271).

RADIO AS A POLITICAL AGENT AND A REFERENCE GROUP

It is difficult to define exactly the individual political preferences of the elderly ladies, let alone to forecast their electoral choices, because of cognitive closure issues and the enduring confusion between leftist economic and right-wing identity dimensions of their political views and subsequent vulnerability to populist slogans (Golec 2011; Golec de Zavala et al. 2010; Pankowski 2010). However, "mohair berets" (also *moheretki*–"mohairets"—or *radiomaryjki*) have been considered to belong to the typical audience of a specific medium. That medium is the Catholic Radio Maryja which is broadly considered "the radical centre for the lost, utopian right and nationalists, linked to the interwar period far right", as the researcher has put it (Osłowski 2009, 166–171). The extremely important role of religion and the Catholic Church in Poland on the public scene and in the media discourses has been extensively covered and compared to the situation in other countries by numerous Polish and European sociologists and political scientists, including Aleksandrowicz (2005), Karolak and Karolak (2013), Krzemiński (2009), Lundskow (2008), Porter-Szucs (2011), Turowski (2005) and others.

The radio named after the Virgin Mary was founded by the Redemptorist Tadeusz Rydzyk in 1991 and very soon became popular as a "Catholic Voice in Your Home" (Krzemiński 2009, 7). Later, the so-called "Family of Radio Maryja" (*Rodzina Radia Maryja*) appeared, "a mass movement organized on a religious basis, with several hundred thousand active members, the majority of them being elderly women", as well as the university with undergraduate and graduate departments to educate "a new generation of nationalist cadres", as Pankowski and Kornak put it (Mudde 2005, 156).

According to the Polish National Broadcasting Council (KRRiT), in 2012 in the capital city of Warsaw 2.7 % of listeners tuned into Radio Maryja, giving it the twelfth place among all the stations (Trochimczuk 2013, 5). At the same time, it was in third place among listeners aged 65–75 with 10.6 % and in general was 2.3 times more popular among women than among men (Trochimczuk 2013, 7, 10). According to the audience rating from the third quarter of 2015, Radio Maryja had 2 % out of 74.5 % radio listeners in Poland, or just over half a million people (Trochimczuk 2015). In the National Broadcasting Council report, Radio Maryja was described as a social and religious (Catholic) radio station with information, documentary and religious programmes, prayers and relaxing music, mostly religious, classical and of Polish origin (Trochimczuk 2013, 16). This radio station was the only one in Poland where more than half of the listeners were female, out of whom more than 40 % were 60–75 years old. For all other stations, elderly listeners were the smallest group with around 15 % (Trochimczuk 2009, 4, 7–8). In the case of Radio Maryja, the elderly listeners were mostly women and almost half of all the listeners were retired and lived in rural areas (Trochimczuk 2009, 9, 11, 15). In 2009, over one third of the listeners of Radio Maryja earned between 601 and 1000 Polish zlotys, which is less than the minimum wage (Trochimczuk 2009, 13).

Taking into account such demographic data, the character of Radio Maryja, its message and especially its listeners represent very specific phenomena. In critical academic research, the moment when the radio was invented is considered to be a "watershed moment for the institutionalisation of the racist extremist ideology as one of the key points of the far right ideologies along with anti-Semitism, ultra-nationalism, ethnic homogeneity or xenophobia" (Langenbacher and Schellenberg 2011, 17; Mudde 2005, 157, 165). Other researchers do not define Radio Maryja and its active listeners as the extreme right. The listeners play an important role in providing indirect support for specific right-wing political parties known for their nationalist, religious and anti-Semitic rhetoric (Karolak and Karolak 2013, 138–139). There have been several other studies of Radio Maryja and its place in Polish society and in the public discourse (Krzemiński 2009). They have revealed the controversial nature of the widespread negative opinions in the media and popular discourse. Such opinions and stereotypes concern both the worldviews represented by the listeners as well as the listeners themselves, especially the female elderly segment.

"Mohair" stigmatization, however, is not only considered to be a stereotypic derogatory expression but is paradoxically accepted as a part of group identity and values. The same term has been used in both denouncing and laudatory contexts (Klimczak 2005). The phrase "mohair berets" rather quickly became an almost normal political term for a certain "mohair worldview", a sort of discursive community. The strong self-identification most probably weakened its qualities as invective. The leader of the "mohair berets" is Tadeusz Rydzyk, one of the most popular Catholic priests and the owner of Radio Maryja and other mass media. He once exclaimed at the conservative Catholic congress: "I see mohair berets! Long live the mohair coalition!" (Hołub 2005). The latter term for a conservative coalition was coined by Donald Tusk in his critical address in November 2005. Some researchers point out anti-women comments by Father Rydzyk among many other controversial ones, including references to well-known public activists and politicians (Marciniak 2011, 126–127). This attitude certainly does not reflect that of his loyal female listeners and activists.

Media Representations and Exclusion

The "mohair" worldview mainly represents the older part of female conservative power in Poland. As one of the researchers on experiencing and imagining old age in Poland puts it, "the link between older women and the conservative nationalism of *PiS* [the Law and Justice party] took the figure of the *moherowe berety*" (Robbins 2013, 17). Therefore, the representation of elderly right-wing women in the public discourse touches on the problem of age discrimination and ageism and in this case also stigmatization in the public discourse. Different discourses on ageing focus on moral and political considerations, but they are not consistent, as Coupland and Coupland point out. The authors underline the need for differentiation in studies of so-called "elderly people". "There is an urgent need to recognise many areas and processes of prejudice and disadvantage that do threaten the self-esteem and quality of life of many older people". Only after careful differentiation can age discrimination be more seriously analysed without any "grandiose moral assessment" (Coupland and Coupland 1999, 177). Societal ageism, however, has a homogenizing character, especially when additional criteria are applied, such as gender or social status. This can lead to the public opinion that all "poor elderly women" are right-wing believers, activists or even devotees. Therefore, ageist prejudices about the nature and experiences of elderly women create "unpleasant images of older people which subtly undermine their personal value and worth" (Coupland and Coupland 1999, 179).

The most important aspect here is the role of ageist assumptions in structuring not only the social status of older people and specifically women but their expectations of themselves or moral personhood, to use Robbins' term (Robbins 2013, 21–22). So many people actually believe that their power, rights and privileges decrease with age. This problem is closely connected to the modern focus on youth, its productivity and independence, so effectively advocated in the media and popular culture. In fact, various ageist assumptions and discrimination of the elderly in general are naturally accepted by elderly people, more than any other "isms" (Coupland and Coupland 1999, 180). Researchers present a natural explanation, which is the lack of strong intragroup identity among elderly people, despite the popular stereotypic image of an exceptionally homogeneous group of solitary individuals. In this picture one can easily recognize the "mohair legion" of right-wing elderly female listeners of Radio Maryja, called "the Family", who strongly self-identify with it (Marciniak 2011, 126). Belonging to the "mohair berets" means being excluded from society, almost marginalized, but closely associated with similar individuals (Robbins 2013, 158–159; Novikova 2015, 67). Exclusion, however, does not apply to the Catholic part of society, especially the Church and its officials. On the 2006 pilgrimage to Jasna Gora, one of these women spoke about the sad problem of exclusion, and the classification of strong Catholic believers as "second class citizens, worse Poland, Poland of the mohair berets, provincial, unfashionable Poland" and at the same time emphasized that "this Poland has not denied Christ, has not followed fashion [...] even during the worst oppression it was loyal to God and Fatherland" (*Jasna Góra: XIV pielgrzymka Radia Maryja* 2006).

Age Stereotypes and Aestheticization

The aesthetic dimension of the mohair beret, that is, a wool cap, relates it mainly to the older generation: it's cheap, easy to do-it-yourself, fashion-independent (or rather old-fashioned), asexual and thus a characteristic of old age in the mass consciousness. As a Polish linguist has admitted, this term was very offensive and rather primitive, especially in the beginning, as terms referring to other people's look, attire or lameness often are (Kamińska-Szmaj and Urbanek 2007). Because it is worn by conservative elderly ladies in Poland, it is frequently mockingly endowed with supernatural powers, such as the ability to receive the Radio Maryja signal by its so-called antenna (the short element at the top of the beret). In general, a mohair beret is considered old-fashioned, not in terms of retro which can be attractive, but in terms of age, ugliness and the lack of sexuality of elderly people. The mohair beret has thus become an integral part of politically involved lookism, closely related to ageism in the popular discourse. In 2009, miniature berets became a symbol, a pin on the clothes of the pilgrims to Jasna Góra (one of the most famous summer pilgrimage destinations), and Father Rydzyk asked his loyal female radio audience to knit them because "those berets have a double meaning. One should be proud of being a person, a believer, a Pole. So the berets are a way to say to people that they should not feel bad, whatever people say". As one of the priests commented when activists handed out the small berets to pilgrims: "we would like to demonstrate our connection to Christian and national values, to Virgin Mary, to the Catholic Church" (*Rodzina Radia Maryja z pielgrzymką na Jasnej Górze* 2009).

This gave rise to many sarcastic articles, posts and comments (e.g. United Colours of Benetton) (*Ojciec Rydzyk ogłasza moherowy wyścig zbrojeń* 2009). There were also references to the "mohair beret" as a sort of organizational outfit (Szarota 2008, 168). A couple of months after promotion of the term in the media discourse, there were some pseudo-economic reports on the difficulties of the "mohair trade market" with obvious headlines, for example, "the end of the mohair beret" (Stangret 2006). Another example is that the whole city where Radio Maryja and other connected media are located is labelled "mohair city".

Other examples of the specific discourse on elderly ladies wearing mohair berets and professing specific political views can be found in satirical pop songs written and performed by rock bands ("Big Cyc"), as well as in comedy sketches where actors dress in mohair berets and behave as the artists, and probably the whole audience, think old ladies behave (e.g. "Neonówka") (Kamiński Łukasz and Alex Kłoś 2005). There have also been art performances, some openly referring to the political provocation, for example the costume ball "Funky Moher", where everyone was expected to wear something made of mohair (Czajkowska 2006).

There was also a comedy play performed in one of the Warsaw theatres under the title "Upiór w moherze" ("Phantom of the Mohair"), echoing the Polish translation of the "Phantom of the Opera" (Upiór w operze"), and the plot included a conflict between a lonely homosexual young man and his elderly and ugly "mohair beret" neighbour, also lonely, who was presented as a very conservative religious zealot (Szczygielski and Rozhin 2012). The crucial fact here is that all these jokes and parodies have become socially acceptable. Voices trying to change the situation and calling for more respect for elderly people are relatively rare. Sometimes, in satirical cartoons, the elderly ladies are shown as envying younger women and girls their youth. One such cartoon, called "The Monthly Guard", shows an angry "mohair beret" lady chasing a journalist, while explaining that she is aggressive only once a month, obviously a double reference to a female physiological condition and the official mourning on the 10th of every month in commemoration of the crash of the Polish Air Force Tu-154 and the death of the Polish president and many Polish state officials in 2010.

Mohair Warriors

The catchphrase "loyal warriors" is strongly connected with the term mentioned earlier: a "legion of mohair berets". It highlights the warlike nature of the circumstances which stimulate active and continuous participation. The beret is still part of a military uniform in the public consciousness. Other military expressions used to refer to the actions of the "mohair berets" include "the mohair ranks", "serried ranks", "mohair terrorists", "grannies go on the warpath every Sunday", "crusade", "revolution", "drinking tea then fighting evil", "mohair arms race", "mohair ninja", "retired squadron" or "mohair guards". The convergence of gender roles brought about by old age seems to have a strong influence on interpretations of the role of the "mohair berets", who are regarded as warriors despite their gender, age and health. It has been said in the media that it is the first headwear to divide Poland into two halves, like two armies at war. However, the division is not clear at all.

In one study of the "mohair berets" phenomenon, the author states that "the huge mohair beret is overloaded, almost splitting, because according to the latest statistics it contains almost 70 % of the Polish population: a 24-year-old student, a 30-year-old lawyer, a famous sociologist, a middle-aged philosopher, a social activist and an 80-year-old lady Aldona listening to Radio Maryja" (Szarota 2008, 171).

Generally, the mainstream media explanation is rather monothematic: manipulation with a touch of lookism, as one of the left liberal weekly magazines has put it. The "mohair berets" and the largely speculative supremacy of Radio Maryja in Polish society are referred to in the headline: "Rydzyk-nation: from cradle to grave". "One does not need anything else to be happy. Father Rydzyk is enough. He will tell you what to think, watch, eat, read, and sing. Over the last twenty years the Toruń Redemptorist has been educating Polish people because his main goal is to create a completely new mankind" (Święchowicz 2011, 6).

Conclusion

The "mohair beret" as the attribute of a loyal female warrior has become the symbol of certain political views and values of a right-wing character, closely connected to the Church and its media institutions. In public discourses on the other side of the political scene, this term is associated with a certain female appearance and symbolic violence. The "mohair beret" has developed not only into a dominant media stereotype but also a powerful discursive construction of politicized gender and aestheticized age. The elderly conservative right-wing women who wear such berets are considered eccentric or even comic figures, and anyone wearing mohair headwear is stigmatized because of the symbolic meaning it has acquired. This has led to exceptionally negative "ageist" and lookist portrayals, and the moral vilification of elderly ladies as political belligerents, as well as their disrespectful treatment in everyday practice, while media discourses and social representations have failed to counteract this development.

NOTE

1. All the original Polish texts are translated into English by the author.

REFERENCES

Aleksandrowicz, Dariusz. 2005. Post-Communist Transition and Catholicism in Poland. In *Democracy and the Post-totalitarian Experience*, ed. Leszek Koczanowicz, and Beth J. Singer, 23–38. Amsterdam: Rodopi.

Bednarek, Antje. 2012. 'Handbagging' the Feminisation Thesis? Reflections on Women in the Scottish Conservative and Unionist Party. In *Whatever Happened to Tory Scotland?* ed. David Torrance, 149–169. Edinburgh: Edinburgh University Press.

Coupland, Nikolas, and Justine Coupland. 1999. Ageing, Ageism and Anti-Ageism. Moral Stance in Geriatric Medical Discourse. In *Language and Communication in Old Age: Multidisciplinary Perspectives*, ed. Heidi Hamilton, 177–208. New York & London: Garland.

Czajkowska, Agnieszka. 2006. Artyści organizują moherowy bal przebierańców. Gazeta Wyborcza, February 07. http://wroclaw.wyborcza.pl/wroclaw/1,35771,3152365.html

Golec, Agnieszka. 2001. Konserwatyzm polityczny a próba poznawczego domknięcia w badaniach polskich. *Studia Psychologiczne* XXXIX: 43–60.

Golec De Zavala, Agnieszka, Aleksandra Cislak, and Elzbieta Wesolowska. 2010. Political Conservatism, Need for Cognitive Closure, and Intergroup Hostility. *Political Psychology* 31(4): 521–541.

Hołub, Jacek. 2005. 10 tys. osób świętuje urodziny Radia Maryja. *Gazeta.pl*. Accessed 14 December 2015. http://wiadomosci.gazeta.pl/kraj/1,34308, 3052995.html

Jasna Góra: XIV pielgrzymka Radia Maryja. 2006. Accessed 20 January 2015. http://www.radiomaryja.pl.eu.org/arch/2006-20xtys.html

Kamińska-Szmaj, Irena, and Mariusz Urbanek. 2007. Zapluty karzeł wiecznie żywy. *Gazeta Wyborcza*, October 17. http://wyborcza.pl/1,76842,4585896.html

Kamiński, Łukasz, and Alex Kłoś. 2005. Moherowe berety w twórczości młodych artystów. Gazeta Wyborcza, November 20. http://wiadomosci.gazeta.pl/kraj/1,34309,3024248.html

Karolak, Magdalena, and Nikodem Karolak. 2013. Globalization and Religious Resurgence: A Comparative Study of Bahrain and Poland. In *Experiencing Globalization: Region in Contemporary Context*, ed. Derrick M. Nault, Dei Dawei, Evangelos Voulgarakis, Rab Paterson, and Cesar Andres-Miguel Suva, 129–152. London & New York: Anthem Press.

Klimczak, Arkadiusz. 2005. Moherowe szaleństwo, czyli co uwiera Polaków w głowy. *Ekumenizm.pl*. Accessed 8 January 2016. http://www.ekumenizm.pl/publicystyka/moherowe-szalenstwo-czyli-co-uwiera-polakow-w-glowy/

Kohn, Marek. 2005. The Mohair Berets are on the March. The New Statesman, December 19. http://www.newstatesman.com/node/152228

Kopecky, Petr, and Cas Mudde. 2012. *Uncivil Society? Contentious Politics in Post-Communist Europe*. London: Routledge.

Koscianska, Agnieszka. 2008. Mohair Berets: The Development of Fundamentalism Within the Catholic Church of Poland. In *The Sociology of Religion: A Substantive and Transdisciplinary Approach*, ed. George N. Lundskow, 363–365. London: Sage.

Krzemiński, Ireneusz. 2009. *Czego nas uczy Radio Maryja? Socjologia treści i recepcji rozgłośni*. Warszawa: WAIP.

Langenbacher, Nora, and Britta Schellenberg. 2011. *Is Europe on the "Right" Path? Right-Wing Extremism and Right-Wing Populism in Europe*. Berlin: Friedrich-Ebert-Stiftung.

Lundskow, George N. 2008. *The Sociology of Religion: A Substantive and Transdisciplinary Approach*. London: Sage.

Marciniak, Katarzyna. 2011. Postsocialist Hybrids. In *Streets of Crocodiles: Photography, Media, and Postsocialist Landscapes in Poland*, ed. Kamil Turowski, and Katarzyna Marciniak. Chicago: Intellect.

Morgan, Leslie A., and Suzanne R. Kunkel. 2011. *Aging, Society and the Life-course*. New York: Springer.

Mudde, Cas. 2005. *Racist Extremism in Central and Eastern Europe*. London: Routledge.

Narbutt, Maja. 2004. Labirynty księdza prałata. *Rzeczpospolita*, dodatek *Plus Minus*, 23: 10. http://archiwum.rp.pl/artykul/511832_Labirynty_ksiedza_pralata.html

Novikova, Kateryna. 2015. Ageizm, uczenie się przez całe życie a samorealizacja: Krytyczny zarys problematyki. *Journal of Modern Science* 3(26): 61–72. http://wsge.edu.pl/files/JOMS/3-26-2015/Joms_3_26_2015.pdf

Ojciec Rydzyk ogłasza moherowy wyścig zbrojeń. 2009. Accessed 14 December 2015. http://glosrydzyka.blox.pl/2009/05/ORydzyk-oglasza-moherowy-wyscig-zbrojen.html

Osłowski, Karol. 2009. Radio Maryja w "Gazecie Wyborczej" w latach 1998–2004. In *Czego nas uczy Radio Maryja? Socjologia treści i recepcji rozgłośni*, ed. Ireneusz Krzemiński, 156–172. Warszawa: WAIP.

Pankowski, Rafał. 2010. *The Populist Radical Right in Poland: The Patriots.* London: Routledge.

Porter-Szucs, Brian. 2011. *Faith and Fatherland. Catholicism, Modernity and Poland.* Oxford: Oxford University Press.

Ritzer, George. 2004. *Encyclopedia of Social Theory.* London: Sage.

Robbins, Jessica C. 2013. Personhood in Places: Aging, Memory, and Relatedness in Postsocialist Poland. *University of Michigan.* Accessed 14 December 2015. http://deepblue.lib.umich.edu/bitstream/handle/2027.42/97929/Jessica_Robbins_Dissertation.pdf?sequence=4&isAllowed=y

Robbins-Ruszkowski, Jessica C. 2015. 'Active Aging' As Citizenship in Poland. In *Generations. Rethinking Age and Citizenship*, ed. Richard Marback, 270–286. Detroit: Wayne State University Press.

Rodzina Radia Maryja z pielgrzymką na Jasnej Górze. 2009. Accessed 14 December 2015. http://www.radiomaryja.pl.eu.org/arch/2009-200tys-2.html

Stangret, Michał. 2006. Koniec moherowego beretu. *Gazeta.pl.* Accessed 14 December 2015. http://wiadomosci.gazeta.pl/wiadomosci/1,114873,3230067.html

Staniszkis, Jadwiga. 2001. *Postkomunizm. Próba opisu.* Gdańsk: Słowo/obraz terytoria.

Szarota, Piotr. 2008. *Od skarpetek Tyrmanda do krawata Leppera.* WAIP: Warszawa.

Szczygielski, Marcin, and Andrzej Rozhin. 2012. Berek, czyli upiór w operze. *Instytut Rozwoju Kultury Alternatywnej.* http://irka.com.pl/portal/Review?review_id=2598&area_id=4

Święchowicz, Małgorzata. 2011. Radio, czyli Dzieło. *Przekrój* 28(11): 6–9.

Thel, Karolina. 2011. Reflection on Redefinition of Elderly People's Role in the Modern Society. Acta Universitatis Lodziensis, Folia Oeconomica 250, http://dspace.uni.lodz.pl:8080/xmlui/bitstream/handle/123456789/608/75-83.pdf?sequence=1

Trochimczuk, Monika. 2009. *Analiza danych radiometrycznych pod kątem modelu słuchania radia z uwzględnieniem wskaźników demograficznych.* Warszawa: Krajowa Rada Radiofonii i Telewizji.

———. 2013. *Rynek programów radiowych w Warszawie preferencje słuchaczy na podstawie danych o słuchalności programów radiowych w 2012.* Warszawa: Krajowa Rada Radiofonii i Telewizji.

————. 2015. *Udział w rynku i wielkość audytorium programów radiowych w III kwartale 2015 r.* Warszawa: Krajowa Rada Radiofonii i Telewizji.

Turowski, Mariusz. 2005. Religion and Politics in Poland: Political Discourse, Toleration, and Neutrality. In *Democracy and the Post-totalitarian Experience*, ed. Leszek Koczanowicz, and Beth J. Singer, 39–47. Amsterdam: Rodopi.

Gender Stereotypes Constructed by the Media: The Case of the National Socialist Underground (NSU) in Germany

Michaela Köttig

INTRODUCTION

In November 2011 the case of a right-wing extremist group which calls itself the National Socialist Underground (NSU) became public in Germany. The far-right background of the case was discovered by chance, in the context of a search for two bank robbers. The bank robbers tried to hide; according to current knowledge, shortly before the police raided their hiding place one of the two shot his accomplice and then himself. The flat in which both of them and a woman had lived exploded just a few hours later. At first the woman could not be found. Four days later she turned herself in to the police. The evidence secured, and a confession video claiming responsibility for certain crimes, revealed that the two dead men and the woman were right-wing extremists wanted by the police. The three, namely, Beate Zschaepe, Uwe Mundlos and Uwe Boehnhardt, had gone underground some 13 years earlier. The evidence suggested that the three individuals were responsible for 15 bank robberies and 2 bomb attacks. In addition, weapons were found in the flat which had been used for killing nine men with an immigrant background in different cities throughout the country, as well as for injuring and shooting two police

M. Köttig (✉)
Frankfurt University of Applied Sciences, Frankfurt, Germany

© The Author(s) 2017   221
M. Köttig et al. (eds.), *Gender and Far Right Politics in Europe*,
DOI 10.1007/978-3-319-43533-6_15

officers. Up to this point, these crimes had not been treated as the deeds of right-wing extremists. Even worse, it was suspected that the perpetrators were to be found among the immigrant communities themselves, where the police searched intensively for them. The press encouraged this one-sidedness by referring to the crimes as "doner kebab murders" (see, e.g. Spiegel 2006, 2011).

In the course of the years an increasing number of inconsistencies and errors came to light in the work of the investigating authorities, which had failed to reveal the connection between these crimes and the extreme-right milieu (see Kleffner 2013). Committees of inquiry on the level of the states involved and on the federal level were set up as a result, but many questions remain unanswered to this day. Police and government authorities are still striving to prove that the crimes were committed by these three persons, together with a very small number of accomplices, despite evidence that the NSU was part of a wide network within Germany and had international contacts (see Köhler 2014).

The proceedings against Beate Zschaepe, accused as a principal offender, and four other women accused of being her accomplices, have been underway since May 2013.[1] The trial is largely limited to proving that the accused are guilty as charged. Supporter networks and open questions concerning the case do not play a significant role. Up to the end of 2015, Beate Zschaepe refused to give evidence and then allowed statements to be read by one of her lawyers. In these statements she denied knowing anything about the murders and constructed an image of herself as a victim of the situation (Forschungsnetzwerk Frauen und Rechtsextremismus 2015).

Gender stereotypes have played an important role in this case. In this article I will examine this issue from different angles. Firstly I will consider the media coverage shortly after the discovery of the NSU and how the media worked with gender stereotypical representations of the three offenders. The analysis of articles in different print media shows that these gender stereotypes are based on right-wing extremist ideology. This leads to the assumption that girls and women cannot be politically active agents.

In a second step I will show how Beate Zschaepe and other witnesses from the NSU network have resorted to gender stereotypical images during the trial to describe themselves and their activities. This has allowed them to water down the political significance of their activities.

The Discovery of the NSU and Its Social Embedding

Right from the beginning, reporting on the NSU has operated with common gender-role stereotypes (see Forschungsnetzwerk Frauen und Rechtsextremismus 2011, 2013, 2015; Kaufhold 2015). I refer here to reports published shortly after the NSU was discovered, and to reduce the complexity of the issue I discuss the reports only on the level of the language used. To understand the embedding of the situation, it is important to realize that German society was confronted "unexpectedly" with this dramatic case, for until then radical right violence and terrorism had not attracted serious attention in Germany (see Lehr 2013). In addition, two deeply rooted convictions in respect of the extreme right in Germany were called into question: firstly, the notion that right-wing extremists are just a few male juvenile thugs who are stupid and/or confused. This assumption was proved wrong, because this group had operated in a clever, strategic manner, planning their actions in such a way as to remain in the shadows, not boasting about their actions. At the same time, the terrorists had succeeded in sowing mutual mistrust within migrant communities. Secondly, there was the fact that a woman could be a part of right-wing extremist violence and live underground for such a long period out of political motives; this challenged people's assumptions that women in general are not capable of acting in accordance with right-wing extremist behaviour strategies (Elverich 2007). The contradiction of common assumptions that until then had prevented any serious debate on right-wing extremism was linked to the public's interest in finding out details about the case. However, the public prosecutors were able to show very few findings, and the media were thus forced to generate reports based on a relatively thin body of evidence. In addition, due to the highly charged nature of the case, it was imperative for all media to pick it up; this meant that journalists who were not experts in the subject were entrusted with reporting. This resulted in speculations across the press landscape on the course of events, the personalities of the offenders and their motives. It is also the reason why some journalists have tried to describe the persons involved on the basis of very limited information on their biographies, as well as their motives and activities. The small amount of available facts was thus compensated by common gender clichés. However, this construction of gender stereotypes had a great effect on the shaping of public perceptions of the three suspects. In addition, it is not impossible that the prosecution authorities have also been influenced by these constructions. On the basis of media reports and expert evidence used in the case, I will show that these constructions of the offenders are based on stereotype gender-role assumptions and also, more specifically, on stereotypes regarding women's and men's roles in right-wing extremism.

THE FOCUSING OF REPORTING ON FEMALE STEREOTYPES

By using selected articles from the yellow press (like the *Berliner Kurier*, the *Hamburger Morgenpost* and the *Bild* newspaper), as well as articles from reputable media (like the *Frankfurter Rundschau*), I will show that the authors fell back on stereotypes that have developed in Germany regarding gender roles and right-wing extremism. When I talk about the construction of gender, I am referring to the concept of "doing gender" introduced by West and Zimmerman in 1987.

With regard to Beate Zschaepe, the yellow press focused clearly, and in a not very subtle manner, on a specific gender role. On 14 November 2011, the *Hamburger Morgenpost* and the *Berliner Kurier* published photos under headlines like "The Bride of Evil[2]". On page 1, below the headline "The cold-blooded killer bride", a report by Ortmann and Böttcher speculates, among other things, that "...Beate Zschaepe is said to have 'alternately' been the girlfriend of one or the other of the two Uwes. Free love among Neonazis?"

The chief columnist of the *Bild* newspaper, Franz-Josef Wagner, sticks to the sexual relationships and Nazi bride status, but expands them, in the sense that he adds the role of subservient housewife as a metaphor. On 15 November 2011, his article was headed "Weird Beate Zschaepe", and he continues by putting a personal question to her: "Who are you? Follower? Obedient accomplice, who shared your bed with the two killer Nazis? What role did you play? Killer-bitch or killer-service-lady, washing dishes, keeping the hiding place in the underground clean? ...You are either a malicious criminal or a deeply distraught woman, who prefers living with murderers to being lonely". Just one day later (16 November 2011), the *Bild* headline reads: "The Nazi bride was rated as a hot item"; this is presented as a statement made by a right-wing extremist who claims he had met Beate Zschaepe at an NPD (National Democratic Party of Germany) Christmas function in Georgsmarienhuette in 2004—at a time when she was already living underground. A day later

(17 November 2011) the *Bild* newspaper published photos showing a sleepy Beate Zschaepe as a juvenile in bed with one of the alleged offenders (Uwe Mundlos), with the headline "The weirdo with bedroom eyes" (Hellmann et al. 2011).

In their texts the authors use classic sexist ascriptions like: being sneaky, an inaccessible beast, sexually insatiable or dependent, the lonely and subservient housewife.[3] These ascriptions are based on bi-polar gender constructions in which the man is conceived as dominant and the woman inferior. These constructions serve to maintain the balance of power between men and women, as Simone de Beauvoir argued as early as 1951. Oelhaf, who presented a critical discourse analysis of the reports in the *Bild* newspaper from 8–18 November 2011, immediately after the suspects were revealed, proves that a sexualization of Zschaepe took place within the framework of the media coverage (Oelhaf 2012, 3). Furthermore, she points out that "Zschaepe's statements concerning her sex life and her relationships take up much space in delineating her character, whereas this is not the case when it comes to characterizing Boehnhardt and Mundlos. The fact that several Neonazis courted her, and her reputation as a 'hottie', made her a sex object for male Nazis. 'Mixing up' by turns with Boehnhardt and Mundlos ascribes promiscuousness to her with a slightly negative undertone. Her right-wing extremism, however, is presented as negligible and of a passive nature: she is considered to be just a follower. None of this paints a picture of a woman who probably killed several human beings on racist grounds" (ibid.). This quotation emphasizes that apart from the construction of sexualization there is another effective dimension, that of constructing stereotypical right-wing female personalities.

THE CONSTRUCTION OF STEREOTYPICAL GENDER ROLES IN RIGHT-WING EXTREMISM

While the focus of the reports is generally on ascriptions of femininity, these are combined with stereotypical gender roles in right-wing extremism. As a central stereotypical gender-role construction of masculinity, Virchow (2010) describes the favoured role of the "military fighter" or "warrior", which is still in existence despite the "failure" of National Socialism in which it played a significant role. This construction is associated with characteristics such as heterosexuality, family breadwinner, intransigence (unwillingness to compromise), hardness, strength, willingness to make sacrifices, fearlessness, braveness and service to the people and the nation, to the point of self-sacrifice (Virchow 2010, 42). It is based on the leader-follower pattern of allegiance, which means it involves both the male elite soldier and the violent proletarian type, suggesting a division into "leaders of thought" and "doers" who put the ideas into practice. These masculine ascriptions exist inside and outside right-wing extremism, although, according to Heilmann (2010, 60), "there are signs of modernization in the sense of a more flexible normalizing adaptation to current forms of civic masculinity". This means that there are very different forms of male self-representation within the field of right-wing extremism.

This also applies to constructions of femininity. Classical right-wing extremist ascriptions of femininity, which may be derived from the National Socialist ideology, refer to women above all as the bearers and educators of the following generation (cf. Bitzan 2011, 116 f.). Women are regarded as incapable of holding autonomous political positions. Their chief fields of activity are relationship building and venerating old customs (ibid.). However, female scholars have been able to reconstruct varying roles and functions of female right-wing extremists, ranging from street fighter, bread-winning ideologist with a dual burden, to the ideologized traditional mother role. It has also been shown that women participate in all right-wing extremist activities, admittedly to a quantitatively smaller extent (cf. Bitzan 2011; Röpke and Speit 2011; Lang 2010; Döhring and Feldmann 2005; Köttig 2004). Yet in spite of these academic and public perceptions, the idea persists that women, through no fault of their own, "slide into" the far-right scene and that they are non-political, inoffensive followers, who "sleepwalk" into a group because their partner is a member of it. This image has also been reproduced by the media (cf. Bitzan et al. 2005).

The reporting outlined above on the group of suspects, who are known in the Federal Republic of Germany as the "right-wing extremist trio", the "Zwickau terrorist cell" or the "Zwickau trio", works with these stereotype constructions of femininity and masculinity in right-wing extremism (Büttner et al. 2012). First and foremost, this is the case in the yellow press: an article entitled "The sick hatred of the Nazi killers" (Kiewel et al. 2011) says: "Uwe Mundlos, the unscrupulous thought leader. Son of a professor, intellectual. His former headmistress describes him as 'unobtrusive and polite'. He pushes his disabled brother in a wheelchair through the neighbourhood. He listens to songs by Lindenberg and attends trials of deniers of the Holocaust. He likes to draw—in his room there is a self-drawn portrait of Hitler's deputy Rudolf Hess. ...Uwe Boehnhardt, the dull gun nut. An unskilled construction worker, uncontrolled and unscrupulous. He nearly always has a 30-cm dagger on him. 'When you see him—run off!' the left scene says. Boehnhardt wears a bomber jacket and bovver boots. 'He stretched out his right arm whenever there was an opportunity', a friend says. ...Beate Zschaepe, the dangerous follower. Trained gardener. She refuses to wear the typical uniform of the brown scene. Several Neo-Nazis compete for her. She has a three-way relationship with Boehnhardt and Mundlos: 'Sometimes she was together with the one, then with the other', a former friend says. At home she hung up the imperial war flag".

Although the *Bild* newspaper's coverage of the NSU, and particularly of Beate Zschaepe, thematizes her co-responsibility (cf. Oelhaf 2012; Lemm 2012), the classical role stereotypes for the two men (the strategic, radical thinker and the brutal thug) and for the woman (a scarcely politicized follower, who acts out of sexual indigence) are exaggerated.

Though an interest in sex and crime is to be expected from the yellow press, more reputable media also use these right-wing extremist gender stereotypes. On the front page of the *Frankfurter Rundschau*, for example, there are photos of the three on 14 November 2011 and captions characterizing each person (Förster and Thieme 2011). The following comment appeared below Beate Zschaepe's photo: "Was one of the few active women in the right-wing extremist scene. She is said to have been not very politically committed". Uwe Boehnhardt's caption says: "Was rated as a gun nut. His right-wing extremist sympathizers assume he could have been the gunman who fired the fatal shots". About Uwe Mundlos we read: "Was rated as the intellectual of the group. He is said to be polite, rhetorically gifted and interested in politics". These constructions are particularly suitable for codifying stereotypes because they are easy to grasp and because of their tradition that has existed since the Nazi period.

While these constructions of right-wing extremist masculinities and femininities are "effective publicity", there are also indications that the prosecution authorities have used similar patterns of classification. An expert report was written by three high-ranking lawyers for the purpose of assessing the actions of the Thuringian authorities who had been charged with the prosecution of the three in the 1990s and the early 2000s, before and shortly after their disappearance. In the report, the biographical development and political activities of the three lead to a general characterization (Schäfer et al. 2012, 54–58). Beate Zschaepe is assessed, among others, as follows: "The Thuringian State Criminal Police Officer, who had also interrogated Zschaepe before her disappearance, described her as being sly and street-smart. When being questioned by the police she had a confident and condescending manner. ...Furthermore: His impression was that she was 'a calculating and callous lady'. ...In the opinion of an officer of the Thuringian State Criminal Police she was supposed to be alternately Boehnhardt's and Mundlos' girlfriend, which was confirmed by an officer for targeted search..." (Schäfer et al. 2012, 57 f.). With regard to Uwe Boehnhardt the expert report says, among other things: "In the opinion of an officer participating in the targeted search, Boehnhardt was supposed to be 'cuckoo', a guy who simply acted, brutally and without foresight. Tino Brandt characterized him as a gun nut with a military interest which had always been his main focus". A few lines later the report continues: "Not overly intelligent with little mental interest" (Schäfer et al. 2012, 55). Uwe Mundlos is summarized as follows: "In contrast, the officer of the Thuringian State Criminal Police rated Mundlos as more deliberate and intelligent. According to the officer for targeted search, Mundlos was highly intelligent ... (He was) A mother-in-law's dream, more deliberate and eloquent. He was also able to adapt" (Schäfer et al. 2012, 57). These generalizing characterizations borrow the clichés of right-wing extremist stereotypical gender roles. It is interesting to observe that these stereotype ascriptions were, and still are, used by women in the context of the NSU.

STEREOTYPE SELF-IMAGES OF WOMEN IN THE CONTEXT OF THE NSU

Before discussing the self-images of women from the environment of the NSU, it is important to stress that the NSU is a well-organized Germany-wide network, as mentioned above. The extreme politicization of right-wing youth in Thuringia in the context of the *Kameradschaft Jena* (Jena Fellowship), later known as *Thueringer Heimatschutz* (Thuringian Homeland Security), in the phase following the reunification of the two German states in the early 1990s, can be regarded as the origin of the NSU (Melzer and Serafin 2013). There are a number of indications that the members of this group were responsible for crimes and that it was on its way to becoming a terrorist association. The group had extended its activities to the whole of Germany and prepared to go underground (see Heerdegen 2016). That Boehnhardt, Mundlos and Zschaepe went underground can be explained by the fact that they were wanted by the police following the discovery of weapons and explosives in the possession of Beate Zschaepe. During this time they were supplied with weapons, identity papers and plenty more by a large number of supporters. The Federal Prosecutor estimates that there were about 100 individuals connected with the NSU (cf. Schmidt 2012), including about 20 women (Sanders 2012).

One reason for the non-detection of the right-wing extremist background of the three can be seen in the fact that they followed common role stereotypes in their social environment. Thus, all witnesses confirm that Beate Zschaepe was the one who fostered contacts while the two men remained more or less invisible. Zschaepe, by acting as she did, defused possible problems in her environment which might arise from living together with two men. She adopted the stereotype of a socially competent, open-minded woman who looks after her cats. In her written statement at the trial, Beate Zschaepe presents herself as a woman who learned about the crimes committed by the two men only later on: "We weren't together from morning to night. Uwe Mundlos and Uwe Boehnhardt often went out without telling me where they were going or what they were planning to do".[4] She stresses her emotional and financial dependence on the two men. Although she was not happy—as proof of this she mentions her excessive drinking—she was incapable of leaving them. In her second statement she even says that she was beaten up by Boehnhardt, "when he ran out of verbal arguments".[5] In the foreground of her statement is the attempt to present herself as being largely innocent, in some respects naive, and a victim of the situation, which corresponds to the stereotype of the unpolitical woman in the background. Her claim that she suffered while living with the two men contrasts with the statements made by her women neighbours, who describe Zschaepe as lively and cheerful.

Like Beate Zschaepe, witnesses connected with the NSU also use the stereotype of the "ignorant and unpolitical woman".[6] Antje P., for instance, says she had no idea that Beate Zschaepe was using her passport. She herself is a founding member of the Blood & Honour Saxony Section. On 14 June 1998 she allegedly proposed to "carry out political attacks from the underground". At the trial, when she was confronted with having said this, she denied it by arguing that at that time she was the mother of a 1-year-old child and would never have suggested anything like that.[7] She said: "I was the only girl in our group, and the boys didn't include me in a lot of things. Basically, women have no say and their place is in the kitchen".[8]

Juliane W., another witness connected with the NSU, and a former girlfriend of one of the accused, frequently claims that she can't remember. She plays down her own role: "I would say that really I was just a follower". She admits that she helped to place stickers but claims she was never so involved that she knew where events were due to take place, and she never helped to prepare them.[9] Mandy St., a central figure in the Nazi scene in Bavaria and Saxony and also an important supporter of the trio, presents similar arguments. She found a flat for the three and she organized health insurance and identity papers for Beate Zschaepe. In the three interrogations she consistently minimizes her own activities in the extreme right: "I was just a 'male appendage', women had no say, they either did what was expected of them or they were laughed at".[10]

That Zschaepe and the other female witnesses who are known to have been (and still be) committed members of an extreme-right network should attempt at the trial to play down their knowledge of, and active participation in, the crimes is understandable in view of the legal consequences involved. However, the fact that these women resort to the stereotype of the "unpolitical woman" in their self-presentations is an indication that they regard such stereotype images of gender roles and right-wing extremism as being functional and useful in a situation where they need to suggest that they could not have been politically active.

CONCLUSION

In this article I have shown how the media in Germany reported the discovery of the National Socialist Underground and its crimes. I have shown that this media coverage and reports by experts contributed to the reproduction of gender stereotypes by male and female right-wing extremists, which as a result were reinforced and not revised. Consequently, women connected with the NSU have been able to use these stereotype constructions of masculinity and femininity as a means of self-defence.

That the media reported the case in this way shortly after the discovery of the NSU can be explained by the fact that there was not enough information available at that time on the background of the individuals involved and their crimes. However, the question arises why a scientific expert opinion does not go into more detail and provide accurate information concerning the dynamics and the specific behaviour of the different participants. If the disclosed facts had been studied more closely, conclusions on the inner structure of the group would have been possible at an early stage. This raises the final question: why has this case, and the circumstances beyond it, not been investigated more closely to this day? This is a question that present-day German society needs to face up to, and inferences can be drawn about how Germany copes with its past.

NOTES

1. See the detailed reports of the trial at: http://www.nsu-nebenklage. de/en/, accessed 19.03.2016. The reports were written by NSU-Watch, part of the Anti-Fascist Press Archive and Education Centre apabiz. Its goal is to promote independent clarification of the facts surrounding the "National Socialist Underground" (NSU) terror cell and its racist murders.
2. All quotations from media reports and the Thuringian expert report have been translated by the author.
3. See the state of the art report by Pozzi, Giulia (Pozzi 2012).
4. See the entire statement at http://m.welt.de/politik/deutsch-land/article149803799/Dokumentation-Die-Aussage-der-Beate-Zschaepe.html, accessed 21.03.2016.
5. See: http://www.zeit.de/gesellschaft/zeitgeschehen/2016-03/beate-zschaepe-nsu-prozess-gewalt-uwe-boehnhardt, accessed 21.03.2016.
6. See also the unpublished lecture by Lang, Juliane and Kaufhold, Charlie. "...und dass Frauen da nicht viel zu sagen haben und eigentlich an den Kochtopf gehören". Geschlechterstereotype in der Selbstinszenierung neonazistischer Akteure Im NSU-Prozess, held on 01.07.2015, Fachschaftsrat Politik der Universität Münster.
7. Record of the 162nd day of the proceedings, 20.11.2014, see: https://www.nsu-watch.info/2014/11/protokoll-162-verhandlungstag-20-november-2014/, accessed 21.03.2016.
8. Record of the 169th day of the proceedings, 10.12.2014, see: https://www.nsu-watch.info/2014/12/protokoll-169-verhandlungstag-10-dezember-2014/, accessed 21.03.2016.
9. Record of the 98th day of the proceedings, 26.03. 2014. See: https://www.nsu-watch.info/2014/04/protokoll-98-verhandlungstag-26-maerz-2014/, accessed 21.03.2016.
10. Record of the 90th day of the proceedings, 27.02.2014, see: https://www.nsu-watch.info/2014/03/protokoll-90-verhandlungstag-27-februar-2014/, accessed 21.03.2016.

REFERENCES

Beauvoir, de Simone. 1951. *Das andere Geschlecht*. Reinbek: Rowohlt-Verlag.

Bitzan, Renate. 2011. 'Reinrassige Mutterschaft' versus 'nationaler Feminismus'—Weiblichkeitskonstruktionen in Publikationen extrem rechter Frauen. In *Rechtsextremismus und Gender*, ed. Ursula Birsl, 115–127. Opladen & Farmington Hills: Barbara Budrich.

Bitzan, Renate, Michaela Köttig, and Berit Schröder. 2005. Vom Zusehen bis zum Mitmorden: Mediale Berichterstattung zur Beteiligung von Mädchen und Frauen an rechtsextrem motivierten Straftaten. *Zeitschrift für Frauenforschung und Geschlechterstudien* 21(2–3): 150–170.

Büttner, Frauke, Juliane Lang, and Johanna Sigl. 2012. Mediale Klischeereproduktion: Zur Berichterstattung über die Neonazistin Zschäpe. *Femina Politica* 1: 23–27.

Döhring, Kirsten, and Feldmann Renate. 2003. Akteurinnen und Organisationen. Die Involviertheit von Frauen in der extremen Rechten. In *Braune Schwestern? Feministische Analysen zu Frauen in der extremen Rechten*, ed. Antifaschistisches Frauennetzwerk/Forschungsnetzwerk Frauen und Rechtsextremismus, 17–34. Münster: Unrast-Verlag.

Döhring, Kirsten, and Renate Feldmann. 2005. Akteurinnen und Organisationen. Die Involviertheit von Frauen in der extremen Rechten. In *Braune Schwestern? Feministische Analysen zu Frauen in der extremen Rechten*, ed. Antifaschistisches Frauennetzwerk/Forschungsnetzwerk Frauen und Rechtsextremismus, 17–34. Münster: Unrast-Verlag.

Elverich, Gabi. 2007. *Rechtsextrem orientierte Frauen und Mädchen—eine besondere Zielgruppe? Die Rolle von weiblichen Neonazis wird bislang unterschätzt.* http://www.bpb.de/politik/extremismus/rechtsextremismus/41506/rechtsextrem-orientierte-frauen-und-maedchen (letzter Zugriff 23.02.2103).

Forschungsnetzwerk Frauen und Rechtsextremismus. 2011. *"Und warum ist das Interessanteste an einer militanten Rechtsextremistin ihr Liebesleben?"–Offener Brief des Forschungsnetzwerks Frauen und Rechtsextremismus zur Berichterstattung über die Rechtsextremistin Beate Zschäpe.* Accessed 19 March 2016. http://www.frauen-und-rechtsextremismus.de/cms/

———. 2013. *Offener Brief zum Prozessbeginn gegen die mutmaßliche Rechtsterroristin Beate Zschäpe und zur Beteiligung weiterer Frauen im Netzwerk des Nationalsozialistischen Untergrunds.* Accessed 19 March 2016. http://www.frauen-und-rechtsextremismus.de/cms/

———. 2015. *Ich habe nichts gemacht, ich war nur in der Küche–Statement des Forschungsnetzwerks Frauen und Rechtsextremismus zur Einlassung Beate Zschäpes im NSU-Prozess am 9.12.2015.* Accessed 19 March 2016. http://www.frauen-und-rechtsextremismus.de/cms/

Heerdegen, Stefan. 2016. Nicht vom Himmel gefallen. Die Thüringer Neonaziszene und der NSU. In *Rechtsextremismus und "Nationalsozialistischer Untergrund". Interdisziplinäre Debatten, Befunde und Bilanzen*, ed. Wolfgang

Frindte, Daniel Geschke, Nicole Haußecker, and Franziska Schmidtke, 195–211. Wiesbaden: Springer VS.

Heilmann, Andreas. 2010. Normalisierung und Aneignung—Modernisierung und Flexibilisierung von Männlichkeiten im Rechtsextremismus. In *Was ein rechter Mann ist…'. Männlichkeiten im Rechtsextremismus*, ed. Robert Claus, Esther Lehnert, and Yves Müller, 53–65. Berlin: Karl Dietz Verlag.

Kaufhold, Charlie. 2015. *In guter Gesellschaft?* Münster: Assemblage.

Kleffner, Heike. 2013. NSU: Rassismus, Staatsversagen und die schwierige Suche nach der Wahrheit. In *NSU-Terror. Ermittlungen am rechten Abgrund*, ed. Imke Schmincke, and Jasmin Siri, 29–42. Bielefeld: Transkript-Verlag.

Köhler, Daniel. 2014. The German 'National Socialist Underground (NSU)' and Anglo-American Networks. The Internationalisation of Far-Right Terror. In *The Post-War Anglo-American Far Right. A Special Relationship of Hate*, ed. Paul Jackson, and Anton Shekhovtsov, 122–141. Basingstoke: Palgrave MacMillan.

Köttig, Michaela. 2004. *Lebensgeschichten rechtsextrem orientierter Mädchen und junger Frauen—Biographische Verläufe im Kontext der Familien- und Gruppendynamik*. Gießen: Psychosozial-Verlag.

Lang, Juliane. 2010. …diese Gemeinschaft von Frauen, unter Frauen, gemeinsam mit Frauen sitzen und sich besprechen und so weiter, tut Frauen einfach gut. Frauen im Rechtsextremismus. In *Was ein rechter Mann ist … Männlichkeiten im Rechtsextremismus*, ed. Robert Claus, Esther Lehnert, and Yves Müller, 127–142. Berlin.

Lehr, F. Peter. 2013. Still Blind in the Right Eye?: A Comparison of German Responses to Political Violence from the Extreme Left and the Extreme Right. In *Extreme Right Wing Political Violence and Terrorism*, ed. Max Taylor, P.M. Currie, and Donald Holbrook, 187–214. London: Bloomsbury.

Lemm, Anne Detje. 2012. *Rechtsextremismus aus der Genderperspektive. Inhaltsanalytische Betrachtung von Darstellungen rechtsextremer Frauen in der medialen Berichterstattung zum ,Nationalsozialistischen Untergrund'.* Unpublished BA thesis, submitted at the Hochschule für Wirtschaft und Recht, Berlin.

Melzer, Ralf, and Sebastian Serafin, eds. 2013. *Right-Wing Extremism in Europe: Country Analyses, Counter-Strategies and Labor-Market Oriented Exit Strategies*. Berlin: Friedrich-Ebert-Stiftung.

Oelhaf, Anna. 2012. Beate Zschäpe in der Bild-Zeitung: Zwischen Nazi-Braut und Nazi-Killer. Der Diskurs um Frauen im Rechtsextremismus am Beispiel des NSU. Duisburger Institut für Sprach- und Sozialforschung *(Diss)-Journal* 23: 6–10. Accessed 22 April 2016. http://www.diss-duisburg.de/2012/08/beate-zschape-in-der-bild-zeitung/

Pozzi, Giulia. 2012. Women and Mass Media. Bruxelles: Amazone. Accessed 21 March 2016. http://www.amazon.be/IMG/pdf/women_and_mass_media-gpozzi.pdf

Röpke, Andrea, and Andreas Speit. 2011. *Mädelsache. Frauen in der Neonazi-Szene*. Berlin.

Sanders, Eike. 2012. Frauen und Männer im Untergrund—Geschlechterverhältnisse im NSU und in seinem Umfeld, *apabiz monitor*, nr. 55: 1–3.

Schäfer, Gerhard, Volkhard Wache, and Gerhard Meilborg. 2012. *Gutachten zum Verhalten der Thüringer Behörden und Staatsanwaltschaften bei der Verfolgung des "Zwickauer Trios" im Auftrag des Freistaates Thüringen.* Accessed 21 March 2016. http://www.thueringen.de/imperia/md/content/tim/veranstaltungen/120515_schaefer_gutachten.pdf

Virchow, Fabian. 2010. Tapfer, stolz, opferbereit—Überlegungen zum extrem rechten Verständnis 'idealer Männlichkeit. In *Was ein rechter Mann ist…'. Männlichkeiten im Rechtsextremismus*, ed. Robert Claus, Esther Lehnert, and Yves Müller, 39–52. Berlin: Karl Dietz Verlag.

West, Candace, and Don H. Zimmerman. 1987. Doing Gender. *Gender & Society* 1: 125–151.

JOURNALISTIC SOURCES

Hellmann, Angelika, Reinhard Keck, Jörg Völkerling, and Olaf Wilke. 2011. *Die Unheimliche mit dem Schlafzimmerblick.* Bild.de, November 19. Accessed 26 March 2016. http://www.bild.de/news/inland/nsu/die-unheimliche-mit-dem-schlafzimmerblick-teil1-21112884.bild.html

Förster, Andreas, and Matthias Thieme. 2011. Terror von Rechts. Frankfurter Rundschau, November 14.

Kiewel, Maximilian, Martina Kurtz, Carolin Lemuth, Oliver Löhr, Julian Reichelt, Schuler Ralf, and Stefan Sievering. 2011. *Der kranke Hass der Nazi-Killer.* Bild. de, November 14. Accessed 26 March 2016. http://www.bild.de/news/inland/nsu/nationalsozialistische-terror-gruppe-20982014.bild.html

Ortmann, Joachim, and Böttcher Marcus. 2011. *Die eiskalte Killer-Braut.* Hamburger Morgenpost/Berliner Kurier, November 14. Accessed 26 March 2016. http://www.mopo.de/panorama/brauner-terror-die-eiskalte-killer-braut,5066860,11148338.html

Schmidt, Wolf. 2012. *Die Hundertschaft der NSU.* taz.de, October 09. Accessed 26 March 2016. http://www.taz.de/Umfeld-des-Neonazitrios/!103214/

Spiegel online. 2011. Twist in 'Doner Killings' Case: Police Find Gun Used in Unsolved Murder Series. Accessed 19 March 2016. http://www.spiegel.de/international/germany/twist-in-doner-killings-case-police-find-gun-used-in-unsolved-murder-series-a-797327.html

———. 2006. A Serial Killer Stalks Turkish Shopkeepers: German Police Step Up Hunt for "Döner Kebab Killer". Accessed 19 March 2016. http://www.spiegel.de/international/a-serial-killer-stalks-turkish-shopkeepers-german-police-step-up-hunt-for-doener-kebab-killer-a-430710.html

Wagner, Franz-Josef. 2011. *Unheimliche Beate Zschäpe.* Bild.de, November 15. Accessed 26 March 2016. http://www.bild.de/news/standards/franz-josef-wagner/unheimliche-beate-zschaepe-21037638.bild.html

A World Without Gender? The Struggle of Austria's Far Right over What It Means to Be Human: An Analysis of Barbara Rosenkranz' Book *MenschInnen*

Boka En, Michael En, and Mercedes Pöll

INTRODUCTION

In this article, we explore discourses on gender in the Austrian far right to provide an insight into the arguments, strategies and networks used to construct, advocate and uphold a very particular gender worldview. We focus on a 2008 publication by Barbara Rosenkranz, current member of the Austrian parliament representing the far-right Austrian Freedom Party (*Freiheitliche Partei Österreichs;* FPÖ). Her book *MenschInnen: Gender Mainstreaming—Auf dem Weg zum geschlechtslosen Menschen (Human/ esses: Gender Mainstreaming—On the way to the genderless human)*[1] supposedly reveals a conspiracy on the part of feminists, capitalists, Marxists, homosexuals, gender pseudo-scientists and the media that has the sole

B. En (✉)
Independent scholar, Vienna, Austria

M. En
Center for Translation Studies, University of Vienna, Vienna, Austria

M. Pöll
Independent scholar, Vienna, Austria

© The Author(s) 2017   235
M. Köttig et al. (eds.), *Gender and Far Right Politics in Europe*,
DOI 10.1007/978-3-319-43533-6_16

purpose of abolishing gender and thereby changing human nature. Taking a closer look at the perspectives Rosenkranz employs, we argue that her book and the discourses she draws on construct an elitist Other to the 'average citizen' and a threat to the continued survival of the Austrian nation and its people.

THE FREEDOM PARTY OF AUSTRIA (FPÖ) AND BARBARA ROSENKRANZ

Founded in the 1950s, the FPÖ has a history of positioning itself firmly on the right of the Austrian political spectrum and is frequently used as an example of a stable and successful right-wing populist party (cf. Harrison and Bruter 2011). Under leader Jörg Haider, the FPÖ took on governing responsibility in a coalition with the centre-right Christian conservative ÖVP (*Österreichische Volkspartei*—Austrian People's Party) in 1999 (cf. Frölich-Steffen 2004; Morrow 2000). In 2005, tensions within the party led Haider to initiate a split from the FPÖ to form the BZÖ (*Bündnis Zukunft Österreich*—Alliance for the Future of Austria). His successor as FPÖ chairman was Heinz-Christian Strache, whose aggressive anti-immigration politics and focus on nationalist interests (Meret and Siim 2013, 81) carried him to significant success in the 2010 and 2015 local elections in Vienna.

The FPÖ's latest party manifesto (FPÖ 2011) sets out their '[l]iberal policy guidelines'. 'Freedom' and the protection of 'our homeland of Austria, our national identity and autonomy' and 'our natural livelihood' prominently underpin the party's efforts. The FPÖ aims, among other things, at ensuring the security of the Austrian territory and its citizens (while preserving Austria's neutrality), understanding Europe as a community of associated, but distinct, 'free peoples and autonomous fatherlands' and upholding the nuclear family.

The FPÖ has frequently been described as being flexible in its ideology and stances on different issues over time; for example, the party's initial support for joining the European Union (EU) was gradually replaced by encouragement of Austrian patriotism to appeal to a specific electorate (cf. Chiantera-Stutte and Pető 2003; Frölich-Steffen 2004). Similarly, the FPÖ has moved from a traditionally anti-clerical position to identifying with Christian (so-called family) values in the face of a perceived Islamic threat (Luther 2005; Meret and Siim 2013). With respect to gender issues,

Geden sees the FPÖ as notable in comparison to most of the European extreme right because of its emphasis on 'women's and family policy issues' (2005, 401). Geden theorises that this is due to the FPÖ's relatively strong position within national politics, necessitating engagement with a range of topics.

At the time of writing (January 2016), Barbara Rosenkranz is a member of the Austrian parliament, working on committees concerned with family, anti-discrimination and EU-related issues (among others). Her political history includes serving as national vice-chairwoman of the FPÖ, party chairwoman for Lower Austria, member of the government of Lower Austria and presidential candidate. Rosenkranz is a polarising figure in Austrian politics. National media portray her as a 'hardliner' and 'national-conservative' (*Die Presse* n.d.), an 'icon of the Right' (*Die Presse* 2010) and even as part of the 'right wing' within her party (Heigl 2013 in *Der Standard*). Often mentioned is her marriage to Horst Rosenkranz, who—as a former politician and publisher—has close ties with the extreme right and with whom she has ten children (cf. Lackner 2010 in *Profil*). Her personal circumstances have led to her often being cast in a maternal role, which aligns with Rommelspacher's (1999) findings that female participants in the political right often experience and operationalise a connection between mothering children and mothering the nation (1999, 55–56; see also Bacchetta & Power, 2002). Rosenkranz has reportedly described herself as "conscious of *Heimat* and committed to values" (*Der Standard* 2010) and has distanced herself from allegations of right-wing extremism during her presidential campaign (FPÖ 2010).

Representative of her politics is her 2013 campaign in the Lower Austrian elections, for which she was FPÖ frontrunner. Her slogan *Politik mit Hausverstand* ('Politics with common sense') (FPÖ-Landesgruppe NÖ 2013) links to many of the discourses we will highlight below.

Understanding *MenschInnen*

MenschInnen gets its title from a corrupted version of '*Mensch*' (human being). In German, most nouns referring to persons can produce a specifically feminine form by adding the ending '*-in*' ('*-innen*' for the plural) to the masculine form. While for a long time masculine forms were considered to be unmarked and to refer to 'both' genders, it has recently become less common to use masculine forms only. While there are several methods for greater inclusivity in German, forms that combine both the masculine and the feminine form into one word by using a capital I have become the most widely used—and the most attacked. While this option works with nouns that have a specifically female-marked form (*'StudentInnen'*—male and female students), Rosenkranz applies it to *'Menschen'* (human beings) even though *'Menschinnen'* is not grammatical. She borrows this strategy from critics who mock feminist language use by producing absurd-sounding words based on actually used gender-inclusive forms.

The expression of (grammatical) gender on the linguistic level of lexis creates a particular challenge in translating quotes from the book. Rosenkranz switches between 'male' forms and 'female only' forms (the latter usually for people whom she sees as proponents of the 'gender ideology'). She also uses joint forms with a capital I (see above) but does so only to 'Other' those she is referring to, often imbued with a sense of mockery (of such language use, as well as of the people who advocate it).

The subtitle of the book, *Auf dem Weg zum geschlechtslosen Menschen* ('On the way to the genderless human') hints at one of Rosenkranz' main arguments. Like other far-right activists, Rosenkranz understands movements for gender equality as part of a bigger plan to rid humans of what are seen as some of their most important—innate—qualities: sex and gender. More than that, gender is seen as a fundamental element of humanity whose loss results in a transformation of humans.

In addition to analysing *MenschInnen*, we have followed up on the authors quoted by Rosenkranz, as well as sources which discuss her ideas (cf. Billig 2004). This allows us to identify similarities and differences between various right-wing discourses on gender (especially German discourses). While it is not possible here to go into details of these additional sources due to restrictions of space, they have enabled us to better understand the contextual embeddedness of *MenschInnen*. We found that *MenschInnen* can in many ways be seen as both a continuation and a repetition of common right-wing, masculinist and religious-conservative discourses on gender and sexuality. In some cases, Rosenkranz reproduces passages from her sources almost literally. However, even though these other texts are written from various and potentially competing perspectives, this is not immediately obvious from *MenschInnen*.[2] It is only through reading Rosenkranz' sources that the different currents in *MenschInnen* become visible.

While many of Rosenkranz' sources position men as victims of feminist suppression, Rosenkranz' main enemy is 'the gender ideology' and its supposed aim of 'creating a new kind of human being'. Similarly, the 'gender conspiracy', which Rosenkranz claims to unmask, is supported by groups that are in stark opposition to each other (e.g., Marxists and capitalists), and she refutes her own claims of a homogeneous conspiracy by citing articles that are critical of Gender Mainstreaming from what she describes as 'left-wing media'. Furthermore, in her understanding, Gender Mainstreaming is at the same time a headless beast and a concerted conspiracy led by a small circle.

However, such inconsistencies are secondary because it is not immediately important to Rosenkranz' 'argument' *who* the Other is, as long as there is an Other that can be constructed in opposition to the *Volk* ('the people')[3] and its *Hausverstand* ('common sense'), and Rosenkranz as their defender. This Other is both diffuse ('the elite', 'the gender ideology') and specific (represented by various exponents such as Judith Butler or the social democratic—and lesbian—MEP Lissy Gröner) but always employs ruthless strategies to achieve its goal of a 'genderless person'. In the form of the 'gender conspiracy', the Other is everywhere, a constant threat to the future of the *Volk* that must be repelled.

ANALYSIS

Gender Mainstreaming

Gender Mainstreaming, focus of Rosenkranz' criticism in *MenschInnen*, is defined by the Council of Europe as 'the (re)organization, improvement, development and evaluation of policy processes, so that a gender equality perspective is incorporated in all policies at all levels and all stages, by the actors normally involved in policy making' (2004, 12).

Rosenkranz, however, dissolves the term into its two lexical components: *gender* and *mainstreaming*. She associates 'gender' with attempts to deconstruct/destruct people's gender and sex (*Geschlecht*[4]). 'Mainstreaming', then, refers to the attempt to make this conception of *Geschlecht* 'mainstream', that is, force it upon everyone. Rosenkranz describes Gender Mainstreaming as an 'ingenious concept summarised with an obfuscating term' (30). The alleged lack of a 'German translation' is seen as a sign that the meaning of Gender Mainstreaming is intentionally veiled: 'The lack of a translation of the "technical" terms into German proves the intention [...] to hide the true reasons behind it from the populace' (40).

Elite vs. People

Throughout the book, Rosenkranz suggests that Gender Mainstreaming is a strategy that is pursued by the elite who intentionally keeps its agenda hidden from 'the people'. Both 'elite' and 'people' are treated as internally coherent and homogenous groups. The oppositional relationship between 'the elite' and 'the people' (14) is made explicit in a chapter title in which their relation to each other is described as antagonistic. This dichotomy is a hallmark characteristic of populist rhetoric (Harrison and Bruter 2011). Gingrich (2006) argues that such discourses are frequently used by what he terms 'new nationalists' (30), which aligns with the FPÖ's overall *Heimat*-focused politics; it furthermore fits into a division of the world into 'good' and 'bad' factions (Wodak 2002, 35)—a very basic distinction that nevertheless is instrumental in positioning the party and its potential voters as fighters for the true desirable state of society.

'The elite' is positioned as being aware of the will of the people, but intentionally ignoring it. They are constructed as 'divorced from everyday life' (120) and blinded by their ideology, which also pits them against the 'common sense' of 'the people'. This idea of a common understanding of what is good, right, acceptable and true is a distinctive feature of Rosenkranz' politics and right-wing politics more generally. Rosenkranz operationalises (national, sexual, gendered, etc.) citizenship as a site of inclusion and exclusion simultaneously (cf. Yuval-Davis and Werbner 1999) and works towards conceptualising images of enemies and allies for (the) people to dis-/identify with and to elicit emotional responses. She specifically elevates the quality of 'common sense' to a virtue of those who agree with a supposedly self-explanatory traditional truth, forging a site of belonging and a basis for safe (because 'well-reasoned' and 'objectively researched') 'dissidence' in relation to the 'politically correct' elite (cf. Auer 2002, 297). Rosenkranz positions herself as both a part of 'the people' and their defender against those in power.

Rosenkranz' depiction of gender theories shows peculiar xenophobic overtones, as she discursively produces an 'ideological "scapegoat"' (Auer 2002, 296) that, on the one hand, is allowed to stand as a hard-to-grasp force against the self-evident common good, and on the other hand, may receive a particular identity (e.g., that of Judith Butler) to bear the brunt of irony, vaguely implied humour or ostensibly innocent incomprehension.

Rosenkranz' focus on anti-establishment discourses in respect to gender illustrates a politics of emotion and protest that locates the perpetrators of a poisonous ideology in the ranks of those in power. The perceived nebulous, and therefore threatening, ideas of the 'gender ideology' are seen as institutionalised on the highest levels of national and EU governments, thereby being forced on the Austrian people. As 'the elite' tries to fundamentally change the way people see *Geschlecht*, their right to self-determination is under attack, providing ground for sentiments of existential anxiety to fester, which right-wing parties traditionally seek to utilise (Betz 1994). By presenting herself in the role of the unraveller, Rosenkranz personifies a defender of the people (who are always implied to adhere to *Hausverstand* views).

The Gender Conspiracy

Although Rosenkranz does not use the word *conspiracy*, allusions to the existence of a concerted effort hidden behind Gender Mainstreaming are sustained throughout the book: 'The propagandists of Gender Mainstreaming act consciously, and keep strictly to the chosen strategy' (97).

The term 'chosen strategy' implies that the conspiracy has a head who chose this course of action and deliberately engineered the situation so as to be perceived differently than it 'really' is. And indeed, elsewhere, Rosenkranz speaks about the 'insiders' (33) of Gender Mainstreaming and suggests that 'if you assume that the true reasons [behind Gender Mainstreaming] are being obscured, you are right' (40).

'Our misguided elites, who think they can ignore the laws of nature, life experience, and all traditions without consequence, take advantage of a sinister magic trick with which they have (so far) been able to paralyse and deceive their naïve subjects—us. They use their monopoly over the media,[5] their obedient academic networks at universities and their subservient teachers and professors to create an image of a public opinion that leads everyone to believe that all those who are well-educated and successful agree on the arbitrariness of sex and gender' (142).

The wealth of different groups that are supposedly part of the conspiracy is surprising: they include feminists, homosexuals, Marxists, capitalists, the EU and the media. Even conservative parties have submitted to or actively take part in the gender conspiracy (110).

Rosenkranz claims that the goal that unites feminists, Marxists and capitalists is having as many women as possible in the workforce. In relation to the role of women in Marxism, she writes: 'The only thing that counts is that the human material[6] can be used for work. People get turned into work tools, objects that can be used at will' (72).

Rosenkranz maintains that Lenin had the same goal the EU has today: 'confusing and destroying "old role models" in order to use women for labour' (72). The link between Marxism and capitalism is their shared belief in 'materialism'. Both capitalism and Marxism are constructed as lacking the values that Rosenkranz claims to protect: 'In both ideologies, a reality beyond the material is not recognised. Both are ideologies without metaphysics' (93).

The media as well as academic institutions are considered another part of the gender conspiracy. This relates to tendencies in the right to portray themselves (and thus the populace whom they seek to be on a par with) as victims of their political opponents. For example, discourses of *Ausgrenzung* ('marginalisation') of right-wing voices were operationalised by Haider and his colleagues as a communicative means to keep a foothold in discussions by accusing non-FPÖ politicians of excluding them and their views from serious consideration (Gotsbachner 2003). As with Gender Mainstreaming, these efforts relied on a capitalisation of feelings of exclusion, being left behind, and not having their (and thus the people's) needs met.

The Gay Agenda

Rosenkranz repeatedly claims that feminists and homosexuals form a close alliance and constructs this link as creating a fundamental incommensurability between the aims of 'the feminist movement' and 'normal women': '[Female] Feminists often were close to the homosexual community[7] [...] This necessarily means that the demands of leftist [female] feminists [...] are different from the wishes of many women, especially in the important domains of family and marriage' (81).

Rosenkranz propagates a perception of the world in essentialist, clearcut and supposedly self-evident terms. Sexual, gendered and therefore political Others (feminists, homosexuals) are conflated into a grouping hostile towards the women that Rosenkranz portrays as 'many' (i.e., the normative majority). She appears to see no reason to elaborate on why the desires of homosexuals in relation to marriage and the family would 'necessarily' differ from those of heterosexuals—this self-evident truth creates space for those who understand and accept it in its obviousness, and in which people get rewarded by inclusion in normative citizenship.

Homosexuality is read as directly counteracting pro-natalist efforts by not allowing for procreation. As a result, homosexuals and their allies are thought not to care about the future of the nation (cf. Edelman 2004); they are concerned with hedonistic and selfish aims, whereas Rosenkranz stands, both politically and as a private (mother-)figure, proudly and determinedly in support of encouraging population growth, and thus the future of Austria.

Using a similar strategy, the gender and sexual properties of supposed proponents of Gender Mainstreaming are put on display to undermine their credibility when talking about gender issues: 'Foucault, who was born in 1926 and died of AIDS in 1984, himself homosexual, tried to deconstruct the naturalness of sexuality' (83).

Furthermore, in many cases, implicit or explicit links are drawn between proponents of 'the gender ideology' and paedosexuality or other deviant sexualities (cf. De Koster and Houtman 2008; Riegel 2005). By denigrating supposed 'enemies' whose existence and outspokenness jeopardise the *Volk*'s on-going survival (i.e., the welfare of its children and the moral 'purity' of people's health and desires), Rosenkranz produces a sense of alarm and imminent danger that underlines the urgency of her argument.

Totalitarianism and Persecutions

As the chapter title 'Resistance is punished' (59) alludes to, Rosenkranz positions 'the gender ideology' as a totalitarian movement reminiscent of 'religious zealotry' (59). The elite suppresses dissenting opinions, 'persecutes nonbelievers' (59) and 'does not shy away from threatening dissidents' (61). Furthermore, this elite supposedly sees counter-arguments as proof of a patriarchal conspiracy; an ironic claim in light of the fear of a gender conspiracy that permeates the book.

By positioning opponents of 'Gender Mainstreaming' as martyrs in the fight against feminism and political correctness, Rosenkranz avails herself of language that has distinctive connotations of curtailed freedom, intentional misleading, persecution of the innocent and injustice targeted at the people. Even though Rosenkranz repeatedly refers to (neo-)liberal ideas, suggesting that the state must not interfere in the private affairs of its citizens, it becomes clear that the desired form of free will is one which corresponds to right-wing or 'common-sense' conceptions of 'what women truly want'. The desired 'will of the people', which is constructed as being the actual will of the people, is naturalised as unquestionably true.

In Rosenkranz' view, 'reality' is heavily linked to fundamental conceptions of humanity; not only is it supposedly natural to prefer a life within a homogeneous community (cf. Meret and Siim 2013), but this understanding of self is rooted in a biologistic determination of gender roles (Geden 2005). Rosenkranz' work can therefore be read in the context of a perceived crisis of gender culture that pervades Austrian society (and Western societies in general).

A New Kind of Human

According to Rosenkranz, the aim of the totalitarian gender conspiracy is the creation of a new kind of human being: ultimately, Gender Mainstreaming is 'a Marxist project to create a "new human being" through the destruction of "traditional gender roles"' (96). The aim of all Gender Mainstreaming 'insiders' is to create a kind of genderless person and to oppress men.

'To most "average people", this may still sound somewhat strange … "Still" because the proponents [of Gender Mainstreaming] have already infiltrated politics, science and society, and work relentlessly to achieve their goal' (92).

This *Neuer Mensch* ('new human') is constructed as being stripped of their individuality by the elite. It can be seen as a metaphor for a new society, one that does not adhere to traditional norms, and where citizenship is opened up to deviants as well as newly transformed former 'good' citizens. The *Neuer Mensch* is a foreign body that infiltrates the secure *Heimat* that is associated with affects of belonging, similarity and reference to a communal nostalgic past. This infiltration and transformation happens socially as well as physiologically as, after all, sex itself is constructed in the 'gender ideology'.

Umerziehung

The elite believes in its goal of creating a new kind of human being because it thinks that *Geschlecht* can be 'reprogrammed' (63). In order to achieve their goal of the 'genderless person', the elites are willing to act not only against 'the people's' will, but also against the needs of children, which are constructed in parallel to mothers' desires. In their pursuit of the genderless person, the elites employ what Rosenkranz calls *Umerziehung* ('re-education'; 132). As 'the gender ideology' is seen as an 'experiment that contradicts all anthropological and scientific knowledge' (142), it is 'obvious that the state needs to get hold of the children and sexualise them as early as possible to achieve the set goal' (142).

The *Umerziehung* of 'innocent' children is linked to the totalitarian state as well as sexual depravity. The far-right encyclopaedia *Metapedia* contains a lengthy article on '*Umerziehung*' in which it is defined as 'a far-reaching political method which manipulates world views and behaviours with the aim of effecting change in ideology in open or subtle ways through forced and systematic indoctrination' (*Metapedia* 2013).

This concept of *Umerziehung* is especially linked to the time after the Second World War when the *Besatzungsmächte* ('occupation forces') used *Internierungslager* ('internment camps') to 're-educate' 'the German people'. Additionally, the term has very strong negative connotations and associations with totalitarian regimes even outside of far-right ideologies (Müller 2010, 81). The *Umerziehung* of Austrian children to mould them to the goals of the gender ideology is therefore seen by Rosenkranz as another sign of a totalitarian conspiracy.

Umerziehung is, notably, not restricted to children: the proponents of the gender ideology also force their will onto mothers by means of 'economic consequences as well as legal regulations and "consciousness-raising"' (22). The use of quotation marks implies that there is actually something else hiding behind what 'gender proponents' call 'consciousness-raising'.

Threats to Identity and Future

The ideology of Gender Mainstreaming is consistently constructed as a threat to the continued existence of the Austrian *Volk*. Rosenkranz argues that if the birth rate of a society is too low, this society 'has to succumb to any other society, however archaic and premodern' (11). In the next paragraph, she cites the high birth rate in Africa (11–2), ostensibly referencing a continent full of such societies. Similarly, there is a chapter entitled 'The demographic threat' (11). This threat to the people/nation is associated with a sense of urgency as the gender conspiracy has almost achieved its goals: '[Proponents of Gender Mainstreaming] decide the prevailing tenor of most media, they teach our children according to their wishes, they concoct strategies and laws in Brussels that are then implemented as legally binding by our local courts, by our parliament' (141).

That Gender Mainstreaming is seen as a 'dogma from Brussels' (28) links to the general anti-EU position the FPÖ adopted in the 1990s (Chiantera-Stutte and Pető 2003) and which it emphasised recently. In parallel to Rosenkranz' claim that the common people have retained their true and rightful will to maintain traditional gender roles and a traditional family life in spite of the onslaught of the gender conspiracy (141), having children is seen as women's duty to protect the integrity of the people and the nation. Women are positioned in the role of the nurturing mother whose primary responsibility is to guarantee the continued survival of the *Volk*, and the gender conspiracy threatens that role: 'If even just a fraction of the attention and means devoted to Gender Mainstreaming were dedicated to our bitterly suffering family politics, we would be freed of all our sorrows' (110).

It is not only the low birth rates that threaten the future of the Austrian *Volk* but also the destruction of traditional and supposedly commonsensical norms by homosexuals, feminists, Marxists, capitalists and other subversive elements, such as immigrants. This dual threat—the extinction of both the biological bodies and the social values that make up the *Volk*—echoes throughout the book. We suggest the term *Überfremdung von innen*, referring to the fear of *being transformed into the Other from the inside*. With this concept, we want to capture a different phenomenon than the more common right-wing fear of the nation's being overrun with (often visually discernible) ethnic, cultural or religious Others: Gender Mainstreaming and its ideological influence endanger the *Volk* from within, doubling a threat to communal identity by adding a gendered and sexual dimension. Upsetting traditional gender norms is a particularly insidious danger to national customs and identity since they are intertwined with the family—the fundamental building block that, through its set structure, upholds society. The family, and with it the *Volk*, can only be sustained by the right norms—those norms that are based on the 'right' *Hausverstand*.

CONCLUSION

Rosenkranz' book and her related politics use many communicative strategies utilised by the national and international far right. The discourses we have commented on in this chapter are centred around notions of gender that are highly assumptive and normative in their construction of roles and behaviours of individual people: men and women are biologically determined in their identities, practices and preferences, and while there might be outliers, they usually prove the rule or find a way to segue into it (just like Rosenkranz' own persona as a successful career politician on the one hand, and a committed wife and mother of ten on the other). Resulting from this is a strong suggestion of how the world *should* be, which is concurrently seen as how 'ordinary people' desire the world to be, and placed in opposition to 'the elite's' totalitarian vision of how *they* want it to be. Utilising populist tactics of interpretation and deliberate re-framing of issues, Rosenkranz positions Austrian culture in a state of crisis in relation to its gender conditions. Here, a firm connection is established between gender and the family, as well as between the family and the continued survival of society. Specifically, the decline in Austria's birth rate is highlighted as a fundamentally dangerous circumstance that Rosenkranz and her party are working hard to reverse.

Austria's prosperity as a nation and a distinct community of people is perceived as being under threat from many sides. This leads to a need for self-defence against cultural, ethnic, racial and religious Others who seek to enter the country from outside (immigrants, refugees), since their merging with the Austrian people potentially pollutes the population's (perceived) purity. However, Rosenkranz also commits herself to uncovering Gender Mainstreaming, an ostensibly hidden conspiracy to change ordinary people from the inside out.

Her identification of numerous perpetrators of this allegedly already very active process leads to the construction of abstract as well as personified enemies of what counts as normal in her vision of ubiquitous *Hausverstand* ('common sense'): feminists, homosexuals, political and bureaucratic elites in Austria and the EU, pseudo-scientists, capitalists, Marxists and the media all supposedly take part in a concerted and frivolous effort to eradicate gender (and sex).

Within her worldview, Rosenkranz' fear is legitimised by the fact that gender relations within the family make up the nuclei that, together, structure and knit together the Austrian people into a coherent, homogeneous whole. From this perspective, the very idea that gender might be deconstructed is preposterous and, at best, laughable, since 'everyone' agrees that gender works in a specific, long-established way.

Rosenkranz implies a recklessness associated with Gender Mainstreaming politics. If ordinary, innocent and good citizens are in danger of being duped into thinking that gender might be different from what it 'is' (or more than that), then a form of societal organisation with heteronormative nuclear families at its heart becomes untenable. In this regard, society is in danger of being manipulated into destroying itself. Simultaneously, 'indigenous' Austrians remain subject to external threats of becoming a minority in their own *Heimat*. This process concerns both material aspects (fewer and fewer babies are born to 'Austrian' parents) and socio-cultural aspects of life. With a deconstruction of gender norms comes a shift in values and morals that could cause Austria's far right's fears to come true. Many of these anxieties can indeed be read as relating to a transformation of the Austrian people as a worst-case scenario. Rosenkranz frequently points out the non-heterosexual orientations or trans* status of 'gender ideologists' in an implicitly negative manner; by cautioning against Gender Mainstreaming, she thereby also warns against an assimilation that will result not only in the people's deviation from normative identities and practices but in their *becoming the Other*. *MenschInnen* therefore exemplifies a fear of what we call *Überfremdung von innen*: the self-inflicted transformation and, therefore, destruction of the nation and its people from within.

NOTES

1. A note on translations: all translations from German to English are ours. This refers to Rosenkranz' book as well as German-language media sources. These translations are not to be understood as neutral, as no translation ever can be (Derrida 1982 [1972], 20; Fawcett and Munday 2009 [1998], 137–138; c.f. Resch 2001; Cooke 2011). We are fully aware that our translation is one option among many (Spivak 1997, lxxxvi), and trust that it will make our analysis understandable for our readers.
2. Interestingly, the very common reference to 'Judeo-Christian' ideas used in Rosenkranz' sources is not apparent in *MenschInnen*. There may be two reasons for this: first, Rosenkranz herself has left the Catholic church (*News* 2010). Second, Rosenkranz attacks the credibility of the gender conspiracy by denouncing it as a purely ideological and unscientific political project, and claims a position of ideological 'neutrality' for herself and 'the people's will'. This position would have been weakened by referring to religious ideologies.
3. *Volk*, especially in a right-wing context, carries racist connotations of cultural and ethnic homogeneity. The *Volk* is the people as much as it is the nation.

4. The term '*Geschlecht*' can refer to gender, sex or both gender and sex at the same time.
5. The media are described as '*gleichgeschaltet*', which implies that they are made to adhere to propaganda strategy. It is linked to the concept of '*Umerziehung*', which will be explored in more depth below.
6. 'Human material' ('*Menschenmaterial*') implies that humans are a resource that can be used and disposed of at will. Humans in '*Menschenmaterial*' are no longer people, but simply resources.
7. '*Szene*', which we translated as 'community' here, has a strong association with being a subcultural Other. It does not encompass the potential positive connotations of 'community'.

References

Auer, Katrin. 2002. 'Political Correctness'—Ideologischer Code, Feindbild und Stigmawort der Rechten. *Österreichische Zeitschrift für Politikwissenschaft* 31: 291–303.

Bacchetta, Paola, and Margaret Power (ed). 2002. *Right-Wing Women: From Conservatives to Extremists Around the World*. London: Routledge.

Betz, Hans-Georg. 1994. *Radical Right-Wing Populism in Western Europe*. Basingstoke and London: The Macmillan Press.

Billig, Michael. 2004. Methodology and Scholarship in Understanding Ideological Explanation. In *Social Research Methods*, ed. Clive Seale, 13–18. London: Routledge. Originally published in Charles Antaki (ed). *Analysing Everyday Explanation: A Casebook of Methods*. London: Sage, 1988.

Chiantera-Stutte, Patricia, and Pető, Andrea. 2003. Cultures of Populism and the Political Right in Central Europe *CLCWeb: Comparative Literature and Culture* 5(4). Accessed 24 February 2013. http://dx.doi.org/10.7771/1481-4374.1198

Cooke, Michèle. 2011. *The Lightning Flash: Language, Longing and the Facts of Life*. Frankfurt am Main: Peter Lang.

Council of Europe. 2004. Gender Mainstreaming: Conceptual Framework, Methodology and Presentation of Good Practices. Directorate General of Human Rights, Strasbourg. Accessed 22 March 2016. http://www.coe.int/t/dghl/standardsetting/equality/03themes/gender-mainstreaming/EG_S_MS_98_2_rev_en.pdf

De Koster, Willem, and Dick Houtman. 2008. 'Stormfront is Like a Second Home to Me': On Virtual Community Formation by Right Wing Extremists. *Information, Communication & Society* 11(8): 1153–1175.

Derrida, Jacques. 1982 [1972]. Semiology and Grammatology: Interview with Julia Kristeva. In *Positions*, ed. Derrida, Jacques, 15–36. Translated and annotated by Alan Bass. Chicago: University of Chicago Press.

Der Standard. 2010, April 21. Rechtsextrem bin ich jedenfalls nicht. Accessed 22 March 2016. http://derstandard.at/1271374800090/Nachlese-Rosenkranz-Chat-Rechtsextrem-bin-ich-jedenfalls-nicht

Die Presse. 2010, February 26. Barbara Rosenkranz: Zehnfache Mutter will Hofburg bevölkern. Accessed 22 March 2016. http://diepresse.com/home/politik/innenpolitik/542752/Zehnfache-Mutter-Rosenkranz-will-Hofburg-bevoelkern?direct=543283&_vl_backlink=/home/politik/innenpolitik/358330/index.do&selChannel

Die Presse. n.d. Rosenkranz: Nationalkonservative Vorzeigemutter kann Fischer nicht gefährden. Image 2. Accessed 22 March 2016. http://diepresse.com/home/politik/hofburgwahl/358330/Rosenkranz_Nationalkonservative-Vorzeigemutter-kann-Fischer-nicht?gal=358330&index=2&direct=&_vl_backlink=&popup=

Edelman, Lee. 2004. *No Future: Queer Theory and the Death Drive.* Durham: Duke University Press.

Fawcett, Peter, and Jeremy Munday. 2009 [1998]. Ideology. In *Routledge Encyclopedia of Translation Studies,* 2 edn, ed. Mona Baker, and Gabriela Saldanha, 137–140. London and New York: Routledge.

FPÖ. 2010, March 08. Eidesstättige Erklärung von Präsidentschaftskandidatin Barbara Rosenkranz. Accessed 22 March 2016. http://www.fpoe.at/news/detail/news/eidesstaettige-erklaerung-von/

———. 2011, June 18. Party Programme of the Freedom Party of Austria (FPÖ). Resolved by the Party Conference. Graz.

FPÖ-Landesgruppe NÖ. 2013. *Mut zur Heimat: Niederösterreich zuerst!* Election Manifesto for Local Elections in Lower Austria. St. Pölten.

Frölich-Steffen, Susanne. 2004. Die Identitätspolitik der FPÖ: Vom Deutschnationalismus zum Österreich-Patriotismus. *Österreichische Zeitschrift für Politikwissenschaft* 33(3): 281–295.

Geden, Oliver. 2005. The Discursive Representation of Masculinity in the Freedom Party of Austria (FPÖ). *Journal of Language and Politics* 4(3): 397–420.

Gingrich, Andre. 2006. Nation, Status and Gender in Trouble? Exploring Some Contexts and Characteristics of Neo-nationalism in Western Europe. In *Neo-Nationalism in Europe and Beyond: Perspectives from Social Anthropology,* ed. Andre Gingrich, and Marcus Banks, 29–49. New York and Oxford: Berghahn Books.

Gotsbachner, Emo. 2003. Normalisierungsstrategien in der Rhetorik der FPÖ: Die politische Alchemie, Kritik in Unterstützung zu verwandeln. *Österreichische Zeitschrift für Politikwissenschaft* 32(4): 457–483.

Harrison, Sarah, and Michael Bruter. 2011. *Mapping Extreme Right Ideology.* Basingstoke: Palgrave Macmillan.

Heigl, Andrea. 2013, February 24. Rosenkranz: 'Mütter kleiner Kinder würden gern viel länger daheimbleiben'. *Der Standard.* Accessed 22 March 2016.

http://derstandard.at/1361240945616/Rosenkranz-Muetter-kleiner-Kinder-wuerden-gern-viel-laenger-daheimbleiben

Lackner, Herbert. 2010, March 06. Rosenkranz-Kandidatur: Erlebt Österreich noch einmal einen Waldheim-Wahlkampf? *Profil.* Accessed 22 March 2016. http://www.profil.at/articles/1009/560/263725/rosenkranz-kandidatur-erlebt-oesterreich-waldheim-wahlkampf

Luther, Kurt R. 2005. Die Freiheitliche Partei Österreichs (FPÖ) und das Bündnis Zukunft Österreichs (BZÖ) Keele European Parties Research Unit (KEPRU), Working Paper 22. Keele University. Accessed 22 March 2016. http://www.keele.ac.uk/media/keeleuniversity/group/kepru/KEPRU%20WP%2022.pdf

Meret, Susi, and Birte Siim. 2013. Gender, Populism and Politics of Belonging: Discourses of Right-Wing Populist Parties in Denmark, Norway and Austria. In *Negotiating Gender and Diversity in an Emerging European Public Sphere*, ed. Birte Siim, and Monika Mokre, 78–96. Basingstoke: Palgrave Macmillan.

Metapedia. 2013. Umerziehung. Accessed 28 February 2013. http://de.metapedia.org/wiki/Umerziehung

Morrow, Duncan. 2000. Jörg Haider and the New FPÖ: Beyond the Democratic Pale? In *The Politics of the Extreme Right: From the Margins to the Mainstream*, ed. Paul Hainsworth, 33–63. London: Pinter.

Müller, Yves. 2010. Gegen Feminismus und »Dekadenz«—die Neue Rechte in der Krise? In »Was ein rechter Mann ist ...«: Männlichkeiten im Rechtsextremismus, ed. Robert Claus, Esther Lehnert, and Yves Müller, 67–87. Berlin: Karl Dietz Verlag.

News. 2010, March 03. Rosenkranz ist alles andere als "heilig": Schon vor Jahren aus der Kirche ausgetreten. Accessed 22 March 2016. http://www.news.at/a/rosenkranz-heilig-schon-jahren-kirche-263408#

Resch, Renate. 2001. Übersetzen als Empowerment: Zum Verhältnis von Text, Diskurs und Macht. In *Übersetzung aus aller Frauen Länder. Beiträge zu Theorie und Praxis weiblicher Realität in der Translation*, ed. Sabine Messner, and Michaela Wolf, 119–126. Graz: Leykam.

Riegel, David L. 2005. Pedophilia, Pejoration, and Prejudice: Inquiry by Insinuation, Argument by Accusation. *Sexuality & Culture* 9(1): 88–97.

Rommelspacher, Birgit. 1999. Right-Wing 'Feminism': A Challenge to Feminism as an Emancipatory Movement. In *Women, Citizenship and Difference*, ed. Nira Yuval-Davis, and Pnina Werbner, 54–64. London and New York: Zed Books.

Rosenkranz, Barbara. 2008. *MenschInnen: Gender Mainstreaming—Auf dem Weg zum geschlechtslosen Menschen*. Graz: Ares Verlag.

Spivak, Gayatri C. 1997. Translator's Preface. In *Of Grammatology*, ed. Jacques Derrida, ix–lxxxvii. Translated by Gayatri C. Spivak. Corrected edition. Baltimore and London: The Johns Hopkins University Press.

Wodak, Ruth. 2002. Discourse and Politics: The Rhetoric of Exclusion. In *The Haider Phenomenon in Austria*, ed. Ruth Wodak, and Anton Pelinka, 33–60. New Brunswick: Transaction Publishers.

Yuval-Davis, Nira, and Pnina Werbner. 1999. Women and the New Discourse of Citizenship. In *Women, Citizenship and Difference*, ed. Nira Yuval-Davis, and Pnina Werbner, 1–38. London and New York: Zed Books.

Pitied Women, Aggressive Men. Images of Muslims in Swedish Christian and Secular News Discourse

Kristian Steiner

INTRODUCTION

This is a descriptive comparative analysis of Swedish media discourses on the use of gender in the construction of Islam and Muslims. The analysis focuses on editorials in two Christian and two secular publications from 2006–2007. The study has three aims; first of all to get a better understanding of how Muslims and Islam are constructed, secondly to examine to what extent and in what ways gender is used to construct this image and thirdly to see to what extent this usage of gender is consensual.

Four media have been selected for strategic reasons: *Dagens Nyheter*,[1] the Swedish morning paper with the largest circulation, is representing liberal and secular Swedish mainstream media. *SD-Kuriren*[2] is a much smaller media product, a journal representing a neo-nationalist political party, the Sweden Democrats. Thus, it deviates from *Dagens Nyheter* in character, with regard to its purpose, size, and independence. However, since *SD-Kuriren* is the leading neo-nationalist journal or newspaper in the Swedish market, it has been selected for analysis.

This is a revised version of 'Images of Muslims and Islam in Swedish Christian and secular news discourse' in Media, War & Conflict, 2015, Vol. 8(1) 20–45.

K. Steiner (✉)
Department of Global Political Studies, Malmö University, Malmö, Sweden

© The Author(s) 2017
M. Köttig et al. (eds.), *Gender and Far Right Politics in Europe*,
DOI 10.1007/978-3-319-43533-6_17

The two remaining newspapers are conservative Christian and comparatively small: *Dagen*[3] is conservative and Evangelical and is sometimes called an ecumenical newspaper. *Världen idag*[4] is formally independent but has close ties to Livets Ord (Word of Life) in Uppsala, a charismatic fundamentalist church.

Although a number of studies on the media image of Muslims and Islam have been undertaken, the gender aspect has been neglected (Navarro 2010:97). Ergo, this is where this study can make a contribution to the debate.

The few studies on the media image focusing on gender all come to similar conclusions: Muslim women are repeatedly depicted as veiled, oppressed, passive (Martin-Muñoz 2002:2; Ehrkamp 2010:24; Macdonald 2006:13; Hebbani and Wills 2012:88), often without control over their sexuality (Ehrkamp 2010:14), submissive (Navarro 2010:98), victims without freedom (Posetti 2006:1f) and in need of Western rescue (Lee Riley 2013:15). They are often also depicted as incapable, being without a profession (Martin-Muñoz 2002:3), and as being absent in the political sphere (Navarro 2010:98).

Of course there is not just one single media image of Muslim women. Particularly in Europe, the hijab has become a symbol of repression (Macdonald 2006:8, 13; Byng 2010:111f; Carøe Christiansen 2011:336f) or 'a highly visible sign of a despised difference' (Macdonald 2006:19) and even of conflicts between cultures (Posetti 2006:1). The only truly positive image of Muslim women, at least in French media, is that of the liberated and rebellious Muslim woman (Navarro 2010:106).

These images are not harmless; they have consequences. Images of *oppressed* Muslim women can evoke our pity (Martin-Muñoz 2002:5) and make media consumers believe that 'they' are in need of 'our' liberation (Posetti 2006:1f). Furthermore, *we* define what liberation means (Macdonald 2006:10, 15), and often it means to unveil (Hebbani and Wills 2012:89). Moreover, the image of Muslim women as being oppressed by a patriarchy (Hoodfar 2006:5) not only constructs the West as superior (Hoodfar 2006:5); it can also be used as a reminder to Western women of 'their relative fortune and an implied warning to curb their 'excessive demands' for equality with men' (Hoodfar 2006:6). Likewise, it can be used to depict Western men as 'liberal and free-thinking, and appreciative of every aspect of female liberation', even as liberators of Muslim women (Lee Riley 2013:3). And lastly, such an image of Muslim women 'serves to reinforce the threat the Muslim man is said to pose to the West' (Razack 2008:107).

In the literature I have found two sets of motives explaining the occurrence of these images of Muslim women. Firstly, in media discourses on Islam, Muslim men are depicted as violent and dangerous. And this image requires an oppressed woman (cf. Hoodfar 2006:8; Navarro 2010:110). The image of Muslim women being oppressed by Muslim men is necessary to this construction. Secondly, in the construction of 'us' as superior, the image of an independent, emancipated Western woman is useful. The emancipation of Western women is a sign of our superiority. The veiled oppressed Muslim woman comes in handy as a point of reference (Bullock and Jafri 2000:35; Ehrkamp 2010:26).

In my research a descriptive, comparative, quantitative content analysis was used. Using such a method enables the results not only to reflect differences and similarities between the news products but also to identify nuances in their respective uses of language (Landmann 2008:4–5). The years under scrutiny, 2006 and 2007, were selected since they were years of intense conflict between Islamophobic groups in the West and Islamists. Furthermore, the political effects of the Danish Mohammed caricatures were evident, resulting in demonstrations and economic boycotts against Denmark. In Sweden, the website of the Sweden Democrats was shut down for a short time after the party had published the caricatures. And finally, parliamentary elections were held both in Sweden and in the Palestinian territories, resulting in a more heated political climate.

I only selected those articles that mentioned Islam and Muslims, Muslim organizations such as Hamas, Muslim terms such as Sharia and Muslim individuals or ethnic groups with a Muslim majority. In the case of *Dagens Nyheter*, *Dagen* and *Världen idag*, I selected only the editorials. In the period 2006–2007, *Dagens Nyheter* published 710 editorials (356 in 2006), of which 169 concerned Muslims and Islam (94 in 2006). *Dagen* published approximately 200 editorials a year, one per issue. Out of these, 76 editorials (41 in 2006) were selected. *Världen idag* published approximately 300 editorials a year, two in each issue. Based on the aforementioned criteria, 127 editorials were selected from the 2006–2007 issues (60 in 2006), which is approximately 21 per cent of all editorials. The selection criteria were expanded in the case of the *SD-Kuriren* so that not only editorials were included but all articles written by any member of the Sweden Democratic party board. In 2006 and 2007, 8 issues of *SD-Kuriren* were published, and in these issues members of the party board wrote 84 articles. Out of these 84 political articles, 34 were selected, making 40 per cent of all the political articles.

Analytically, the study has developed and refined a method based upon Entman 1993 keywords *diagnosing*, *evaluating* and *prescribing*, and likewise uses the same keywords to organize the study into three sections. In some sections, I develop more specific attendant operational questions.

THE DIAGNOSES

Editorials and ideological articles are usually spurred on by political problems. Success stories are rarely an inspiration. That problems characterize these articles is not necessarily a consequence of anti-Muslim attitudes *per se*. Nevertheless, a problem arises when European Muslims do not possess the tools to articulate alternative public images. Statements go unchallenged and contribute to an anti-Muslim discourse. Moreover, it is difficult to categorize editorials according to their diagnoses; sometimes there is more than one, and sometimes the diagnosis is unclear. The editorials are therefore classified inductively, identifying the most pertinent diagnoses without using predefined categories, the reason being that at this early stage this makes the articles appear open-ended and existing in their own right.

In the case of *Dagens Nyheter*, the most common diagnosis concerns the national policies, domestic or foreign, of different states. Furthermore, *Dagens Nyheter* mainly uses a non-religious discourse. Muslim actors are portrayed as politicians with a political, not a religious, agenda. This also holds true in the case of future Iranian nuclear capability (*Dagens Nyheter*, 16 January 2006).

The situation of Muslim women only once becomes the diagnosis of an editorial in *Dagens Nyheter*. In this article (*Dagens Nyheter*, 25 June 2007), the oppression of women in Iran and Saudi Arabia is emphasized, as well as the fear that such oppressive norms could also come to Sweden as an effect of immigration. 'We', particularly Swedish schools, are supposedly 'nonplussed' by these challenges, and we need to distinguish between unimportant issues, such as the veil, and important ones.

In *Dagen*, the dominant theme is the secularization of Swedish society, particularly of Swedish schools. Another major topic is the relationship between Muslims and Christians or the Western world. In this category threats are present. However, Islamism, not Islam, is defined as an inspiration for terrorism in Sweden (Thureson, 5 May 2006) and is said to be 'advancing' (Thureson, 8 June 2006) or responsible for terrorism in the UK (Österberg, 11 August 2006; Sandlund, 5 July 2007). In one editorial, the killing of a Catholic nun is discussed (Cyrillus, 20 September

2006). However, this is depicted as a case of religious persecution rather than of Muslim misogynism.

Världen idag's editorials frequently discuss the oppression of women in Muslim societies, but always as an element within a wider discussion. It is never the main theme. Rather, it is used as one of many arguments to illustrate Islam's violent and threatening character and its inability to democratize. By far the most common theme concerns different Muslim threats, particularly physical threats posed to the West. A second theme appearing in some editorials is the retreat of various Western elites from important Christian or democratic values, particularly when facing a Muslim threat. This retreat is described in a typically populist vein. It is supposedly caused by Muslim immigration as well as ignorant and naïve Western elites fearing Muslim immigrants. A third diagnosis is the perceived incompatibility between Islam and democracy. Islam is described as genuinely undemocratic. Muslim societies are supposedly unable to adopt democratic values (Tunehag, 27 February 2006).

An analysis of *SD-Kuriren* shows major rhetorical similarities with *Världen idag*, but also some differences. One important difference is that Western women are vulnerable to the threats that Muslim men allegedly pose. One article, 'The "new rape wave"' (Jomshof 74a, 2007), focuses completely on sexual assaults on women committed by 'immigrants'. The motives presented are the foreigners' racism and culture.

A general tendency in *SD-Kuriren* is the dominance of the Muslim threat as a theme. This threat is the dominating problem, or one of two dominating problems, in more than 60 per cent of the selected political articles. This is a larger proportion than in *Världen idag*. Unlike *Världen idag*, *SD-Kuriren* never claims that Islam as such is incompatible to democracy. However, just like *Världen idag*, *SD-Kuriren* dwells on the idea that Muslims in Europe constitute a threat to democracy. Furthermore, the writers return to the idea that the Muslim threat is permanent and growing, since 'they' are here, their number is growing and since 'they' are assumedly getting more radical. The number of Muslims is said to be growing very fast through 'mass immigration and high birth rates' (Jomshof 69a, 2006) and 'will cause very big problems in the future' (Jomshof 69a, 2006), as they will demand 'antidemocratic Sharia laws', Muslim autonomy and segregation (Jomshof 69d, 2006).

Just as in *Världen idag*, in *SD-Kuriren* Muslims are also portrayed as violent and irrational. The threat they constitute is not merely a threat to democratic ideas, but they also supposedly constitute a real physical threat and a threat to law and order. *SD-Kuriren* stresses that crime and sexual violence are yet another kind of Muslim threat and an outcome of Islam. In the mindset of *SD-Kuriren*, crime is not merely a social or legal issue if the perpetrator is Muslim. Crime is understood as part of a global war between the Muslim world and the West (Karlsson 74, 2007; Karlsson 68, 2006) and is seen as an outcome of Islamic attitudes, since 'Muslim violence against infidels to a large extent is based upon attitudes towards women, men, sex, and violence thriving in Muslim societies' (Jomshof 74a, 2007).

Another reoccurring theme in *SD-Kuriren* is the retreat of Western elites. Herein lies *SD-Kuriren*'s populist dimension, shared by *Världen idag*, voicing a mistrust of national elites and depicting them as ignorant and blind to the massive threats posed by the Islamic presence in the West. Just like *Världen idag*, *SD-Kuriren* sometimes uses historical analogies, comparing contemporary actors to those in the 1930s and 40s. The Scandinavian media are described as appeasers (Wiklander 67, 2006), and similarly, Dutch media allegedly 'suppress and belittle' the riots outside Utrecht (Jomshof 72b, 2007).

EVALUATION OF MUSLIMS' MORAL CHARACTER

The second phase in Entman 1993 framing method concerns the moral evaluation of actors in a discourse. This extensive section is divided into subsections based on more specific attendant operational themes. The first section analyses *explicit* claims regarding Muslims' moral character, and the second examines *implicit* ones.

EXPLICIT DESCRIPTIONS OF MUSLIMS

The analysis of the usage of labels denoting Muslims deals with the denotative precision and connotative value of labels (Ottosen 1995:100). Combining negative connotations with vague denotations is an effective strategy for inciting prejudice. In this case, no major differences between the four media appear. All of the newspapers seem to consciously avoid dysphemisms and other labels with negative connotations. However, that does not mean that the usage of labels is identical, as a few qualitative examples might illustrate. As in the other media, neutral or vague labels dominate in *Dagens Nyheter*, and 46 per cent of the labels denote ambiguity. Furthermore, the fact that the editorials use secular language also has implications for the use of labels depicting Muslims—they are usually secular. In the labels with negative connotations, about 17 per cent, *Dagens Nyheter* regularly avoids emphasizing their Muslim character. Regimes, governments, terrorists and presidents are rarely referred to as 'Muslim' regimes or a 'Muslim' government, and so on. When 'fanatics' are discussed, they are not referred to as 'Muslim', and 'extremists' are referred to as 'extremists on both sides' (*Dagens Nyheter*, 7 February 2006). And lastly, there are very few labels in the texts referring to Muslim women, Benazir Bhutto being the only exception, and no labels depict Muslim men as oppressors of women or Muslim women as victims. One negative label, referring to a Muslim woman, refers to Benazir Bhutto as a 'filthy figure' (*Dagens Nyheter*, 8 August 2007).

The use of labels in *Dagen* resembles that in *Dagens Nyheter* to a large extent. Here, too, very few labels refer to Muslim women; the Social Democratic politician Nalin Pekgul, Helena Benaouda, the chairperson of the Muslim Council of Sweden, and Benazir Bhutto, who is labelled as 'the leader of the opposition', are the only exceptions. Furthermore, no labels referring to Muslim men depict them as misogynic. Still, since *Dagen* is Evangelical, it has a tendency to use more religious language, to Islamize labels designating Muslim actors, turning militant actors into 'militant Muslims' (Thureson, 1 February 2006) and regimes into 'theocratic Arab countries' (Cyrillus, 15 November 2006). This is a bit surprising since *Dagen* tends to have a more benign outlook on Islam and Muslims in other respects.

Världen idag's editorials have significantly more labels for Muslims than *Dagens Nyheter* which publishes significantly more editorials. Of these labels, 13 per cent fall into the category of labels with an unequivocally negative connotation, the same proportion as *Dagen*. And labels with vague or neutral connotations dominate, as in other media. Labels with positive connotations are exceptionally rare. Lastly, Muslim women are largely absent and no labels are used to depict Muslim men as misogynic or women as oppressed.

Of course, the most problematic category is the one combining derogatory connotations with unspecific denotations, and here we find 'Islamic extremists' (Björk, 13 January 2006), 'this religion of violence' (Stenström, 6 February 2006), 'dangerous religion', (Stenström, 6 February 2006), 'the wolves' (Björk, 8 May 2006), 'the terrorists' (Tunehag, 6 September 2006) and 'these bawlers' (Tunehag, 18 September 2006). One label, 'Islamic despotic oppressors of women' (Tunehag, 3 May 2006), clearly depicts Muslim leaders as broadly misogynic.

SD-Kuriren's use of labels is consistent with the other media. In 34 articles, 184 labels denoting Muslim actors have been found, 12 per cent being classified as negative. This means that, just like the other media, *SD-Kuriren* does not allow labels with negative connotations to dominate. Likewise, vague or neutral labels dominate the editorials in *SD-Kuriren*. And here, too, labels denoting Muslim women are uncommon; no labels depict Muslim women as oppressed or men as misogynic. In one case, however, Nalin Pekgul, a Social Democrat with a Kurdish and Muslim background, is called a 'new Swede', in an attempt to depict her as an outsider (Jomshof 2007f).

In all the publications except *Dagens Nyheter*, there is a tendency to ambiguity. In *SD-Kuriren* 54 per cent of the labels denoting Muslims are ambiguous, possibly indicating that the writers generalize to some extent, but avoid using negatively charged labels. The dominant category is labels combining an ambiguous denotation with a neutral or vague connotation, such as 'Muslims' (Jomshof 6a, 2006; Jomshof 72b, 2007; Jomshof 74b, 2007), 'increasing numbers of Muslims' (Jomshof 67a, 2006; Jomshof 69a), 'strong Muslim forces' (Söder 67, 2006) and 'Islam' (Söder 67, 2006; Söder 69, 2006; Jomshof 72a, 2007).

The most ethically problematic labels, those combining a denotative ambiguity with negative connotation, represent 8 per cent of the total. In the case of *Världen idag*, many of these labels are clear dysphemisms. In *SD-Kuriren* all the dysphemisms are borderline cases, less malicious dysphemisms, such as 'a too large Muslim population in Sweden' (Jomshof 69a, 2006; Jomshof 74b, 2007), 'Muslim fundamentalists' (Jomshof 74b, 2007) and the 'alleged moderate Muslims' (Karlsson 72b, 2007).

All in all, this implies that the four media in many ways coincide in the use of labels as an instrument for describing Muslims; although the labels are ambiguous, they are considerably more offensive in the case of *Världen idag*.

IMPLICIT DESCRIPTIONS OF MUSLIMS

Presumably, debaters and writers avoid making explicit claims and assaults. Therefore, in this section, another linguistic layer will be considered, studying the implicit moral assessment of Muslims. Here, allegations regarding Muslim behaviour will be analysed. This section examines the moral standard of behaviour attributed to Muslim actors by analysing verbs, direct objects and adverbs. Here again, we can see a striking resemblance between *SD-Kuriren* and *Världen idag*. These two media repeatedly relate morally questionable behaviour to ambiguous Muslim actors, making Muslims in general responsible. This linguistic technique is the one where Muslims are consistently depicted in negative terms.

Dagens Nyheter connects Muslim actors with negative behaviour in 42 per cent of the cases, but more often with a well-defined actor, making individual leaders or organizations responsible, not Muslims in general. However, in 15 per cent of the cases, ambiguous actors are connected to negative behaviour, particularly in the heated Mohammed caricature debate, in statements like 'Muslims all over the world demand respect from Denmark' (*Dagens Nyheter*, 11 January 2006). The actions of Muslim men are rarely described as misogynic. In one editorial, the sexual freedom of Muslim children, particularly girls, is discussed. However, the criticized actors are 'parents', not fathers (*Dagens Nyheter*, 2007-06-25). The Taliban's kidnapping of South Korean nurses and teachers in the summer of 2007 is also discussed, but the gender of the victims is not mentioned. The kidnapping is not depicted as misogynic, but as a conflict between Islamist organizations and the West, especially Evangelical Christianity (*Dagens Nyheter*, 28 July 2007). In a few editorials, Muslim women are present as political actors, most importantly the Pakistani politician, Benazir Bhutto, and the Swedish Social Democrat, Nalin Pekgul.

The editorials in *Dagen* are slightly different in one important aspect. Although *Dagen* also associates Muslim actors with morally dubious behaviour, this is done less frequently. In 13 per cent of the cases, wide categories of Muslims are made responsible for negative behaviour, which in comparison to other media is relatively few cases. Moreover, negative behaviour is more often associated with well-defined actors.

The editorials in *Dagen*, just as in *Dagens Nyheter*, occasionally describe behaviour attributed to Muslim actors as commendable, although some comments are ambiguous (Thureson, 8 June 2006). And, in some cases, Muslim behaviour is depicted as ethical: Swedish Muslim representatives are said to support Christian values in the educational system (Österberg, 30 November 2006) and Arab states are said to criticize Hamas' policies (Thureson, 18 July 2006). In *Dagen*, statements made by female actors are sometimes approved of. The female actors are relatively powerful, representing a major Muslim organization in Sweden (Helena Benaouda), a political party (Benazir Bhutto) and the Swedish Social Democrats (Nalin Pekgul). No acts are mentioned that turn women into victims of Muslim male violence.

The two remaining media products are drastically different. *Världen idag* frequently makes Muslim actors accountable for morally questionable behaviour (Table 6c); 65 per cent of Muslim behaviour is morally doubtful; a mere 7 per cent is morally acceptable. 28 per cent of the behaviour depicted is morally vague or neutral. Furthermore, morally negative behaviour is repeatedly combined with ambiguous subject labels, making an undefined and large Muslim group responsible for the behaviour in question. The two most common behaviours attributed to Muslims are 'murder' and 'making demands'. During the observation period, Muslims are said to have committed murder more than 20 times. Secondly, Muslims 'make demands', and their demands are unjust, directed towards the West and part of a zero-sum game. Everything 'they' demand is at 'our' expense.

Also the role of women is different in *Världen idag*. First of all, women appear in 12 cases as victims of Muslim misogynic behaviour, perpetrated either by Muslim regimes, groups/citizens or individual men. In some cases the victims are *Christian* women, ergo 'our' most vulnerable individuals are used in order to construct a Muslim threat. Tunehag reports: 'recently a Christian women was stoned to death by a Muslim mob. ... she had testified about her faith in Jesus' (Tunehag, 12 July 2006). In some cases Muslim women's or even girls' violent behaviour and attitudes are used to accentuate the brutality of Islam. Saima, a Palestinian girl, is reported as saying, 'I want to die as a martyr for Allah' (Tunehag, 11 July 2007).

Basically *SD-Kuriren* uses the same linguistic strategy as *Världen idag*, perhaps even more harshly: 69 per cent of alleged Muslim behaviour is categorized as negative; 30 per cent of Muslim behaviour is categorized as morally neutral or ethically unclear. In the case of *SD-Kuriren* the most common behaviour ascribed to Muslims is that they 'mean' (14 cases) and 'participate' (9 cases). 'Mean' has more or less the same function as 'making demands' in the case of *Världen idag*, indicating unjust attitudes, such as Muslims 'mean' that Swedish society should adapt to them (Jomshof 69d, 2006).

Women play a similar role in *SD-Kuriren* as in *Världen idag*; Muslim and Western women are victims of Muslim male violence. Muslim fundamentalists allegedly kill women and children without mercy (Jomshof 67, 2006), an imam condones wife assault (Jomshof 69, 2006), British imams defend this oppression and call for beating girls who do not use the hijab (Helset and Jomshof 71, 2007) and a pregnant women is molested by Muslim gangs (Jomshof 72, 2007). One entire article concerns the reported rampant increase of gang rapes in Sweden, and the article makes African, Middle Eastern and Muslim men responsible (Jomshof 74a, 2007).

In three cases the behaviour of influential Muslim women is criticized: Nalin Pekgul's *schadenfreude* over political problems within the Sweden Democrats (Jomshof 73a, 2007), the behaviour of Egypt's Ambassador to Denmark during the Muhammad cartoons controversy (Jomshof 67c, 2006) and the lack of credibility of Helena Benaouda's negative attitude to Sharia laws (she is the chairperson of the Muslim Council of Sweden) (Karlsson 72b, 2007).

PRESCRIPTIONS AND SOLUTIONS

Entman 1993 framing analysis implies that frames are also revealed in suggested solutions to vital problems. Accordingly, different solutions put forward in the articles will be analysed; more specifically, to what extent the solutions are of a problem-solving kind or based on critical theory calling for reform and emancipation. A problem-solving theory does not believe in fundamental changes to societal structures, but 'takes the world as it finds it, with the prevailing social and power relationships and the institutions into which they are organized, as the given framework for action' and only tries to 'make these relationships and institutions work smoothly by dealing effectively with a particular source of trouble' (Cox 1981:128–129). Critical theory, on the other hand, 'does not take social and power relations for granted but calls them into question' (p. 129).

In editorials and political articles, very few solutions concern Muslim or non-Muslim women. In some of these texts, the solutions do not really concern Muslims at all. They are not the principal objects of political measures, and therefore the solutions in these items do not reflect political attitudes to Muslims and cannot be classified. In items that concern alleged Muslim threats, Muslims are usually the object of suggested political measures and reveal attitudes to Muslims. Consequently, in the case of *Dagens Nyheter*, *Världen idag* and *SD-Kuriren*, editorials and political articles on Muslim threats will be analysed, since they reveal whether the writers advocate problem-solving or emancipatory solutions. In the case of *Dagen*, another selection had to be made: Articles concerning 'attitudes to Muslims in Sweden', 'the relationship between Muslims and Christians or the Western world', 'the Israeli-Palestinian conflict' and 'threats against freedom of expression' were selected since they represent a conflictual relationship.

The analysis yields three important results. Firstly, all media products repeatedly avoid making explicit prescriptions. Yet, in many of these articles, the ideology of the media is clear and can tacitly imply a solution. Secondly, there is a rift between *Dagens Nyheter* and *Dagen* on the one hand, and *SD-Kuriren* and *Världen idag* on the other. In *SD-Kuriren* and *Världen idag* no articles with emancipating solutions appear. *Dagen*'s solutions are more often precise and emancipatory. Even in editorials concerning conflicts between the Western and Muslim world, an attitude of reform and emancipation is present, the only exception being an editorial commenting on a planned terror attack on the church Livets Ord in Uppsala (Thureson, 5 May 2006).

As previously stated, *SD-Kuriren* and *Världen idag* clearly deviate since they never suggest emancipating solutions. Furthermore, the suggested measures are often imprecise comparatively; it is not stated who is going to act, the measures are not clearly defined and not based on problem-solving theory. The readers are not requested to understand Muslims or Islam, or to establish a constructive relationship with Muslims. On the contrary, readers are encouraged to dissociate themselves from this group, and it is urgent to deter them from further aggression, to regain control over Western areas and free them from Muslim influence and to explicitly express dissatisfaction with policies in Muslim countries.[5] By far the most common linguistic tool used in *Världen idag*, which makes the solutions imprecise, is the use of implied prescriptions (Ejvegård 2005:29) such as expressive exclamations (pp. 26–27).

In one editorial, Stenström poses numerous rhetorical questions, provoking the reader to find solutions of a problem-solving kind. Later, Stenström draws her own conclusions: 'European countries with major Muslim populations ... must ... prepare a strategy for the future. ... The civilized world must brace itself for a united resistance to this dangerous madness' (Stenström, 6 February 2006). Interestingly enough, although oppression of women in the Muslim world is mentioned a few times, the solutions hardly ever concern them.

SD-Kuriren's rhetoric on solutions to Muslim issues resembles that in *Världen idag*; the solutions tend to be problem-solving and in some cases imprecise. Without explaining who is supposed to act, or what kind of actions should be undertaken, Richard Jomshof makes an implicit prescription: 'Just as the democratic world took the fight against Nazism in the 1930s and 40s, we must now take the fight against the Islamists'

(Jomshof 67b, 2006). This sentence is repeated in three additional articles in 2006 and 2007 (Jomshof 69c, 2006; Jomshof 69d; Jomshof 74b, 2007), the last time adding 'it is now time not merely to react, but also to act'. *SD-Kuriren* also argues that Muslims are unable to live in harmony with the rest of the population. Reform is not an option. And just as in the case of *Världen idag*, the solutions concern women only very vaguely. Not even the article that entirely focuses on rape offers a solution to this crime (Jomshof 74a, 2007).

A third result concerns the relatively high prevalence of problem-solving solutions in *Dagens Nyheter*. This requires some comments though. First of all, these solutions generally concern Iran's nuclear programme. Secondly, the solutions are unambiguous. The target is the Iranian regime, and the actors, as well as the measures, are well defined. The paper suggests boycotts (*Dagens Nyheter*, 16 January 2006) or travel bans for Iranian officials (*Dagens Nyheter*, 26 February 2007). And lastly, the target of these measures, the Iranian regime, is defined as an immoral political actor, never as a Muslim one. Interestingly enough, the cases where *Dagens Nyheter's* solutions are both problem-solving and ambiguous in character concern the oppression of women. It is stated, 'We cannot accept that women are oppressed' (*Dagens Nyheter* 24 September 2006), and 'Sweden must stand up for certain values' (*Dagens Nyheter*, 25 June 2007).

Conclusions

As stated in the introduction, this study aims at providing a better understanding of how Muslims and Islam are constructed, to what extent and in what ways gender is used to construct this image and lastly to see to what extent this usage of gender is consensual.

First of all, it is clear that there is a rift in the Swedish media landscape regarding descriptions of Muslims and Islam. However, this rift is not between conservative Swedish Christian media and secular ones. Instead, the rift divides Christian as well as secular media. Liberal *Dagens Nyheter* and conservative and Evangelical *Dagen* avoid describing Muslims and Islam as a threat and usually seek constructive solutions to different challenges. *Dagen* also sees both Christians and Muslims as victims of the forces of secularization. *Dagens Nyheter* describes conflicts between Muslim and Christian actors in political, not religious, terms. In a similar way, there is common ground between the neo-nationalist journal *SD-Kuriren* and fundamentalist charismatic *Världen idag*. These two media repeatedly make generalizing assertions and describe Islam and Muslims as violent and irrational, making unacceptable demands at 'our' expense, and as a danger and threat to Christians, and to the Western world, primarily its democracy. Western leaders are allegedly submissive to Muslim demands and retreat before them. *Världen idag*, unlike *SD-Kuriren*, additionally claims that Islam is permanently inconsistent with democracy. Whether this actually portends a possible alliance between neo-nationalist movements and conservative Christianity could be a starting point for future research.

Secondly, gender is not used to any great extent in this endeavour. It is rarely a diagnosis in the data, labels rarely depict Muslim men as misogynic, the behaviour of Muslims in the data rarely indicates that Muslim men are dangerous to women and, lastly, the solutions hardly ever address situations where Muslim men constitute a problem to women, Muslim or non-Muslim. Such are the general trends. Still there are some differences. In a few cases, *Världen idag* and *SD-Kuriren* depict women as both victims and as brainwashed perpetrators, and men appear as misogynic and a threat to all women, Muslim and non-Muslim alike. Thus, the aforementioned rift between *Dagen* and *Dagens Nyheter* on the one side, and *SD-Kuriren* and *Världen idag* on the other reappears also here.

And thirdly, although there are some differences between the papers, a commonality is that gender plays only a small role in the construction of Islam, particularly compared to the results of previous research. One reason for this could be that the period under scrutiny in this study was not a period when gender-related issues were discussed, as they were during the debates over the veil.

Notes

1. *Dagens Nyheter*, founded in 1864, is the largest morning newspaper in Sweden with a weekday circulation of 285,000 and 330,000 on Sundays. It is regarded as an independent liberal paper and an important leader of public opinion in Sweden since the Second World War.
2. *SD-Kuriren* is a periodical with four annual issues and was founded in 1991 as the official organ of the Sweden Democrats. It has a circulation of about 28,000. Occasionally it is accessible on the Internet.
3. The leader of the Pentecostal movement founded *Dagen* in 1945. Currently the paper has 18,000 subscribers. It is Norwegian-owned and is regarded as Evangelical or ecumenical.

4. *Världen idag* was founded in 2001 and currently has about 6600 subscribers. The newspaper is part of the faith movement and the Swedish Christian right.

5. Some editorials deviate, as the writers turn to an imagined Muslim audience (Tunehag, 18 September 2006) and to Swedish politicians (Björk, 11 August 2006).

REFERENCES

Bullock, K.H., and G.J. Jafri. 2000. Media (Mis)Representations: Muslim Women in the Canadian Nation. *Canadian Woman Studies* 20(2): 35–40.

Byng, M.D. 2010. Symbolically Muslim: Media, Hijab, and the West. *Critical Sociology* 36(1): 109–129.

Carøe Christiansen, C. 2011. Contesting Visibilities: Sartorial Strategies Among Muslim Women in Danish Media. *Journal of Intercultural studies* 32(4): 335–353.

Cox, R.W. 1981. Social Forces, States and World Orders: Beyond International Relations Theory. *Millennium* 10: 126–155.

Ehrkamp, P. 2010. The Limits of Multicultural Tolerance? Liberal Democracy and Media Portrayals of Muslim Migrant Women in Germany. *Space and Polity* 14(1): 13–32.

Ejvegård, R. 2005. *Argumentationsanalys.* Lund: Studentlitteratur.

Entman, R. 1993. Framing: Toward Clarification of a Fractured Paradigm. *Journal of Communication* 43: 51–58.

Hebbani, A., and C.-R. Wills. 2012. How Muslim Women in Australia Navigate Through Media (Mis)Representations of Hijab/Burqa. *Australian Journal of Communication* 39(1): 87–100.

Hoodfar, H. 2006. The Veil Their Minds and on Our Heads: The Persistence of Colonial Images of Muslim Women. *RFR/DRF* 22(3/4): 5–18.

Landmann, T. 2008. *Issues and Methods in Comparative Politics: An Introduction,* 3rd edn. London: Routledge.

Lee Riley, R. 2013. *Depicting the Veil, Transnational Sexism and the War on Terror.* London: Zed Books.

Macdonaldm, M. 2006. Muslim Women and the Veil: Problems of Image and Voice in Media Representations. *Feminist Media Studies* 6(1): 7–19.

Martin-Muñoz, G. 2002. Islam's Women under Western Eyes. Open Democracy 2002-10-09.

Navarro, L. 2010. Islamophobia and Sexism: Muslim Women in the Western Mass Media. *Human Architecture: Journal of the Sociology of Self-Knowledge* 8(2): 95–114.

Ottosen, R. 1995. Enemy Images and the Journalistic Process. *Journal of Peace Research* 32(7): 97–112.

Posetti, J. 2006. Media Representations of the Hijab: Case Study 1. *Journalism in Multicultural Australia*. http://www.reportingdiversity.org.au/case_studies.html

Razack, S. 2008. *Casting Out: The Eviction of Muslims from Western Law and Politics*. Toronto: University of Toronto Press.

EDITORIALS

DAGENS NYHETER

Dagens Nyheter. 2006. Avrätta inte Saddam Hussein (editorial), 6 November.

———. 2006. Demokratin är fortsatt utmanad (editorial), 7 July.

———. 2006. Demokratin hann försvara sig (editorial), 11 August.

———. 2006. En svensk tragedi valåret 2006 (editorial), 19 April.

———. 2006. Inget öppet samhälle utan hädelse (editorial), 11 January.

———. 2007. Iran trotsar vidare (editorial), 26 February.

———. 2006. Iranska kärnvapen vore en mardröm (editorial), 16 January.

———. 2007. Ond mix i Pakistan (editorial), 14 November.

———. 2007. Slöjan hotar ingen (editorial), 27 September.

———. 2006. Stoppa trängseln vid stubintråden (editorial), 7 February.

———. 2006. Än är Turkiet inte förlorat (editorial), 13 May.

DAGEN

Cyrillus (Olsson), Erika. 2006. FP sviker kristna skolor (editorial). *Dagen*, 22 August.

———. 2006. Påven öppnar för dialog (editorial). *Dagen*, 28 November.

———. 2006. Stoppa palestinskt blodbad (editorial). *Dagen*, 14 June.

———. 2006. Vansklig fredslösning (editorial). *Dagen*, 15 November.

Grahn, Daniel. 2006. Dialog—inte demonisering (editorial). *Dagen*, 10 February.

Sandlund, Elisabeth. 2007. När doktorn blir terrorist (editorial). *Dagen*, 5 July.

Thureson, Birger. 2006. En misslyckad strategi (editorial). *Dagen*, 1 August.

———. 2006. Israel bör haka på (editorial). *Dagen*, 11 May.

———. 2006. Israel efter Ariel Sharon (editorial). *Dagen*, 10 January.

———. 2006. Kanske är fred möjlig (editorial). *Dagen*, 18 July.

———. 2006. Krig ett dåligt vapen (editorial). *Dagen*, 8 June.

———. 2006. Legitimera inte islamism (editorial). *Dagen*, 17 May.

———. 2006. Svårartad kulturkrock (editorial). *Dagen*, 1 February.

———. 2006. Terrorism på svenska (editorial). *Dagen*, 5 May.

Österberg, Thomas. 2007. Ensidighet hindrar fred (editorial). *Dagen*, 5 June.

———. 2006. Farligt nej till julspel (editorial). *Dagen*, 30 November.

———. 2007. Hopp och tvivel om fred (editorial). *Dagen*, 21 November.

———. 2006. Hot mot 'blomstertiden' (editorial). *Dagen*, 13 June.
———. 2006. Irak allt svårare för Bush (editorial). *Dagen*, 26 September.
———. 2007. Lång väg kvar till fred (editorial). *Dagen*, 4 April.
———. 2006. Registrera inte tro, Säpo (editorial). *Dagen*, 26 January.
———. 2006. Sårbarheten finns kvar (editorial). *Dagen*, 11 August.
———. 2006. Vapenvila utan segrare (editorial). *Dagen*, 17 August.

VÄRLDEN IDAG

Agnarsson, Ruben. 2006. Hatet mitt ibland oss (editorial). *Världen idag*, 27 January.
———. 2006. Övningen i Boden (editorial). *Världen idag*, 18 January.
Björk, Hans-Göran. 2006. Dödshoten islams rätta ansikte? (editorial). *Världen idag*, 13 January.
———. 2006. Falsk rapportering är förödande (editorial). *Världen idag*, 9 August.
———. 2006. Hamas fick legitimitet i Sverige (editorial). *Världen idag*, 8 May.
———. 2006. Sluta flirta med terrorister (editorial). *Världen idag*, 11 August.
———. 2006. Ursäkten blev kapitulation (editorial). *Världen idag*, 3 February.
Stenström, Carin. 2006. Nu krävs samordnat försvar (editorial). *Världen idag*, 6 Februay.
Tunehag, Mats. 2006. Demokratin går framåt och bakåt (editorial). *Världen idag*, 13 December.
———. 2006. Folkpartister talar klarspråk (editorial). *Världen idag*, 6 September.
———. 2006. Iran, kärnvapen och den 12:e imamen (editorial). *Världen idag*, 22 February.
———. 2006. Islam hotar Danmark—Persson tiger (editorial). *Världen idag*, 2 January.
———. 2006. Islams benägenhet till våld (editorial). *Världen idag*, 25 September.
———. 2006. Islams fyrkantiga cirklar (editorial). *Världen idag*, 31 March.
———. 2006. Islamsk intolerans når nya höjder (editorial). *Världen idag*, 1 February.
———. 2006. Islamska republiken Sverige (editorial). *Världen idag*, 8 March.
———. 2006. Jämtin och muren i Saudiarabien (editorial). *Världen idag*, 4 September.
———. 2006. Kan islam moderniseras? (editorial). *Världen idag*, 27 February.
———. 2007. Kebab utan sharia, tack (editorial). *Världen idag*, 31 January.
———. 2006. Kristna lever farligt (editorial). *Världen idag*, 12 July.
———. 2006. Lika goda kålsupare (editorial). *Världen idag*, 8 November.
———. 2006. Mecka-kyrka och Malmö moské (editorial). *Världen idag*, 14 June.
———. 2006. Ny regering, ny utrikespolitik (editorial). *Världen idag*, 13 September.
———. 2006. Påven och islam (editorial). *Världen idag*, 18 September.

———. 2006. Sekularister banar väg för jihadister (editorial). *Världen idag*, 7 Juni.

———. 2006. Ska alla tvingas följa islam? (editorial). *Världen idag*, 13 February.

———. 2006. Skamfläckar och hot (editorial). *Världen idag*, 10 March.

———. 2006. Sopspioner mot terrorister? (editorial). *Världen idag*, 14 Augusti.

———. 2006. Val inte lika med demokrati (editorial). *Världen idag*, 30 January.

SD-KURIREN

Jomshof, Richard. 2007. Den 'nya våldtäktsvågen'. *SD-Kuriren* 74a.

———. 2007. Göteborgsmoské byggs med pengar från Saudiarabien. *SD-Kuriren* 72a.

———. 2006. Islamiseringen av Sverige. *SD-Kuriren* 69a.

———. 2007. Islamiseringen av Sverige. *SD-Kuriren* 74b.

———. 2006. 'Muhammed har avbildats tusentals gånger genom historien'. *SD-Kuriren* 67a.

———. 2006. 'Muhammed har avbildats tusentals gånger genom historien'. *SD-Kuriren* 69b.

———. 2007. Muhammedkonflikten fortsätter. *SD-Kuriren* 74c.

———. 2006. Muslimska protester mot Danmark. *SD-Kuriren* 69c.

———. 2007. Om yrkesapartheid och självförakt. *SD-Kuriren* 71.

———. 2006. Protester mot Danmark. *SD-Kuriren* 67b.

———. 2007. Rondellhunden Muhammed stopped. *SD-Kuriren* 73.

———. 2006. SD-Kuriren granskar och avslöjar islam i Sverige. *SD-Kuriren* 69d.

———. 2006. Sharia oförenligt med demokrati. *SD-Kuriren*, 68.

———. 2007. Upplopp i Nederländerna. *SD-Kuriren* 72b.

Jomshof, Richard and Söder Björn. 2006. Kravaller skakade Europa. *SD-Kuriren* 67.

Karlsson, Mattias. 2007. Rätt av Åkesson att ta debatten. *SD-Kuriren* 72a.

———. 2007. Ungdomsrånen—ett krig mot svenskarna. *SD-Kuriren* 74.

———. 2006. Universitetsstudie: Ungdomsrånen är ett krig mot svenskarna. *SD-Kuriren* 68.

———. 2007. Upprorisk tonåring eller mammas flicka?. *SD-Kuriren* 72b.

Söder, Björn. 2007. Fegisarna diskuterar. *SD-Kuriren* 73.

———. 2006. Söder: Vi måste våga ifrågasätta islam. *SD-Kuriren* 67.

———. 2006. 'Vi måste våga ifrågasätta islam'. *SD-Kuriren* 69.

Wiklander, Tony. 2006. Ecce homo Muhammed. *SD-Kuriren*, nr 67.

Åkesson, Jimmy. 2007. Att ta den berömda debatten... *SD-Kuriren* 72.

PART IV

Discourses on the Issues
Antifeminism and Masculinity

At the Mercy of *Femocracy?* Networks and Ideological Links Between Far-Right Movements and the Antifeminist Men's Rights Movement

Alva Träbert

INTRODUCTION

In this article, I will examine the antifeminist men's rights movement and its ideological interconnections with *völkisch* far-right movements.[1] My analysis builds on research which originally focused on organized online antifeminism in Germany and Switzerland between 2010 and 2011.[2] The original study has been translated and expanded to include a brief comparison with organized online antifeminism in Austria and the UK. I will outline the antifeminist men's rights movement, introduce its strategies and main ideologies, then carve out the most prominent threads of antifeminist discourse and compare them with their counterparts in far-right and new-right ideologies.

THE ANTIFEMINIST MEN'S RIGHTS MOVEMENT

In contemporary organized antifeminism, traditional antifeminist ideology is merged with a more novel *männliche Opferideologie* (ideology of masculine victimhood), with social actors mobilizing primarily online.

A. Träbert (✉)
School of Social and Political Science, Sociology, University of Edinburgh, Edinburgh, UK

© The Author(s) 2017   273
M. Köttig et al. (eds.), *Gender and Far Right Politics in Europe*,
DOI 10.1007/978-3-319-43533-6_18

While these networks often claim to be part of a social movement, they lack a collective identity and critical mass. Although antifeminist networks[3] have a common opponent in feminism, they lack clearly formulated aims. Some men's rights activists (MRAs) proclaim their hate of women, while some emphasize their wish to restore masculine dominance in society. Others argue that feminism was once a valid pursuit, but is now obsolete. Networks are heterogeneous and mobilize support across far-right, conservative and moderate liberal circles. Although online antifeminist networks do not qualify as a social movement in the terms discussed above, in this chapter we will retain the label of antifeminist men's rights movement to reflect the participants' self-perception and the networks' self-presentation. Many participants describe themselves as MRAs. This could be interpreted as campaigning for human rights from a masculine perspective, compatible with a pro-feminist standpoint; for example, most non-domestic violence is committed by men against men, and most feminists would endorse supporting male victims of violence by taking a stand against male aggression. However, for MRAs, nearly all the (perceived) challenges men experience have their root in feminism.

The internet is virtually the only platform on which interventions are staged, and the anonymity it offers shapes the strategies employed. The number of groups or individual actors striving for academic recognition is very small.[4] Strategic use of personal insults and/or libel against political opponents is much more frequent. However, their main strategy is most accurately described as hate speech, including threats of death and rape against women and children, and of death and castration against men.[5] While, at this point, no case is known of a member of the antifeminist men's rights movement physically attacking a political opponent, this does not mean that none of them resort to physical violence. Women's refuges are a huge issue within antifeminist circles, and some have gone so far as to publicize the locations of safe houses.[6]

MAIN IDEOLOGIES

Antifeminism as a Uniting Ideology

Antifeminism is distinct from critiques of feminism which differentiate between feminist approaches and address the complex politics under the "feminism" umbrella. Antifeminism does not engage with the diversity of feminist approaches, instead constructing a heterogeneous "enemy", which is attacked through superficial arguments. Feminism is presented as fundamentally antagonistic to men, avoiding the question of whether men could benefit from gender equality. It is conceptualized as omnipotent, as wielding political power in the shape of a "femocracy". This goes hand in hand with holding feminism responsible for social and legal structures, the creation of which it has not significantly impacted. Arne Hoffmann suggests that the majority of German media are effectively controlled by the women's movement.[7] Christine Hamprecht argues that Germany is entirely under feminist control, making it a "femocracy".[8] The inability to differentiate between democratic agency and despotism is paired with the assumption that female public functionaries devote themselves entirely to women's interests, providing no justice for men in their "femisystem". In online interventions, this ideology is often expressed in a combination of four different threads of discourse: Antifeminism, Anti-Genderism, men as traitors to their sex, and Anti-Political Correctness. I will briefly outline how these terms are used.

Antifeminism: A discursive example is the assertion that all (female) judges are feminists, deciding in favour of the mother in custody cases as a matter of principle.[9] Antifeminism is often accompanied by homophobia.

Anti-Genderism: One component of the antifeminist men's rights movement's rhetoric is their opposition to the term *gender* and the idea of *Gender Mainstreaming (GM)*.[10] The basic aim of *GM* is to move on from the idea of promoting women to the promotion of gender equality more generally, including men's issues. However, MRAs claim that the focus of *GM* remains predominantly on the promotion of women. Some portray it as an instrument of feminist oppression on a European level. *Gender* is seen as oppressive. Rather than welcoming the increased diversity of gender models, there is mistrust of any human ability to deal in a self-reflexive manner with one's own gender. Neither theoretical work[11] nor empirical research[12] that supports the existence of more than two genders (and sexes) is received or acknowledged. For most antifeminists, freedom equals orientation along "natural", essentialist ideas of gender, without a component of choice. The concept of malleable gender identity is seen as dangerous.

Men as traitors to their sex: The disparaging use of "female" and terms associated with femininity to describe male individuals is a long-standing tradition in Western discourse, often used as an instrument of political power.[13] Colloquial language provides many disparaging terms, such as pussy, fairy or bitch. While in English, emasculating slurs often have an added homophobic connotation, this is not true to the same extent for the most common German slurs. Antifeminist networks also coin their own terms. In German, the term *Lila Pudel* (purple poodle) is an extreme example. Within networks, these terms have a double function as an everyday insult and as a political slur to be used against male opponents.[14]

Anti-Political Correctness: Opposition to the concept of political correctness ties into the construction of feminism as all powerful. The conclusion is that men are oppressed and forbidden to speak out against male discrimination, because feminism only opposes female discrimination. Following this logic, opposing feminism becomes an issue of freedom of speech.

Ideology of Masculine Victimhood

The most prominent idea introduced by antifeminists is the trope of male or masculine victimhood: the assumption that all men are victimized by feminism. In extreme cases, men are described as "the Jews of the Federal German Republic".[15] The ideology of masculine victimhood works with different premises: Firstly, existing structural disadvantages experienced by some groups of men are taken out of context and sometimes drastically exaggerated. An example of this is the claim that the education system is designed to fail boys. Secondly, the ideology of masculine victimhood is based on denying issues facing other, particularly female, demographic groups. Thirdly, it requires the construction of feminism as an omnipotent enemy, preventing masculine victimhood from being interpreted as individual weakness. Fourthly, it promotes traditional, essentialist gender norms as part of the suggested solution.

The ideology of masculine victimhood has its benefits as a strategy against feminism. It is an extreme example of the discursive figure of masculinity in crisis, which can be found both in the mainstream and the far right, making multiple affiliations possible. The concept of masculinity in crisis essentializes masculinity, reducing it to a pre-determined biological attribute that is endangered by social change and the women's movement. However, hegemonic masculinity can justify militant, aggressive traits only in opposition to a constant threat, real or imaginary. In contrast to the "masculinity in crisis" discourse, the ideology of masculine victimhood assumes not merely a crisis of masculine identity that is manifest in certain constellations of dependency but rather a structural oppression of men in all areas of life.

The expansion of the traditional masculinity-in-crisis discourse brings strategic advantages. The construction of feminism as all powerful provides a convenient enemy, making social mobilization easier than it would be based on socio-political analysis. The second advantage is the ease with which such an ideology can superficially tie in with the hegemonic discourse around equality: discrimination against men requires the same social intervention as discrimination against women.

COUNTRY COMPARISON

In Germany, the antifeminist men's rights movement consists of three major organizations, a small number of high-profile individuals and associated intellectuals in key positions within the media. The main players, however, are the organizations. There are two registered organizations, *agens* and *MANNdat*, as well as the online platform *wgvdl.com*, short for "*Wieviel Gleichberechtigung verträgt das Land?*" (How much equality can this country bear?).

The main activities of *MANNdat* are promotion via their website and occasional events, such as panel debates. The organization's aims and policies centre around notions of masculine victimhood. It sees gender politics as biased, partial to women's issues and deliberately discriminating against men.[16] *MANNdat* presents itself as a respectable and homogeneous organization, and members mainly connect to each other and the wider movement through its online forum and chat room.

Agens has published two books on gender politics and men's rights and runs a website.[17] The organization strives for an academic reputation, but its publications have been criticized for their methodological shortfalls.[18] Eckhardt and Ramona Kuhla, the group's chairman and treasurer, link *agens* to fundamentalist Christian and pro-life organizations. The rhetoric of both the online platform and the publications is antifeminist, essentialist and in parts openly homophobic.[19]

Wgvdl.com is the largest player in the German-speaking scene and a platform for far-right and racist ideas.[20] The website is affiliated with *Wikimannia*, an antifeminist counterpart to Wikipedia, and a blog by the name of *FemokratieBlog* (femocracy blog), arguing that the German state is controlled by feminists.[21] *Wgvdl.com* is highly influential within the antifeminist men's rights movement in terms of networking and building an ideological canon. Overall, *MANNdat* and *agens* are more moderate antifeminist organizations in comparison with *wgvdl.com*, which is best described as extreme.

The Austrian scene focuses more specifically on fathers' rights, with hardly any openly antifeminist organizations. The so-called *Väterplattform* (fathers' platform) is a major actor. One organization using this platform is the *Männerpartei* (men's party), which is fairly unknown when it comes to elections, but significantly impacts the way men's rights are spoken about. For strategic reasons, the party does not use openly antifeminist rhetoric, but the ideas promoted are clearly antifeminist.

There are differences in tactics and content nationally, but the German-speaking scene illustrates that groups are willing to work together whenever it benefits them. In both countries, there are links to right-wing and far-right organizations. In Germany, antifeminist spokespeople such as Arne Hoffmann and Eugen Maus have given interviews to the right-wing newspaper *Junge Freiheit* (Young Freedom).[22]

Examining English-speaking antifeminist men's rights platforms is significantly more complex, as it is often not immediately obvious where they are based. This only becomes clear when referring to specific political structures, for example when calling for policy change.

One UK-based forum is antimisandry.com, the main purpose of which is the sharing of personal stories about perceived cases of misandry, both in the public eye and in contributors' personal lives. The terms of use prohibit any "female-centric" threads, or anything that is "non male, father, boy, husband". The language used conveys the idea that men face systematic oppression and hate and are organizing as a matter of self-defence. It is reminiscent of the rhetoric of masculine victimhood found in the German-speaking forums.[23]

In contrast, *Fightingfeminism*, a blog mainly authored by Mike Buchanan, makes its opposition to feminism explicit and is divided into two subsections addressing different issues.[24] The material in the first is largely based on his experience at the boardroom level of multinational corporations. The blog rallies against quotas for women, discrediting them as "tokenism", and provides a platform for the publication of articles and comments by similarly minded men across the British press. Buchanan has published three books arguing against affirmative action in the workplace and across management structures, with little success. A section of the platform is dedicated to opposing "militant feminism", which has "long assaulted individuals and institutions including the following: men, women, marriage, the family, the justice system, academia, the media, government, business, and much else". The language used compares to the more extreme German counterparts described above.

Thirdly, *register-her.com*, a UK-based website with links to the US-based antifeminist platform avoiceformen.com, allows users to register "individuals that have caused significant harm to innocent individuals either by the direct action of crimes like rape, assault, child molestation and murder, or by the false accusation of crimes against others for personal gain in one form or another".[25] Mugshots of the "offenders", sometimes taken from social media and a summary of their "crime", are accompanied by links to relevant media coverage, perpetuating the notion of women exploiting a supposedly gender-partisan political system, for instance by making false rape accusations.

The vast number of English-speaking antifeminist platforms makes a brief overview challenging. However, the three examples described above show that the English-speaking movement exhibits a range of ideas and strategies close to their German counterparts, including the notion of female- or feminist-dominated media and political sphere, and the concept of masculine oppression.

Ideological Interconnection with Far-Right Ideologies

Further analysis first requires a distinction between different currents of extreme-right ideology. The following discussion focuses on German-based *völkisch*, racial ideologies, which place a particular emphasis on traditional gender concepts as they relate to the idea of a *Volksgemeinschaft* (*völkisch* collective) based on ethnic lineage and place the racial nuclear family at the heart of this reproductive system.

It is not always possible to clearly distinguish between the new and extreme right, so I will examine a range of ideological positions that can be found across both circles. One prominent example of antifeminist ideas within the far right is the website free-gender.de, affiliated with the extreme-right initiative *Raus aus den Köpfen—Genderterror abschaffen* (Out of their heads—abolish gender terror), registered to Mareike Bielefeld.[26] In terms of ideological content, the initiative closely matches the results of recent research into right-wing extremism.

ANTIFEMINISM WITHIN THE RIGHT?

The importance of the antifeminist stance for right-wing and neo-fascist circles cannot be emphasized enough. The so-called *Volksgemeinschaft*, basis of far-right ideology, presumes and requires a traditional gender dichotomy,[27] though far-right circles do not subscribe to a uniform image of femininity. Some far-right groups call for gender equality in the workplace in order to mobilize more potential members. Such demands are interwoven with ideas around the *Volksgemeinschaft;* consequently, any demands for equality within far-right groups cannot be seen as feminist, as they negate emancipatory efforts outside the *Volksgemeinschaft.*[28] Overall, the extreme right can be characterized as antifeminist. Although feminism is not the main "enemy", and far-right music, for instance, centres around the threats imposed by immigrants, Jews, punks, the left wing, the state and the police, arguments are often phrased along antifeminist lines.[29] The *RNF* (a *völkische* women's organization) explicitly aims to provide "anti-feminist answers" to the gender debate, and *free-gender.de* lists feminism as a distinct category.[30]

Although antifeminist ideas can be found in right-wing circles, more discursive emphasis is placed on *GM*, which is seen as a "giant re-education project" and is a bogeyman for many extreme-right organizations.[31] The anti-*GM* discourse in far-right circles is very similar to that used by anti-feminist men's rights activists. They, too, criticize *GM* on a functional level, arguing that it represents the advancement of women exclusively. Its purpose is ultimately perceived as the abolition of men.[32] It is presented as endangering heterosexual, Christian, nuclear families, which in extreme-right circles is extended to mean the German *Volksgemeinschaft*. This risk is described as "*Volkstod*" (ethnic death), assuming that "*genderism*" catalyses demographic change.[33]

MALE VICTIMHOOD IN THE FAR RIGHT

Within the far right, there has been almost no reception of the masculine victimhood ideology, which may be because masculinity is associated with strength in accordance with essentialist gender constructs. Among other factors, this strength is based on the ideal of masculinity as being in control of, rather than a slave to, desire. The discourse around masculinity in crisis is very much anchored in far-right ideology; it strengthens the idea of the male fighting for the nation and its nuclear component, the hetero-sexual family.[34]

Summary of Links Between the Antifeminist Movement and the Far Right

Although the antifeminist men's rights movement displays some ideological links with the new right, it is best described as self-contained, currently working independently of extreme-right groups. However, the ways in which the antifeminist men's rights movement is appropriating new-right structures and strategies with regard to placing themselves and their body of thought in the mainstream[35] is highly concerning: there is a real danger that the links between the two may grow.

Conclusion

Firstly, it is clear that organized antifeminism is a form of sexism. Large parts of the antifeminist men's rights movement use heterosexist and misogynist arguments, and all antifeminist ideology that I have examined is used to protect the existing male hegemony. My further conclusions are less easily generalized. My samples are from groups of organized white antifeminists in wealthy, Western countries. I can draw no conclusions about antifeminism within marginalized groups and cannot offer a global comparative perspective.

My second conclusion concerns the nature of the antifeminist men's rights movement. While the networks described are small, their intervention strategies, such as hate speech and ideological interconnections with the political mainstream and far right, pose a real danger. A growing connection between these three discourses may strengthen antifeminist and heterosexist sentiments in society as a whole and may also strengthen racist ideologies.

Thirdly, I believe it is important to point out that a critique of the antifeminist men's rights movement should not place its main focus on networks and ideological links with far-right or new-right groups. Rather, the focal point should be the movement's primary ideologies and strategies, taking them seriously as issues in their own right. Their danger lies precisely in the fact that they are not merely connected to transparently far-right groups.

Finally, we need society-wide debate and education on antifeminist activism, similar to the way in which increasing awareness of racism and nationalism has been an important factor in fighting far-right activism. I believe that future research should focus on antifeminist sentiments within the political and cultural mainstream, both in order to provide better tools to counter the antifeminist men's rights movement, and more importantly, heterosexism and misogyny where it affects vast numbers of diverse individuals, namely, in mainstream culture.

NOTES

1. Völkisch refers to a racial understanding of nation, as used in national-socialist propaganda. While right-wing ideologies relying on cultural racism can do without antifeminism, those that build more strongly on völkisch ideas and biological essentialism need the reference to 'traditional' family values, meaning a gendered division of labour in the nuclear family. For the latter, producing offspring of the 'right race' is at stake, which is why they often harness antifeminist ideas.
2. Hinrich Rosenbrock, Die Antifeministische Männerrechtsbewegung (Berlin: Heinrich Böll Stiftung, 2012).
3. Oxford Dictionary of Media and Communication defines a network as an interconnected group of people. Due to the often anonymous nature of the online contributions in the forums we examined, it is difficult to be more precise about the contributors.
4. "Was wollen wir", agens, accessed January 30, 2013, http://agensev.de/was-wollen-wir/
5. Hinrich Rosenbrock, "Hate speech: Hass als Emotion und Strategie", in: Die Maskulisten. Organisierter Antifeminismus im deutschsprachigen Raum, ed Andreas Kemper (Münster: Unrast, 2012) pp 139–142.
6. For instance "Ein Ratgeber für Männer und Väter", IGAF, accessed August 30, 2011, http://www.antifeminismus.ch/familie/frauen-hausluege/index.php, WGVDL Forum, Accessed February 16, 2012, http://www.wgvdl.com/forum/forum_entry.php?id=215721&page=0&category=0&order=last_answer
7. s.a., p. 119.
8. Christine Hamprecht, FemokratieBlog, accessed January 30, 2013, http://femokratie.com/

9. "Familiengericht", Trennungsfaq. Accessed January 30, 2013, http://www.trennungsfaq.de/nachtrennung.html#familiengericht
10. Regina Frey, "Von Mythen und Vermischungen – Zur Konstruktion des «Genderismus»", in: Gender, Wissenschaftlichkeit und Ideologie. Argumente im Streit um Geschlechterverhältnisse, ed Regina Frey (Berlin: Heinrich Böll Stiftung, 2013).
11. Judith Butler, Körper von Gewicht. Die diskursiven Grenzen des Geschlechts (Berlin: Suhrkamp Verlag, 1995) p. 21.
12. See for instance Susanne Schröter, FeMale. Über Grenzverläufe zwischen den Geschlechtern (Frankfurt am Main: S. Fischer Verlag, 2002), Martin Whyte, The Status of Women in Preindustrial Societies (Princeton: 1978), Ilse Lenz and Ute Luig, Frauenmacht ohne Herrschaft. Geschlechterverhältnisse in nichtpatriarchalischen Gesellschaften (Berlin: Campus Verlag, 1990).
13. Paul Julius Möbius, Über den psychologischen Schwachsinn des Weibes (München: 1905) p. 27.
14. Thomas Gesterkamp, Geschlechterkampf von rechts. Wie Männerrechtler und Familienfundamentalisten sich gegen das Feindbild Feminismus radikalisieren (Berlin: Friedrich-Ebert-Stiftung, 2010) p. 12, wikimannia c, WGVDL Forum 2010 d).
15. "Hassideologie", WGVDL Forum. Accessed January 30, 2013, http://www.wgvdl.com/forum/forum_entry.php?id=134593. (translation: Träbert).
16. "Unsere Leitgedanken", MANNdat, accessed February 16, 2012, http://manndat.de/ueber-manndat/unsere-leitgedanken
17. "Bücher", agens, accessed January 30, 2013, http://agensev.de/bucher/
18. Marc Gärtner, "Doppelstandard—Zur politisch interessierten Selektivität der Vorwürfe", in: Gender, Wissenschaftlichkeit und Ideologie. Argumente im Streit um Geschlechterverhältnisse, ed Regina Frey (Berlin: Heinrich-Böll-Stiftung, 2013), Rolf Pohl, "Männer – das benachteiligte Geschlecht? Weiblichkeitsabwehr und Antifeminismus im Diskurs über die Krise der Männlichkeit", in: In der Krise? Männlichkeiten im 21. Jahrhundert, eds. Mechthild Bergseil, Anke Neuber (Münster: 2010) p. 10.
19. Hinrich Rosenbrock, Die Antifeministische Männerrechtsbewegung (Berlin: Heinrich Böll Stiftung, 2012) p. 57.
20. Thomas Gesterkamp, Geschlechterkampf von rechts. Wie Männerrechtler und Familienfundamentalisten sich gegen das

Feindbild Feminismus radikalisieren (Berlin: Friedrich-Ebert-Stiftung, 2010) p. 12.

21. Christine Hamprecht, FemokratieBlog, accessed January 30, 2013, http://femokratie.com/

22. André F. Lichtschlag, "Junge Freiheit": ef-Gleichstellungsbeauftragter Arne Hoffmann im Interview", Junge Freiheit, accessed January 30, 2013, http://ef-magazin.de/2007/11/15/junge-freiheit-ef-gleichstellungsbeauftragter-arne-hoffmann-im-interview, Thomas Gesterkamp, Geschlechterkampf von rechts. Wie Männerrechtler und Familienfundamentalisten sich gegen das Feindbild Feminismus radikalisieren (Berlin: Friedrich-Ebert-Stiftung, 2010) p. 13.

23. Anti Misandrie 2013, accessed January 30, 2013, antimisandry.com

24. Fighting Feminism 2013, accessed January 30, 2013, http://fightingfeminism.wordpress.com

25. Register Her 2013, accessed January 30, 2013, register-her.com, A Voice for Men 2013, accessed January 30, 2013, avoiceformen.com

26. Hinrich Rosenbrock, Die Antifeministische Männerrechtsbewegung (Berlin: Heinrich Böll Stiftung, 2012) p. 125, Andrea Röpke and Andreas Speit, Mädelsache! Frauen in der Neonazi-Szene (Berlin: Christoph Links Verlag, 2011) p. 122, Blick nach Rechts 2010.

27. Esther Lehnert, "«Angriff auf Gender Mainstreaming Und Homo-Lobby»—der moderne Rechtsextremismus und seine nationalsozialistischen Bezüge am Beispiel der Geschlechterordnung", in: Männlichkeiten im Rechtsextremismus, ed Robert Claus (Berlin: Rosa-Luxemburg-Stiftung, 2010) p. 90.

28. Wehler-Schöck, Anja, "Rechtsextreme Frauen zwischen Tradition und Emanzipation, Rezension des Buches «Braune Schwestern»" querelles-net Rezensionszeitschrift für Frauen- und Geschlechterforschung, No. 17 (2005), http://www.querelles-net.de/index.php/qn/article/view/383/39

29. Henning Flad, "Trotz Verbot nicht Tod. Ideologieproduktion in den Songs der extremen Rechten", in: RechtsRock. Bestandaufnahme und Gegenstrategien, eds. Christian Dornbusch, Jan Raabe (Bielefeld: 2002) pp. 112–120.

30. Andrea Röpke and Andreas Speit, Mädelsache! Frauen in der Neonazi-Szene (Berlin: Christoph Links Verlag, 2011) p. 54.

31. Esther Lehnert, "«Angriff auf Gender Mainstreaming Und Homo-Lobby»—der moderne Rechtsextremismus und seine nationalsozialistischen Bezüge am Beispiel der Geschlechterordnung", in: Männlichkeiten im Rechtsextremismus, ed Robert Claus (Berlin: Rosa-Luxemburg-Stiftung, 2010) p. 97.

32. Yves Müller, "Gegen Feminismus und »Dekadenz«—die Neue Rechte in der Krise?", in: Männlichkeiten im Rechtsextremismus, ed Robert Claus (Berlin: Rosa-Luxemburg-Stiftung, 2010) p. 79.

33. "Volkstod der Familie", free gender, accessed August 30, 2011, http://www.free-gender.de/sexualisierung/volkstod-der-familie-durch-immer-mehr-in-homosexuellen-partnerschaften-lebenden-kindern/

34. Yves Müller, "Gegen Feminismus und »Dekadenz«—die Neue Rechte in der Krise?", in: Männlichkeiten im Rechtsextremismus, ed Robert Claus (Berlin: Rosa-Luxemburg-Stiftung, 2010) p. 86.

35. *Oxford English Dictionary* defines 'mainstream' as the ideas, attitudes and activities that are regarded as conventional, and the dominant trend in opinion.

References

Butler, Judith. 1995. *Körper von Gewicht. Die diskursiven Grenzen des Geschlechts.* Berlin: Suhrkamp Verlag.

Claus, Robert. 2012. Maskulistische Geschichtskonstruktionen, kollektive Identität und Erfahrung. In *Die Maskulisten. Organisierter Antifeminismus im deutschsprachigen Raum*, ed. Andreas Kemper, 122–138. Münster: Unrast.

Claus, Robert, and Yves Müller. 2010. Männliche Homosexualität und Homophobie im Neonazismus. In *«Was ein rechter Mann ist …» Männlichkeiten im Rechtsextremismus*, ed. Robert Claus, 109–126. Berlin: Rosa-Luxemburg-Stiftung.

Edathy, Sebastian, and Bernd Sommer. 2009. Die zwei Gesichter des Rechtsextremismus in Deutschland – Themen, Machtressourcen und Mobilisierungspotentiale der extremen Rechten. In *Strategien der extremen Rechten: Hintergründe Analysen Antworten*, ed. Stefan Braun, 45–57. Wiesbaden: VS Verlag für Sozialwissenschaften.

Flad, Henning. 2002. Trotz Verbot nicht Tod. Ideologieproduktion in den Songs der extremen Rechten. In *RechtsRock. Bestandaufnahme und Gegenstrategien*, ed. Christian Dornbusch, and Jan Raabe. Bielefeld: Unrast.

Frey, Regina. 2013. Von Mythen und Vermischungen – Zur Konstruktion des «Genderismus». In *Gender, Wissenschaftlichkeit und Ideologie. Argumente im*

Streit um Geschlechterverhältnisse, ed. Regina Frey, 16–27. Berlin: Heinrich-Böll-Stiftung.

Gärtner, Marc. 2013. Doppelstandard – Zur politisch interessierten Selektivität der Vorwürfe. In *Gender, Wissenschaftlichkeit und Ideologie. Argumente im Streit um Geschlechterverhältnisse*, ed. Regina Frey, 53–66. Berlin: Heimrich-Böll-Stiftung.

Gesterkamp, Thomas. 2010. *Geschlechterkampf von rechts. Wie Männerrechtler und Familienfundamentalisten sich gegen das Feindbild Feminismus radikalisieren.* Berlin: Friedrich-Ebert-Stiftung.

Hausen, Karin. 1981. Family and Role-Division. The Polarization of Sexual Stereotypes in the Nineteenth Century. An Aspect of Dissociation of Work and Family Life. In *Social History of the Family in Nineteenth and Twentieth Centuries Germany*, ed. Richard J. Evans, 51–83. London: Croom Helm.

Kemper, Andreas. 2012. Maskulinismus als Virtualität. Breiviks Antifeminismus. In *Die Maskulisten. Organisierter Antifeminismus im deutschsprachigen Raum*, ed. Andreas Kemper, 101–120. Münster: Unrast.

Kiepels, Sandra. 2013. *Antifeminismus im Zeitungsdiskurs von 1980–2013: Untersuchung und Vergleich der antifeministischen Diskursstrategien in den Zeitungsdebatten über den 'Backlash', 'Political Correctness', 'Gender Mainstreaming' und die Frauenquote.* Hamburg: Diplomica Verlag.

Lehnert, Esther. 2010. 'Angriff auf Gender Mainstreaming Und Homo-Lobby'— der moderne Rechtsextremismus und seine nationalsozialistischen Bezüge am Beispiel der Geschlechterordnung. In *«Was ein rechter Mann ist …» Männlichkeiten im Rechtsextremismus*, ed. Robert Claus, 89–99. Berlin: Rosa-Luxemburg-Stiftung.

Meier, Stefan. 2008. *(Bild-)Diskurs im Netz. Konzept und Methode für eine semiotische Diskursanalyse im World Wide Web.* Köln: Herbert von Halem.

Möbius, Paul Julius. 1990. *Über den psychologischen Schwachsinn des Weibes, Nachdruck der Ausgabe von 1905.* München.

Müller, Yves. 2010. Gegen Feminismus und 'Dekadenz' – die Neue Rechte in der Krise? In *'Was ein rechter Mann ist …' Männlichkeiten im Rechtsextremismus*, ed. Robert Claus, 67–88. Berlin: Rosa-Luxemburg-Stiftung.

Röpke, Andrea, and Andreas Speit. 2011. *Mädelsache! Frauen in der Neonazi-Szene.* Berlin: Christoph Links Verlag GmbH.

Rosenbrock, Hinrich. 2012a. *Die antifeministische Männerrechtsbewegung.* Berlin: Heinrich-Böll-Stiftung.

———. 2012b. Die Hauptideologien der Männerrechtsbewegung. In *Die Maskulisten. Organisierter Antifeminismus im deutschsprachigen Raum*, ed. Andreas Kemper, 58–78. Münster: Unrast.

———. 2012c. Hate speech: Hass als Emotion und Strategie. In *Die Maskulisten. Organisierter Antifeminismus im deutschsprachigen Raum*, ed. Andreas Kemper, 139–145. Münster: Unrast.

Schröter, Susanne. 2002. *FeMale. über Grenzverläufe zwischen den Geschlechtern.* Frankfurt am Main: S. Fischer Verlag.

Stegbauer, Christian, and Roger Häußling. 2010. *Handbuch Netzwerkforschung.* Wiesbaden: Springer.

Volz, Rainer, and Paul Zulehner. 2009. *Männer in Bewegung. Zehn Jahre Männerentwicklung in Deutschland. BMFSFJ Forschungsreihe Bd. 6.* Stuttgart: Bundesministerium für Familie, Senioren, Frauen und Jugend.

Whyte, Martin. 1978. *The Status of Women in Preindustrial Societies.* Princeton: Princeton Legacy Library.

Wippermann, Carsten. 2009. *Männer: Rolle vorwärts, Rolle rückwärts? Identitäten und Verhalten von traditionellen, modernen und postmodernen Männern.* Opladen: Verlag Barbara Budrich.

Zastrow, Volker. 2009. *Gender. Politische Geschlechtsumwandlung.* Waltrop: Manuscriptum.

INTERNET SOURCES

A Voice for Men. 2013. Accessed 30 January 2013. avoiceformen.com

Was wollen wir. agens. Accessed 30 January 2013. http://agensev.de/was-wollen-wir/

Bücher. agens. Accessed 30 January 2013. http://agensev.de/bucher/

Anti Misandrie. 2013. Accessed 30 January 2013. antimisandry.com

Entlarvendes Frauenbild. Blick nach Rechts. Accessed 30 August 2011. http://www.bnr.de/content/entlarvendes-frauenbild

Suche Volksverräter. Deutsche Lobby. Accessed 30 January 2013. http://deutsch-elobby.com/?s=volksverräter

Fighting Feminism. 2013. Accessed 30 January 2013. http://fightingfeminism.wordpress.com

Es lebe das Matriarchat. Free Gender. Accessed 30 August 2011. http://www.free-gender.de/gleichstellungspolitik/%E2%80%9Ees-lebe-das-matriarchat%E2%80%9C/#more-121

Volkstod der Familie. Free Gender. Accessed 30 August 2011. http://www.free-gender.de/sexualisierung/volkstod-der-familie-durch-immer-mehr-in-homosexuellen-partnerschaften-lebenden-kindern/

Christine Hamprecht, FemokratieBlog. Accessed 30 January 2013. http://femokratie.com/

Ein Ratgeber für Männer und Väter. IGAF. Accessed 30 August 2011. http://www.antifeminismus.ch/familie/frauenhausluege/index.php

1 Jahr IGAF. IGAF. Accessed 30 August 2011. www.antifeminismus.ch/downloads/1-jahr-igaf.pdf

Authors' list of Junge Freiheit. Accessed 30 August 2011. http://www.jungefreiheit.de/Autoren.52.0.html

James Kirkup. Middle Classes to Lose Out Under Harman's Equality Plan. Daily Telegraph. Accessed 9 September 2009. http://www.telegraph.co.uk/news/uknews/6159537/Middle-classes-to-lose-out-under-Harmans-equality-plan.html

Plenarprotokoll 5/38. Landtag Mecklenburg-Vorpommern. Accessed 3 July 2008. http://www.dokumentation.landtag-mv.de/Parldok/

Lichtschlag, André F. Junge Freiheit: ef-Gleichstellungsbeauftragter Arne Hoffmann im Interview. Junge Freiheit. Accessed 30 January 2013. http://ef-magazin.de/2007/11/15/junge-freiheit-ef-gleichstellungsbeauftragter-arne-hoffmann-im-interview

Register Her. 2013. Accessed 30 January 2013. register-her.com

Michail Savvakis. Der Maskulist. Accessed 30 August 2011. www.maskulist.de

Pressemitteilung: Wahl des '22. Unwort des Jahres'. Sprachkritische Aktion UNWORT DES JAHRES. Accessed 15 January 2013. http://www.unwortdesjahres.net/fileadmin/unwort/download/pressemitteilung_unwort2012.pdf

Familiengericht. Trennungsfaq. Accessed 30 January 2013. http://www.trennungsfaq.de/nachtrennung.html#familiengericht

Wehler-Schöck, Anja. 2005. Rechtsextreme Frauen zwischen Tradition und Emanzipation, Rezension des Buches «Braune Schwestern» querelles-net Rezensionszeitschrift für Frauen- und Geschlechterforschung, No. 17. http://www.querelles-net.de/index.php/qn/article/view/383/39

West, Lindy. Oh God, Please Don't Let White Male Victimhood Be the Next Big Social Movement. Jezebel. Accessed 12 April 2012. http://jezebel.com/5965429/oh-god-please-dont-let-white-male-victimhood-be-the-next-big-social-movement

Hassideologie. WGVDL Forum. Accessed 30 January 2013. http://www.wgvdl.com/forum/forum_entry.php?id=134593

WGVDL Forum. Accessed 16 February 2012. http://www.wgvdl.com/forum/forum_entry.php?id=215721&page=0&category=0&order=last_answer

——— 16 February 2012. http://www.wgvdl.com/forum/forum_entry.php?id=215474

——— 16 February 2012. http://www.wgvdl.com/forum/forum_entry.php?id=218407

Bombe: die IGAF und der Stüssi … WGVDL Forum. Accessed 9 October 2014. http://webarchiv.wikimannia.org/wgvdl.net/forum/41701.htm

Wer kann Frauenhausadressen in Ludwigshafen kontrollieren? WGVDL Forum. Accessed 9 October 2014. http://www.wgvdl.com/forum2/forum_entry.php?id=202961

Gender Mainstreaming. Wikimannia. Accessed 30 January 2013. http://wikimannia.org/Gender_Mainstreaming

Lila Pudel. Wikimannia. Accessed 30 January 2013. http://wikimannia.org/Lila_Pudel

Songs That Sound "Right"

Marko Stojanovska Rupčić

Introduction

The official website (Perkovic Thompson 2015d) of the Croatian singer Marko Perković Thompson features an embedded video on its main page with a simple title "Who is Marko Perković Thompson?". The video, which is available through the Croatian Music Channel's[1] YouTube account (*Tko Je Marko Perković Thompson?* 2013), aims to answer the title question through a chronological narrative that could be summarized by the expression *per aspera ad astra*. The narrator mentions Thompson's economically deprived background and offers a guided tour though his career, which commenced during the war in Croatia and had blasted off by the end of that decade. In the words of the narrator, "a young man that used songs to seduce girls from Čavoglave, grew into a big music star".[2] Although the video offers a romanticized visual biography which accentuates Thompson's achievements in the music industry and culti-

This paper is the result of my involvement in this topic which started some years ago as research for my MA thesis at the Central European University. I am especially grateful to Jean-Louis Fabiani and Marija Stojanovska Rupčić for their comments and encouragement, as well as to the editors of this volume.

M. Stojanovska Rupčić (✉)
Budapest, Hungary

© The Author(s) 2017
M. Köttig et al. (eds.), *Gender and Far Right Politics in Europe*,
DOI 10.1007/978-3-319-43533-6_19

vates an affirmative outlook of him as a personality, it does not fail to mention contrasting voices. These voices are, according to the narrator, kindled in Thompson's work by the centrality of "Catholicism, family and homeland"[3] (*Tko Je Marko Perković Thompson?* 2013). Thus, the issue of gender is far from being peripheral in this discordance and, as will be elaborated upon later, Thompson's take on this is harmonious with anti-emancipatory sentiments. The narrator's interpretation is coherent with that of the singer who does not refute the altercations which he generates, relating them to wider and more fundamental strife in Croatian society (Kovačević 2009, 26) However, according to Catherine Baker, he conspicuously embraced the aforementioned ideas only in the new millennium (Baker 2009a, 96). Then, as Baker points out, he became the embodiment of "the archetypal veteran" and "a guardian of war memory and Croatian values" (Baker 2009a, 96). This corresponds to what Zambelli understands as a re-evaluation of this nascent state's backbone (Zambelli 2010, 1661). Similarly, articles by Lamont and Pavlaković vividly describe the tumultuous times when the country had to re-evaluate some aspects of the war which marked its nascency (Pavlaković 2010, 1707–1738; Lamont 2010, 1683–1702). Baker further explains that Thompson fortified these ideas with his active membership in the Croatian military during the war (Baker 2009a, 96; Baker 2009b, 40). Interestingly, Rivera shows that those coming to Croatia on holiday will not easily be able to get acquainted with the bloodshed that the country witnessed soon after the Berlin wall fell (Rivera 2008, 620). It is, she explains, intentionally swept under the rug (Rivera 2008, 620), leading to implications for people like Thompson with such past military records. Furthermore, Baker compares the attitudes displayed by Thompson with those expressed by the late first Croatian president and argues for their homology (Baker 2009a, 96). The same author mentions other important parts of this music "machine" such as his animosity towards Tito's Yugoslavia and its regime, as well as a benevolent and affirmative attitude towards domestic Fascist collaboration during World War II[4] (Baker 2010, 174). Whether Thompson has altered these attitudes in recent times, in particular his stance on gender-related topics, is the main question that this chapter will address.

THE CONTEMPORARY THOMPSON

This text provides a fresh glance at Thompson's latest work and his public activities, relating them to relevant academic writings. Firstly, through a review of the existing literature, the background of this phenomenon will be elaborated upon. After giving an outline of the scenery in which Thompson and some comparable musicians dwell, the spotlight of this text will turn to current topics related to the singer. Thus, his latest release[5] is scrutinized with particular emphasis on gender representations in his lyrics. This information is then compared to Baker's findings which date back several years and refer to the previous two decades (Baker 2009a, 125). Moreover, this text will go beyond mere analysis of the lyrics of Thompson's latest release by including some of his public statements as well as several messages transmitted through his official Facebook page. Finally, the prevalence and interpretation of "Catholicism, family and homeland" (Tko Je Marko Perković Thompson? 2013) in the aforementioned material is analysed.

GRASPING THE BACKGROUND

Baker has investigated this phenomena in a broader perspective, keeping in mind the temporal dimension and, looking back over almost two decades of "patriotic popular music production" in this young country, she detects several peaks in its prevalence (Baker 2009b, 36). According to her, it gained prevalence concurrently with the country's birth, half a decade later, and around the turn of the millennium (Baker 2009b, 36). She says that the peak which commenced around fifteen years ago was still prominent at the time she wrote her article (Baker 2009b, 36). Although the scope of her article does not extend spatially to the borders of the whole country, her text sheds light on the temporal dimension of the phenomenon and illuminates its dynamism (Baker 2009b). She says that "almost every active professional musician in Croatia joined in a wave of patriotic popular music production" spurred by the violence which accompanied the formation of the country (Baker 2009b, 36). The outcome of that endeavour, according to Senjković and Dukić, was a number of recycled tropes (Senjković and Dukić 2005, 52). Although Thompson's video biography (*Tko Je Marko Perković Thompson?* 2013), as well as Baker's academic texts (for instance Baker 2013, 416 or Baker 2009a, 37), mentions that Thompson was on this bandwagon, they both argue that he found his way onto the large stages around the turn of the millennium (*Tko Je Marko Perković Thompson?* 2013; Baker 2009b, 40; Baker 2009a, 95–99).

Such music, according to Anton Shekhovtsov and Catherine Baker, is not specific to a single country or historical period (Baker 2013, 410; Shekhovtsov 2013, 330–331). Through a summary of relevant texts, Shekhovtsov shows that nationalist ideas had been converted into audio formats for more than a hundred years (Shekhovtsov 2013, 330–331). Baker makes the same point and similarly argues that "[m]usic and nationalism are intimately connected" (Baker 2013, 410). Hence, it shouldn't come as a surprise that Mavra and McNeil highlight this phenomenon while scrutinizing the nascent Croatia (Mavra and McNeil 2007, 1–18), and László Kürti[6] says that this kind of music can also be found in present-day Hungary (Kürti 2012). Another example of this both spatially and temporally diverse phenomenon comes from Wanner's chapter on the "Ukrainian nationalist song festival" (Wanner 1996, 136). The aforementioned cases further fortify the ideas laid out by Shekhovtsov and Baker, who point out that such songs are not only manufactured concurrently and in the same spot (Shekhovtsov 2013, 330–331; Baker 2013, 410) but, as Kaplan argues, this manufacturing does not rely exclusively on domestic ingredients and external ones can be harnessed and "domesticated" (Kaplan 2012, 217–234).

THE LOUDNESS OF ANTI-EMANCIPATORY SENTIMENTS

While analysing the literature, Baker shows that similar songs, written at the time of Tuđman's presidency, were predominantly homologous with the officially promoted views "of women as peaceful and innocent Others to the masculine soldier" and "women as mothers and men as soldiers and providers" (Baker 2009a, 27). Goldstein also points out that these views were pervasive during that period (Goldstein 1999, 260). According to him, the general tendency was to celebrate women in the domestic setting and to emphasize their reproductive role, to underscore the importance of religion and to adopt a benevolent stance towards the domestic Nazi past (Goldstein 1999, 260). Kunovich and Deitelbaum have extensively analysed this topic and they argue for a symbiosis of these orientations with broader dispositions that include, among other things, animosity towards socialism as well as burgeoning religious and national affiliations (Kunovich and Deitelbaum 2004, 1091–1104). They also highlight the importance of war in Croatia, and the ethnic distance that accompanied it, as an element that enabled such a stance to become pervasive (Kunovich and Deitelbaum 2004, 1102–1104). According to them, these types of anti-emancipatory orientation and their outcomes should not be seen as exclusively Croatian, but rather as part of a larger wave in post-socialist Europe (Kunovich and Deitelbaum 2004, 1092). Nevertheless, they do say that there are variations in magnitude between different countries (Kunovich and Deitelbaum 2004, 1092). Kunovich and Deitelbaum further mention that, after the Berlin wall crumbled, emancipatory efforts lost precedence in such countries and argue that the capitalist economy could be seen as one of the elements that contributed to the proliferation of anti-emancipatory perspectives (Kunovich and Deitelbaum 2004, 1091–1092). Their text shows that a specific climate can spur anti-emancipatory ideas and that Thompson's statements (Kovačević 2009, 26–27) are well suited to this climate. Furthermore, Baker says that "[f]riendship and male family ties played an important role in patriotic music such as Thompson's, where women only mattered if they were mothers (socializing males), fairies (guiding males), the Virgin Mary (both roles combined) or an exemplary figure like the Diva Grabovčeva" (Baker 2009a, 125). Thus she shows that, even in the first decade of the new millennium, anti-emancipatory sentiments were also being promoted through his songs.

Just as Kunovich and Deitelbaum brought attention to the negative impact of the war in Croatia on the emancipation of women (Kunovich and Deitelbaum 2004, 1102–1104), Shekhovtsov argues "that [...] in times of conflict and war, the power of music to set the in-group against the Others increases" (Shekhovtsov 2013, 331). This is an important notion that enables us to grasp the temporal aspect of such songs which, in the case of Croatia, was tackled by Baker as well as Mavra and McNeil (Baker 2009b, 36; Mavra and McNeil 2007, 1–18). Moreover, Baker says "that music can also be used as a tool of conflict" (Baker 2013, 410) and argues that walls between embattled groups can also include bricks made of songs (Baker 2013, 411).[7] Furthermore, in order to properly scrutinize a specific song, Shekhovtsov requires it to be embedded in its habitat (Shekhovtsov 2013, 332). Hence, according to this author, Thompson's lyrics, statements and actions should be couched in the relevant domain.

UNDERSTANDING WHEN THE TIME IS "RIGHT"

Shortly before his latest record was released,[8] Thompson talked about it and other issues with a journalist from "Hrvatski Tjednik" (Černivec 2013). He told her that his musical products are homologous with his personality (Černivec 2013, 21–22). Moreover, Thompson pointed out that he aims to disseminate a "worldview that has been present within our people for centuries" (Černivec 2013, 22). The text published in Hrvatski Tjednik also tackled the temporal issue of this release (Černivec 2013, 22), which didn't go unnoticed and was touched on by one of the online

reviewers (Oršolić 2016). He illustrated the point with a Facebook cita-
tion (Oršolić 2016) and this issue is further explored in the lines that
follow.

In one section of the aforementioned text from "Hrvatski Tjednik",
space is given to the record label's director who said that the new release
would hit the shops with a short delay (Černivec 2013, 22). He explained
that it would be pressed abroad in order to capture its quality properly,
so that the initial release date was being put off (Černivec 2013, 22).
The official website of Croatia Records features an article published on
April 11 with the title "Thompson's album 'Ora et labora' on sale from
today" (Croatia Records 2013). However, the previous day the editors
of Thompson's official Facebook page[9] had published a short amateur
video showing the fresh CD accompanied by the following text: "Dear
friends, we are proud to inform you that today, 10th April 2013 at 19:00
hours, Thompson's new album "Ora et labora" was released. Attached[10]
one of the first albums with Marko's signature" (Perkovic Thompson
2013a). This, at first glance trivial, information gains importance if one
opens a history book such as the works by Goldstein or Tanner and finds
out that this day marks the foundation of the Axis-allied Croatian regime
(Goldstein 1999; Tanner 1997). According to Tanner "[t]he first acts
of the NDH made it clear that the new state was to be a carbon copy of
Nazi Germany" (Tanner 1997, 144). In Croatia this reference is not so
enigmatic, as Oršolić's online text shows (Oršolić 2016). Some of the
comments under that Facebook post,[11] which was "liked" by close to one
thousand people, confirms this (Perkovic Thompson 2013a). For example, one of the commentators wrote "10th April... ['grin emoticon']
super!!" clearly hinting at the importance of the timing. This comment
received more than 30 'likes'. Another one read "I knew it would [come
out] today! bravo Marko!". It was also interesting to read a comment
that was not celebratory: "He shouldn't have [released it] on this day.
Again they will denounce him and have arguments for that..." (Perkovic
Thompson 2013a). Although not all comments under this video tackled
the temporal issue, these few examples clearly show that some members
of his audience recognized what the timing implied, or could imply.
Moreover, precisely one year later, Thompson's official Facebook page
featured an image from the cover of his last CD accompanied by the following text: "We congratulate you on the first anniversary of the release
of the Ora et labora album" (Perkovic Thompson 2014). The lower part
of the image features "10th April 2013 [-]10th April 2014" on top of

each other (Perkovic Thompson 2014). The text that accompanies this image in a celebratory tone speaks about Thompson's musical piece and mentions that "[t]his album was officially last year's bestselling album in Croatia [and the] bestselling Croatian release on iTunes in 2013" (Perkovic Thompson 2014). The same text also points out that many people convened for the live performances that followed his latest release (Perkovic Thompson 2014). The text vividly describes the eminence of this singer and clearly indicates that he remains in vogue. Moreover, some of the comments under this post confirm the argument that the timing of this project and its implications were recognized by at least some segments of his audience (Perkovic Thompson 2014). The editors of Thompson's official Facebook page did a similar thing in 2015 by posting an image almost identical to the album cover with his name pushed to the top of the image, and at the bottom they added a text that read "A.D. 2013. 10th April." (Perkovic Thompson 2015a). This time, as in the previous year, the accompanying text aims to celebrate the highlights of his recent career. Some of the comments from visitors to his Facebook page again reflected on the issue of timing. For example, a comment that received more than fifty "likes" summarized this issue in a very simple and straightforward manner: "10. 4. 1941.-10. 4. 2013.-10. 4. 2015. ['heart emoticon']" (Perkovic Thompson 2015a). This example reinforces the argument in Shekhovtsov's article that it is necessary to explore the terrain in which a song is entrenched (Shekhovtsov 2013, 332). Shekhovtsov argues for a frame of academic scrutiny that is not too tight and which strives to capture and translate important references (Shekhovtsov 2013, 332). According to him, it is crucial to scrutinize the habitat of a specific song and comprehend what he calls "the historical and cultural baggage" (Shekhovtsov 2013, 332). Similarly, in this text, we saw that seemingly trivial information regarding the timing of Thompson's fresh release has powerful undertones which are recognized by some of his audience, as well as being mentioned in an online review (Oršolić 2016). Finally, Dragan Markovina reminds us that Thompson has already done the same thing in the past (Bakotin 2012).

THOMPSON'S THOUGHTS ON THE ISSUE OF GENDER

In the Hrvatski Tjednik article discussed above, Thompson says that he looks at his old material with pride, but he also praises his latest work (Černivec 2013, 21). Thompson explains that although the musical aspect of his material fluctuates, the lyrics are always homologous (Černivec 2013, 22–23). The interviewer touches upon the issue of gender, commenting that "[o]n every album there is one female name", and mentions that "[o]n the new album you dedicated one of the songs to your wife" (Černivec 2013, 23). Thompson's response vividly illustrates his view of the family and its gender dimension when he says that "I dedicated one song to my wife because she is one of the most important people in my life. She gave birth to my five children and she dedicated her whole life to them and me. With [this] song I give her a crumb of the love that she gives to all of us" (Černivec 2013, 23). This response clearly shows that Thompson's thoughts on gender are in line with the ideas summarized by Baker which, according to the scholarly work she cites, were pervasive throughout society and in similar songs during Tuđman's presidency (Baker 2009a, 27). Furthermore, Thompson's recent statement, if compared to Baker's view of his work from several years ago, indicates consistency with regard to this issue (Baker 2009a, 125). This does not come as a surprise since Thompson, as mentioned earlier, highlights the congruity of his lyrics over time in the same interview (Černivec 2013, 22–23). Baker also noticed that, what she calls "romantic songs about direct male-female relationships" almost completely vanished from his set-lists (Baker 2009a, 125). Thompson reflected on such trends in his discography and pointed out that it is a result of his temporary preoccupation with "higher priority themes" (Černivec 2013, 23). This statement corresponds to one of the dispositions that Kunovich and Deitelbaum mention (Kunovich and Deitelbaum 2004, 1092). Their text then suggests that Thompson's views are far from being exceptional in the anti-affirmative discourse.

"ORA ET LABORA" UNDER THE SPOTLIGHT

Several different reviewers (Oršolić 2016; Gall 2013; Jagatić 2013; Horvat 2013; Dragaš 2013) gave unfavourable feedback to this release which, considering the text by Senjković and Dukić, should come as no surprise (Senjković and Dukić 2005, 59). Their evaluations highlight the saturation of this record with the tropes that, according to his video biography, Thompson embraced (*Tko Je Marko Perković Thompson?* 2013), as well as the hawkish atmosphere (Gall 2013; Oršolić 2016; Jagatić 2013; Horvat 2013; Dragaš 2013).

"The falcon's cry" [Sokolov krik] (Perkovic Thompson 2013b),[12] the album's "curtain-raiser", tackles the issue of a life filled with godly devotion on a rather general level. The singer describes the common ground that "Christian people" share, as well as what their goals should be. The latter aspect rings through the chorus in which Thompson promotes the idea expressed in the name of his album. The bird in the title is highlighted by Senjković and Dukić as an element "of Balkan folklore" and "oral epic" that the singer has already used (Senjković and Dukić 2005, 52).

The second song, "Welcome" [Dobrodošli], begins with an important political reference, a sound bite from a Tuđman address from the mid-nineties. His views on the rising imperilment expressed there are, according to Blanuša, "the most notorious conspiracy theory in the recent Croatian past" (Blanuša 2014, 202). Blanuša points out that this address warns the audience of disloyal and hostile agitators, and the imperilment is, as he argues, the eventual nullification of the juvenile state (Blanuša 2014, 202–204). Following this sound bite, the music starts and the lyrics of this song could be compared to an older song, *"Don't let anyone touch my little part of the universe"*,[13] which Baker discusses (Baker 2009a, 123–124). According to her, the older song is Thompson's backlash against antagonistic interpretations of his work (Baker 2009a, 123–124). Similarly, in the song "Welcome" he sings about the hostile environment for people like him.

The following song, "God and Croats" [Bog i Hrvati], tells the story of the often dire past of his people and highlights the importance of ecclesiastical devotion and humility. The song chronologically follows the path of his people who often faced a long ordeal after their godly and patriotic zeal waned. Among the dreadful moments in history, that appear in these verses, Thompson does not refer to the collaboration of Croats with Hitler's regime. However, this song also contains a reference to the "Virgin Mary" which suggests that Baker's assertion (Baker 2009a, 125) is still valid.

"Light a fire" [Zapali vatru] is another song that has ecclesiastical undertones. It sends an optimistic message to anguished people that faith and a positive attitude are the remedy for agony.

"Maranatha", the fifth song on the album, is thematically close to his song "God and Croats". It intertwines accentuated pious melodies with strong patriotic rhythms. The text suggests that the integration of these two elements would bring about the much-desired harmony. An additional ecclesiastical element is the fact that, as mentioned on the website of his record label, a bishop is the author of these verses (Croatia Records 2013). The same clergyman also contributed to a book dedicated to the singer (Ivas 2009). As in the case of "God and Croats", one of the verses of this song mentions the "Virgin Mary".

The following song, according to his record label, was "a single for the European football championships" (Croatia Records 2013) and its fusion of patriotic and ecclesiastical ingredients was presumably meant to energize both the team on the pitch and the audience. The music video for this song, "Always faithfully yours" [Uvijek vjerni tebi] (Cro Rec 2012), blends wartime images with ones depicting players in the national team and the fans. It aims to draw a symbolic connection between the war efforts of Croatian soldiers and success on the football pitch. The main message seems to be that the fundamental motive for both is the same.

According to Thompson's official website, the next song, with the simple title "Bosnia" [Bosna], is an expression of the unbreakable bond with his compatriots living there (Perkovic Thompson 2015c). This bond, as the explanation goes, was downplayed for some time and Thompson tries to amend that (Perkovic Thompson 2015c). His portrayal of Bosnia could be understood as an irredentist claim that Baker noted with reference to his previous work (Baker 2009b, 40). However, on his official website he explicitly recognizes Bosnia's multicultural character (Perkovic Thompson 2015c). In the lyrics, he depicts it as "wounded" and "crucified" as well as "the cradle of Croats".

The eighth song on the album was "Hit of the year"[14] (Porin 2015) and in it Thompson celebrates romantic devotion that continues after the death of a partner. On his official Facebook page he mentions that it is "a song which he dedicated to his wife Sandra"[15] (Perkovic Thompson 2015b). The lyrics are written in the first person and in one verse the protagonist says he is content with his life ending, but expresses concern for his partner without his guardianship. In one verse he depicts a hostile environment "full of wolves" and her as a vulnerable "fawn". The lyrics of this song fit the pattern described by Baker (Baker 2009a, 27). Nevertheless, the song does not completely follow the artistic trajectory which Baker detected (Baker 2009a, 125).

"Never surrender" [Nema predaje], the penultimate song on the album, juxtaposes the alienated political elite and the numerous patriots in the country. It tells of a dire situation where those in charge are estranged from the people and working against their interests. However, his song maintains an optimistic outlook on the situation and Thompson urges the people "never [to] surrender".

He closes the album with the song "Road to heaven" [Put u raj], whose lyrics offer guidance for reaching this destination. The song promotes godly virtues that one should embrace in order to achieve this goal. This final song of the album emphasizes again the importance of ecclesiastic zeal for Thompson. The whole album (Perkovic Thompson 2013b), as the aforementioned reviews (Oršolić 2016; Gall 2013; Jagatić 2013; Dragaš 2013; Horvat 2013) as well as my own examination demonstrate, is flavoured with "Catholicism, family and homeland" (*Tko Je Marko Perković Thompson?* 2013).

CONCLUSION

Close to a quarter of a century after the inception of his career, Thompson seems to be far from being forgotten in someone's attic, which calls for an investigation of his recent work. In this chapter I have demonstrated how Thompson has stuck with his magical formula and a few major tropes over the last couple of years, and that Catherine Baker's description of him is still valid today. The temporal aspect of his latest release is another potential bone of contention in his book which, given what has already been written about him, does not come as a surprise. Thompson's recent statements, as well as the content of his latest album, show a firm anti-emancipatory orientation which corresponds to Baker's elucidation of his earlier career. "Catholicism, family and homeland", mentioned in his video biography, remain the inexhaustible ink that he generously spills in writing down his latest verses.

NOTES

1. The video also features the logo of "Croatia Records", Thompson's record label (Croatia Records 2015), in the top right-hand corner.
2. See also (Senjković and Dukić 2005, 59).
3. These notions are also discussed by Senjković and Dukić (2005, 51–52).
4. See also Baker 2009a, 101–109.
5. This text covers the period up to the end of 2015.

6. In one of the footnotes, Kürti mentions Thompson as being congruent with some artists coming from Hungary (Kürti 2012, 109).
7. See also Cloonan and Johnson 2002, 27–38.
8. This article covers the period up to the end of 2015.
9. These data were checked on May 29, 2015.
10. Referring to the video.
11. See also Oršolić 2016 who refers to another post.
12. See also Oršolić 2016; Gall 2013; Jagatić 2013; Horvat 2013; Dragaš 2013 for their views on some of these songs.
13. Translation is taken from Baker 2009a, 123. The original text is also italicized.
14. See also Kirchmayer Bilić 2016.
15. See also Kirchmayer Bilić 2016.

References

Baker, Catherine. 2009a. *Sounds of the Borderland: Popular Music, War, and Nationalism in Croatia since 1991*. Burlington, VT: Ashgate Popular and Folk Music Series.

———. 2009b. War Memory and Musical Tradition: Commemorating Croatia's Homeland War Through Popular Music and Rap in Eastern Slavonia. *Journal of Contemporary European Studies* 17(1): 35–45.

———. 2010. 'Death to Fascism Isn't in the Catechism': Legacies of Socialism in Croatian Popular Music After the Fall of Yugoslavia. *Narodna Umjetnost* 47(1): 163–183.

———. 2013. Music as a Weapon of Ethnopolitical Violence and Conflict: Processes of Ethnic Separation during and after the Break-up of Yugoslavia. *Patterns of Prejudice* 47(4–5): 409–429.

Bakotin, Jerko. 2012, August 06. Oluje u Čavoglavama: ustaštvo ili hrvatstvo? Deutsche Welle. Accessed 15 January 2016. http://www.dw.com/hr/proslava-oluje-u-%C4%8Davoglavama-usta%C5%A1tvo-ili-hrvatstvo/a-16146713

Blanuša, Nebojša. 2014. Political Unconscious of Croatia and the EU: Tracing the Yugoslav Syndrome Through Fredric Jameson's Lenses. *Journal of Balkan and Near Eastern Studies* 16(2): 196–222.

Cloonan, Martin, and Bruce Johnson. 2002. Killing Me Softly with His Song: An Initial Investigation into the Use of Popular Music as a Tool of Oppression. *Popular Music* 21(1): 27–39.

Croatia Records. 2015. Main Page. Accessed 18 October 2015. http://www.crorec.hr/crorec.hr/uwe_index.php

————. 2013. Od danas u prodaji Thompsonov album 'Ora et labora'. Accessed 28 December 2013. http://www.crorec.hr/crorec.hr/vijest.php?OBJECT_ID=728736

Cro Rec. 2012. Thompson—Uvijek Vjerni Tebi (Official Video). Accessed 28 December 2012. https://www.youtube.com/watch?v=nxBY2NQ9QVc

Černivec, Andrea. 2013, March 28. Novi album 'Ora et labora' pravi je dragulj. Hrvatski Tjednik.

Dragaš, Aleksandar. 2013, April 16. Aleksandar Dragaš: O čemu pjeva Thompson Zarobljen u prošlosti i mitovima, problemi Hrvata ga ne zanimaju. Jutarnji List. Accessed 27 October 2015. http://www.jutarnji.hr/thompson--zarobljen-u-proslosti-i-mitovima--problemi-hrvata-ga-ne-zanimaju-/1097339/

Gall, Zlatko. 2013, April 21. MP THOMPSON Ora et Labora. Slobodna Dalmacija. Accessed 3 December 2015. http://www.slobodnadalmacija.hr/misljenja/parangall/clanak/id/199245/mp-thompson-ora-et-labora

Goldstein, Ivo. 1999. *Croatia: A History*. Montreal: McGill-Queen's University Press.

Horvat, Hrvoje. 2013, April 15. Thompson; dobrodošli u građanski rat. Muzika. hr. Accessed 3 December 2015. http://muzika.20minuta.hr/clanak/41220/komentari/thompson-dobrodosli-u-gradanski-rat.aspx

Ivas, Ante Mons., and Bishop of Šibenik. 2009. Marko Perković Thompson iliti 'Ilija od Kljaka.'. In *Thompson u očima hrvatskih intelektualaca. Bilo je i to jednom u Hrvatskoj...*, ed. J. Pečarić, and M. Kovačević, 12–15. Fortuna.

Jagatić, D. 2013, May 10. Što je zajedničko Thompsonu i Dubioza Kolektivu? tportal.hr. Accessed 4 December 2015. http://www.tportal.hr/showtime/glazba/259570/Sto-je-zajednicko-Thompsonu-i-Dubioza-kolektivu.html

Kaplan, Danny. 2012. Institutionalized Erasures: How Global Structures Acquire National Meanings in Israeli Popular Music. *Poetics* 40(3): 217–236.

Kirchmayer Bilić, Eva. 2016 Hrvatski narod je odlučio: Porina dobivaaaaa: MARKO PERKOVIĆ THOMPSON!!! Accessed 3 January 2016. http://thompson.hr/osvrt/174-hrvatski-narod-je-odlucio-porina-dobivaaaaa-marko-perkovic-thompson

Kovačević, Mate. 2009. M. P. Thompson: Ne će me zaustaviti! In *Thompson u očima hrvatskih intelektualaca. Bilo je i to jednom u Hrvatskoj...*, ed. J. Pečarić, and M. Kovačević, 18–31. Fortuna.

Kunovich, Robert M., and Catherine Deitelbaum. 2004. Ethnic Conflict, Group Polarization, and Gender Attitudes in Croatia. *Journal of Marriage and Family* 66(5): 1089–1107.

Kürti, László. 2012. Twenty Years After: Rock Music and National Rock in Hungary. *Region: Regional Studies of Russia, Eastern Europe, and Central Asia* 1(1): 93–129.

Lamont, Christopher K. 2010. Defiance or Strategic Compliance? The Post-Tuđman Croatian Democratic Union and the International Criminal Tribunal for the Former Yugoslavia. *Europe-Asia Studies* 62(10): 1683–1705.

Mavra, Miroslav, and Lori McNeil. 2007. Identity Formation and Music: A Case Study of Croatian Experience. *Human Architecture: Journal of the Sociology of Self-Knowledge* 5(2): 2, 1–20.

Oršolić, Marijan. 2016. Dossier Thompson: analiza najnovijeg albuma 'Ora et Labora'. Fanfo.org. Accessed 3 February 2016. http://fanfo.org/2013/04/25/dossier-thompson-analiza-najnovijeg-albuma-ora-et-labora/

Pavlaković, Vjeran. 2010. Croatia, the International Criminal Tribunal for the Former Yugoslavia, and General Gotovina as a Political Symbol. *Europe-Asia Studies* 62(10): 1707–1740.

Perkovic Thompson, Marko. 2013a. Novi album 'Ora et labora.' Accessed 29 November 2013. https://www.facebook.com/video.php?v=4601659893705 &theater

———. 2013b. Thompson Ora et labora. Accessed 25 November 2013. http://www.crorec.hr/crorec.hr/izdanje.php?OBJECT_ID=726520

———. 2014. Na današnji dan prošle godine izašao je album 'Ora et labora.' Accessed 18 November 2014. https://www.facebook.com/marko.perkovic.thompson/photos/a.187389567984204.47264.151454118244416/67743365231312 4/?type=1

———. 2015a. ČESTITAMO 10. TRAVNJA-DAN IZLASKA ALBUMA 'ORA ET LABORA'!. Accessed 21 November 2015. https://www.facebook.com/marko.perkovic.thompson/photos/a.187389567984204.47264. 151454118244416/861580233898464/?type=1

———. 2015b. Na znanje vranama, šišmišima i sličnim medijima. Accessed 29 November 2015. https://www.facebook.com/marko.perkovic.thompson/posts/526814224041735

———. 2015c. Tekst pjesme Bosna, sa novog albuma 'Ora et Labora.' Accessed 29 November 2015. http://www.thompson.hr/arhiva/95-bosna

———. 2015d. Thompson: Službene stranice Marka Perkovića Thompsona. Accessed 16 January 2015. http://www.thompson.hr/

Porin. 2015. Dobitnici nagrade Porin 2014. Accessed 29 November 2015. http://www.porin.org/content/dobitnici-nagrade-porin-2014

Rivera, Lauren A. 2008. Managing 'Spoiled' National Identity: War, Tourism, and Memory in Croatia. *American Sociological Review* 73(4): 613–634.

Senjković, Reana, and Davor Dukić. 2005. Virtual Homeland? Reading the Music on Offer on a Particular Web Page. *International Journal of Cultural Studies* 8(1): 44–62.

Shekhovtsov, Anton. 2013. Music and the Other: An Introduction. *Patterns of Prejudice* 47(4–5): 329–335.

Tanner, Marcus. 1997. *Croatia: A Nation Forged in War*. New Haven: Yale University Press.

Tko Je Marko Perković Thompson? 2013. Accessed 28 December 2013. https://www.youtube.com/watch?v=9H9ele4ELOs&feature=youtube_gdata_player

Wanner, Catherine. 1996. Nationalism on Stage: Music and Change in Soviet Ukraine. In *Retuning Culture: Musical Changes in Central and Eastern Europe*, ed. M. Slobin, 136–155. Durham: Duke University Press.

Zambelli, Nataša. 2010. A Journey Westward: A Poststructuralist Analysis of Croatia's Identity and the Problem of Cooperation with the International Criminal Tribunal for the Former Yugoslavia. *Europe-Asia Studies* 62(10): 1661–1682.

The Far Right's Ideological Constructions of 'Deviant' Male Sexualities

Robert Claus and Fabian Virchow

INTRODUCTION

Sexuality—its conceptualization as heteronormative and its regulation by state institutions as part of a broader biopolitical approach to strengthen the '*Volksgemeinschaft*'—has always played a decisive role in far-right world-views and politics (Bacchetta and Power 2002; Maiwald and Mischler 1999; Smith 1994; Schoppmann 1991). One of the best mobilizing topics of the far right in Germany in recent years has been the issue of 'paedo-sexual perpetrators'. For example, on September 25, 2012, one day after a report in the tabloid *Bild*, that a six-year old boy had become a victim of sexual abuse in the small Saxonian town of Riesa, the local branch of the National Democratic Party of Germany (NPD) was able to mobilize some 300 people to attend a demonstration demanding capital punishment for the offender. In the aftermath, Jürgen Gansel, at that time NPD represen-tative in the state parliament of Saxony, called this a 'mobilization success', due primarily to 'the arousing and emotionalizing issue' (Gansel 2012, 17).

R. Claus (✉)
Berlin, Germany

F. Virchow
Department of Social Sciences and Cultural Studies, University of Applied Sciences Düsseldorf, Düsseldorf, Germany

© The Author(s) 2017
M. Köttig et al. (eds.), *Gender and Far Right Politics in Europe*,
DOI 10.1007/978-3-319-43533-6_20

Addressing the issue of child molesting and sexual abuse, the far right has found a topic to which it can relate several of its main political messages, like creating order, protecting children and the family, and calling for harsh punishments.

From a historical perspective, however, the German far right's thematization of an issue relating to sexuality is not without precursors (Weißmann 2010). Already in the 1960s it agitated against the upcoming spread of pornography, and in the 1980s it addressed the issue of homosexuality in general, and HIV in particular. Far-right narratives and actions have always drawn a clear line between an alleged 'natural' heteronormative sexuality, from which the imagined national community ('*Volksgemeinschaft*') benefits, and 'perverse' or 'abnormal' sexuality as a threat to society's stability, future and peace. Thus, pornography, homosexuality and paedo-sexual offenders are held responsible for the alleged problem of a decadent society that suffers from low moral values and destruction of the heterosexual family.

In recent decades, sexuality has become a widely discussed issue in the social sciences (see for example Duggan & Hunter 1995). For the purpose of our research, the definition provided by Uwe Sielert (2005, 37–51) has proved helpful. He distinguishes four dimensions of sexuality. First, there is the topic of identity and self-perception of one's body. Second, the issue of relations and concepts of (sexual) community are important. Third, he points to desire and the question what people find attractive about each other. Fourth, he mentions the category of reproduction, not only as a biological procedure but also as a source of happiness and mental wellness.

We will follow these categories in our analysis and use them to show how sexuality and deviance are constructed. Our underlying assumption is that each category is dominated by the construction of a normative male and a normative female body, as well as that of a normative, child-producing family.

In this chapter, we will investigate the construction of 'abnormal' male sexual behaviour in far-right political thought and narratives in post-war Germany. We start with some basic considerations and theoretical reflections about the place of sexuality in far-right political thought. This is followed by a brief reconstruction of far-right perspectives on sexual liberalization in general, and pornography in particular, in the 1960s and 1970s, and on HIV in the 1980s. While these issues have lost their importance and have disappeared almost totally from far-right discourses, male homosocial bonding, such as the issue of all-male student associations, homosexuality and paedo-sexual behaviour are of great importance today in far-right political thought and practice.

THE FAR RIGHT AND SEXUAL POLITICS

Sexual politics in narratives and actions of the far right have been the subject of several studies over the past few decades. From a historical perspective, one could go back to Wilhelm Reich's 'The Sexual Revolution' (1945) or Klaus Theweleit's 'Male Phantasies' (1987). More recently, a broad range of German academic literature has been published on gender roles (Bitzan 1997, Forschungsnetzwerk Frauen und Rechtsextremismus/ Antifaschistisches Frauennetzwerk 2005) and gender regimes in far-right scenes, not least regarding the construction of the 'Volksgemeinschaft' (Lehnert 2010). While the discussion was initially dominated by femininity and gender roles, as well as women's careers in far-right movements, it has been complemented by investigations on masculinity in recent years (Claus, Müller and Lehnert 2010; Virchow 2010). Moreover, gender has started to become part of the discussion on prevention of violence and far-right extremism (Birsl 2011; Radvan 2016). The far-right construction of a normative heterosexuality as the basis of the racial family has been part of the analysis, especially when this is focused on family politics.

Besides this, far-right narratives and actions on sexual or 'sexually deviant' issues have been an issue in only a very few publications. Rosa von Praunheim, a well-known observer of the gay scene in Germany, has produced a documentary film entitled 'Men, Heroes, Gay Nazis'[1] (von Praunheim 2005). Among other issues, the film portrays three homosexual far-right activists, who apparently live an everyday contradiction between their sexual preferences on the one hand and the ideological view of 'abnormal' homosexuality in their political environment on the other. The same contradiction has been analysed by Claus and Müller (2010) in an essay on homophobia and homosexuality in German neo-Nazism. The authors state that there is a contradiction between the official propaganda against homosexuality and the existence of homosexual neo-Nazis. They focus especially on Michael Kühnen's 'National Socialism and Homosexuality' (Kühnen 1986). In this booklet, Kühnen tried to create a space for homosexuality in the ideology of the 'Volksgemeinschaft' by arguing that male bonding and camaraderie are a necessary precondition for human development, a view that created controversial debate and fierce fighting inside German neo-Nazism (Claus and Müller 2010). Ulrich Overdieck (2010) made the construction of 'racial disgrace' in far-right discourses the centre of his research. He concludes that the term, regularly used in Nazism to discredit sexual relationships involving Whites and People of Colour, mostly concerns White women who are not allowed to have sexual contact with Men of Colour. Therefore, it mostly serves the control of feminine sexuality as a central element of hegemonic masculinity. Jentzsch and Sanders (2011) discuss whether the latest appearance of the 'autonomous nationalist movement' and its vague political theory tends to open far-right structures to more liberal gender concepts: non-creational sexuality or women participating in street fights. They conclude that these tendencies only exist during a first phase of politicization. In the long run, they serve to recruit more people who will keep the boundaries of ideology and standardization as tight as they have ever been.

The Far Right's Attitude to Pornography and HIV

In the 1950s, a growing minority of Germans considered eroticism and sex the epitome of the (albeit still future) better life, as an available experience and as the promise of the 'American way of life'. Although society was dominated by a conservative idea of family grounded in Christian beliefs, and a sexual morality closely linked to marital coitus, men and women had easy access to erotic and sexual information. This was also true for contraceptives, erotic literature and photographs that were obtainable through mail order and in this way entered millions of households. The increasing sexualization of consumption, the translation of the Kinsey Reports into German in 1954 and 1955 and their popularization by newspapers and magazines, as well as marriage guidebooks containing chapters on eroticism and sex, made sex a broadly discussed topic (Eder 2007). Access to the birth control pill and a growing range of sex education films, as well as the commodification of sexual needs, also contributed to a development called the 'sex wave' by contemporary observers. Against this background, the 'sexual revolution' of the late 1960s and 1970s in West Germany was the liberalization of a sexual order which had been 'revolutionized' in the behaviour and attitudes of many people for years (Eder et al. 2015).

However, there were also widespread reservations about, and opposition to, sexual liberation in German society. Ultra-conservative and far-right political forces agreed in believing that sexual liberation was eroding taboos necessary for an orderly coexistence of people, and going against the norm that sex should take place exclusively in the context of a loving relationship (Ehlers 1973; Strub 2011). Manfred Roeder, who practised as a lawyer in a small town in Hessen, may serve as an outstanding example of a far-rightist fighting sexual liberalization. He started his political career as an activist in the 'Citizens' initiative against moral and political anarchy'. In August 1970 he threw bags filled with paint as a protest during the first adult entertainment convention organized in post-war Germany. Several weeks later he attacked an erotic shop in Nuremberg with butyric acid. In 1971, he organized a series of direct actions and brought criminal charges against events and individuals he considered were responsible for the morale decline caused by sexual liberation. In one of his talks he lamented that 'while the memoirs of a prostitute are released as not harmful to minors, the memoirs of an officer from the last war are put on the index' (quoted from Anti-Roeder-Arbeitskreis 1978, 21). Roeder's action created some media attention and was cheered broadly by far-right groups like the 'Gesellschaft für freie Publizistik' (GfP) or the 'Deutsches Kulturwerk europäischen Geistes' (DKEG), and echoed in far-right magazines like *MUT* (N.N. 1972).[2]

In 1981, HIV was clinically observed in the United States. Two years later, doctors in West Germany recorded it as a cause of death for the first time. From the mid-1980s, HIV became an issue for the German far right, resulting in a broad campaign starting in 1987. In accordance with far-right critique of the pluralization of sexual desire, HIV was deemed another outcome of the 'decadent society' (Mattausch 1987, 25). Characterized as the 'most devastating health disaster in history' (Sichelschmidt 1988, 5), the disease was attributed to migration from African and Asian countries to Europe (Hansen 1987) and to homosexual men (Ames 1996). Accordingly, the far right brought forward two main political demands relating to the 'correlations between the epidemic nature of AIDS, the sexual behaviour of certain groups or races, and between race and recent AIDS infections' (Mattausch 1987, 21). One was a demand that the alleged policy of open borders should be revised in order to prevent Europe from 'becoming African' (Dehoust 1987, 4). The other demand was for comprehensive reporting of HIV-infected people in order to get a huge number of male homosexuals registered, the application of the Federal Disease Act and the committal of patients in closed institutions. Other approaches to dealing with the problem, like education, data protection and the consideration of civil liberty rights, were denounced by the far right as characteristic of a liberalistic society and a weak state.

Interpreting HIV as a fundamental threat to conventional concepts of normality, the far-right propagated concepts in which the family, marital fidelity and heterosexual practices are the ideal (Hafeneger 1988, 19).

THE FAR RIGHT: HOMOPHOBIA AND GAY NAZIS

Homophobia constitutes a central element of hegemonic masculinity, as well as the conception of manhood in far-right gender regimes. The construction of family in particular and '*Volksgemeinschaft*' in general is located in a sexual and racial setting that is heteronormative and white (Maiwald and Mischler 1999, Sanos 2013). However, this hegemonic discourse is confused by the existence of homosexual Nazis and has historically been discussed with reference to Michael Kühnen's 'National Socialism and Homosexuality'. In this booklet Kühnen tries to connect same-gender desires with the idea that male homosocial bonding is a necessary precondition for the creation of civilization. This contradiction is constantly marginalized, as the following analysis shows.

On the one hand homosexuality is brought into position against the ideal of the white, heterosexual, 'down-to-earth' family: 'While more and more people don't know how to feed their families by their work, left parties (…) seriously think about ways to legalize perverse affections and make them socially acceptable' (Zasowk 2012). Although the quotation mainly refers to paedophilia, it connects with the discourse on homosexuality. Especially the public show of homosexuality meets strong opposition; accordingly, the 2008 Christopher Street Day in Munich was heavily criticized on the far-right newswire 'de.altermedia.info', which argued that 'the excessive encouragement of the gay and lesbian scene by local authorities is a scandal without equal, while there is no money for single parents and families with children' (altermedia 2008).[3] Furthermore, homosexuality is associated with multiculturalism and migration: 'Discriminated, marginalized and defamed in the first place are those who don't want the overflowing gay propaganda, multicultural excesses of 'integration' and the millions spent on funding them.' Consequently, homosexuality is fitted into a larger picture of a 'degenerate society' which constantly seems to produce artificial identities and a tremendous lack of values, disconnecting human life from its biological and natural basis.

On the other hand, such public discourses do not reflect the internal discussions on homosexual 'comrades' in far-right scenes, which are quite ambivalent. As mentioned above, Rosa von Praunheim (2005) interviewed far-right activists who are out of the closet. One of them, Alexander Schlesinger, said that 'we are not interested in what our members do in their beds or behind their doors'. Moreover, he did not see any contradiction to the ideal of masculinity that is prominent in neo-Nazi circles: 'Personally, I am a very intolerant gay. I don't understand such "Tatütata-Huschen".[4] I did not become gay because I like feminine types. I became gay because I like tough guys.' His ideal of masculinity affirms values such as strength and brawniness. Another interviewee, Skinhead André, underscores this: 'The struggle against gays is not a struggle against men who go to bed with other men, but a struggle against unmanliness'.[5] Homophobic dismissal of 'feminine attitudes' or weakness is central to this construction of gay Nazis—hypermasculinity legitimates certain expressions of homosexuality.

In this discourse, partial 'tolerance' should not be confused with acceptance or emancipation. Homosexual far-right activists have to avoid any kind of effeminacy if they want to be respected as full members of their movement. The contradiction of being a 'gay Nazi' has to be rendered insignificant by pointing out the person's merits as a comrade who has served the neo-Nazi movement.

A Neo-Nazi's Approach to Defending Male Homosexuality

During the Nazi dictatorship, male homosexuality was described as morbid and was brutally persecuted. Denouncing someone as 'gay' was used as a means to outcast or eliminate political opponents and competitors (Koch 1986; Zur Nieden 2005, 147–192). In the same way, 'homosexuality' was instrumentalized by the far right in post-war West Germany. Only with the booklet 'National socialism and homosexuality' written by Michael Kühnen—one of the most prominent activists of the far right until he died from HIV in 1992—did a different approach appear. Although written as early as 1981—in the aftermath of the *Feme* murder of far-right and homosexual activist Johannes Bügner—Kühnen did not publish the booklet until 1986 due to the danger of a split in the neo-Nazi movement.

In the booklet, Kühnen tries to create a space for male homosexuality in the ideological construction of the '*Volksgemeinschaft*' and therefore uses a long pseudo-scientific history of societies characterized by male bonding, which, as he puts it, is what created leadership as the basis for huge civilizations (1986, 39–46). According to Kühnen, these male societies were formed by homosexuality because men had a reasonable interest in the stable power of their male leaders and did not want this development to be disturbed by women. Moreover, he defines '*Volksgemeinschaft*' as a 'form of state and culture, which for *all* racial members means home and a way of life that can develop in the place they inhabit due to their skills and affections, as well as their altruistic and comradely work to create a natural high culture' (Kühnen 1986, 64). Consequently, even homosexuals should have a place in neo-Nazism.

Although this debate opened a small space for rare reflections on masculine ideals in the far-right movement, the benchmarks are the same for all authors: the strong, brave soldier as bearer of a higher culture, who does his duty to the racial nation, controls feminine sexuality and has a civilizing mission (Kühnen 1986, XX). Kühnen tried to find a place for repressed masculinity in the charts of right-wing masculinities but failed. Nowadays, the debate on homosexuality in right-wing circles is marginalized because it is hard to resolve the contradiction between a violent heteronormative ideology and the existence of homosexual comrades.

THE FAR RIGHT ON 'CHILD ABUSE'

In the early 1990s, the neo-Nazi group 'Deutsche Frauenfront' (DFF) addressed the issue of child prostitution. The DFF was part of a broader West German neo-Nazi network and its foundation was intended to attract more women to the movement (Schwarzmeier and Wunderlich 1995). These authors claimed that the main cause of child prostitution was the desire of young girls for material goods such as expensive brand products. This attitude was attributed to an alleged Americanization of German society, which had led to the marginalization of 'German idealism' in favour of consumerist thinking (Deutsche Frauenfront 1990). Yet, not a single word mentioned the fact that prostitution supplies a demand, in other words men who seek sexual services and are willing to pay (mostly) women for these services.

By contrast, men and their criminal behaviour have been at the core of multiple far-right campaigns in recent years. On many occasions, the disclosure of a sexual offence or the fact that a sexual offender has taken up residence nearby after release from prison has been taken by neo-Nazi groups as an opportunity to stage public demonstrations. Far-rightists are particularly active when the victims are children. Regularly, speakers and participants at such demonstrations demand the death penalty for the perpetrator or deny him the right to find a new home. They claim that the state authorities are too soft in the case of sexual offences committed against children (see, for instance, widerstandnord 2002).

This attitude is shared by many German citizens who are in favour of severe punishments. They distrust the judicial authorities, they demand more law and order, and they are strongly opposed to immigration (Cochran and Piquero 2011). Far-rightists make use of the emotional dimension of this issue in order to make their authoritarian solution more acceptable (Schuermans and De Maesschalck 2010). In some cases, there has been a violent atmosphere of vigilantism, turning the demonstration into a 'reactionary crowd' (Drury 2002; Pardy 2011).

This mechanism partly works by portraying the suspect as non-human. This includes not only pejorative wording such as 'perverse', 'swine', 'scum' or 'monster'. It also contains the construction of a dark and evil male sexuality. The neo-Nazi rock band 'Aufmarsch' sings: '... but there in the dark, a sable figure, it is too late, it's getting cold'.[6] The far right often presents perpetrators, or suspected perpetrators, of sexual violence against children as 'the Other' and as pathologically driven. Both messages are empirically wrong, but serve political purposes. Only a small percentage of those misusing children are paedo-sexuals; the vast majority want power and control over children; they know that they harm children and that they are in a position to decide not to abuse them. In principle, medical, psychological or educational support could help them to change their behaviour. Insofar, there is an alternative to the death penalty that is regularly demanded by the far right (Quinn et al. 2004).

Defining perpetrators as 'the Other', which in many cases is linked to defining them as 'foreigners' (Keskinen 2011), avoids closer investigations of the repressive relations and acts of sexual abuse by men in the social environment of the victim (Heiliger 2000). From a far-right perspective, this helps to defend the (traditional) idea of the family as the core unit of the '*Volksgemeinschaft*'.

Moreover, the far right tries to emotionalize the entire debate on paedo-sexual offenders. It sees a higher likelihood of mobilizing a 'critical mass' by reaching people in their personal fears and needs. To achieve this kind of emotionalization, it uses different means and strategies. They can be divided into three categories: images of unprotected children, dehumanization of the offender and connecting the issue to the menace of an unstable and fluid society in general.

Far-right propaganda on the issue of paedo-sexual offenders focuses on unprotected, lonely children who are not able to defend themselves in a threatening society. This is most explicit in images of female children with a strong reference to the traditional gender conception of weak women who need protection (Hawkes and Dune 2013). In their song 'Alptraummann' ('Nightmare Man') the neo-Nazi music group 'Störkraft' sings: 'That naked young chicken flesh, the ribbon on her braid (...) she is the woman for you because she can't defend herself.'[7] It is true that a vast majority of women are concerned by sexual violence and that children are less able to protect and defend themselves than adults, so that the lyrics here are intended to create a strong urge to protect the innocent bodies of girls. It is also suggested that the protagonist best able to protect young girls and stop their abuse is the 'nationalist movement'.

The far right's rhetoric of failed protection, unstable families and lack of order is not limited to the debate on paedo-sexual offenders. It is part of a more general discourse of the alleged destruction of moral values and the decay of stable identities and communities through the decadence of modern, liberal and capitalistic times. Correspondingly, the far-right band 'Saccara' sings: 'These decadent times have distorted you as well, you are such a perverted swine, attracted by children'.[8] The topic of decadence connects the issue of paedo-sexual offenders to other issues of social politics, such as the 'crisis of the family', the 'crisis of masculinity' or the 'demographic crisis of the German people' in general. The issue of crisis is central to far-right discourses. At the same time, the far right presents its concept of the 'German family' as an important line of political action. 'Avoid the looming death of the German people by a just family policy' is the subtitle of an article in the monthly magazine of the NPD, where it is argued: 'Families have been culpably disregarded for many decades by the political class and pushed to the margins of society' (Köster 2012).

CONCLUSION

In general, male sexuality cannot be considered without taking the construction of female sexuality into account. Especially in a heteronormative system, they are both constructed as being related to and depending on each other. Therefore, our analysis of right-wing discourses on ('abnormal') sexuality includes both perspectives. Coming back to the dimensions of sexuality introduced at the beginning, this leads us to the following conclusions:

Identity: Right-wing discourses always construct 'soft' and sexually accessible women on the one hand, and tough masculinity on the other. This becomes especially clear in the debates on homosexuality—gay Nazis still follow a traditional ideal of manliness and masculinity.

Relationship: The idea of the heteronormative family as the 'inner core of the nation' is the unquestioned and dogmatic focus point. In the family—according to right-wing discourses—sexual violence does not exist and it guarantees reproduction of the nation.

Desire: This is only possible inside the boundaries of the '*Volksgemeinschaft*' structured in accordance with heteronormative gender arrangements. On the individual level, homosexual Nazis exist, but they are rendered invisible in right-wing discourses and narratives. Values such as faithfulness, family and togetherness are placed first on the agenda. Sexual practices are not an issue, and cleanliness counts as an aim.

Reproduction: On a biological as well as on a mental level, reproduction is only legitimate within the framework of the family in the traditional sense. This model is set as the norm.

In conclusion, the construction of 'abnormal sexuality' mainly serves to set the boundaries of sexual practices in the idealized '*Volksgemeinschaft*'. This does not happen by people reflecting and discussing their own position, but by drawing a line between themselves and a constructed threat. The heteronormative nuclear family is set up as a means of protection against loss of values, decadence, pornography, polygamy, homosexuality and 'child abuse'.

All of these issues and the dimensions of sexuality are part of a patriarchal system which aims to establish a clear line of descendance inside the ethnic boundaries of a '*Volksgemeinschaft*'. The control of a 'healthy sexuality' is part of masculinity and its requirements. Boundaries, which may be flexible in some cases, like gay Nazis, are firmly set in the debates on pornography, homosexuality and 'child abuse'. In these discourses, femininity is constructed at two poles. On the one hand, it is a threat; pornography counts as a sin, becoming feminine is a menace of homosexuality. On the other hand, femininity is a promise, related to caring within the family (Walton 2012). Masculinity mostly counts as something good, as protective and respecting the boundaries. This only changes in the discourse on 'child abuse', where masculinity appears as a sexual threat.

Notes

1. This is a video documentary produced by the German public broadcasting corporation *NDR* and published by *absolut Medien*. Rosa von Praunheim wrote the script and was the director. Rosa von Praunheim See: http://www.rosavonpraunheim.de/werke/rosafilme/05maen/maen_1.html and: https://absolutmedien.de/film/849/Rosa+von+Praunheim+Box (accessed 22.03.2016).
2. The 'Gesellschaft für freie Publizistik' ('Society for free journalism') was founded in 1960 by former members of the NSDAP and the SS. It became the leading far-right association for writers, journalists, publishers, and book-sellers. The 'Deutsche Kulturwerk europäischen Geistes' (German Culture Guild of European Spirit), founded in 1950, dissolved in 1996) offered former Nazi writers and poets a platform for presenting their works.
3. See: de.altermedia.info/general/fn-munchen-nationaler-protest-gegen-csd-in-munchen-130708-15153.html, accessed 2012. The neo-Nazi portal 'Altermedia' was banned in Germany in 2016 (see: http://www.fr-online.de/politik/rechtsextremismus-im-internet-neonazi-portal--altermedia--verboten,1472596,33623946.html (accessed 22.03.2016)). Access is currently not possible. The sources used in this paper, however, were all documented.
4. This expression is a slang term for 'feminine' gay men.
5. See: https://absolutmedien.de/film/849/Rosa+von+Praunheim+Box (accessed 21.03.2016).
6. See: https://www.youtube.com/watch?v=q-dp2WEnlwE (accessed 21.03.2016).
7. See: https://www.gugalyrics.com/lyrics-132933/st%C3%B6rkraft-alptraummann.html (accessed 21.03.2016).
8. See: https://www.youtube.com/watch?v=0PZ7iWwnVxU (accessed 21.03.2016).

References

Original Sources

Dehoust, Peter. 1987. Aids. *Nation Europa* 37(8): 3–4.
Deutsche Frauenfront—aktuell. 1990. Kinderprostitution—ein Problem unserer Zeit. Leaflet.

Ehlers, Hans. 1973. Mohler räumt den Sex-Shop auf. *Deutscher Studenten-Anzeiger* 13(1–2): 5.

Gansel, Jürgen. 2012. Facebook-Mobilisierung gegen Kinderschänder. *Deutsche Stimme* 37(11): 17.

Hansen, Klaus. 1987. AIDS bedroht uns alle. Warum unternimmt Bonn nichts? *Der Republikaner* 4(1): 3.

Köster, Stefan. 2012. 'Deutsche Kinder braucht das Land!' Eine Trendumkehr ist möglich: Den drohenden Volkstod durch eine gerechte Familienpolitik verhindern! *Deutsche Stimme* 37(2): 8.

Kühnen, Michael. 1986. *Nationalsozialismus und Homosexualität*. Paris.

Mattausch, Christian. 1987. AIDS—Symptom einer Weltanschauung. *Nation Europa* 37(8): 19–26.

N.N. 1972. Sex als politische Waffe. *MUT* 7(57): 36–39.

Sichelschmidt, Gustav. 1988. Todesseuche greift weiter um sich. *Deutscher Anzeiger* 31(13): 5.

Weißmann, Karlheinz. 2010. Sexpol—Die Linke, der Sex und die Politik. *Sezession* 36: 10–15.

Widerstandnord. 2002. Missbraucht! Von Typen wie dem? 300.000* und das politische System 'produziert' immer neue Kinderschänder. Leaflet. Hamburg.

Zasowk, Ronny. 2012. Verkommene Gesellschaft. *Deutsche Stimme* 37(6): 2.

LITERATURE

Ames, Lynda J. 1996. Homo-Phobia, Homo-Ignorance, Homo-Hate: Heterosexism and AIDS. In *Preventing Heterosexism and Homophobia*, ed. Esther D. Rothblum, and Lynne A. Bond, 239–253. Thousand Oaks: Sage.

Anti-Roeder-Arbeitskreis. 1978. *'NSDAP'-Propagandisten unter der Lupe*. Hamburg: Reents.

Bacchetta, Paola, and Margaret Power (ed). 2002. *Right-Wing Women: From Conservatives to Extremists Around the World*. New York: Routledge.

Birsl, Ursula (ed). 2011. *Rechtsextremismus und Gender*. Opladen: Budrich.

Bitzan, Renate (ed). 1997. *Rechte Frauen: Skingirls, Wallküren und feine Damen*. Berlin: ElefantenPress.

Claus, Robert, and Yves Müller. 2010. Männliche Homosexualität und Homophobie im Neonazismus. In *'Was ein rechter Mann ist ...'—Männlichkeiten im Rechtsextremismus*, ed. R. Claus, E. Lehnert, and Y. Müller, 109–126. Berlin: RLS.

Cochran, Joshua C., and Alex R. Piquero. 2011. Exploring Sources of Punitiveness Among German Citizens. *Crime & Delinquency* 57(4): 511–571.

Drury, John. 2002. 'When the Mobs Are Looking for Witches to Burn, Nobody's Safe': Talking About the Reactionary Crowd. *Discourse & Society* 13(1): 41–73.

Duggan, Lisa, and Nan D. Hunter. 1995. *Sex Wars: Sexual Dissent and Political Culture*. New York/London: Taylor & Francis.

Eder, Franz X. 2007. The National Socialists' Healthy Sensuality Succeeded by the American Influence. Sexuality and Media from National Socialism to the Sexual Revolution. In *Sexuality in Austria*, ed. G. Bischof, A. Pelinka, and J. Köstlbauer, 102–131. New Brunswick: Transaction Publishers.

Eder, Franz X., Peter-Paul Bänziger, Pascal Eitler, and Magdalena Beljan (ed). 2015. *Sexuelle Revolution? Zur Geschichte der Sexualität im deutschsprachigen Raum seit den 1960er Jahren*. Bielefeld: Transcript.

Forschungsnetzwerk Frauen und Rechtsextremismus/Antifaschistisches Frauennetzwerk. 2005. *Braune Schwestern? Feministische Analysen zu Frauen in der extremen Rechten*. Münster: Unrast.

Hafeneger, Benno. 1988. Die extreme Rechte und AIDS. *Vorgänge* 91: 17–20.

Hawkes, Gail, and Tinashe Dune. 2013. Narratives of the Sexual Child: Shared Themes and Shared Challenges. *Sexualities* 16(5–6): 622–634.

Heiliger, Anita. 2000. Täterstrategien und Prävention. Sexueller Mißbrauch an Mädchen innerhalb familialer und familienähnlicher Strukturen. Ergebnisse einer empirischen Untersuchung. In *Das Forschungsjahr 1999*, ed. Deutsches Jugendinstitut, 51–55. München: DJI.

Jentzsch, Ulli, and Eike Sanders. 2011. AN und Gender. In *Autonome Nationalisten*, ed. A. Häusler, and J. Schedler, 135–153. Wiesbaden: VS.

Keskinen, Suvi. 2011. Borders of the Finnish Nation: Media Politics and Rape by 'Foreign' Perpetrators. In *Media in Motion. Cultural Complexity and Migration in the Nordic Region*, ed. E. Eide, and K. Nikunen, 107–124. Abingdon: Ashgate.

Koch, Friedrich. 1986. *Sexuelle Denunziation*. Frankfurt/Main: Syndikat.

Lehnert, Esther. 2010. *Gender und Rechtsextremismusprävention*. Berlin: Metropol.

Maiwald, Stefan, and Gerd Mischler. 1999. *Sexualität unter dem Hakenkreuz. Manipulation und Vernichtung der Intimsphäre im NS-Staat*. Hamburg/Wien: Europa Verlag.

Overdieck, Ulrich. 2010. Der Komplex 'Rassenschande' und seine Funktionalität für Männlichkeitskonstruktionen in rechtsextremen Diskursen. In *'Was ein rechter Mann ist ...'—Männlichkeiten im Rechtsextremismus*, ed. R. Claus, E. Lehnert, and Y. Müller, 100–108. Berlin: RLS.

Pardy, Maree. 2011. Hate and Otherness. Exploring Emotion Through a Race Riot. *Emotion, Space & Society* 4(1): 51–60.

Quinn, James F., Craig J. Forsyth, and Carla Mullen-Quinn. 2004. Societal Reaction to Sex Offenders: A Review of the Origins and Results of the Myths Surrounding Their Crimes and Treatment Amenability. *Deviant Behavior* 25(3): 215–232.

Radvan, Heike. 2016. *Rechtsextreme Frauen in der Gegenwart. Analysen und Handlungsempfehlungen für die Soziale Arbeit und Pädagogik.* Leverkusen: Budrich.

Reich, Wilhelm. 1945. *The Sexual Revolution.* New York, MD: Orgone Institute Press.

Sanos, Sandrine. 2013. *The Aesthetics of Hate: Far-Right Intellectuals, Antisemitism, and Gender in 1930s France.* Stanford: Stanford University Press.

Schoppmann, Claudia. 1991. *Nationalsozialistische Sexualpolitik und weibliche Homosexualität.* Pfaffenweiler: Centaurus.

Schuermans, Nick, and Filip De Maesschalck. 2010. Fear of Crime as a Political Weapon: Explaining the Rise of Extreme Right Politics in the Flemish Countryside. *Social & Cultural Geography* 11(3): 247–262.

Schwarzmeier, Antje, and Eike Wunderlich. 1995. Politische Aktivistinnen für Volk und Vaterland. In *Kameradinnen. Frauen stricken am Braunen Netz*, ed. Fantifa Marburg, 39–80. Münster: Unrast.

Sielert, Uwe. 2005. *Einführung in die Sexualpädagogik.* Juventa: Weinheim.

Smith, Anna Marie. 1994. *New Right Discourse on Race & Sexuality.* New York: Cambridge University Press.

Strub, Whitney. 2011. *Perversion for Profit. The Politics of Pornography and the Rise of the New Right.* New York and Chichester: Columbia University Press.

Theweleit, Klaus. 1987. *Male Fantasies.* Minneapolis: University of Minnesota Press.

Virchow, Fabian. 2010. Tapfer, stolz, opferbereit—Überlegungen zum extrem rechten Verständnis 'idealer Männlichkeit'. In *'Was ein rechter Mann ist ...'— Männlichkeiten im Rechtsextremismus*, ed. R. Claus, E. Lehnert, and Y. Müller, 39–52. Berlin: RLS.

von Praunheim, Rosa. 2005. *Männer, Helden, schwule Nazis.* Berlin: Absolut Medien.

Walton, Stephen J. 2012. Anti-feminism and Misogyny in Breivik's 'Manifesto'. *NORA—Nordic Journal of Feminist and Gender Research* 20(1): 4–11.

Zur, Nieden Susanne. 2005. *Homosexualität und Staatsräson. Männlichkeit, Homophobie und Staatsräson in Deutschland 1900–1945.* Frankfurt/Main: Campus.

Men in the Battle for the Brains: Constructions of Masculinity Within the "Identitary Generation"

Alice Blum

Introduction

"Of all the fights you have fought, your fight against gender was the most repugnant. Where once the strong and the beautiful sexes were happily united, you have created an alliance of hermaphrodites, a coalition of halves, a union of nothing" (Willinger 2013, 21).[1] This is a quotation from one of the first publications by an activist in the new-right group "Identitäre Bewegung Deutschlands" (IBD).[2] It sounds like the familiar reactionary position of conservative, anti-feminist and extreme-right thinkers. But, as shown in this volume, the extreme right is becoming increasingly differentiated. In addition to classical far-right parties, such as the NPD in Germany, the Golden Dawn party in Greece (see Alvanou in this volume) or Jobbik in Hungary (see Felix in this volume), there are modern autonomous nationalists or right-wing terrorist groups like the NSU (see Köttig in this volume), as well as loose associations which become active, for instance, in the context of anti-gender protests.

Research in this field mostly concentrates on describing group structures. If gender is studied as a category in the extreme right, usually the

A. Blum (✉)
Frankfurt University of Applied Sciences, Frankfurt, Germany

© The Author(s) 2017
M. Köttig et al. (eds.), *Gender and Far Right Politics in Europe*,
DOI 10.1007/978-3-319-43533-6_21

321

focus is on women, including "their functions, careers and roles" (Claus et al. 2010, 9). Men, or rather "masculinities", in the extreme right have received very little attention. One reason for this could be that for a long time the extreme right was considered as "male" practically by definition; in other words "masculinity" was one of its constitutive elements (ibid.). The images discussed by Hechler of the stereotype male Neonazi who always cultivates a military image could be another reason why no one has attempted to investigate the role of men in the far right from a more differentiated perspective (Hechler 2015). A first move in this direction in the German discourse was made by Claus, Lehnert and Müller, who in 2010 published a number of studies relating to this thematic field in an edited volume entitled "'Was ein rechter Mann ist ...' Männlichkeiten im Rechtsextremismus" ("'What makes a proper man...' Masculinities in the extreme right"). This volume shows the plurality of constructions of masculinity in different far-right scenes and sheds light on processes of change. Since this book was published, the extreme right, and especially the "New Right", has undergone rapid transformation. It is therefore necessary to take a new look at these phenomena.

In this chapter I will contribute to the discussion by examining ideas of masculinity in the so-called New Right. My study of the roles and functions of masculinity is focused on a very recent grouping in Germany, the "Identitäre Bewegung" (IB).[3] After briefly outlining the background of the New Right, I will discuss the Identitäre Bewegung and its activism, paying special attention to the question of gender roles and conceptions of masculinity and femininity as an ideological issue and identity-forming moment. I adopt an intersectional approach to the categories of *race and gender*, which are essential to the group's political positioning. I borrow the term "hegemonial masculinity" from Conell (2006) and try to weave into my study intersectional perspectives on the ideological orientation of the group.[4]

THE NEW RIGHT

I will look first at the structural background or political origin of the Identitäre Bewegung: the New Right. The term "New Right" first appeared in 1968/69 as an alternative name for the "Young Right". It was the term preferred by young intellectuals in the far-right Nationaldemokratische Partei Deutschlands (German National Democratic Party, NPD). They accused the party leaders of not being able to step out of the shadow of National Socialism (see Speit 1999, 17 f.) and used the new name to distance themselves from the old incrusted structures. This development was later underpinned by the pamphlet "Abschied vom Hitlerismus (Farewell to Hitlerism)" published by two right-wing terrorists, Hepp and Kexel (1982). In it they "distance themselves from the 'three bad habits of nationalism', namely 'Hitlerism', 'middle-class nationalism' and 'NS and uniform fetishism', which 'do more harm than good to the cause of our people, the anti-imperialist liberation struggle'. They conceived of themselves as 'neither right nor left'" (Hübner 2011). This idea has been taken up by the Identitäre Bewegung and the New Right in general and used for their own purposes in the sense of a *Querfront* (cross-front) strategy. "The concept of *Querfront* is an attempt to resolve differences by resorting to a *völkisch* concept of society as a 'united community'. Over many years this has resulted in the development of an alliance strategy to overcome the problem of marginality, which mainly finds resonance in the (extreme) right, but also occasionally among leftists" (Culina and Fedders 2016, 11). Attempts are made to pacify critics of the concept of nationalism, which is usually closely associated with national socialism, in order to obtain a broad basis for the ideology of a "national identity".

The term New Right is more than just an expression of the modernisation of the extreme right. It stands for an "ideological and programmatic transformation" (Stöss 2007) and is thus to be distinguished from the "Old Right" or extreme right. The term New Right is actually misleading, for the ideas are not new, but go back to the anti-democratic theories of the "Conservative Revolution" in the Weimar Republic. Although the combination of the terms "conservative" and "revolution" may appear to be contradictory, this is not the case "when the conservative element in this thinking is related not to the existing state of affairs, but to a condition of society yet to be created through changes to come" (Pfahl-Traughber 1998, 48). The supporters of this movement in the Weimar Republic envisioned an elite of intellectual and political "leaders of opinion" who would set up a new system in place of the democratically constituted state (see Sontheimer 2004, 23). Following the ideas of Gramsci, an Italian Marxist, the main task of these intellectual leaders of opinion was to conquer the pre-political space. In the Identitäre Bewegung this is expressed as follows: "The German Identitäre Bewegung is not a party and will not become a party in the foreseeable future. We are above party politics; in the metapolitical anteroom we discuss certain topics without beating about the bush.

Our aim is to serve as a creative source of inspiration, to provoke thought and suggest solutions".[5,6]

However, the New Right cannot be described as a homogeneous group, neither in the past nor in the present. On the contrary, there are big differences in the self-images of the actors, and what unites them can best be summed up by what they reject. The common elements include: "1. ethnopluralist thinking, 2. anti-liberalism, 3. anti-Americanism, 4. self-understanding as an intellectual elite, 5. rejection of accepted ideas of 'political correctness'" (Borstel 2009, 60). There is a striking difference here between the classical extreme right and the New Right, in that the former usually includes anti-intellectualism as an inherent part of its ideology. For the New Right, its self-image as an "intellectual elite" is of critical significance in the way it approaches constructions of masculinity, as I will show below. In this, members of the Conservative Revolution, including Carl Schmitt, Arthur Moeller van den Bruck, Oswald Spengler, Ernst Jünger and Ernst Niekisch, serve as a model for today's New Right and stickers or T-shirts are produced bearing their portraits.[7] These authors also influence theoretical and substantive discussions in the IB.

THE HISTORY OF THE IDENTITÄRE BEWEGUNG IN EUROPE

The Identitäre Bewegung (IB) originated in France, a country in which the present-day New Right also began with the think tank GRECE (Groupement de recherche et d'études pour la civilisation européenne/ Research and Study Group for European Civilisation). This theoretical group is closely linked to the names of Dominique Venner and Alain de Benoist, who is considered as the "guiding spirit" of the New Right in France (see Scholz 2009). From here a number of groups and organisations developed which can be considered as belonging to the New Right. As the youth organisation of the "Bloc Identitaire" (Identitary Bloc), the "Génération Identitaire" (Identitary Generation, IG) made its first public appearance on 20 October 2012 when it occupied the roof of a mosque in Poitiers. The protest was directed against "Islamisation" and "mass immigration" in Europe; it was argued that the "national identity" must be preserved instead of creating a "multicultural Europe". The place and date of the action were no coincidence but were chosen to commemorate the battle in which Charles Martel in 732 stopped the advance of the Moors from the Iberian Peninsula. In New Right discourses this battle is regarded as the victory of Europe against the Muslims. The year 732 is used for propaganda purposes by the IB and appears, for instance, on stickers or in the name of a web blog.[8] This contributes to building an image of militant men who function as hypermasculine and heroic models. In addition to commemorating battles, the Identitäre Bewegung uses other references which contribute to creating this masculine image. In addition to its political message, the occupation of the mosque by the IG supplied a model for actions by the Identitäre Bewegung and for its "corporate identity". Thus, its banner was black and yellow, and the lambda rune, a Greek letter shown in yellow on a black background, appeared for the first time, in imitation of the shields of the Spartans. This was the starting point of a style of action, in this case the occupation of a building, borrowed from left-wing protest strategies, as well as the symbolism and colours which became the badge of identitary groups (see Bruns et al. 2014, 62) in Austria, the Czech Republic, Italy, France, the Netherlands or Switzerland, which today are closely networked.[9] In January 2013 the Génération Identaire published its manifesto on Youtube as a video entitled "Déclaration de Guerre"[10] in which its ideology is elaborately staged. This video has been translated into various languages, and on the Facebook pages and blogs of European identitary groups, it is recognised as a "declaration of war" on Europe's multicultural society and the generation of 1968.

Today these groups carry out actions every week all over Europe, but they have the character of events produced for an inner circle rather than for the general public: a few people meet at unfrequented locations and produce photographs of themselves holding up a banner, for instance. These images are then presented on the internet. The photos and videos produced by the IB suggest that it is mainly young men who are attracted by the movement. One reason for this could be the milieu from which they are recruited. Like many members of the New Right, a large number of Identitary Generation activists in the German-speaking countries come from student societies or fraternities which do not admit female members. All IB actions and groups have certain references and symbols in common, such as the use of the lambda rune. The name itself suggests a special interpretation of "identity", although this is not further explained. One slogan is "not left, not right, but 100 % identitary", and another: "100 percent identity—0 percent racism". In the following section I will examine the meaning of these terms and slogans.

IDENTITARY GENERATION—WHAT IS MEANT HERE BY
IDENTITY? ON THE POLITICAL IDEOLOGY
OF THE IDENTITÄRE BEWEGUNG

Identity is the keyword of the Identitäre Bewegung. It stands for the ideal of a *völkisch* collective, a rejection of the generation of 1968, a homogenising concept of culture and a racist conception of ethnopluralism. Markus Willinger, who considers himself as a member of the Identitäre Bewegung in Austria, is the author of the book "Die Identitäre Generation. Eine Kriegserklärung an die 68er" ("The Identitary Generation. A Declaration of War on the Generation of 1968"), which has become a point of reference for the IB. He sees in the term "identity" a tradition-bound territory in which certain cultural practices should be observed. The ideal he describes is a multiplicity of cultures living peacefully together, but without being amalgamated into multicultural societies (Willinger 2013, 67f.). The IB makes the following statement: "With the word identitary we mean our local belonging to a regional culture, our belonging to our people and our self-understanding as Europeans. These identities complement and reinforce each other. Today it is clear that the world does not stop at Germany's borders and we need a strong, united Europe, from Spain to Russia, from Greece to Iceland, in order to protect our ethnocultural identity".[11] This is based on an interpretation of "culture" which is related to history or language, is "ethnic" and homogeneous and thus functions as an "essentialist category of difference and identity" (Osterloh and Westerholt 2011, 412). With this concept of culture, members of the Identitäre Bewegung can effectively invoke the dangers threatening the "identitary Europe" they conjure up. They argue that the German and European collective identity has been destroyed by the generation of 1968 which made the "German collective" a "victim of re-education". This rejection of "political correctness" by making explicit reference to feminist struggles and today's diversity education is a constitutive element of the New Right. Willinger writes: "You have deprived men of their masculinity. Reduced them to feeble teddy bears, with no energy, no courage or strength, in short: no will to power" (Willinger 2013, 21). This is based on a biologistic understanding of masculinity. In other words, men seek power by nature, but a "wrong education" has robbed them of this "natural" characteristic. Within the Identitäre Bewegung, this idea makes it possible to admit other forms of masculinity besides "typical" men; although they must be seen as "deviating from nature", there is always a chance that they may be returned to the right path. Thus, the group is able to accept a variety of masculinities. Men who do not correspond to the ideals of strength and martiality find justification and can fit into the group. Identity here means not only a cultural, or *völkisch* identity, but also a gender identity, which for the Identitäre Bewegung is a static construct, or overarching goal. The categories gender and nationality are interdependent. In order to understand this better, it is worth taking a look at other arguments of the Identitäre Bewegung within their political orientation.

WITH RACISM AGAINST A BLURRING OF GENDER ROLES

In recent years the IB has repeatedly warned against the "great exchange".[12] By this is meant the abolition of culture and "replacement" of the local people by immigrants. However, this static concept of culture is only a variant of the concept of race; it also attributes "natural" properties and special characteristics to certain constructed groups. This is a form of Othering in which there is always a dichotomous division into "us" and "them" involving implicit value judgements (see Osterloh and Westerhold 2011, 414). It is linked to the conception of ethnopluralism, which is promoted by the New Right. This is a concept in which homogeneous, closed *völkisch* units exist side by side without any hierarchy. On the website of the German IB, the Middle East conflict is used as an example to explain this idea: "Neither kippah nor pali scarf"—"As genuine ethnopluralists we recognise the right to life of all peoples and see them as part of the family of peoples on a common planet. Our enemies are only those who threaten our identity, no imaginary axes of evil or global conspiracies".[13] The group explicitly distances itself here from the anti-Semitism of the classical extreme right, or "old right". On the contrary, in the fight against the enemy, Israel is regarded as a partner, as the last bastion of the West against the enemy. The alleged enemy who threatens an imagined cultural identity is clear: members of the Identitäre Bewegung always see themselves as threatened by "Islamisation" which they claim will replace German or European culture, the latter being understood exclusively as "Western and Christian".[14] In this, the IB stands side by side with right-wing populist parties in Europe. These parties "paint apocalyptic scenarios in which our monetary and social systems are about to collapse and hordes of criminal foreigners are pouring into European countries. Blame is laid on the EU, which disempowers and regulates the European peoples, abolishes border controls and drives national economies into ruin. The nation state is the best defence against these developments, only one's nationality can provide warmth and stability in the globalised world" (Gensing 2014). Besides frequent interpretations of what is foreign, all too often in terms of skin colour and language, the image of "culture" and "ethnic belonging" drawn here has "a static, material and essentialist character", "which precedes action and justifies it" (Osterloh/Westerhold 2011, 413).

Anti-Muslim racism is characteristic of many of the IB's symbolic references. For example, the Reconquista, which is referred to positively by the German Identitäre Bewegung in flyers or stickers,[15] can be read as a symbol of "the close interlinkage of anti-Islamic racism, anti-Semitism, and colonial racism" (ibid., 45). The symbol of the Identitäre Bewegung, the lambda rune, is also a reference to the anti-Muslim worldview of the IB. The Greek letter in black on a yellow background, taken from the film "300", gives the group a kind of brand recognition and functions as the movement's label. In 2007 the comic book "300"[16] was filmed, which tells the story of the battle of Thermopylae in which the Spartans defeated the Persian invaders. The film uses hypermasculine images, men as warriors and defenders. The IM uses the film's symbolism as a "metaphor of their struggle as Europeans against immigration" (Schlüter 2013). This is the primary concern of the Identitäre Bewegung. Willinger even devotes a whole chapter to Islam in which he describes the threat posed to Europe by Muslims (Willinger 2013, 60f.). This is accompanied by a relativisation of the Shoah. Willinger writes for example: "Don't quote the Second World War and Hitler when it is Mehmed and Mustafa we are talking about. And don't say foreigners are just like us, when we see every day that they are not. [...] We don't want Mehmed and Mustafa to become Europeans. We don't want immigrants to assume our identity" (Willinger 2013, 32). It is striking here that only men are seen as posing a threat. Women are not put forward as evidence of "infiltration". This split has a special purpose, as I will show in the section on female images in the IB. Men are portrayed here in the first place as active agents. This image is also found in accusations of "imported crime".[17] In addition, Muslim men, or men regarded as being non-German, are frequently represented as being "sexually aggressive and as preventing the reproduction of German men. Through this denigration of foreign men, the we-group of German men is constructed as having contrasting, positive qualities. In extreme-right ideology, foreign men and German men are engaged in a battle over sexual relationships and reproduction" (Overdieck 2014), as Overdieck has observed in respect of the classical extreme right. This argumentation affects conceptions of masculinity within the IB itself. With regard to the accusation of having lost gender identity through an emancipatory gender policy, Willinger writes: "We will not repeat your mistakes. And slowly but surely we are shaking off your foolish theories and want to be masculine men and feminine women again. […] For women *want* to be taken by storm. Deep inside they wish for the One who can win them and bind them. But instead of heroic knights, you send them good friends and feeble cowards" (Willinger 2013, 21, italics in original). This explains why a strong gender identity is needed to counter the aggressiveness and stealing of identity by Muslim men. While the role of men seems to be unambiguous, both on the side of the enemy and on the home side, the image of women within the Identitäre Bewegung is more ambiguous, and I will discuss it briefly in the next section. Although this chapter is devoted to images of masculinity, it must be remembered that masculinity as a construct exits "only in relation to femininity and (…) can be defined only in contrast to it and in relation to it" (Brandes 2002, 18).

IMAGES OF WOMEN IN THE IDENTITÄRE BEWEGUNG

As Bruns et al. have shown, the Identitäre Bewegung exploits the concept of "sex sells" as is customary in the world of advertising. It works with images of young women who meet the socially accepted ideal of beauty to publicise Identitary messages. With the help of "erotic poses and naked skin as objectivised projection surfaces for its promotional messages" (Bruns et al. 2014, 213), the Identitäre Bewegung attracts the attention of a broad, mainly male, public. These images are often in contradiction to the image of women propagated by the IB, which is that of the traditional homemaker. In contrast to conceptions of masculinity based on the classical notions of strong men, warriors and providers, the image of women is less clear. They are expected to play different roles: mother, active combatant and desirable sexual object. On the one hand, it is made quite clear that women must be caring mothers. This is justified mainly in biologising terms, women being a natural factor in the "reproduction of the people". On the other hand, the Identitäre Bewegung paints a picture of women as self-assured, militant actors in the social struggle. Here there is a contradiction between reactionary ideology and real practice in everyday life. Despite the use of a "sex sells" strategy, "German" women are presented as being more emancipated than women in Islam. This is explained as being due to the fact "that in Muslim societies women are oppressed because Islam is a patriarchal religion. That circumcision, early and forced marriage, honour killings and full-body veils are considered as normal"[18] (IB 2015). Within such interpretations and debates, "women are homogenised [...] in a monolithic image of Islam consisting of the oppression of women and male dominance" (Kuhn 2015, 62). Here we again see the interdependence between racism and sexism; women's roles are ascribed to them with biologistic arguments, but these roles are played off against each other and set in relationship to each other following a racist logic.

Conclusion: Masculinities in the Identitäre Bewegung

In this chapter I have shown that the Identitäre Bewegung promotes classical conceptions of masculinity. As in other far-right discourses, its ideal is "a German, heterosexual maculinity that is an expression of hardness, power of decision, ability to act following the principles of command and obedience, self-denial and self-sacrifice, and fearlessness in battle or heroism" (Overdieck 2014). That this is no longer the norm is explained as being due to the feminisation of education policies. This argument makes it possible to include men who do not correspond to this ideal in political debates and activities. In addition, the IB borrows arguments from the New Right according to which the political struggle, unlike in the "Old Right", is not necessarily a physical fight, but above all an intellectual one, a battle to achieve intellectual leadership of opinion. Thus, they introduce a form of masculinity which can be seen as complementing effeminised and hegemonial masculinities. It is clear that gender identity is linked to cultural identity; at the same time, we also see here the interdependency of racism and sexism as power relations, which are constitutive elements of the ideology of the far right. The complexity of constructions of masculinity in the Identitäre Bewegung makes it attractive for a larger number of people. By adopting women's rights discourses, it has made itself interesting to people who have always distanced themselves from the far right. The opportunity to do theoretical work such as developing theories or publishing texts, and at the same time the option of being able to participate in male and militant activism, appeals to both hypermasculine types and marginalised masculinities. Any attempt to counter far-right influences must therefore include a consideration of the factors that move people to join far-right groups, not only in terms of gender research but also in terms of the content of practical educational activities.

Notes

1. All German quotations translated by R. Schubert.
2. In Germany, Austria and Switzerland the group call themselves "Identitäre Bewegung", what means something like 'Identitary Movement'. In English-speaking contexts they call themselves 'Generation Identity'. In this article, I will use the chosen form 'Identitäre Bewegung' to make it clear that these are German-speaking groups.
3. The question of whether the Identitäre Bewegung should be regarded as part of the New Right or extreme right has given rise to heated international debates. I have studied this question in respect of the German-speaking countries and have come to the conclusion that it should be counted as part of the New Right. This article is based on this assumption (see Blum 2015).
4. This article is based on my thesis entitled "Die Identitäre Bewegung in Deutschland zwischen gesellschaftlicher Mitte und extremer Rechter. Gegenstrategien und Handlungsansätze im Umgang mit den Modernisierungsbestrebungen der Neuen Rechten" with additional arguments reflecting new developments. I rely heavily on the book published by Markus Willinger, and articles by Martin Sellner, one of the main actors in the Identitäre Bewegung in the German-speaking countries and a key figure linking this group to other New Right groups, as well as articles and blogs by the Identitäre Bewegung.
5. The Identitäre Bewegung is a group that is still being formed and seems to be very open to change. Facebook pages and blogs are frequently deleted, so that it is difficult to follow its development in detail over the past few years. However, I have kept screenshots of all texts quoted here as documentary evidence.
6. https://www.facebook.com/photo.phpfbid=726736577344404 &set=a.583269085024488.1073741828.581482171869846&ty pe=1&theater, accessed on 17.5.2014.
7. For stickers, see https://www.facebook.com/photo.phpfbid=335 169336608341&set=a.276942382431037.1073741829.244767

705648505&type=1&theater, accessed on 12.03.2016. For clothing, see 'Phalanx': https://phalanx-europa.com/de/80-herrenshirts, accessed on 12.03.2016.

8. http://generation732.files.wordpress.com/2013/07/732-110. jpg%3Fw%3D155%26h%3D110%26crop%3D1, accessed on 12.03,2016.

9. http://www.identitaere-bewegung.de/struktur/, accessed on 12.03.2016.

10. http://www.youtube.com/watch?v=5Vnss7y9TNA, accessed on 12.03.2016.

11. https://identitaerebewegung.wordpress.com/positionierungen/ unser-weg-fuhrt-nach-europa/, accessed on 12.03.2016.

12. https://deraustausch.iboesterreich.at/, accessed on 12.03.2016.

13. https://identitaerebewegung.wordpress.com/positionierungen/ weder-kippa-noch-palituch/, accessed on 19.5.2014.

14. https://deraustausch.iboesterreich.at/, accessed on 12.03.2016.

15. http://i1.ytimg.com/vi/P-2RafCUh7A/hqdefault.jpg, accessed on 12.03.2016.

16. A large number of blogs, commentaries and newspaper articles have wondered whether the author of the comic, Frank Miller, is a supporter of the far right and whether a consistent racist and fascistoid style can be detected in his works. See for instance the discussion at: http://www.tagesspiegel.de/kultur/frank-miller-ab-in-die-hoelle/7359566.html, accessed on 12.03.2016 or http:// www.comicgate.de/cmdb/db_300_bw.htm, accessed on 12.5.2014.

17. https://deraustausch.iboesterreich.at/, accessed on 12.03.2016.

18. https://www.facebook.com/identitaere/posts/1108574315827 293?fref=nf, accessed on 12.03.2016.

REFERENCES

Blum, Alice. 2015. Neue Rechte als Herausforderung für politische (Jugend-Bildungsarbeit). In *Journal für politische Bildung: Unzufriedene Demokraten—radikalisierte Überzeugungen*, 44–52. Schwalbach/Ts: Wochenschau Verlag.

Borstel, Dierk. 2009. Geländegewinne? Bilanz rechtsextremer Erfolge und Misserfolge. In *Strategien der extremen Rechten. Hintergründe—Analysen—Antworten*, ed. Stefan Braun, Alexander Geisler, and Martin Gerster, 58–74. Wiesbaden: VS-Verlag.

Brandes, Holger. 2002. Der männliche Habitus. In *Männerforschung und Männerpolitik*, vol 2. Wiesbaden: VS Verlag für Sozialwissenschaften.

Bruns, Julian, Kathrin Glösel, and Natascha Strobl. 2014. *Die Identitären. Handbuch zur Jugendbewegung der Neuen Rechten in Europa*. Münster: Unrast-Verlag.

Claus, Robert, Esther Lehnert, and Yves Müller. 2010. '*Was ein rechter Mann ist ...' Männlichkeiten im Rechtsextremismus*. Berlin: Karl Dietz Verlag.

Connell, Robert W. 2006. *Der gemachte Mann. Konstruktion und Krise von Männlichkeiten, Geschlecht & Gesellschaft*, vol 8, 3rd edn. Wiesbaden: VS Verlag für Sozialwissenschaften.

Culina, Kevin, and Jonas Fedders. 2016. *Im Feindbild vereint. Zur Relevanz des Antisemitismus in der Querfront-Zeitschrift Compact*. Münster: Edition Assemblage.

Gensing, Patrick. 2014. Stimmen gegen Europa Rechtspopulisten bilden bizarre Koalitionen. In *Jüdische Allgemeine*. Accessed 12 March 2016. http://www.juedische-allgemeine.de/article/view/id/19223

Hechler, Andreas. 2015. Beharrliche Bilder. Bildsprache und geschlechterreflektierte Neonazismusprävention. In *Geschlechterreflektierte Pädagogik gegen Rechts*, ed. Andreas Hechler, and Olaf Stuve, 223–237. Opladen/Berlin/Toronto: Verlag Barbara Budrich.

Hübner, Carsten. 2011. Abschied vom 'Hitlerismus' In den 80er Jahren: Rechtsterrorist Odfried Hepp nutzt Kanäle nach Nahost und in die DDR. Accessed 12 April 2014. http://www.neues-deutschland.de/artikel/213950.abschied-vom-hitlerismus.html

Kuhn, Inva. 2015. *Antimuslimischer Rassismus. Auf Kreuzzug für das Abendland*. Köln: Papyrossa Verlag.

Osterloh, Katrin, and Nele Westerholt. 2011. Kultur. In *Wie Rassismus aus Wörtern spricht. (K)Erben des Kolonialismus im Wissensarchiv deutsche Sprache. Ein kritisches Nachschlagewerk*, ed. Susan Arndt, and Nadja Ofuatey-Alazard, 412–416. Münster: Unrast-Verlag.

Overdieck, Ulrich. 2014. Männliche Überlegenheitsvorstellungen in der rechtsextremen Ideologie. Accessed 12 March 2016. http://www.bpb.de/politik/extremismus/rechtsextremismus/197016/maennliche-ueberlegenheitsvorstellungen-in-der-rechtsextremen-ideologie

Pfahl-Traughber, Armin. 1998. *"Konservative Revolution" und "Neue Rechte". Rechtsextremistische Intellektuelle gegen den demokratischen Verfassungsstaat*. Opladen: Leske+Budrich.

Schlüter, Margarete. 2013. Identitäre Inszenierung. In *Jungle World*, Nr 9. Accessed 12 March 2016. http://jungle-world.com/artikel/2013/09/47217.html

Scholz, Robert. 2009. Die "Nouvelle Droite" in Frankreich—die "Mutter" der deutschen "Neuen Rechten". Accessed 12 March 2016. http://www.

endstation-rechts.de/news/kategorie/allgemeines-1/artikel/die-nouvelle-droite-in-frankreich-die-mutter-der-deutschen-neuen-rechten.html

Sontheimer, Kurt. 2004. Die Kontinuität des antidemokratischen Denkens. In *Die Neue Rechte—eine Gefahr für die Demokratie?* ed. Wolfgang Gessenharter, and Thomas Pfeiffer, 19–29. Wiesbaden: V.S. Verlag für Sozialwissenschaften.

Speit, Andreas. 1999. Schicksal und Tiefe—Die Sehnsüchte der Neuen Rechten. In *Jenseits des Nationalismus—Ideologische Grenzgänger der "Neuen Rechten"—Ein Zwischenbericht*, ed. Jean Cremet, Felix Krebs, and Andreas Speit. Münster: Unrast-Verlag.

Stöss, Richard. 2007. Die "neue Rechte" in der Bundesrepublik. Accessed 8 April 2014. http://www.bpb.de/politik/extremismus/rechtsextremismus/41435/die-neue-rechte-in-der-bundesrepublik?p=all

Willinger, Markus. 2013. *Die Identitäre Generation. Eine Kriegserklärung an die 68er.* London: Arktos Media Ltd.

PART V

Counter Strategies

Disengagement and Deradicalization Work with Girls and Young Women—Experiences from Germany

Michaela Glaser

INTRODUCTION

The topic of this chapter is disengagement and deradicalization[1] work with female members of right-wing-oriented or right-wing extremist scenes[2] in Germany. According to experts' estimations, girls and young women are still clearly underrepresented in these scenes. However, with an estimated 7 to 27 per cent female membership of party organizations and 10 to 30 per cent of other groups (cf. Bitzan 2008; Baier et al. 2009), they are no negligible group either. And although their active participation in violent right-wing extremist acts is comparatively low, research has shown that they support or initiate violent attacks in various ways (cf. Bitzan et al. 2003; Bruhns and Wittmann 2002).

Especially because females are regarded to be far less violent and politically ideologized than their male counterparts, they also play a specific role within modern right-wing extremism: they (seem to) represent the moderate, more 'civilized' part of the movement—and thus contribute to

Thanks to Sally Hohnstein for translation support.

M. Glaser (✉)
German Youth Institute, Halle/Saale, Germany

M. Köttig et al. (eds.), *Gender and Far Right Politics in Europe*,
DOI 10.1007/978-3-319-43533-6_22

337

the spread and (social) acceptance of far-right ideas in mainstream society (cf. Bitzan 2008; Röpke and Speit 2011).

It therefore seems highly plausible that disengagement and deradicalization work in this field—as an approach to combating right-wing extremism by supporting young people's reintegration into democratic society—should not only concentrate on young males but should also supply adequate approaches and concepts for working with the female members of these scenes.

In which ways current disengagement and deradicalization work in Germany meets these demands and what challenges professionals face in working with—or trying to work with—girls and young women from these scenes will be discussed in this chapter. In doing so, I will mainly rely on findings from interview-based research among practitioners working in the field of disengagement and deradicalization, conducted at the German Youth Institute (cf. Glaser et al. 2016; Hohnstein and Greuel 2015).[3]

The article is structured as follows: First, I will give a short description of the database and the most common project types found in this field (1). Next, I will describe the roles played by girls and women from right-wing-oriented or right-wing extremist scenes within these working contexts (2). Then, I will discuss specific challenges and difficulties arising in project work with female members of these scenes: which difficulties can be identified regarding access to female clients (3)? Which challenges are connected with specific forms of female involvement in these scenes—and how do professionals respond to these challenges when working with girls and women (4)? Finally, I will end by outlining certain demands concerning the further conceptual development of this kind of deradicalization work (5).

DATABASE AND PROJECT TYPES

The DJI research project "Pedagogical support of disengagement processes"[4] was aimed at identifying appropriate pedagogical approaches to support disengagement from right-wing-oriented or right-wing extremist scenes, as well as outlining preconditions for successful work in this field. Interviews were conducted with people involved in projects that are

- working with right-wing extremist-oriented young people or with young people at risk of becoming right-wing extremist;
- aimed at initiating and supporting disengagement and deradicalization processes among this target group.

At the time of writing this chapter, information has been collected from a total of 18 projects. Professionals from 12 projects had been questioned in short telephone interviews, asking for main approaches, target groups, and the relevance of "gender" in their work. In addition, people from eight projects have been interviewed in face-to-face situations lasting 2.5 to 3 hours, in order to explore practical work performance and related experiences more deeply (all of these eight projects are also in contact with female members of right-wing-oriented or right-wing extremist scenes).[5]

Additionally, a workshop with interview partners has been organized (where, among other topics, the role of "gender" and "gender-sensitive work approaches" were discussed in one session). Finally, members of the research team have attended two national meetings of projects active in this field (the annual meeting of the state-run disengagement programmes and the East German Annual Meeting of Streetwork Projects (OBST).

But before discussing some of this research project's findings on disengagement work with female clients, we will first give a short description of the main types of projects to be found in this field and of the target groups they are working with.

Youth Work with Young People "At Risk"

Outreach Work/Streetwork Projects
Streetwork projects are designed to work in public spaces with cliques of young people who cannot be reached by other youth work or social work programmes. These projects, according to their own professional understanding, do not work with organized right-wing activists, but with young people regarded as being at risk of becoming right-wing extremists. Members of these groups may display right-wing extremist symbols, listen to right-wing music, and—most problematic—may act violently towards "foreigners" and other minorities. Although these cliques do not belong to political right-wing extremist organizations, individual members may have contacts in such organizations; the violent groups in particular have to be regarded as a potential transition zone towards organized, political right-wing extremism (cf. Kohlstruck 2012). The formal education level of these young people is often low, and many of them suffer from severe deficits in social integration, as well as having problematic family backgrounds (cf. Möller and Schumacher 2007; Glaser 2013).

Pedagogical settings include work with the whole group but also interpersonal one-to-one settings (cf. Möller 2002; Rieker 2009).

Cooperation-Based Individual Guidance Work
In recent years it has become increasingly difficult for social professionals to identify and reach right-wing-oriented cliques in public spaces. This is due to certain changes, not only in right-wing-oriented youth cultures but also in young peoples' social activities. For instance, there is a less visible dress code and right-wing-oriented youth has a less "offensive" appearance, but there has also been a shift of young peoples' leisure and social activities from the public to the semi-public and virtual domains (cf. Glaser and Greuel 2013).

As a result, a new type of pedagogical work has emerged, also designed to help right-wing-oriented youth. Projects of this type identify and approach their target group with the help of professionals from other youth-related professions (schools, vocational training, regular youth work, etc.). When they identify possible signs of right-wing orientation, these professionals try to initiate a meeting with the person in question and with project leaders, thereby acting as a "bridge" between project and potential client. Pedagogical work in these projects usually takes place in individual face-to-face-settings. The social backgrounds and education level of the clients show a broader variety than in streetwork projects (cf. Hohnstein and Greuel 2015).

Projects Supporting Exit from Right-Wing Extremism

Disengagement Programmes
Disengagement programmes, more commonly known as exit projects, aim at supporting and accompanying people who have decided to exit right-wing extremist groups (so called "dropouts", in German "*Aussteiger*"). Like the projects described above, they also refuse to work with people who are still actively engaged in the scene. To be accepted in the programme, candidates have to stop all contacts and activities connected to it. Some of these programmes are civil initiatives and organizations, but the majority of them are state-run, either by the police, the intelligence service, or youth welfare agencies. Clients are usually of an older age than those in the groups mentioned above, ranging from fellow travellers to frontier activists.

Those programmes usually work with clients in individual case work settings (see Möller 2010; Glaser et al. 2014).

Training Courses

Another type of programme aiming to support disengagement from (violent) right-wing extremism is anti-aggression training, especially developed for working with right-wing extremist perpetrators of violence. These training courses put a strong focus on violent behaviour and violence-supporting attitudes, but—unlike other kinds of anti-aggression training—also aim at reflecting on the prejudiced and ideological views of the participants. They usually take place in group settings, most of them in prisons (cf. Hohnstein and Greuel 2015).

Though these different types of projects have different target groups, and work under different conditions and in different ways, some common elements of their work can be identified. First, they all target disengagement by stabilizing their clients socially and emotionally, for instance, by establishing new contacts, by integration into the educational system and labour market, by giving support in coping with drug or violence problems, and so on. Second, they also—though with different emphasis—aim at the deradicalization of attitudes, for instance, via critical confrontation with beliefs and behaviour, by developing socioemotional competences, or by encouraging reflection on personal (long-term biographical and short-term) motives for joining these groups (cf. Glaser 2013).

In the following section, on the basis of reports by project staff, I will discuss the presence of girls and women in these projects and how they act within this environment.

PRESENCE OF GIRLS AND WOMEN IN THESE PROJECTS

What first strikes the eye is the fact that girls and women are clearly underrepresented in disengagement and deradicalization projects. This underrepresentation manifests itself not only in total numbers but also by comparing the number of female project participants with the (estimated) number of females in the (organized) right-wing extremist scene.

As mentioned at the beginning, according to experts the number of female members of right-wing extremist scenes currently ranges between 7 and 30 per cent. However, the percentage of female participants in the examined projects was significantly lower. Some practitioners even declared that—at least at the time of our interviews—they had not yet reached women in their work.

Another remarkable aspect is the female role types these projects are confronted with in their work. During the last few years, a broadening of female role concepts within the right-wing extremist scene has been noticed and described, as well as a growing number of women who play an active role in this scene (Bitzan 2000; Bitzan 2008; Döring and Feldmann 2005). However, this development does not seem to affect the projects we studied. According to our interviewees, the most prominent female role type appearing in these projects still corresponds to traditional role arrangements and subordinate positions, which often goes together with a self-image of being non-political, "not right-wing", and only "the girl-friend of".[6] Additionally, all project professionals in our sample reported that female clients have often experienced forms of physical and sexual violence within the scene and in their partnerships and that many of them had also been victims of sexual abuse in earlier years, during their childhood.

These tendencies and manifestations constitute certain challenges for professionals, when working, or trying to work, with female members of these scenes.

DIFFICULTIES IN ACCESSING FEMALE CLIENTS

As the underrepresentation of girls and women in the projects indicates, one major challenge in working with females in this field is simply initializing contact with them. It is thus worth taking a closer look at the strategies used by project professionals to get in contact with their target groups.

Streetwork projects, as mentioned above, recruit their clients by establishing contact with youth groups they meet in the public sphere, either in the streets or in (self-run) youth clubs. These youth groups can *generally* be described as being weakly attended by females, as girls tend to spend more of their leisure time in non-public surroundings and show a preference for more intimate friendships and forms of social gathering (Fuchs et al. 2003, 178). Girls who do join these groups often remain less closely attached to them, hopping from one to another group more often than their male peers, which makes it more difficult for practitioners to get in touch and build up stable working bonds with them.

For *projects supporting disengagement* (exit projects and trainings) an important approach to potential clients is provided by the criminal justice system and its institutions: contacts are often initiated by the police, judges, and probation officers. This holds true especially for state-run programmes and training courses. Clients in these projects have usually been found guilty of having committed at least one crime with a right-wing extremist background.

Yet, the percentage of women involved in registered crimes is relatively small: according to police crime statistics, it ranges between 6 and 10 per cent (Buschbom n.d.; Stöss 2010, 154). And these are mostly cases of suspicion only, registered by the police; there is evidence that the percentage of criminal convictions is even lower (cf. Bitzan et al. 2003). On the one hand, this is good news (though it does not necessarily exclude the possibility that higher percentages of women might be involved in these crimes. They may not be identified because of gendered perceptions within criminal justice system or may not be registered because they participate in indirect ways that are not documented in official crime statistics). However, it also implies that potential female clients of disengagement programmes are only poorly reached in this way.

In summary, we can say that streetwork projects, disengagement programmes, and training courses face specific difficulties in accessing girls and women. Their established methods for approaching young people who are engaged in, or are at risk of becoming engaged in, right-wing extremist scenes show clear limits when it comes to accessing female members of these scenes.

Compared to these approaches, cooperation with other pedagogical professions seems to offer better opportunities for reaching out to right-wing-oriented females. This holds true especially for cooperation with school professionals, as schools are attended by females and males alike.

However, the projects of this type which we examined also showed a disproportional dominance of young males among their clients. According to practitioners' explanations, this could be due to the fact that multipliers are more aware of open, aggressive ("male") right-wing behaviour and are less successful in identifying more typical "female" forms. Teachers in particular—in the view of our interviewees—are more likely to respond to offensive or violent behaviour in the classroom, and don't pay much attention to problematic views and social contacts, if they don't go along with "disturbances" of that kind.[7]

CHALLENGES IN WORKING WITH FEMALE CLIENTS

However, the staff of these projects do not always fail to establish contact with female clients. They work with girls and young women on different occasions and in different ways. Therefore, in this section we will examine the various approaches employed in work with females and the challenges connected with this work.

As mentioned above, female clients in these projects often show certain characteristics: they have often suffered in different ways from male dominance and male violence in their lives and may still do so (in other words, they often were, and still are in many ways, victims themselves). Also, they often express their political, racist views less openly (cf. Pingel and Rieker 2002, 41) and are involved in political and violent activities more indirectly and less visibly (cf. Bruhns and Wittmann 2002, 156; Pingel 2002; Lutzebäck et al. 1995).

As studies on this issue show, this might lead professionals to tendentially overlook the problematic views of female group members as well as their specific forms of involvement in political and violent activities (cf. Pingel and Rieker 2002).

It might also have the consequence—and in our sample we find some evidence of this—that professionals interacting with female clients concentrate on the role of females as victims. In their professional reactions, they might focus on a supporting and encouraging approach, aimed at helping these women to overcome experiences and structures of male dominance and male violence (e.g. by organizing shelter from a violent partner, by supporting females in following their own educational or work career, or by encouraging them to reappraise experiences of domestic violence and sexual abuse with professional help).

A side remark: This focus on women as victims also applies to gender-reflective work in these settings. In contrast to results of an earlier study (Pingel and Rieker 2002) that couldn't identify any gender-reflective approaches in this working field, our interviews indicate that since then a critical reflection of gender constructions has started to play a certain role in this work. Though not in all projects, and most often not on a conceptual level, gender-reflecting elements can be found, for instance in professionals' attempts to act as positive role models, in critical reflections of partnership constellations, or in discussions on future perspectives of female clients. However, these approaches still focus on reflecting on female subordination and its negative implications for women's lives.

It seems plausible that such supporting and gender-reflective approaches may encourage and support women who suffer from right-wing group structures or violent right-wing partners in their *disengagement* from these problematic social contexts. Yet we also know from different research findings that many of these women not only hold racist and right-wing extremist views themselves but even have specific female motives for joining right-wing extremist scenes—and some of these motives go along very well with traditional, subordinate female role images, including a specific female racism, rooted in the projection of (experienced) male violence on "foreigners", or a longing for male protection and for clearly identified role concepts (cf. Beckmann 2008).

What these professional reactions are therefore lacking is a confrontation with these women's own racist views and their motives and interests for joining and staying in right-wing extremist scenes. They are lacking, in other words, pedagogical elements of *deradicalization*—elements that respond to (specific) female motivational bonds with a right-wing extremist ideology.

However, the observed deficit of practical approaches in following this aim is not solely due to a lack of professional sensitivity or will to address these issues. Professionals trying to confront female clients with their own problematic beliefs and behaviour might also have to face the problem that these females do not regard themselves as political persons but just as "girlfriends of". In the words of one practitioner: "When I try to talk about these issues, they say, 'But I am not right-wing—what does this have to do with me?'" (Interview-Alpha, 01: 23:42–3).

Thus, not only a change in the professional perception of female scene members is needed but also the development of conceptual solutions enabling practitioners to involve "non-political" female clients in critical reflection processes of this kind.

Summary and Perspectives

Our interview findings suggest that current work with members of right-wing-oriented or right-wing extremist scenes is in need of several changes. Firstly, this work needs new strategies for accessing female scene members, taking into account specific female forms of social gathering and political engagement.

Secondly, it requires a greater sensitivity among cooperation partners (but sometimes among staff members as well) for less obvious forms of right-wing extremist orientation and behaviour.

Thirdly, there is a need for (the development of) appropriate approaches combining support for women in overcoming their subordinate and violent circumstances with reflection on the problematic, discriminating, and violence-supporting views and attitudes their self-images and role concepts may include.

Finding ways to meet these needs will be a difficult task. However, a first step might be to refuse to accept and share these women's self-images of being only non-political "girlfriends of".

NOTES

1. There are different definitions of the term "deradicalization" to be found in the academic literature (cf. Della Porta/LaFree 2012). Whereas some research strands define "deradicalization" with reference to both behavioural and cognitive elements, in this chapter the term is used in contrast to the term "disengagement" (here mainly referring to ending extremist activities and group memberships), stressing cognitive aspects (such as attitudes and believes) of a person's distancing from extremism (cf. Horgan 2008).

2. In this chapter the term "right-wing-oriented or right-wing extremist scenes" refers to the whole spectrum of groups, which—in the German debate—are regarded either as being part of the organized German right-wing extremist movement or as being in danger of becoming so. This includes right-wing extremist party organizations, Neonazi groups, and so-called Kameradschaften (comradeships, fraternities) (cf. Stöss 2010) as well as the so-called right-wing extremist youth culture, made up mainly of informal, only loosely organized groups (Hafeneger/Becker 2007, 23). For some of these youth groups right-wing ideology or fragments of it might play an important role for group identity; others are only poorly ideologized, demonstrating their belonging to this youth culture mainly by showing and wearing certain right-wing symbols and by consuming right-wing music (cf. Hafeneger/Jansen 2001; Pfeiffer 2007).

3. The German Youth Institute (DJI) is a non-university social science research institute in the area of children, young people, and the family in Germany.

4. This research project, running from 2012 to 2014, was located at the Research Centre for the Prevention of Right-wing Extremism and Xenophobia (Arbeits—und Forschungsstelle Rechtsextremismus und Fremdenfeindlichkeit) in the German Youth Institute. Members of the research team were Frank Greuel, Sally Hohnstein, and the author.

5. The final sample included 22 projects. Staff members of all of them were interviewed in face-to-face interviews. Several of these projects, however, reported no, or almost no, experience with female clients.

6. These practitioners' observations may be influenced by their own gendered perceptions of reality, lacking sensitivity for the different forms of female engagement in the right-wing extremist scene, as suggested for instance by Wasniewski (2007). But even taking into account such an effect, these descriptions are still strong evidence for these patterns being the dominant ones of female appearance and engagement in these groups.

7. This also leads to an underrepresentation of less aggressive, less openly acting right-wing-oriented males in these projects.

REFERENCES

Baier, Dirk, Christian Pfeiffer, Susann Rabold, Julia Simonson, and Cathleen Kappes. 2009. Kinder und Jugendliche in Deutschland: Gewalterfahrungen, Integration, Medienkonsum. *KFN-Forschungsbericht* 109.

Beckmann, Kathinka. 2008. *Rechtsextremismus: Männersache? Geschlechtsspezifische Differenzen im Umgang mit rechtsextremem Gedankengut*. Norderstedt: Books on Demand.

Bitzan, Renate. 2000. *Selbstbilder rechter Frauen. Zwischen Antisexismus und völkischem Denken*. Tübingen: Edition Diskord.

———. 2008, January 23. Frauen im Rechtsextremismus. In *Theorie und Praxis, Impulsreferat auf der Veranstaltung "Brave Mädels und echte Kerle? Theorie und Praxis von Geschlechterrollen im Rechtsextremismus"*. Forum Berlin: Friedrich-Ebert-Stiftung.

Bitzan, Renate, Michaela Köttig, and Berit Schröder. 2003. Mediale Berichterstattung zur Beteiligung von Mädchen und Frauen an rechtsextrem motivierten Straftaten. *Zeitschrift für Frauenforschung und Geschlechterstudien* 21(2, 3): 150–170.

Bruhns, Kirsten, and Svendy Wittmann. 2002. *Ich meine, mit Gewalt kannst du dir Respekt verschaffen. Mädchen und junge Frauen in gewaltbereiten Jugendgruppen*. Opladen: Leske + Budrich.

Buschbom, Jan. n.d. *"Walküren, Mädels, Mütter"—Frauen und Mädchen in der extremen Rechten*. www.politische-bildung-brandenburg.de/extrem/frau.htm

Della, Porta Donatella, and Garry LaFree. 2012. Processes of Radicalization an De-Radicalizatio. *International Journal of Conflict and Violence* 6(1): 4–10.

Döhring, Kirsten, and Renate Feldmann. 2005. Akteurinnen und Organisationen. Die Involviertheit von Frauen in der rechtsextremen Szene. In *Braune Schwestern? Feministische Analysen zu Frauen in der extremen Rechten*, ed. Antifaschistisches Frauennetzwerk, Forschungsnetzwerk Frauen und Rechtsextremismus, 17–34. Münster.

Fuchs, Marek, Siegfried Lamnek, and Ralf Wiederer. 2003. *Querschläger. Jugendliche zwischen rechter Ideologie und Gewalt*. Opladen: Leske + Budrich.

Glaser, Michaela. 2013. Ansetzen an den Problemen, die die Jugendlichen haben
.... Zur Rolle individueller Problembelastungen rechtsaffiner und rechtsori-
entierter Jugendlicher in der Distanzierungsarbeit. In *Jugend an der roten
Linie—Analysen von und Erfahrungen mit Interventionsansätzen zur
Rechtsextremismusprävention in Hessen*, ed. Reiner Becker, and Kerstin
Palloks, 252–266. Schwalbach/Ts: Wochenschau Verlag.

Glaser, Michaela, and Frank Greuel. 2013. Jugendarbeit und Rechtsextremismus.
In *Enzyklopädie Erziehungswissenschaft Online (EEO), Fachgebiet Jugend und
Jugendarbeit*, ed. Thomas Rauschenbach, and Stefan Borrmann. Weinheim:
Beltz Juventa.

Glaser, Michaela, Sally Hohnstein, and Frank Greuel. 2014. Ausstiegshilfen in
Deutschland—ein vergleichender Überblick über Akteure und Vorgehensweisen.
In *Hilfe zum Ausstieg? Ansätze und Erfahrungen professioneller Angebote zum
Ausstieg aus rechtsextremen Szenen*, Hrsg. Peter Rieker, 45–76. Weinheim:
Opladen.

Glaser, Michaela, Frank Greuel, and Sally Hohnstein. 2016. Preventing Entry,
Assisting Exit. In *Tumblr, DJI International*. http://dji-international.tumblr.
com/post/134911589666/preventing-entry-assisting-exit-differentiated

Hafeneger, Benno, and Reiner Becker. 2007. *Rechte Jugendcliquen. Zwischen
Unauffälligkeit und Provokation. Eine empirische Studie*. Schwalbach/Ts:
Wochenschau Verlag.

Hohnstein, Sally, Frank Greuel, unter Mitarbeit von Glaser Michaela. 2015.
*Einstiege verhindern, Ausstiege begleiten. Pädagogische Ansätze und Erfahrungen
im Handlungsfeld Rechtsextremismus*. Halle: Deutsches Jugendinstitut.

Horgan, John. 2008. Deradicalization or Disengagement? A Process in Need of
Clarity and a Counterterrorism Initiative in Need of Evaluation. *Perspectives on
Terrorism* 2(4): 3–8.

Kohlstruck, Michael. 2012. Pädagogische und soziale Arbeit mit rechtsextrem
gefährdeten   jungen   Leuten.   Interventionen.   *Zeitschrift   für
Verantwortungspädagogik* 1(1): 5–13.

Lutzebäck et al. 1995. Mädchen in rechten Szenen. Erfahrungen aus der Praxis
'akzeptierender' Jugendarbeit. *deutsche Jugend* 12: 545–525.

Möller, Kurt. 2002. *Pädagogische und sozialarbeiterische Ansätze der Stärkung von
Integrationspotenzialen   zur   Bearbeitung   von   Rechtsextremismus,
Fremdenfeindlichkeit und Gewalt auf dem Hintergrund von Anerkennungszerfall
und Desintegration*. Bielefeld and Esslingen.

———. 2010. Ausstiege aus dem Rechtsextremismus—Wie professionelle
Ausstiegshilfen Themen- und Bearbeitungsdiskurse über Rechtsextremismus
(re)produzieren und modifizieren. In *Doing Social Problems. Mikroanalysen der
Konstruktion sozialer Probleme und sozialer Kontrolle in institutionellen
Kontexten*, ed. Axel Groenemeyer, 220–245. Wiesbaden: VS Verlag.

Möller, Kurt, and Nils Schumacher. 2007. *Rechte Glatzen. Rechtsextreme Szene-und Orientierungszusammenhänge—Einstiegs-, Verbleibs- und Ausstiegsprozesse von Skinheads.* Wiesbaden: VS Verlag für Sozialwissenschaften.

Pfeiffer, Thomas. 2007. Menschenverachtung mit Unterhaltungswert. Musik, Symbolik, Internet—der Rechtsextremismus als Erlebniswelt. In *Erlebniswelt Rechtsextremismus*, ed. Stefan Glaser, and Thomas Pfeiffer, Schwalbach/Ts..: Wochenschau Verlag, 36–52.

Pingel, Andrea. 2002. *Rechtsextremismus bei Frauen und Mädchen—eine Übersicht zu Diskussionen und Befunden (Kurzfassung).* Halle: unveröffentlichtes Manuskript (erstellt im Rahmen des DJI-Projektes: Rechtsextremismus und Fremdenfeindlichkeit—Jugendpolitische und pädagogische Herausforderungen).

Pingel, Andrea, and Peter Rieker. 2002. *Pädagogik mit rechtsextrem orientierten Jugendlichen. Ansätze und Erfahrungen in der Jugendarbeit.* Halle: Deutsches Jugendinstitut.

Rieker, Peter. 2009. *Rechtsextremismus: Prävention und Intervention. Ein Überblick über Ansätze, Befunde und Entwicklungsbedarf.* Weinheim and München: Juventa.

Röpke, Andrea, and Andreas Speit. 2011. *Mädelsache! Frauen in der Neonazi-Szene.* Berlin: Ch. Links Verlag.

Stöss, Richard. 2010. *Rechtsextremismus im Wandel.* Berlin: Friedrich Ebert Stiftung.

Wasniewski, Cathleen. 2007. Eine Landesarbeitgemeinschaft, die LAG Mädchen und junge Frauen Sachsen e.V., befragte PädagogInnen zu Ursachen zunehmender Rechtsorientierung von Frauen. In *Bundesarbeitsgemeinschaft Mädchenpolitik e.V. Mädchen und Frauen im Spannungsfeld von Demokratie und rechten Ideologien*, 38–45. Berlin: Grin Verlag.

Gender Might Be the Key. Gender-Reflective Approaches and Guidelines in Prevention of and Intervention in Right-Wing Extremism in Europe

Silke Baer, Oliver Kossack, and Anika Posselius

Introduction: Why Gender?

It is beyond doubt that the extreme right has changed over the last few decades. Right-wing extremists have ceased to be the bunch of mostly young male neo-Nazi skinheads who march the streets and commit violent hate crimes—if the picture ever was that simple in the first place. The success of the French extreme right party leader Marine Le Pen, or Beate Zschäpe, the only surviving member of the core of the German neo-Nazi terror cell "National Socialist Underground", have revealed that women are an important part of the extreme right—and that they are not only followers but also activists in crucial positions and perpetrators of extreme right violence in Germany (Köttig 2004).

S. Baer (✉)
Berlin, Germany

O. Kossack
Berlin, Germany

A. Posselius
Berlin, Germany

© The Author(s) 2017
M. Köttig et al. (eds.), *Gender and Far Right Politics in Europe*,
DOI 10.1007/978-3-319-43533-6_23

351

Nevertheless, the stereotypical image of the right-wing skinhead prevails in the media and even in some scholarly works—often without applying any gender perspective at all. Yet, adding such a perspective to the study of right-wing extremism can bring issues and questions to the surface that can easily be overlooked otherwise. What are the roles of men and women in the extreme right? Have these roles changed over time, and if so in what ways? What do such changes imply for the internal cohesion and external appeal of the extreme right? Shifting the perspective to the field of prevention, the question arises whether there are (or should be) gender-reflective and/or gender-specific approaches to prevention and intervention—and what are good practices that could also work elsewhere?

These have been some of the questions that *Cultures Interactive's WomEx* (2013–14) project tried to address in two years of research in different fields. By reviewing theoretical and practical work related to women and gender in (right-wing) extremism, conducting field research and interviews with social workers and other practitioners involved in the prevention of (right-wing) extremism, as well as former members of the extreme right, and collecting good practices in gender-reflective prevention and intervention, the project aimed at shedding light on some of the above-mentioned questions, identifying crucial fields for prevention, and presenting strategies for and approaches to prevention for each of these fields.

WomEx focused its research first and foremost on Germany. An international dimension was added through contact with members of the *Radicalisation Awareness Network (RAN)*, a European network of practitioners working in various fields relating to the prevention of radicalisation. This chapter focuses on the project's findings concerning prevention work, particularly in the areas of youth work; exit, distancing and disengagement work; social and anti-violence training; and community work.

We start with a brief review of gender issues and gender roles in the extreme right and continue with general observations regarding the gender-reflective prevention of right-wing extremism. These general observations are followed by the more specific findings and recommendations for prevention work in the aforementioned fields of pedagogical work, including specific guidelines for good practice.

GENDER ROLES AND THE ROLE OF GENDER IN RIGHT-WING EXTREMISM

The *völkisch* community is still a core concept of extreme right ideology[1] that offers a specific and traditional set of biologically defined roles for men and women. In this ideological framework, men are supposed to be the breadwinners and care for the family's safety by defending their family and territory. Moreover, political action is also deemed to be a male domain. Women, however, should be concerned first and foremost with caring for the family, especially the children. When it comes to political and social activities, they should concentrate on their everyday environment—often seen as the "pre-political" sphere—in the sense of the family, or the children's education (kindergarten, school, sports club, etc.), and work as volunteers (Rommelspacher 2011: 51). Nevertheless, by appearing as caring and engaged mothers, or friendly and communicative neighbours, they should try to communicate their ideological norms and values to people beyond the extreme right. Hence, women may also be politically active in public, but while for men political activity is understood as an obligatory duty, for women it is only an additional option after fulfilling their obligations in the private sphere (Lang 2010: 133).

Yet, even though these gender roles may still dominate within extreme right groups, they have been contested for quite some time. Similar to developments in society at large, a greater diversity of ideas regarding both female and male gender roles in extreme right groups has slowly taken hold. On the one hand, this means that women assume a more active function, including political activism and even violence. They form their own girls' and women's groups within their larger organisation, run campaigns, take part in demonstrations or other events, and commit violent acts—often targeted at other girls. Men, on the other hand, do not always fit the image of the extreme right fighter or outspoken and radical political activist (Lehnert 2013: 201; Radvan 2013: 16f; Möller 2011: 141f). This pluralisation of gender roles and the resulting extension of possibilities for women contribute to an increasing attractiveness of the extreme right scene (Lang 2010: 142).

Moreover—and in spite of the growing diversification of gender roles within the extreme right—gender issues have become a topic of extreme right politics. The societal discourses on gender equality and feminism are perceived as a threat to the traditional, biologically defined gender roles of the *völkisch* community which are still dominant within the extreme right. However, the opposition to gender mainstreaming, feminism or equal rights for LGBTIQ people is not limited to the extreme right. In these views, extreme right groups overlap and often join forces with various conservative milieus (Lehnert 2010: 98f). Yet, it needs to be emphasised that gender issues alone are not the core of extreme right politics but one of many exclusionary ideological elements, first of all racism.

It has frequently been stressed that congruence between personal views and ideological positions of an extreme right group is usually not the primary motivation for (young) people to join these groups. The following sections will therefore address the reasons people have for becoming a member of the extreme right, which is an important issue for prevention work that aims at avoiding or reversing this process.

Rommelspacher stresses that the reason for joining the extreme right cannot be found in a few causal factors but is constituted by complex and case-specific combinations of socio-structural, cultural and individual factors. In this process, the ideology of the predominance of one's own (ethnic) group or "nation" can either function in a compensatory way, that is, experienced affronts can be compensated, or in an affirmative way, confirming and preserving one's own privileges. At this point gender is relevant: for both males and females a hierarchical self-interest is important, and both tend to solve personal, social or political problems or conflicts by degrading others in order to upgrade themselves. In doing so, they share common values and ideologies, but their motivations and ways of enforcing their interests differ (Rommelspacher 2011: 45ff).

Nevertheless, many authors agree on the fact that members of extreme right groups and people who hold extreme right attitudes have not necessarily experienced socioeconomic hardships but may come from stable social environments (Baer 2008; Birsl 2013: 146f). This leads Birsl to the conclusion that there are no specific experiences of socialisation for either women or men that inevitably turn them into right-wing extremists but that there is always a combination of individual factors and structural conditions ("opportunity structures") that encourage young people to adopt an extreme right ideology and join such groups. While an intact democratic and human rights-oriented environment that offers modes of participation for young people will strengthen their resilience to the extreme right, an active extreme right organisation in their home town or village, for instance, and the absence of a democratic civil society may facilitate their entry into the extreme right (see Birsl 2013: 147ff)

Köttig highlights the fact that such a perspective is fraught with the danger of perceiving women as passive "victims" of their socialisation and external opportunity structures. It fails to acknowledge a person's active decision to join an extreme right group (Köttig 2004: 56f). Women might perceive their involvement in the extreme right as an improvement of their personal situation and as an opportunity to give importance to their lives. Members of the scene actively decide to share and promote the ideas, values and activities of the extreme right groups they join—at least to a certain degree.

GENDER AS A DIMENSION OF PREVENTIVE WORK

As shown above, gender is a relevant factor in understanding individual motivations for joining the extreme right. These groups offer gender-specific appeals and have picked up on current societal discourses on gender in their ideology and actions. Accordingly, a gender-specific analysis of right-wing extremism should be fruitful in order to achieve a better understanding of the scene, as well as individual motivations of its members, which can, in turn, provide insights for successful preventive work.

The demands on prevention work are manifold; it has to deal with existing exclusionary attitudes and practices and prevent them, but it also has to strengthen pro-democratic, human rights and antiracist attitudes in society as a whole. Hence, the differentiation of prevention work into primary, secondary and tertiary prevention and appropriate approaches provides a useful systematisation.[2]

Some first recommendations for work with extreme right adolescents, and those who show at least some signs of group-focused enmity, include basic principles to be applied in the three fields of prevention work, such as a profound knowledge of current right-wing extremism, building trust and a personal relationship with clients based on personal appreciation, regardless of their ideological position, and confidently having and showing democratic and human rights attitudes (Baer 2014: 59). Several of the above-mentioned authors have also formulated recommendations for gender-reflective pedagogical and preventive work. One general assumption is that gender is one of the most important factors in individual socialisation. Hence, this issue needs to be addressed as cross-sectional task by reflecting on socially constructed and stereotypical gender roles, questioning them and offering alternative ways of acting ("undoing gender"). If such a gender-reflective perspective is missing, the phenomenon of right-wing extremism is usually perceived as mainly a male affair, and gender roles not fitting into the scheme of martial and violent men or social and family-oriented women are simply overlooked (Radvan 2013: 19; Möller 2011).

According to Köttig, the ways (young) people cope with their socialisation and environment may or may not foster extreme right attitudes and activities (Köttig 2004: 56f). Here, she points to the crucial importance of biographical work which helps to understand why certain experiences and circumstances result in right-wing extremists in some cases but not in others, and how prevention work can intervene in this process. Sigl also supports the claim that a biographical approach is crucial for retracing women's ways into as well as out of the extreme right. When interviewing (former) female right-wing extremists, both authors found that factors like bad relationships with parents, a failure to deal with family history during National Socialism or a failure on the part of people in their social environment to confront their extreme right attitudes contributed to the involvement of young women in the extreme right scene (Sigl 2013: 282ff).

Finally, we would argue that a gender-reflective approach is necessary not only in pedagogical work but also for the pedagogues themselves. Constant reflection on one's own person and actions in terms of gender roles is necessary in order to create appropriate and authentic gender-specific educational programmes. If pedagogues themselves reject a binary understanding of gender roles, they will be able to question and deconstruct practised gender roles and fixed classifications. In doing so, they will open up spaces for males and females to develop and live individual gender roles. This boosts plurality and in turn strengthens democratic values (Lehnert and Radvan 2014: 94ff).

WomEx Guidelines for Relevant Working Fields in Prevention and Intervention

Even though general guidelines for including a gender-sensitive perspective in prevention work already exist, as well as organisations working according to these guidelines, there is still no overarching strategy for how to implement these recommendations across the different fields of preventive work—and filling this gap was one of the major goals of *Cultures Interactive's WomEx* project.

One of the project's results is the systematic overview of the relevant fields of prevention work shown in the figure below. Due to limited space, we cannot go into detail of all these fields of work. Instead, we will sum-marise some of the projects' results, such as general observations, promising practices and recommendations for practical prevention and intervention work, especially youth work, exit, distancing and disengagement work, social and anti-violence training and community work. More information on these fields of work and on those not included in this chapter, as well as an overview of the good practices of NGOs (mainly based in Germany), are available on the project's website at *womex.org* (Fig. 1).[3]

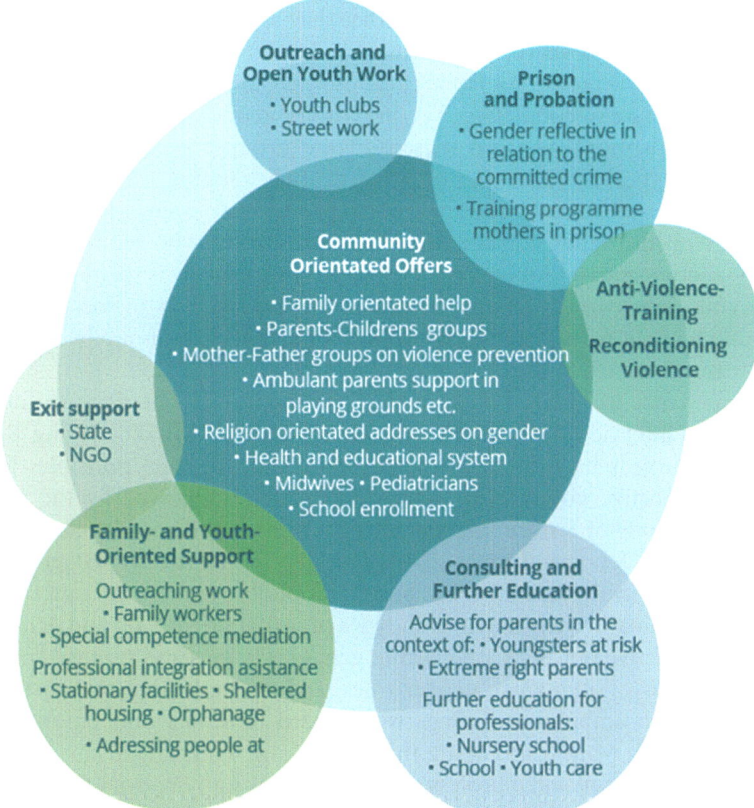

Fig. 1   Relevant fields of prevention and disengagement work. *Source*: Cultures Interactive e.V. (2015)

Youth Work

In recent years, the importance of youth work for primary and secondary prevention of right-wing extremism and group-focused enmity has been frequently pointed out, not least by youth workers and social workers themselves. They are important support persons in youth clubs, they are known and trusted by young people, and therefore they are in a good position to strengthen human rights attitudes and address young people directly in order to tackle different forms of group-focused enmity and antidemocratic attitudes.

Concerning right-wing extremism, youth workers from different cities and rural areas said in interviews that they are mainly confronted with mixed-gender groups that are, however, dominated by males regarding numbers and hierarchy. All-female groups or groups dominated by women are a rather rare phenomenon. Yet, in terms of gender, youth work is confronted with more than just these different group constellations. There are many types of right-wing-oriented women, ranging from aggressive and militant women who assume equal positions to men, to silent supporters or girlfriends of male right-wing extremists, who see themselves only as companions. An upcoming problem in Germany is the number of extreme right women among trainees, staff and students in social work. Young woman with extreme right attitudes and affiliations are becoming increasingly active in the field of youth work.

Experience from vocational training courses and information provided in group interviews conducted with German youth workers during the *WomEx* project have revealed the following fundamental principles for gender-reflective youth work, which are further supported by the recommendations of Kathrin Debus, Olaf Stuve and Andreas Hechler from *Dissens e.V.* (Debus and Stuve 2013; Hechler 2014): special pedagogical intervention in the case of sexist and homophobic comments, open and non-discriminatory treatment of all types of sexual orientation and gender identities, active reflection on existing gender relations and strengthening of awareness of alternative gender roles, and strengthening the capacity to cope with ambivalent feelings with regard to sexual orientation and gender. Youth work teams doing this challenging work should also have a long-term strategy and a professional network of support from the youth care system, security, education and their own organisation.

In addition to working directly with young people, it is also necessary to have sufficient time available for reflection and follow-up. Without supervision, case consultation and financial resources—which make it possible to introduce targeted interventions and gender-specific activities—it will be hardly possible to have an impact. With regard to the staff, it is important to have gender-mixed teams, room for reflection on one's own ideas about gender roles, professional exchange on possibilities of gender-reflective work with adolescents belonging to various groups, and further training on the importance of gender and gender roles in right-wing extremism and other movements hostile to human rights (Wiechmann 2014).

EXIT, DISENGAGEMENT AND DISTANCING WORK

Even though gender has always been a relevant topic in exit work, since gender roles and related expectations and ideas about masculinity and femininity are important in the activities of the extreme right scene, gender aspects have not been systematically and conceptually considered by those working in the field of exit support—but they have often been followed intuitively. For instance, the *Arbeitsstelle Rechtsextremismus und Gewalt* (ARUG) in Lower Saxony, Germany, and the federal working group of German exit programmes have begun to develop specific action plans for girls and women.

On the practical level, interviews with exit workers and their clients have shown that a major gender issue in disengagement work is the team composition. Helping (young) people to exit the scene is a very intense process with an average duration of one to two years. Therefore, it is important to have somebody the client can trust and who is able to address the client's motives for joining the scene, taking gender into account. In practice, some clients react better to an exit worker of the same gender, while others prefer someone of the opposite gender.

One of the most important conclusions from the *WomEx* project regarding exit work is that to date women have not received targeted help or offers of assistance to exit the scene at the right place. Women need to be addressed at different places than men and in gender-specific ways. Exit programmes for women need to target them particularly in situations of personal change, for instance during pregnancy or after a birth, when they are in contact with support structures such as family counselling centres, youth welfare institutions or mother-and-child homes. Such institutions and women's shelters are also a place that women may turn to after having experienced domestic violence and abuse in a relationship. Given the mainly traditional understanding of gender roles in the extreme right and its inherent sexism, this is not a rare experience for extreme right females. Therefore, these structures should not only provide women with a safe place to stay but also offer them the chance of making a sustainable exit from both the extreme right scene and domestic violence, as these are hardly separable in such instances.

There are, however, particular challenges in working with parents when only one of them wishes to exit the scene. Exit work may have to be connected with parent counselling. Child welfare and protecting the children from the possible negative effects of belonging to the scene are a key focus of this work. The exit of mothers can prove to be especially difficult due to threats of violence, harassment or child abduction. A functional network with youth and family welfare workers, as well as criminal justice workers, seems wise as all practitioners need to be aware of the particular difficulties involved when parents separate or divorce as a result of exit processes.

Moreover, there is room for improvement regarding the traditional partners of exit programmes, such as the police, secret service, prison and probation officers. It is necessary to sharpen perceptions of the meaning and roles that women play in extreme right scenes. The activities of extreme right women often go unpunished because they seem to be nonviolent. This—and stereotypical thinking concerning gender roles—creates "gender blindness" among the police and judiciary that leads to underestimating or overlooking female perpetrators.

SOCIAL AND ANTI-VIOLENCE TRAINING

Anti-violence work is usually a measure used for juvenile delinquents and offenders or as a part of the probation process. Anti-violence training includes exercises and settings in which the clients deal directly with their patterns of aggression and violent behaviour. The goal is to enable people to reflect on the deeply rooted social mechanisms of self-exclusion. They can act out their anger and process this together with others in the group and with the facilitator. At the same time, social skills like empathy and personal reflection are strengthened.

Anti-violence work with right-wing extremists is an important element of the disengagement process, since violence is a crucial part of the ideology and self-understanding of many right-wing extremists. Furthermore, many (young) men and women who decide to join the extreme right have had previous experience of violence. In countries where no exit programmes have been established so far, anti-violence training courses are an important intervention tool. Facilitators from the Slovak Republic and Slovenia, for instance, reported at the *RAN* practitioner meetings that they are often confronted with racist and right-wing extremist ideologies.

Given the gender gap[4] regarding the perpetrators of right-wing violence, it is hardly a surprise that 90 to 95 per cent of those who attend anti-violence training courses are men. In Germany only a few organisations, such as the *Institut für genderreflektierte Gewaltprävention (ifgg, Institute for gender-reflective violence prevention)* and *Denkzeit e.V.* in Berlin, or the *Initiative für Münchner Mädchen (IMMA e.V., Initiative for Girls in Munich)*, provide specific anti-violence training for girls and women. These usually take place in individual settings, not least due to the low number of cases. Organisations that offer group training for girls often have difficulties reaching the minimum number of participants.

However, practitioners have stressed the fact that gender roles are a crucial issue connected to extreme right violence, since male perpetrators often seek confirmation by acting out the stereotypical role of the violent male right-wing extremist, while girls or women may try to oppose these "classical" gender roles by using violence as an act of rebellion. Therefore, personal gender stereotypes of masculinity and femininity have to be addressed. How important is the use of violence to the personal self-understanding of being a "real man"? Are there alternative options? Looking at the biography of the clients, we can ask who or what might have influenced their aggressive behaviour. Absent fathers, or parents who have used physical or psychological violence, often come up in the biographical work. Moreover, there are women-specific characteristics, such as self-injury, eating disorders and sexual violence which, although also recorded, are less common among young men (and therefore possibly more difficult to address). Another gender-related issue is the low social status perceived by many young women, which may be a reason why they seek to gain recognition from the group by committing criminal and violent acts. Working with young women also differs in that they often employ subtle forms of passive-aggressive provocation, which motivate others (young men) to commit violent acts. This again creates the problem that girls or women are less recognisable as perpetrators.

COMMUNITY WORK

Community work includes specific features like community centres, group work and community policies to deal with right-wing extremism. The main issues to address are the recognition of right-wing extremism, sensitivity in terms of gender, and the cooperation of actors and institutions in the fields of prevention and intervention. The issues of equality, gender roles and gender identity have barely been considered in community-oriented prevention and intervention work so far, although there are good reasons to do so: female representatives of extreme right movements have been an important factor in improving the image of right-wing extremism in recent decades. Especially on the local level, women engage themselves voluntarily and assume specific functions in parents' associations, social work, nursery school and honorary offices and associations within the community. There they promote gender-related aspects of their extreme right ideology, such as that women should stay at home and care for their families, that gender mainstreaming and the equality of homosexual people contradicts the nature of human beings, that there should not be refugee camps in the neighbourhood because of the risk that local girls will become victims of sexual abuse, or that the democratic government does not care for its "own" people and families. These statements often resonate with sexist, homophobic and racist attitudes that reach far into the heart of the community and work as door-openers for new supporters.

Communities need strategies to counteract the influence of right-wing extremists. The poor recognition of females (and their violent activities) is one reason why training in respect of "gender and right-wing extremism" is necessary for youth welfare offices, the police and judiciary and social services, as they need to become aware of the different forms of violent and nonviolent right-wing extremism that girls and women engage in. Teachers and kindergarten staff are not normally trained to deal with right-wing extremist parents and colleagues, so that further education is needed here as well.

In the *RAN* guidelines, interagency approaches have been identified as especially effective for communities, such as the combination of counselling, capacity building, prevention and intervention measures, as well as cooperation between NGOs and governmental institutions. Particularly in Denmark and the Netherlands, cross-sector local teams and integrated ways of working have been established; the police and secret service, social work (fan work, street work, clubs, etc.), penal services, schools and youth services (drug counselling, social skills training, leisure time oriented services, career counselling) and health services (social psychiatric services), all communicate closely with one another at the local level. These different services have developed useful forms of quick information exchange and intervention (see, e.g. the *Infohouses* in Aarhus, Denmark).

In Germany, various *mobile counselling teams* (*Mobile Beratungsteams*) for the purpose of strengthening civil society have been established all over the country since the end of the 1990s. They combine activities such as monitoring, awareness raising, general information and counselling of local civil societies and communities. Organisations like the *Fachstelle für Gender und Rechtsextremismus* (*Specialist Unit for Gender and Right-Wing Extremism*) in Berlin, or *Lidice House* in Bremen, do monitoring, offer information and training for the public but also counselling for parents of adolescents who have entered the neo-Nazi scene.

One other promising area of gender-reflective prevention and intervention work at the intersection between community and family-oriented work is the establishment by NGOs of groups for fathers, mothers or parents, to help them with processing experiences of violence and gender-repressive traditions.

CONCLUSION

This chapter has aimed at drawing attention to the fact that a gender perspective can contribute significantly to a better understanding of the extreme right and to developing successful prevention and intervention strategies. Many practitioners and researchers have come to subscribe to this idea and apply a gender-reflective perspective in their work. In the media, as well as in public and political discourses, the role of women and gender in right-wing extremism is still an underrepresented topic—not least since attention is still focused on the violent actions of organised groups. However, this article underlines that even within extreme right groups gender roles are not monolithic structures. Some groups contest traditional ideas of the *völkisch* community, in which men are political activists and defenders of the family, while women's activities are mostly restricted to raising and educating children. More and more women, however, are becoming politically active. Since their activities do not always take place in the street, and are less connected with violent behaviour, they tend to be overlooked, even though they are equally effective as a means of promoting right-wing ideologies.

In sum, a gender-reflective analysis of right-wing extremism would be useful, at least in the following areas: (1) ideologies and strategies of right-wing extremist scenes; (2) the gender-specific appeal of extreme right groups, and the roles and fields of action they offer for women and men, in addition to general social conditions that may support or prevent people from joining extreme right groups; and consequently (3) the inclusion of gender-specific and gender-reflective practices and perspectives in prevention and intervention work.

The latter aspect is the main focus of this chapter. It can be concluded from the research conducted in the framework of the *WomEx* project, and by other scholars, that primary, secondary and tertiary prevention work should take into account the fact that women stress different aspects in respect of their activities within the radical right than men, and they often join these groups for different reasons. This implies a need for different approaches in preventive work with male and female clients. Since gender roles within the radical right are becoming more diverse, challenging stereotypical gender roles and offering alternative ones could be a viable strategy for many fields of preventive work.

Furthermore, it might be helpful to extend prevention measures to institutions and fields of social work that already have access to clients coming from, or attracted by, the extreme right, such as prison and probation services, stationary and outreach youth work, child and family support, women's shelters, mother-and-child homes, parents' counselling, mental health service or substance abuse counselling.

When it comes to the community, it is not sufficient to provide isolated help; a successful prevention strategy must include all the above-mentioned measures. Counselling, information and training must be provided for various target groups, and cooperation between all stakeholders and professional workers is essential.

Even though gender is only one among other exclusionary features of the ideology of right-wing extremists, this chapter has provided insights into how gender might be the key to effective prevention work. By drawing on research and existing good practice, we hope to have provided useful recommendations for practitioners in different fields that may help them deal with right-wing extremism in their everyday work. This is surely not the final word on this matter. Perhaps our conclusions may serve as an impulse for researchers and practitioners alike to share their experience and develop further recommendations and good practices for the prevention of right-wing extremism. In view of the rise of right-wing extremism and populism across Europe, there is an urgent need to do so.

Notes

1. The authors of this chapter understand right-wing extremism as an ideology based on the exclusionary idea of a homogeneous nation as the most viable definition for prevention work, not least because it draws attention to exclusionary attitudes and practices in society well beyond manifest extreme right organisations and mere opposition to the democratic system, and thereby widens the target group for prevention work (Decker and Brähler 2006; Heitmeyer 2012; Zick et al. 2011; Mudde 2007: 18; Minkenberg 1998: Chap. 1.2).

2. This systematisation of prevention work derives from the healthcare sector: the first, primary prevention, aims at preventing problematic attitudes and behaviour in advance; approaches are located in the fields of human rights, civic and diversity education, usually in non-formal contexts and open youth work. The field of secondary prevention comprises approaches seeking to combat existing extreme right attitudes and behaviour. Approaches working on ideologically consolidated attitudes are located in the field of tertiary prevention and are usually put into practice in youth work, individual case assistance or in prisons and during probation.

3. www.womex.org (accessed 18 March 2016).

4. International studies have shown only slight differences between the attitudes of men and women with respect to group-focused enmity (Rommelspacher 2011: 44f; Birsl 2011a; Zick et al. 2011: 68ff.). The gender gap grows when behaviour is included: all over Europe, women are underrepresented among the voters of extreme right parties and the gap grows even more with respect to membership of extreme right parties and groups (Givens 2004; Norris 2005: 144ff.; Félix 2015; see also Mudde 2007: Chap. 4). The gap is most visible when it comes to the general acceptance and perpetration of violence (Möller 2010: 27; Birsl 2011b; Bitzan 2006: 111ff): Women's acceptance of right-wing extremism depends on its connection with violence (Rommelspacher 2011: 45).

References

Baer, Silke. 2008. Rechtsextremismus und Jugendgewalt im Kontext psychologisch fundierter Biografieforschung (Review Essay). *Forum: Qualitative Sozialforschung* 9, n.p. Accessed 15 March 2016. http://www.qualitative-research.net/index.php/fqs/article/view/427/925

————. 2014. Pädagogische Zugänge in der Rechtsextremismusprävention und Intervention—Entwicklungen und Standards in Deutschland und Europa. In *Verantwortlich Handeln: Praxis der Sozialen Arbeit mit rechtsextrem orientierten und gefährdeten Jugendlichen*, ed. Silke Baer, Kurt Möller, and Peer Wiechmann, 47–66. Opladen, Berlin, and Toronto: Budrich.

Birsl, Ursula. 2011a. Rechtsextremistisch orientierte Frauen und Männer: Persönlichkeitsprofile, Sozialisationserfahrungen und Gelegenheitsstrukturen. In *Rechtsextremismus und Gender*, ed. Ursula Birsl, 171–185. Opladen and Farmington Hills: Budrich.

————. 2011b. Rechtsextremistische Gewalt: Mädchen und junge Frauen als Täterinnen? Wissenschaftliche Erkenntnisse und offene Fragen in geschlechtervergleichender Perspektive. In *Rechtsextremismus und Gender*, ed. Ursula Birsl, 241–264. Opladen and Farmington Hills: Budrich.

————. 2013. Rechtsextremistisch orientierte Frauen und Männer. Persönlichkeitsprofile, Sozialisationserfahrungen und Gelegenheitsstrukturen. In *Gender und Rechtsextremismusprävention*, ed. Heike Radvan, and Amadeu-Antonio-Stiftung, 131–150. Berlin: Metropol.

Bitzan, Renate. 2006. Rechte Frauen und Mädchen. In *Pädagogische Interventionsstrategien gegen Rechtsextremismus. Erfahrungen und Ergebnisse aus vier Veranstaltungen, Aspekte Jugendsozialarbeit*, ed. Bundesarbeitsgemeinschaft Katholische Jugendsozialarbeit, 111–118. Düsseldorf: n.p.

Cultures Interactive e.V. 2015. *WomEx—Women and Girls in Extremism. Aspects of Gender in Right Wing Extremism and Religious Fundamentalism. Guidelines for Specific Sectors of Prevention and Intervention.* Berlin: Cultures Interactive.

Debus, Katharina, and Olaf Stuve. 2013. Geschlechterreflektierende Arbeit mit Jungen als Prävention rechtsextremer Einstellungen und Handlungsmuster. In *Gender und Rechtsextremismusprävention*, ed. Heike Radvan, and Amadeu-Antonio-Stiftung, 169–196. Berlin: Metropol.

Decker, Oliver, and Elmar Brähler. 2006. *Vom Rand zur Mitte. Rechtsextreme Einstellungen und ihre Einflussfaktoren in Deutschland.* Berlin: Friedrich-Ebert-Stiftung.

Félix, Aniko. 2015. Old Missions in New Clothes: The Reproduction of the Nation as Women's Main Role Perceived by Female Supporters of Golden Dawn and Jobbik. *Intersections* 1: 166–182.

Givens, Terry E. 2004. The Radical Right Gender Gap. *Comparative Political Studies* 37: 30–54.

Hechler, Andreas. 2014. Männlichkeitskritische Neonazismusprävention. In *Verantwortlich Handeln: Praxis der Sozialen Arbeit mit rechtsextrem orientierten und gefährdeten Jugendlichen*, ed. Silke Baer, Kurt Möller, and Peer Wiechmann, 103–113. Opladen, Berlin, and Toronto: Budrich.

Heitmeyer, Wilhelm (ed). 2012. *Deutsche Zustände, Folge 10.* Frankfurt am Main: Suhrkamp.

Köttig, Michaela. 2004. *Lebensgeschichten rechtsextrem orientierter Mädchen und junger Frauen. Biographische Verläufe im Kontext der Familien- und Gruppendynamik.* Gießen: Psychosozial-Verlag.

Lang, Juliane. 2010. ‚...diese Gemeinschaft von Frauen, unter Frauen, gemeinsam mit Frauen, gemeinsam mit Frauen sitzen und sich besprechen und so weiter, tut Frauen einfach gut.' Frauen im Rechtsextremismus. In *Was ein rechter Mann ist...' Männlichkeiten im Rechtsextremismus,* ed. Robert Claus, Esther Lehnert, and Yves Müller, 127–142. Berlin: Karl Dietz Verlag.

Lehnert, Esther. 2010. Angriff auf Gender Mainstreaming und Homo-Lobby'— der moderne Rechtsextremismus und seine nationalsozialistischen Bezüge am Beispiel der Geschlechterordnung. In *Was ein rechter Mann ist... 'Männlichkeiten im Rechtsextremismus,* ed. Robert Claus, Esther Lehnert, and Yves Müller, 89–99. Berlin: Karl Dietz Verlag.

Lehnert, Esther. 2013. Parteiliche Mädchenarbeit und Rechtsextremismusprävention. In *Gender und Rechtsextremismusprävention,* ed. Heike Radvan and Amadeu Antonio-Stiftung, 197–210. Berlin: Metropol.

Minkenberg, Michael. 1998. *Die neue radikale Rechte im Vergleich: USA, Frankreich, Deutschland.* Wiesbaden: Opladen.

Möller, Kurt. 2010. Männlichkeitsforschung im Rahmen von Rechtsextremismusstudien. Ausgangspunkte, Ansätze, Ergebnisse und Perspektiven. In *Was ein rechter Mann ist...' Männlichkeiten im Rechtsextremismus,* ed. Robert Claus, Esther Lehnert, and Yves Müller, 25–38. Berlin: Karl Dietz Verlag.

———. 2011. Konstruktion von Männlichkeiten in unterschiedlichen Phänomenbereichen des Rechtsextremismus. In *Rechtsextremismus und Gender,* ed. Ursula Birsl, 129–145. Opladen and Farmington Hills: Budrich.

Mudde, Cas. 2007. *Populist Radical Right Parties in Europe.* Cambridge: Cambridge University Press.

Norris, Pippa. 2005. *Radical Right: Voters and Parties in the Electoral Market.* Cambridge et al.: Cambridge University Press.

Radvan, Heike. 2013. Geschlechterreflektierende Rechtsextremismusprävention. Eine Leerstelle in Theorie und Praxis? In *Gender und Rechtsextremismusprävention,* ed. Heike Radvan, and Amadeu-Antonio-Stiftung, 9–36. Berlin: Metropol.

Radvan, Heike, and Esther Lehnert. 2014. Geschlechterreflektierende Arbeit mit rechtsextrem Orientierten. In *Verantwortlich Handeln: Praxis der Sozialen Arbeit mit rechtsextrem orientierten und gefährdeten Jugendlichen,* ed. Silke Baer, Kurt Möller, and Peer Wiechmann, 89–101. Opladen, Berlin, and Toronto: Budrich.

Rommelspacher, Birgit. 2011. Frauen in Männer im Rechtsextremismus—Motive, Konzepte und Rollenverständnisse. In *Rechtsextremismus und Gender,* ed. Ursula Birsl, 43–68. Opladen and Farmington Hills: Budrich.

Sigl, Johanna. 2013. Lebensgeschichten von Aussteigerinnen aus der extremen Rechten. Gender-spezifische Aspekte und mögliche Ansatzpunkte für eine ausstiegsorientierte Soziale Arbeit. In *Gender und Rechtsextremismusprävention*, ed. Heike Radvan and Amadeu Antonio-Stiftung, 273–289. Berlin: Metropol.

Wiechmann, Peer. 2014. Hako_reJu: Ein Handlungskonzept für die Offene Jugendarbeit mi trechtsextrem gefährdeten und orientierten Jugendlichen im ländlichen Raum Ostdeutschlands. In *Verantwortlich Handeln: Praxis der Sozialen Arbeit mit rechtsextrem orientierten und gefährdeten Jugendlichen*, ed. Silke Baer, Kurt Möller, and Peer Wiechmann, 189–206. Opladen, Berlin, and Toronto: Budrich.

Zick, Andreas, Beate Küpper, and Andreas Hövermann. 2011. *Die Abwertung der Anderen*. Berlin: Friedrich-Ebert-Stiftung.

Postscript

Alice Blum and Michaela Köttig

PROPAGATED AND LIVED GENDER ROLES—MANY ANSWERS BUT ALSO NEW QUESTIONS

As our work on this book comes to end, the European project is show-ing signs of strain. The goal of uniting all European nations is no lon-ger undisputed. On the contrary, politically the countries of Europe are drifting apart. And many of them are split internally: those who are in favour of a pluralistic and liberal-minded Europe on the one hand and adherents of a narrow-minded and *völkisch* nationalism on the other. This was clearly seen in the most recent elections, the Austrian presidential elections and the referendum in Great Britain on leaving the EU, the so-called 'Brexit'. Extreme right-wing parties are moving from one success to the next and gaining a foothold in the middle classes and in the parlia-ments. From the beginning it was our hope that this book would help to counter these tendencies. The articles are based on sound research and provide a handle for developing action strategies, both on the academic and on the political level, and especially on the level of civil society. We were not to know that the relevance of this topic would become even

A. Blum (✉) • M. Köttig
Frankfurt University of Applied Sciences, Frankfurt, Germany

© The Author(s) 2017   369
M. Köttig et al. (eds.), *Gender and Far Right Politics in Europe*,
DOI 10.1007/978-3-319-43533-6_24

greater. And although we have been able to present a wide spectrum of research, the latest developments leave us dissatisfied. We have not been able to reveal enough about the close entanglement of different levels: global social developments, family background or individual circumstances such as social status and gender-specific reasons for adopting right-wing opinions. Any attempt to offer adequate explanations is quickly taken over by events. The process of publishing this book took several years, and although we have given many answers, we are faced with a whole lot of new questions. Instead of succumbing to feelings of impotence, we should let these questions be the inspiration for new ideas and further research.

The articles in this book show that in many European countries the far right is taking on new forms and in many cases is becoming stronger. Many right-wing groups are modernising themselves, not only in respect of their image or their political ideas but also in respect of a plurality of lived and propagated gender roles. In research and educational work it has been assumed for a long time that far-right groups are based on traditional gender arrangements. Men are seen as 'politically active' and 'potentially violent', and women as followers or supporters of the men (see Sigl 2013). But in practice it is hard to find justification for these stereotype gender ascriptions, as shown in many of the chapters in this volume. Indeed, a variety of different gender constructions can be observed, so that it can no longer be taken for granted that the far right embodies traditional, one-sided conceptions of gender. This is important for academic research, for a democratic, emancipatory civil society, and for gender-reflective educational and prevention work, if adequate counter strategies are to be developed. Research dedicated to gender constructions, gender conceptions and lived gender realities in the far right, on the national and the European level, is only just beginning. In this book an attempt has been made to bring together the first results of such academic research. However, in many European countries there are still no studies which can be used in order to develop appropriate counter strategies. We argue that far-right ideologies should be studied not only in the politically organised sphere but also in informal contexts such as the family as a space of political socialisation. Here, too, it would be important to look at gender roles and images within far-right families and how right-wing ideologies are communicated.

Diversity of Far-Right Structures

It is clear that far-right movements in Europe are not homogeneous. Their diversity and different political orientations can be illustrated, for example, by the 'National Front', Le Pen's extreme right-wing party in France (see Scrinzi in this volume) and her 'national socialism', and the German right-wing populist party 'Alternative for Germany', which propagates ideas that can be described as 'watered-down right-wing radicalism'. Besides these, there are groups whose only political message is a rejection of Islam, and others that are devoted entirely to a struggle against the prevailing 'gender madness' (see Kovats in this volume). Far-right groupings such as the 'Autonomous Nationalists' prefer to develop a subcultural lifestyle. Thus, there is a broad spectrum and many opportunities for different people to identify themselves with a group. There are also attractive opportunities for women, for this diversity offers a chance to be many things. Women can be intellectual theoreticians, they can be active on the streets, they can be leading political figures, strategists in dealing with the public, or mothers, and thus position themselves in the political landscape (see Elverich 2007). The same applies to constructions of masculinity in the far right. Here, too, the new flexibility of right-wing groups opens up possibilities of identification for men who might not find acceptance in the neo-Nazi scene (see Blum in this volume). The study of masculinities in the far right is a field of research that has been even more neglected than the study of femininities. Besides more studies of women's roles in the far right, research into constructions of masculinity is also needed. This means taking a closer look at gender roles and gender constructions in milieus to which too little attention has been paid, such as the 'New Right', the '*Völkisch* Right' or right-wing groups among immigrants like the Turkish *Bozkurtlar* (Grey Wolves), who are active in many European countries.

International Networks

The diverse groupings are becoming more flexible and forming networks that go beyond national borders. Networks formed through digital media are of particular interest: right-wing extremists in different countries communicate with each other through social networks. For women, the digital media offer an ideal platform for the strategic placing of right-wing ideologies (see Radvan 2015). Digital media make it much easier to expand and consolidate international organisations, as can be seen in the case of the neo-Nazi group 'Blood and Honour' (see Obermaier and Schulz 2013), or the networking of right-wing football fans.[1] There is a real need for research on these far-right network structures and gender relations within them. Newer right-wing groups, such as the Identitary Movement or anti-feminist groupings, also form international networks. They share similar forms of protest as well as similar aims. By forming networks they are able to acquire more supporters. This can be observed, for instance, in the case of the anti-feminist group 'Demos for all', a group that started in France under the name 'La Manif Pour Tous' and in 2013 succeeded in mobilis-ing more than 1.5 million people to join in street demonstrations (see Brustier 2014). This concept has been imitated in Germany, for instance by anti-feminist, evangelical or extreme right-wing groups, involving large numbers of people from different milieus and various European countries, such as Switzerland, France, Austria and beyond.[2] Since 2013 similar phe-nomena have been observed in the USA (see Solty 2015). This kind of international mobilisation must be watched critically, and, as this example shows, it is important to observe where the different groups overlap in terms of the people involved and their political aims. It is also important to take parliamentary structures into account. In the European parliament, there is a growing number of groups formed by conservatives and EU sceptics, such as the 'European Conservatives and Reformers', or by right-wing populists and right-wing extremists, such as 'Europe of Freedom and Direct Democracy' or 'Europe of Nations and Freedom'.[3] Topics such as the political struggle against gender mainstreaming or the tightening of EU asylum rules serve as a link between very different extreme-right groups in different European countries.

SHARED TOPICS—THE FAR RIGHT'S ABILITY TO JOIN THE SOCIAL MAINSTREAM

It can be observed that, despite the options open to men and women to assume various roles and functions in right-wing groups, the binary nature of gender is generally not questioned and that gender, especially the category of masculinity, still seems to be a constitutive element of far-right ideologies (see Claus et al. 2010, 9). Indeed, one of the main topics currently shared by right-wing actors is combating gender studies or edu-cational programmes based on gender-reflective practices from a queer or

deconstructivist perspective. With their criticism of the alleged 'early sexu-
alisation' of children and of so-called 'genderism', as currently expressed
by anti-feminists in France or Germany, the extreme right is capable of
joining the conservative mainstream (see Kovats and Põim 2015)—a wor-
rying development which can be countered using insights gained from
gender studies.

But far-right organisations in Europe capture votes not only with their
"attitudes in respect of family and gender" (Kemper 2014, 9)—as in the
case of the 'Alternative for Germany' party—but also, and above all, with
their views on immigration (see Fedders 2016). Currently, as a result of
the so-called 'refugee crisis' in Europe, extreme-right and right-wing
popular parties and groups have gained increasing support. In elections
they mobilise voters with anti-Muslim slogans and calls for restricting the
intake of refugees who have fled their homes in the face of poverty, war
and terror. The drastic increase all over Europe of attacks on refugees and
on hostels prepared for them shows that far-right propaganda leads not
only to rejection and exclusion but also to active aggression. However,
there has been little academic research on the significance of gender and
gender relations in the context of violent crimes committed by right-wing
extremists. There are hardly any reliable figures, and no study has been
made from a gender perspective of the reasons why men and women join
violent groups, the recent publication by Sigl being an exception (see
Sigl 2016). It would also be necessary to examine, both theoretically and
in practice, the intersectional entanglement of racism and sexism, which
affects the dominance hierarchies in societies and in the far right. This
raises the question of 'feminism from the right', its function and its implementation in the far right.

WHAT REMAINS …

The developments discussed above give rise to various questions: what
kind of studies are needed in order to gain a deeper understanding of the
far right and the reasons why people take up right-wing positions? This
means looking for gaps in existing research and possible blind spots and
asking about transnational networks. We want to understand what makes
far-right scenes and attitudes attractive, especially gender-specific factors,
and how these factors are interconnected with other lines of difference on
the European level. How can we counter oversimplified explanations of
causes or a tendency to trivialise the importance of gender constructions?

How can we, from the ivory tower of academia, make emancipatory feminist ideas and concepts attractive (again) for the majority society? At what points can prevention and intervention strategies be applied? What is the role of research and how can the discussion between science, politics and civil society be improved?

It is clear that there are many potential fields of research that have been neglected for too long. This book can therefore offer no more than a first overview of some topics relating to the theme of 'gender and the extreme right in Europe'. Our aim was to take a first step towards filling some of the gaps. A better understanding of gender constructions and gender-specific reasons for joining the far right will make it possible to tailor appropriate solutions for prevention and exit work in order to protect and preserve democratic societies in which there is room for diversity. This requires permanent research on cross-cutting topics relating to the far right, and interdisciplinary and international cooperation between researchers, if the gaps are to be filled. Research on far-right movements always involves a critical examination of state structures. There is a need for closer studies of homophobic ideologies like racism or anti-Semitism, the intersectional constitution of global inequalities and international interconnections.

These are not the exclusive tasks of academic researchers, but it is their job to provide a sound knowledge basis for dealing with right-wing extremism. If Europe is to be a symbol of diversity, we must promote and accept it by listening to minoritised citizens and accepting diversity as the natural state of things. We must speak out against inequality and processes of exclusion. This requires political will, and continuing research on far-right movements, in order to create strong, active and critical civil societies in each country and across borders. This volume is a step in this direction.

Notes

1. See: http://www.spiegel.de/sport/fussball/gewalt-im-fussball-rechtsextreme-aus-oesterreich-vernetzen-sich-in-koeln-a-950741.html (accessed 21 March 2016)
2. See: https://demofueralle.wordpress.com/eine-seite/wer-wir-sind/ (accessed 21 March 2016)
3. See: http://www.europarl.europa.eu/aboutparliament/de/20150201PVL00010/Aufbau-und-Arbeitsweise%C2%A0 (accessed 21 March 2016)

REFERENCES

Brustier, Gaël. 2014. *Le mai 68 conservateur. Que restera-t-il de La manif pour tous?* Paris: Le Cerf.

Claus, Robert, Lehnert, Esther, and Müller, Yves, eds. 2010. Einleitung. In *"Was ein rechter Mann ist …" Männlichkeiten im Rechtsextremismus.* Berlin: Karl Dietz Verlag.

Elverich, Gabi. 2007. Rechtsextrem orientierte Frauen und Mädchen—eine besondere Zielgruppe?. Accessed 20 March, 2016 http://www.bpb.de/politik/extremismus/rechtsextremismus/41506/rechtsextrem-orientierte-frauen-und-maedchen?p=0

Fedders, Jonas. 2016. Die Wahlerfolge der "Alternative für Deutschland" im Kontext rassistischer Hegemoniebestrebungen. In *Die Alternative für Deutschland. Programmatik, Entwicklung und politische Verortung,* ed. Alexander Häusler, 163–178. Wiesbaden: Vs-Springer.

Kemper, Andreas. 2014. Keimzelle der Nation? Familien- und geschlechterpolitische Perspektiven der AfD—eine Expertise. FES, Forum Politik und Gesellschaft. Accessed 20 March, 2016 http://library.fes.de/pdf-files/dialog/10641-20140414.pdf

Kovats, Eszter, and Põim Maari. 2015. *Gender as Symbolic Glue. The Position and Role of Conservative and Far Right Parties in the Anti-Gender Mobilisation in Europe.* Budapest: Foundation for European progressive studies and Friedrich-Ebert-Foundation. Accessed 16 March, 2016 http://library.fes.de/pdf-files/bueros/budapest/11382.pdf

Obermaier, Frederick, and Schulz, Tanja. 2013. Neonazis feiern "Tag der Ehre". Accessed 21 March, 2016 http://www.sueddeutsche.de/politik/verbotene-organistation-blood-honour-neonazis-feiern-tag-der-ehre-1.1596621

Radvan, Heike. 2015. Neonazi–Frauen in Sozialen Medien. Eine Annäherung. Accessed 10 April, 2016 http://www.netz-gegen-nazis.de/artikel/neonazi-frauen-soziale-medien-facebook-10522

Sigl, Johanna. 2013. Mädchen und Frauen in der extremen Rechten Baustein zum Einsatz in der Politischen Bildung. Arbeit und Leben Hamburg.

———. 2016. Female Right-Wing Dropouts and Meanings of Violence. In *Mulheres e violência. Civitas—Revista de Ciências Sociais,* eds. Santos, Hermilio and Köttig, Michaela, 71–85. Heft 2. Accessed 28 June, 2016 http://revistaseletronicas.pucrs.br/ojs/index.php/civitas/article/view/24072/14417, English version.

Solty, Ingar. 2015. Öffentliche Schulbildung, Sexualerziehung und rechter Widerstand gegen kulturelle Liberalisierung. Lassen sich die Bewegung gegen den Bildungsplan 2015 in Baden Württemberg und die Bewegung gegen die "Common Core State Standards Initiative" in den USA vergleichen? In *Unheilige Allianz. Das Geflecht von christlichen Fundamentalisten und politisch Rechten am Beispiel des Widerstands gegen den Bildungsplan in Baden-Württemberg,* ed. Lucie Billmann. Berlin: RLS.

INDEX

© The Author(s) 2017

M. Köttig et al. (eds.), *Gender and Far Right Politics in Europe*, DOI 10.1007/978-3-319-43533-6

377

The manufacturer's authorised representative in the EU is Springer
Nature Customer Service Centre GmbH, Europaplatz 3, 69115 Heidelberg,
Germany. If you have any concerns regarding our products, please
contact ProductSafety@springernature.com

Printed and bound by CPI Group (UK) Ltd, Croydon, CR0 4YY

27/04/2026

02097560-0006